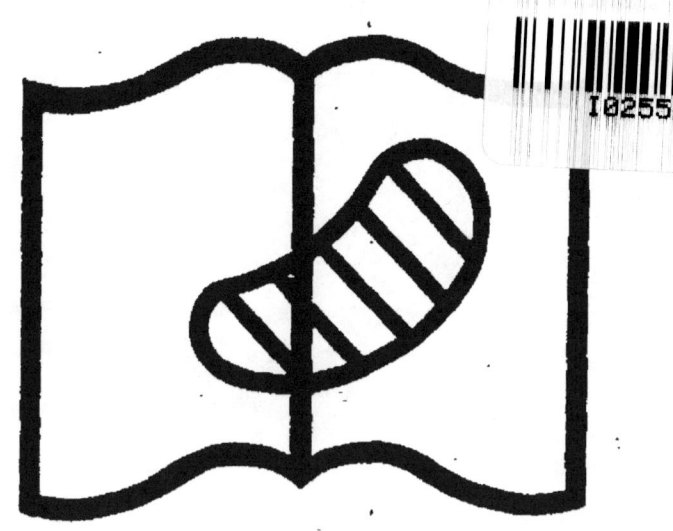

Original illisible
NF Z 43-120-10

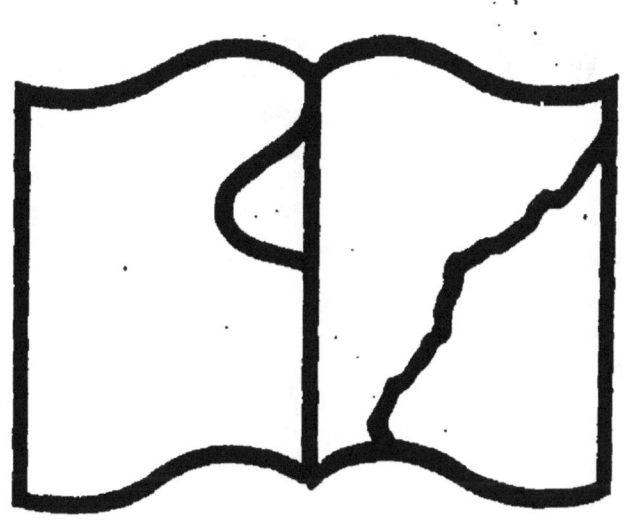

Texte détérioré — reliure défectueuse
NF Z 43-120-11

"VALABLE POUR TOUT OU PARTIE
DU DOCUMENT REPRODUIT".

OLD WINE IN NEW BOTTLES.

OLD WINE IN NEW BOTTLES:

OR,

Spare Hours of a Student In Paris.

BY

AUGUSTUS KINSLEY GARDNER, M.D.

The use of traveling is to regulate imagination by reality; and, instead of thinking how things may be, to see them as they are. JOHNSON.

The moment that you anticipate your pen in forming a sentence, you get as stiff as a gentleman in stays; I use my pen as my horse; I guide it, and it carries me on.
D'ISRAELI.

NEW-YORK:
C. S. FRANCIS & CO., 252 BROADWAY.
BOSTON:
J. H. FRANCIS, 128 WASHINGTON-STREET.
1848.

Entered, according to Act of Congress, in the year 1847,
BY C. S. FRANCIS & CO.,
In the Clerk's Office of the District Court for the Southern District of New-York.

Printed by
MUNROE & FRANCIS,
BOSTON.

CONTENTS.

	Page.
DEDICATION,	ix
PREFACE,	xi

I.
Diary at Sea—Arrival at Havre—Custom-House Agreeabilities—Ancorville and its Gardens, — 1

II.
Traveling in France—Rouen—Paris, — 8

III.
Latin Quarter—Hospital of Hotel-Dieu, — 18

IV.
Catholic Religion—French Hospitals—Hotel-Dieu—Nuns—Hospital Practice—Mons. Blandin—Dr. Mott, of New-York, — 22

V.
Bal Masqué, — 27

VI.
Condition of Women—Hair Market at Caen—Bourgeois Party—Funerals of the Rich and the Poor, — 32

VII.
Musard—Mardi-Gras—Père Gorlot—Louis Philippe—Bastringues—Traiteurs—Feasts—Fasts—Clergy—Confessions—Order of the "Holy Cross," — 38

VIII.
Weather—Fuel—Poor—Grand Opera—Viennese Dancing Girls—Carlotta Grisi—Duchess d'Aumale—Princess and Prince de Joinville—Persiani—Mario—Julia Grisi, — 44

IX.
Love of Country—Danger of Assassination—Tapis-Francs—Prevalence of Crime—The Morgue—Henri Herz—Concert of Sixteen Pianos and Thirty-two Players—Priests—Midwifery—Artificial Arm, — 50

X.
Fashions—Birth-Day of Washington—Ball of the American Minister—Expenses of the Embassy—Ball of the Café Tortoni, — 56

XI.
The Prado—New-Year's Day—Greetings in Private Life—To Military Officers of the National Guard—To the King, by Fifteen Hundred Drummers!—Champs Elysées—Place Concorde—Obelisk of Luxor—Goat Carriages—Learned Dogs—Punch and Judy, — 62

XII.

Further Account of the Hotel-Dieu—Roux—Chomel—Magendie—Ecole Pratique d'Anatomie—Museum of Dupuytren—Shocking Effects of Secret Vice, - - - - - - - - - 67

XIII.

French Politeness—Etiquette—Necessary Expenses of Living—Cost of Various Articles of Dress, - - - - - - - 71

XIV.

Medical Officers in French Hospitals—In American Hospitals—Reason of the Difference in their Characters—System of Concours—Sketch of Velpeau's Life and Person, - - - - - 77

XV.

The Grisette—Lorette—Fille Publique—Hôpital Lourcine—Mons. Hugier—Hôpital du Midi—Ricord—Disgusting Effects of Certain Diseases—American Students, - - - - - - 83

XVI.

Gobelin Manufactory of Tapestry and Carpets—Insane Hospital "La Salpêtrière," for Aged and Poor Women, - - - - 88

XVII.

Superstition—Holy Relics—Michelet—Felicien David—His Concert—Fête of Long Champs—Gen. Tom Pouce—Time and Place for Making Fashions—Conservatoire Royal de Musique—Its Concert—Madame Dorus-Gras, - - - - - - - 93

XVIII.

Common Schools—Colleges—Liberty—M. Michelet—Prisons—The Dépôt de La Préfecture de Police—The Conciergerie—Marie Antoinette, - - - - - - - - - - 99

XIX.

Prisons of Paris—St. Lazare—An Actress off the Stage—Filles Publiques—Debtors' Prison, - - - - - - - - 109

XX.

Place de la Bastille—Column of July—Hotel de Ville—Palm Sunday—Education—Louvre—Relics—Horse Market—Thiers, - 117

XXI.

English—Washing Establishment—St. Sulpice—The "Swiss"—Chamber of Peers—Traits in French Character, - - - 123

XXII.

Arc de Triomphe—Wall of Paris—Duke of Orleans—His Death and Mausoleum—Consequences—Successor to Louis Philippe, - 129

XXIII.

Exhibition of Flowers and Fruit—Love of Flowers—Flower Girls—Horse Races—Auber—War between England and America, - 135

XXIV.

Prisons of Paris—St. Pelagie—La Force—Nouvelle Force—Its Singular Construction—Maison Centrale d'Education Correctionnelle—Remarkable Form and Peculiar Discipline - - 141

XXV.

Methods of getting a living among the Poor—Bread—Chiffoniers—Dogs, - - - - - - - - - - - 147

XXVI.

Hôpital La Charité—Gerdy—Andral—Rayer—Cruveilhier—Fouquier—Bouillard—Course of Medical Study in Paris and America compared—Importance of a Special Attention to a Single Branch—Difficulties of American Physicians—The French and American Practitioner contrasted—American Students at Paris, 156

XXVII.

Celebration of the King's Birth-Day, - - - - - 165

XXVIII.

Versailles—The Palace—Its Cost—Desecration in 1792—Its Restoration by Louis Philippe—Its Embellishments, Pictures, and Statues—Napoleon as he Lives on the Canvas—Effects of these Paintings on a Spectator, - - - - - - - 176

XXIX.

Pictures, Coins, &c., in the Palace at Versailles—Chapel—Louis XIV.—Opera Room—Grand Gallery of Glass—Fountains—Parterre d'Eau—Ancient Orange Tree—Bassin de Neptune—Fountain of Latona—Chariot of the Sun—Bassin d'Encelade—Bosquet des Bassins d'Apollon—Bassins des Eufans—America and her Artists, 183.

XXX.

Grand Trianon—Little Trianon—Private Apartments—French Gardens—Cooper, the Pioneer American Novelist—Freedom of the Press, - - - - - - - - - - - 190

XXXI.

Prison des Jeunes Detenus—Results of the Solitary System—Dépôt de Condamnés—Personal Appearance of the Convicts—The Face an Index of Character—Employments, Privileges, and Manners of the Prisoners—The Sympathising Turnkey, - - - 195

XXXII.

The Clinique—Nelaten—Midwifery—Paul Dubois—Hospital for Orphans—Sisters of Charity—Private Lecturers—Chassaignac—Cazeaux—Longet—Chailly—Breschet—Lamartine—His Speech on the Removal of Napoleon's Body—Rumor of his Visit to this Country—Manner of Treating Foreigners of Distinction, - 202

XXXIII.

Spring—French Mothers and Children—Squares in Paris—Their Great Utility—Thalberg—His Concert—Motion not Music—Spontini, the Composer, - - - - - - - 210

XXXIV.

Coste on Embryology—Party at Mr. D.'s—Donné's Lectures on the Circulation of the Blood—Oxygen and Hydrogen Microscope—Photo-Electric Microscope—English Episcopal Church—Palais-Royal—Healey, the Painter—Veterinary School—Scientific Cruelty to Horses, - - - - - - - - 216

XXXV.

Comparison of the Parisian and American Prisons—Society for the Aid of Boys quitting the House of Correction—Society for the Aid of Abandoned Girls leaving the House of Correction, - 223

XXXVI.

Church at St. Denis—The Sepulchre of the French Sovereigns—Tomb of Lafayette—Père la Chaise, - - - - - 230

XXXVII.

Royal Institution of the Deaf and Dumb—Abbé de L'Epée—Sicard—Royal Institution for the Blind—Artesian Well at Grenelle—Comparison of the Royal Institution for the Blind, and the Asylum for the Blind at South Boston—Thomas Handasyd Perkins, 242

XXXVIII.

Rachel—Her Performance in Virginius—Execution by the Guillotine—Jardin des Plantes—Governor of Coney Island—Military Music—The King—Count de Paris, - - - - - 252

XXXIX.

The Garden of Plants—School of Botany—Menagerie—Men and Monkeys—Beneficial Effects from Alcohol, - - - - 264

XL.

Hôpital de la Pitié—Lisfranc—Velpeau—Louis—Bourgeois Marriage and Wedding Festivities—The Two Milliners—A Tender-hearted Lawyer, - - - - - - - - - 274

XLI.

How do you like Paris?—Style of the Buildings—Fires—Fire Department—Water—Common Sewers, - - - - - 281

XLII.

Answer to "How do you like Paris?" concluded—Religion—Cookery—Utility of a Temporary Residence in Paris, - - 287

XLIII.

Flower Markets—The Pantheon—Paintings by Gros—Tombs of Voltaire, Rousseau, Lagrange, and others, - - - - 295

XLIV.

Mint—Repugnance to the Use of Steam Power by Government—Gregory XVI.—Cabinet of Coins—Medals—Jewelers—Academy of Industry, - - - - - - - - - 302

XLV.

Chaumière—Mons. Coste—Fourierites—La Democratie Pacifique—Mons. Bureau and Family—Frederika Bremer—Prof. Longfellow—Observatory—Mons. Arago, - - - - - 309

XLVI.

Hôpital de Bicêtre, and its Occupants—The Morgue, - - 317

XLVII.

Royal Lunatic Hospital—Dr. Foville—Price of Board—Treatment—Curious Practice in a part of France—Pyramidal Heads—Flat Heads—Blockheads—Ill Treatment of Infants—New-Jersey Hospital for the Insane—Departure from Paris, - - - 324

TO

PAUL DUBOIS,

CHEVALIER OF THE LEGION OF HONOR; PROFESSOR OF THE PARIS FACULTY OF
MEDICINE; MEMBER OF THE ACADEMY OF MEDICINE, PARIS; CHIRURGIEN ACCOUCHEUR
TO THE HOPITAL DES CLINIQUES AND THE MAISON D'ACCOUCHEMENT, ETC.,

THROUGH WHOSE KINDNESS, A GREAT OPPORTUNITY

FOR PROFESSIONAL IMPROVEMENT WAS AFFORDED HIM,

THIS WORK

IS GRATEFULLY INSCRIBED

BY

THE AUTHOR.

PREFACE.

THE Letters, comprising the present volume, were written in Paris to the Editor of the Newark Daily Advertiser, in which print they were originally published. The commendation, which they received at the time from the newspaper press throughout the country, has encouraged the issue of them in this form.

Though the writer's residence in the French metropolis was designed for his improvement in medical science, he deemed it not incompatible with this great object to make himself familiar with the language and characteristics of the great and interesting people, with whom he was sojourning, and whom we ourselves resemble, in some respects, perhaps, more than any other nation. And he felt, in communicating his own impressions to the public, and his friends at home, that he was making the former the participators of his acquisitions—such as they were; and the latter, of some of his pleasures; while, at the same time, the evanescent forms of a multitude of objects and events obtained "a habitation and a name" in his memory, by being daguerreotyped in the very moment of their vanishing away forever.

Hastily prepared, as these letters were, immediately on returning from the scenes described, with a body fatigued, and an excited brain, they were evidently unfit for publication, without considerable revision. This was performed by the author's father, SAMUEL J. GARDNER, ESQ., to whose care and talents is due much of the credit which they have received.

After all, no one must be so unreasonable, as to look for new discoveries in a city, which has become the paradise of travelers, with their hundred eyes and tongues. All, that now remains possible, is to observe the changes of the social kaleidoscope, and copy the old materials, as they group themselves in new attitudes and forms. Such is the characteristic of the book, as its title was intended to express.

Save an occasional explanatory paragraph, the letters are now reprinted from the columns of the newspaper, without change. Much as they would be benefited by a revisal, the author has shrunk from a labor, which would interfere too much with his daily professional duties.

A. K. G.

NEW-YORK, *November*, 1847

OLD WINE IN NEW BOTTLES.

I.

DIARY AT SEA—ARRIVAL AT HAVRE—CUSTOM HOUSE AGREEABILITIES—ANCORVILLE AND ITS GARDENS.

AT SEA, October 6th.

'T IS a week since my departure from New York, and I rejoice to be on deck again, able to write you a few lines, with a horrible nausea, however, still upon me.

TUESDAY, 8th October. Lat. 41° 45'.

A fresh attack of sickness sent me below, and, in addition, heavy gales have since rendered it useless to attempt to write. Yesterday morning I saw a very beautiful rainbow, apparently only a few rods from the ship, spanning an entire arch. I remembered the old proverb, but the day proved beautiful notwithstanding. On Friday last, a sudden squall of wind and rain struck and nearly capsized us. Three men at the wheel, the captain being one, could not move it for some moments. All hands were soon on deck, and the sails were rapidly and successfully clewed up, taken in, reefed, &c., and the danger was past; soon all was fair again. On Sunday night the captain was taken severely sick, and I prescribed for him as well as my dizziness would permit. The wind freshened into a gale and blew much harder than on the day I intended to have sailed. I went on deck several times, and beheld the beauty and grandeur of the waves.

After the wind had been blowing a gale all day, toward night the sea was literally mountainous; nor were the waves more remarkable for size, than color. Just as they broke, their dark blue changed to—what shall I call it?—another shade of blue, perhaps, but so indescribably resplendent and dazzling, that I am convinced the sublime pencil of Titian himself never caught so celestial a tint. To-day a large hawk, perhaps an eagle, lighted for some minutes on our yards, but, as if in derision of our white canvass, soon spread his wings, and sailed around and off.

FRIDAY. Lat. 41° 54' Long. 45° 25'.

Several days, you see, are passed since I last wrote, and I cannot perceive that I am any nearer the promised land, than before. The captain jocosely remarks, that we are now about "half seas over," and then—"what then?" as Sterne says. We have an excellent captain, crew and ship.

SUNDAY, 13th.—How tiresome is a sea life! I cannot conceive, how a bustling yankee can ever get inured to it.

TUESDAY, 22d Oct.—While you are imagining me near my port of destination, I am, on the contrary, many hundred miles away, viz: in long. 18° lat. 43° 5'. We have had, since I last wrote, a succession of squally weather and head winds, &c. It seems to me, that there is but one place, to which I desire to go sufficiently to make another voyage, and that is—Home. Methinks I shall have grey hairs before I see France.

"A life on the ocean wave, and a home on the rolling deep,"

is very good poetry, but to my taste an indifferent sort of housekeeping. "The cloud-kissing waves," and the "foam-crested sea," one may imagine to look very pretty, but—when the waves kiss the clouds, because the latter stoop to the embrace, and when the bowels of the spectator yearn, not with sympathy and tenderness, but sea-sickness—'t is quite a different matter.

SUNDAY, 27th.—Doubtless you are figuring to yourselves my occupation in Paris; but, alas, I am yet many a mile distant. The smart S. W. winds, which have blown for the last two days have buoyed us along the Scilly Isles. Last evening the wind changed to S. E. by E. which entirely prevents our entering the Channel, and here we lie, beating about with a heavy sea, in the company of several vessels. I have been amused during the last week in watching some porpoises gamboling around our ship; and this morning was wet through while standing on deck, by the spray from a wave, which broke against our side.

WEDNESDAY.—Last evening spoke a London packet, who will probably report us. The English far-famed fog envelops us closely. A very heavy rolling sea causes a return of sickness.

SATURDAY EVENING, Nov. 2d.—Still in the Channel—wind yet ahead—over 33 days out. Last night it blew the heaviest gale we have had yet, and we had a lee shore. Butter, potatoes and fresh provisions long ago gone. Shall we ever get in? The Lord only knows.

SATURDAY, Nov. 3d.—This is truly a fine day, though it has snowed, and the heavens are filled with clouds, and the weather very cold; for I have seen land—the pilot is on board—and to-morrow, (what a blessed word to-morrow is!) I shall go on shore! The St. Nicholas, being one day ahead, has been in port eight days, having entered the Channel just before we were blown off. My fingers and feet are covered with chilblains, and my red nose projects fiercely through my mustache and beard.

WEDNESDAY, 6th.—*Havre*, where I arrived last evening at five P. M. still retains me. Sunday morning we arrived in the Roads, and there we lay till last evening, as the water was not high enough for the ship to enter the dock gates.

After so long a period spent on ship-board, one could almost find happiness on a barren island. A ship has been compared to many things—I would give it the title of menagerie, for besides whales, porpoises and sharks, you see strange beasts there, which, though inferior in size, do not affect the feelings less. Such is the bed-bug, " the red rover of the sea," and the more agile flea, which always swarm in cotton laden ships. Both are rare " phlebotomizers." The little dark weevil finding his kingdom in the crevices of the ship-bread " taken from him and given to a stranger," flies for his life, as you raise it to your lips. To these one soon becomes accustomed as well as to the rats, who nightly open avenues through your clothes to the dainty crumb concealed in some of their folds. Sea-sickness may be enjoyed a fortnight together on your back, and also a sudden translation from the berth to the middle of the cabin floor, as the ship may chance to take a sudden lurch—when they are over.

We must leave these things, however pleasant in the recollection, and observe the ship, as she enters the dock. Sunday morning, we arrived in the Roads, and there we lay till last evening, as the water was not high enough to enter the dock gates. These docks are but large basins of water confined by gates, not differing, except in magnitude, from those of our canals. The tide here rising and falling twenty feet, the rush of water otherwise would leave them exposed to danger from the bottom, when heavily laden, from its shallowness at ebb tide. Into this dock we rushed with all the speed, which a flood tide, a strong wind behind and a stronger swell from the Channel could give us. To the unaccustomed eye, we were in constant danger of running into the pier-head, whose massive buttresses project far into the sea, or the shipping moored along its sides. Fortunately, just as the danger seemed imminent, a hawser, apparently stretched by unknown hands, restrained our headlong course. The quay is crowded with people, whose uncouth garments divert the attention from the imaginary danger.

The pier is the grand promenade for the city; and ladies, soldiers, peasants—the whole community almost, are gathered there to witness the entrance of two large American ships and other smaller craft. We hastened from the ship to the hotel, fortunately escaping the search by the police, a fate which my trunk suffered most unmercifully the next morning. The numerous soldiery, who throng the city, seem to have little else to do, except poking into trunks and carpet bags, stirring up the dirty clothes, and snuffing every odor, while on the scent for tobacco. The manufacture and sale of this noisome weed are a monopoly of the king, and the search is therefore very severe. Notwithstanding this, three thousand cigars were smuggled ashore in the following ingenious manner. Two carpet bags were obtained similar to one another. Both were carried to the custom house.

One contained the greater part, and the other a quarter box only. This last was openly displayed in the mouth of the bag and the duties promptly paid. Gulled by this stratagem the other was scarcely opened. At a subsequent period, a bearer of despatches to our embassy, covered the boxes with the yellowish paper, tied with red tape, sealed with numerous red wax seals, stamped with the eagle found on a half dollar, and thus passed some thousands of cigars, unquestioned, through the hands of those who did not know that on the American coat of arms, there were no "50 cents" stamped at the bottom.

I am at Wheeler's Hotel, a very comfortable house, where English is spoken, and have employed myself to-day in traversing the city, and noting its peculiarities; the women, who are employed in every menial service—scraping the streets—riding the little jackasses, behind two immense panniers, stuffed with all kinds of provisions—the peculiar shaped houses—dark and dirty, frequently seven and eight stories high. Linen bed clothes this season of the year are no addition to the warmth of their elastic beds. Fires are in general use, so cold it is. I shall leave for Rouen by the diligence day after to-morrow, the boat having ceased running. Found an agreeable companion in an English clergyman, who described the theatre to me, and a particular play with great fervor. Saw also this morning a funeral—a priest followed by a boy bearing a pine coffin covered with a black cloth, and a man following, probably the mourner, but who was gazing around with great unconcern. At eight P. M. a band of thirteen drummers marched through the streets, calling the soldiers to their quarters for the night.

The city of Havre contains but little worthy of notice. The church of Notre Dâme, the docks and the hospital, are the principal objects of interest. A building for a museum is now erecting. It is made of a soft native stone. The walls are made of the large pieces placed in proper order, but unhewn and almost shapeless. After these are erected, the stone is then worked and pillars are hammered out and ornamented with Corinthian capitals, &c.

The village of Ancorville, separated from the city by a wall and moat, is the residence of the wealthy. It is situated on a high bluff, commanding a fine view of the city proper, with the bay and river Seine stretching for several miles. The buildings are much finer than those in the city, though not pleasing to the American eye, accustomed to white houses and green blinds. They are built of half-burned brick, with walls nearly two feet in thickness, and covered with plaster of such a dingy color, that, noticing shavings, &c. around a house, it is difficult to tell, whether they are building a new or repairing an old one. The gardens, however, make up the deficiency. I visited several, one very splendid, belonging to Jeremiah Winslow, a Boston man. Its winding walks were ornamented by the immense ribs and vertebræ of the whale. Even at this late season, it was covered with flowers. Among them was the Bengal rose, which we call the double Dutch, similar to C.'s, growing in great profusion, full of blossoms. It is left out of doors all winter, and blooms ten months in the year. The Laurestinus, too, with its fragrant flowers, resists the frosts of winter, uninjured. They are both frequently in bloom on Christmas. Rhododendrons, Cape Jessamines, are evergreens. The far-famed Holly and Ivy are also abundant. The former has a very rich green leaf, scolloped, bearing on each point a thorn. I also visited a small private green-house, not very showy at present, and quite similar to our own.

The soldiers stationed here number three hundred, and constitute the most striking objects of notice. They officiate as sentries, police, and custom house officers. Their uniform is in horrible taste. The only excuse for it is its alleged cheapness. They look, as if, roused from their slumbers by a fire in their own dwelling, they had seized the first clothing near them, and appear in scarlet flannel drawers, but partially concealed by a blue surtout. Such coat-tails must certainly impede locomotion.

The antiquarian may hasten to see the old tower, so conspicuous as we enter, which the guide books say was the place where Mazarin confined the princes of Condé and Conti, and where Francis I. was entertained by the early inhabitants. He may pore over the falling stones, and pick up a rusty nail for a souvenir;—my taste seeks rather for the living and breathing works of the present, than the dilapidated monuments of the past.

After two days' experience, I find that I have less difficulty each day in speaking the little French I have occasion for. I think I shall soon acquire it. To-morrow I shall visit the Hospital, and at five dine with Mr. R. E., brother of G. B. E., of Boston, to whom I had a letter, directed to Paris, whence he has lately arrived. You would be amused to see me walking about the streets, ever and anon consulting a small dictionary for aid in understanding some notice at the corners; or, when asking the way, stopping to look out a word in the midst of my speech. The horses are of the large Normandy breed, much larger than the Pennsylvania horse; I saw one to-day going apparently with much ease, drawing on a truck, like those at Boston, two hogsheads of molasses and five boxes of sugar, a half of which in Boston is a load for two.

11 o'clock.—I have just returned from the theatre, the old one was burnt, and this has been open but a fortnight; I therefore saw it in all its freshness. It is said to be a tasteful building, though small. "They did" the Opera of La Dame Blanche, with an orchestra of thirty-three instruments, played finely. The singing was not so good as I expected. I have postponed my departure for Rouen till Saturday morning, where I shall remain for three or four days, and then—for Paris.

II.

Travelling in France—Rouen—Paris.

Leaving Havre, as I told you, I embarked for Rouen, in the far-famed Diligence, which is associated with so many tales of joy and sorrow. A queer vehicle it is, I assure you, propelled sometimes by five horses, sometimes by nine, and I do not despair, after being here a few days more, of finding as many as often have the honor of drawing, in my own dear country, some symbol of a great principle on our grand procession fêtes. The cattle I am now speaking of, however, as far as I can see, have the task of transporting only a quantity of heavy luggage and sundry fat and lean people, as the case may be. For this purpose, five are the least number on the Diligences at a time; two at "the wheel," and three abreast, "on lead." The next additional horse goes on the wheel. The next three ahead of all; these are always governed by a postilion. With you, the driver has a rein for every beast, you know; but here, there are never more than four reins, and these are attached to the outer horses. A postilion sometimes rides on the "near leader." But the outfit is not yet complete. As the soldier is omnipresent in France, one rides, of course, on the banquette, which is a top with a covering like a chaise. An imposing office this, for he pays each driver his daily stipend of twenty-five cents, and shouts to the passengers that intercept the way, with a stentorian voice, who all turn out to make room for the coming avalanche. The inside is divided into three apartments, variously furnished. More room is allowed in some than in others, and the price is proportionate. This is my introduction to the principle of graduation, which is by no means offensive, while submission to it is voluntary, as it is here and on the railways. Accordingly, I ascended to the banquette to obtain the best view of the rich scenery, that is spread out on every side. It affords a complete shelter from the weather, and the glass windows, which can be dropped in front, open to the view of the stranger the country through which we are passing. It is the second or third division in point of expense. The prospect is exceedingly striking. Every object wears the air of novelty—the fertile fields, so exquisitely green—the thatched cottage—the flocks of corbeau, or raven, differing, I think, from our crow in tameness as well as appearance. Occasionally, a hare is seen scudding along, or an old and venerable church, heavenward pointing its grey spire. The driver jabbers to his horses perpetually, keeps his immense whip in constant use, making the narrow streets of the cities echo with its loud explosions.

As we approached Rouen, the most conspicuous objects were the lofty towers and spires of the Cathedral, one of the most celebrated in the world, by some supposed to be founded by William the Conqueror. The first mention of this city is made by Ptolemy, who lived in the second century. It is doubtful whether its population of a hundred thousand is greater now than then; its character, however, has changed. Then, it was inhabited by a people whose name has become a by-word—the ancient Goths; now, its numerous churches proclaim it a Christian nation.

No person who is travelling for pleasure, fails to spend several days in the examination of the curiosities of this old town. The first among these, is the before-mentioned cathedral, commenced in the XIIIth century, and finished in the XVIth. I wish I could portray the beauty and grandeur of this building, four hundred and fifty feet long, one hundred and ten wide, and to the top of the lanthorn, from the inside, two hundred feet.

My first impressions were received by a visit made there in the night. The outside was not visible in the darkness, and the interior, partially lighted by the votive tapers burning at the shrines of saints, lost none of its grandeur and solemnity. There were not more than twenty persons present in this immense building. All was still, save the voice of a priest in one of the distant chapels, and the sighs and the sobs of a penitent worshipper near me. A religion, which draws from their comfortable dwellings so many persons through the rainy streets, to spend an hour or more in the cold damps of a gloomy church, cannot but deeply impress one with a feeling of respect, which I fear is too rarely felt by the Protestant for the Catholic faith.

But it was necessary to have a bright day to see in perfection the grandeur of this edifice. One hundred and thirty windows of stained glass to light it, represent the occurrences in the life of our Saviour, the Apostles and "holy men made perfect,"—one window sometimes containing an entire scene, such as the crucifixion of our Saviour between the two thieves, for example, and sometimes many scenes in the life of an individual, much smaller of course. The perfect expression of these pictures exceeded anything I had ever imagined. I witnessed the grand mass, in which the archbishop officiated.

Among other ornaments, there is a silver lamp of large size, weighing forty marks, before the altar—the gift of the city—a thank-offering for the cessation of the plague in 1637. Here, in the Chapel of the Virgin, is the statue which formerly decorated the tomb of the celebrated Cœur de Lion, which had long been buried. But on the 30th of July, 1838, searches were made for it, and, guided by historical traditions, it was happily discovered. It is hewn out of a single block of freestone, and is six and a half feet long. It represents King Richard in a recumbent position, his head supported by a square cushion, wearing a crown encircled with precious stones; his feet are supported by a crouching lion. On his left hand was a sceptre, of which we only see the remains; the right has been destroyed. The prince's mantle descends nearly to his ancle in wide folds. It is over a tunic which reaches up to the neck, and is bound round the body by an embroidered belt. The researches, continued on the following day, discovered the heart of Richard, enclosed in a double box of lead with the following inscription:

𝕳𝖎𝖈 : jacet : cor : 𝕽𝖎𝖈𝖍𝖆𝖗𝖉𝖎 : regis :
𝕬𝖓𝖌𝖑𝖔𝖗𝖚𝖒 :

Near this, are statues of the husband of Diana of Poictiers, and of the cardinals of Amboise. Pillars, sculptures, galleries, bas-reliefs, statues, and paintings, are without number. The outside is not deficient in interest. Three lofty towers ornament it, the tallest of which, destroyed by fire in 1822, is being replaced, at an expense of $100,000, by one of iron. It will weigh 1,200,000 lbs., and will be four hundred and thirty-six feet high—thirteen feet less than the loftiest pyramid of Egypt.

Leaving now this magnificent cathedral, of which it is impossible to give an adequate description, we will follow the guide—who earns his dollar by conducting us, by the nearest route through the city, to the various places of note, and there giving his stereotyped descriptions—to the churches of St. Ouen, (which contains a window of colored glass unsurpassed in the world,) St. Maclou, St. Patrice, and many others of great beauty. Many of the beautiful churches are no longer used for religious services—one is a stable, and another a storehouse. Their lofty domes and elegant carvings still remain, though mutilated. In many of the others, the broken windows are replaced by modern manufactures of very inferior merit.

It is impossible in the space I have allotted for the hasty description of Rouen, even to attempt an enumeration of the objects of interest in this city, celebrated as the birth place of Corneille, Fontenelle, Boieldieu, the composer, and many others; some of whose statues, as well as that of Joan of Arc, who was here burnt as a witch, ornament its public squares. The town hall contains a collection of portraits, and a public library enriched with manuscripts of distinguished beauty. One of these, the famous illuminated Gradual or Music Book, by Daniel d'Aubonne, richly repays the time, and money (one franc) expended in seeing it. It contains more than two hundred vignettes, and occupied in its construction thirty years of the life of its monkish author. It is not only a monument of devotion and perseverance, but a specimen of writing and pen embellishment unequalled.

On returning to dinner, tired and cloyed with endless novelties, galleries of pictures and statues, views of the city from various points, carved walls and doors, large bells, &c., I fell into the company of some ladies from Brighton, in England, who, after inquiring my country, made me the compliment of speaking English very well, which I politely returned by saying, that they conversed in good American; at which they appeared not a little puzzled. Happening to observe three quarter dollars, (fortunately they were not eagles,) which I had, they begged them of me, as curiosities, and placed them among some Catholic communion wafers, which they had obtained during the day. When they get home they will doubtless all figure advantageously in their cabinet of choice articles of virtu, collected in their travels

On the 11th of November I quitted Rouen, taking the cars for Paris. What a magical agent is money! Two families, for instance, live side by side for years. One of them is worth a million, the other not a thousand. A person, who did not know the world, would innocently imagine, that these two families were neighbors. There cannot be a greater mistake; it is nothing but an optical illusion, I assure you, sir. The difference of their fortunes has rolled an ocean between them, so that these two families actually pass their lives without being at all aware even of the existence of one another.

A freak of money, somewhat similar, though by no means so extraordinary, occurred at the cars for Paris. There are two classes of them at least, and probably more. The first class is designed to accommodate eight only, with seats lined with velvet, and fitted up in other respects to correspond. The second class is equally spacious, but lined with linen, admitting ten persons with abundance of room for all. The price paid for seats in the former was but a trifle more than in the others; yet the effect of that little more upon the passengers was wonderful. Among them there was an English gentleman, and two daughters, who had, on the present excursion, for the first time in their lives left their native island. Under the powerful operation of their national proclivity, they assumed the velvet cushions of course. A party of gentlemen and ladies, also English, of equal rank and fashion, happened to be there too on their return from St. Petersburgh. Having traveled over the whole of Europe, they had by this time acquired a tolerable knowledge of "matters and things," and accordingly chose the cars of the second class. They evidently felt no preference for velvet over linen to sit upon for an hour or two. Indeed, I find that the intelligent, though wealthy, do by no means invariably manifest a preference for what is of the highest price, on that account alone. But the effect of this procedure of the experienced travellers upon the gentleman with the two daughters was very amusing. Doubtless, owing to the cause to which I have alluded, the already turned-up noses of the two daughters now turned up to an elevation, that I had not before believed to be possible. But how extreme was their mortification, when they discovered on our arrival at Paris, that the distinction in the cars was of the most transitory nature, for we all went together from the depot in the same omnibus to the same hotel, and dined at the same table. This was the hotel Mirabeau, situated in the Rue de la Paix, which is very central.

As we approached this great capital, nobody was needed to tell us of our progress; the rapidly augmenting charges were abundantly sufficient to give information. And the bills, to which I am now subjected daily, leave me not in the least doubt whatever of my safe and happy arrival in the modern Athens. It is a great mistake, that everything is cheaper here than in the United States. Clothing, especially cotton, is higher, and woolen also. Linen is cheaper, but not so much so as in England.

The Palace of Luxembourg is but a step from my present residence. It is a square edifice, with an ample portico in the centre. A noble pavilion surmounts the principal building, and terminates in a dome, composed of the Doric and Ionic orders. This palace, like most of the houses, is built in the form of a hollow square. One reason for this mode of construction may be found in their situations; in streets, dirty, narrow, and noisy; among groups of poor buildings, where the luxury of a prospect, except from some of the palaces, is rarely or never enjoyed. The best apartments are, consequently, those which face inward on the square enclosed, which is embellished, according to the means and taste of the owners; with shrubbery, statues of stone, among the rich, and plaster among the poorer proprietors. The centre of the Luxembourg palace is a court-yard flagged, and without any other ornament than the architecture of the building itself. On entering the door, one is met by a sentry, who is stationed at every public building, and, instead of crossing the square, I generally go through along the passage, bordered on both sides by immense orange and lemon trees, ascend two flights of stairs, and enter the picture gallery, which is a receptacle of such works of living artists only, as have been purchased by the government.

These paintings are, some of them, twenty feet square, beautifully executed, with surfaces as smooth as glass. Strangers are admitted every day gratuitously; and students, male and female, may always be seen copying the whole or parts of a picture; and sometimes several at work upon the same.

In this building are also the chambers of the ministers, the councillors of state, &c. Behind it is a large public garden, adorned with statues, and variegated with ponds and other embellishments. On Sunday, the great holiday of Paris, the galleries of paintings in the Luxembourg and Louvre are opened to all, and numerously frequented. In this manner the good taste of the French is kept alive. Those, who can spare the time, promenade every day; and on Sundays, everybody. The shops are then closed at an early hour, and all resort to the Boulevards, or some of the many gardens scattered in all quarters of the city. The garden of the Tuilleries, being the most central, is the point of principal resort, certainly of the aristocracy. On those occasions almost every one has a dog, and the fashions of all classes may be seen, from the puppy of two legs to one of four. These dogs (the quadrupedian I mean) are generally conducted by a string or a small chain. A silk dress has one kind of dog, a fustian has another.

The "Jardin des Plantes" pleases me the most. It is wanting, to be sure, in the numerous statues of the others, which appear indecent to the eye of a stranger, but possesses, in their stead, objects of superior attraction. The other gardens are nearly level; this is diversified by hill and dale—by winding paths and quiet groves. Here, and indeed throughout the country, the grass possesses an intensity of green unknown to you. Trees and shrubs, though now bereft of their foliage, abound in endless variety, as well as animals, birds, and reptiles; but the latter are found in a different direction.

The peculiar dress and habits of the people; the women sweeping the streets (the dirtiest of all highways) and carrying enormous bundles on their heads; the cumbrous vehicles, relics of a barbarous age; and the horses, equally unwieldy, with their useless, ponderous trappings, conspire to render the city avenues a vast museum for the entertainment of the pedestrian. You must not be surprised, therefore, if I am sometimes lost in exploring the recesses of these labyrinths.

Notre Dâme, the metropolitan church, the only Gothic structure of note in Paris, is situated in the cité, the oldest part and centre of the capital, and rises to a great height above all the buildings which surround it. It is no less than four hundred and fourteen feet in length; its width is one hundred and forty-four, and its towers two hundred and four feet high. It is so old, that the date of its erection is unknown. Its walls are crusted over with the smoke of ages, and, of all the edifices in Paris, the cathedral of Notre Dâme conveys to us the most lively impressions of the massiveness and durability of ancient architecture. When I visited this venerable church, every nook was occupied by a priest, who was expatiating to a crowd around him. Some of them seemed to regard the fair countenances of their young hearers with looks far from devotional. This church is filled with paintings and carved work, and, though bearing the evidence of injuries, inflicted by the violence of the populace in revolutionary times, still challenges admiration for its grandeur and beauty.

On Saturday evening, I went to the Italian Opera, and had an opportunity to see a fair specimen, I imagine, of French beauty. But I must decline to express any opinion upon this very delicate subject, (almost as dangerous a topic, as the peculiar institutions of our Southern States,) as well as on the equally tender one of the French *cuisine*, till a longer residence has ripened my judgment. There is a single branch of the latter, however, so interesting, that I cannot wait to have my beard grow, (any longer than it is now at least,) before I give vent to my feelings of delight; namely, the *café au lait*. It is indeed delicious! Listen to the process. Two pots are brought; from one of which your cup is half filled with café, clear, strong and hot; from the other, they fill it up with boiling milk. A little silver plate contains some lumps of white sugar to sweeten it to your taste, or to make *eau de sucre*, which the French are very fond of. This is merely cold water, made sweet with sugar.

But I was speaking of the opera. It was Rossini's Il Barbiere di Siviglia ; and, when sung by such persons, as Mad'lle Persiani, and Messrs. Lablache, Mario, Ronconi, Morelli, &c, with the orchestral accompaniment by about one hundred performers, all of whom are exceedingly skilful, you cannot doubt, that I preferred it, even to the singing of Miss ———. I was indeed delighted.

If my friends should come to see me, I fear I should need a formal introduction; for the razor has not "scraped acquaintance" with my face, since I left the pleasant shores of New Jersey. Though neither neat, nor agreeable, such is the universal fashion here, and saves trouble. What a luxury to me would be your pretty parlor stove with its peach orchard, or lehigh, instead of my wide-mouthed fire place, voraciously devouring the principal part of the caloric, generated by the combustion of two or three sticks of wood, and some Newcastle coal laid thereon. And when it is considered, too, that the windows and doors, and indeed the whole panel-work, afford a pretty easy passage to the air, the contest maintained within, against the external cold, must be acknowledged to be somewhat an unequal one. The want of attention to the economy of heat is the more surprising, since fuel bears so high a price.

But this is not the only inconvenience. The partition walls between rooms are frequently nothing but laths, which sounds and odors penetrate with ease. Just as I go to bed at night at twelve o'clock, for instance, a neighbor of mine expends his surplus enthusiasm upon a pianoforte. I find no fault with the instrument or player, for both are good, but I can't help thinking, that he who breaks my sleep by making a noise after twelve at night, is guilty of an assault and battery, and ought to be sentenced to undergo the penalty, for each offence, of spending a day in the house of some Orpheus, just beginning to learn to play on the trombone.

III.

Latin Quarter—The Hospital of Hotel-Dieu.

Away from the palaces, gardens, statues, galleries of paintings, and even from the fashion and respectability of the city, lies the *Latin quarter*. Let us hurry through its generally dirty and narrow streets, and visit its numerous hospitals, colleges, schools of medicine and law, dissecting rooms, museums, and botanical gardens. Here also are the dwellings of the poor and destitute, the student, and of that class, known only in Paris—the grisette. All these are found almost exclusively in this quarter, which is separated from the habitations of the wealthy and fashionable by the river Seine.

The hospitals of Paris deserve the fame, which they enjoy throughout the world, of being the best in existence, on every account. They are the best for the physicians, who there acquire their reputation and subsistence; best for the student, who can there see every species of disease, that afflicts humanity any where, treated with consummate skill by the most scientific professors of the age; and, finally, best for the patient, who, coming from the highways and byways of life, and from the haunts of misery, penury, and vice, finds all here, which money, religion, and skill can bestow, to make him comfortable, though suffering from the anguish of disease. It is impossible too highly to prize or praise such noble institutions.

A long list of illustrious names commemorates the benefactors of these charities, the origin of which is veiled in impenetrable obscurity, though it can be traced back more than a thousand years. When at home we can calmly take up a book, and read of the effeminacy of one king, and the cruelty of another; we can believe all the vices which are ascribed to a monarch, and shrink with horror from the contemplation of crimes, magnified and colored, if not invented, by some political historian; and we congratulate ourselves, that such enormities cannot be committed in our own favored country. But, when contemplating these buildings, founded by a Mazarin, or Richelieu, and supported and enlarged by a long line of sovereigns, whose characters have been portrayed in the blackest hues, we cannot but suspect them, in many instances, to be injured men, and that their histories, which now exist, are too often the offspring of the malicious imagination of partizan writers. It is difficult to imagine such contradictory conduct, so strange a union of virtue and vice, so incongruous a conjunction of cruelty and humanity. The monuments of their benevolence remain, and, therefore, it is but justice, that we should examine the evidence of their atrocities with cautious impartiality.

The oldest hospital in Paris, and, among the first in extent, stands the Hotel-Dieu, or Hospice D'Humanité. There are twenty other institutions, or more, of this nature, in the city, for the accommodation of patients of every description, on the most soothing and liberal principles. The noble buildings of the Hotel-Dieu have no claim to architectural elegance, being chiefly remarkable for solidity. The work of several ages, their uncertain origin is attributed to St. Landri, Bishop of Paris in the seventh century. This hospital has been successively enlarged by Philip Augustus, Louis XIII, XIV, XV, and XVI. It extends, at present, along both sides of the river Seine, the buildings being united by a tunnel passing under it. Numerous changes are in constant progress, having for their object the ultimate enlargement of the institution, and the substitution of new buildings in modern style. This, however, has for the present reduced the number of beds from 1200 to 800. The different halls are embellished with the statues and portraits of the distinguished physicians and surgeons, who have here spent a large portion of every day in attending the sick and suffering, among which are those of the celebrated Bichat and Dupuytren.

Into this establishment the sick and wounded of all descriptions are received, with the exception of children, incurable and insane persons, and those who are afflicted with cutaneous and syphilitic diseases. The annual average number of patients is eleven thousand, and the average mortality, one in eight hundred and seventy-two. Beside numerous house pupils (*internes*) the daily service of nine physicians and three surgeons is required. Drs. Chomel and Magendie, and surgeons Roux and Blandin are the most eminent. The hospital is open only to students, who have received a diploma, and desire to see the practice and hear the cliniques of these celebrated men. Strangers with passports are admitted to view every day, and the public twice a week.

In order to obtain a more particular knowledge of the appearance and customs of the place, you must follow me in imagination in my diurnal visit. Rising at seven o'clock in the morning, I hasten to arrive at the Hotel-Dieu, a distance of a mile from my lodgings, by half-past seven o'clock. At the door I am stopped by the guard, whose cocked hat and uniform are the evidences of his authority. On showing a ticket, given by the officers of the institution, or, on the exhibition of my diploma, admittance is instantly granted. The medical gentleman from the United States must not neglect to bring his diploma with him, as he will find it quite necessary, on frequent occasions, to the free and proper prosecution of his studies.

Passing through this building, the court-yard, and under the river, I arrive at the edifice devoted to the females. Each of the doors, forming the entrances into the various wards, has over it a name, being that of some saint. On entering, I find myself in a long hall, extending as far almost, as the eye can reach. Upon both sides is a row of beds, numbering nearly a hundred, making a striking appearance to an American. The bedsteads are constructed of iron, which however are concealed from sight by curtains. This iron frame work effectually excludes all vermin. Many hospitals in the United States, supplied with wooden bedsteads, and admitting patients from similar classes of society, are much annoyed by them. The curtains answer the double purpose of temporary seclusion and a screen from the light. The objections, which have been offered by many physicians in the United States in regard to the detrimental influence of curtained beds upon the sick, by confining the air, rendered impure by the breathing of the patients, and the exhalations from the body and open wounds, do not apply to these. The top is left uncovered, which consequently admits a free passage of the atmosphere. At the foot of this hall is perceived, either a painting, a plaster, or perhaps a carved oak representation of the Virgin Mary, or of the patron saint, to whom it is dedicated. This is surrounded by flowers real and artificial, candles, and other emblems of catholic worship.

The description of the practice in this hospital will be given in my next letter.

IV.

CATHOLIC RELIGION—FRENCH HOSPITALS—HOTEL-DIEU—NUNS—HOSPITAL PRACTICE—MONS. BLANDIN—DR. MOTT, OF NEW-YORK.

COMING from a country where harsh judgments are hazarded on the tendency of the Catholic religion, and the hypocrisy of its professors, it gives one the pleasure of a surprise to visit a hospital in France, and witness the hold which it has upon the public mind. However strongly one may be convinced of the erroneousness of many of their doctrines, he cannot, after such a sight, but be less egotistical and self-sufficient; less disposed to condemn others, and to exalt his own judgment, as the only certain standard of right and wrong. I pronounce not on their articles of faith, of which they surely have abundance, nor on the merits of their works, which few will affirm to be inferior to those of others in the daily walks of life. But the heart has its prerogatives, which will not be slighted, and does not wait before it feels, to inquire whether it is right or not.

In this hospital, as in almost every other in France, may be witnessed the unremitting care of the *religieuses*. That which I visited at Havre, is under the general direction of the nuns, the Lady Superior herself giving £400 sterling a year for its support in addition to her undivided attention. There I saw seven hundred beds, and in one of them a sailor, who had fallen from the top of a New-York and Havre packet on her passage out. He struck upon the sky-light, and when taken up, his leg was found to be completely separated from his thigh, and was left on deck, while he was carried below. Sixty *religieuses* of the order of St. Augustine devoted their whole time and attention to the suffering in the Hotel-Dieu alone. Undistracted by the amusements of the world, they find "their meat and their drink" in bathing the burning brow, and moistening the parched lip; in pointing the convalescent to a nobler sphere of duty, in a different path from that in which they have been travelling; in whispering to the dying of Christ's love, and directing their wandering thoughts "to the bright realms of peace and happiness in another and a better world." When I see these women thus engaged, I forget, that they are attendants and nurses, and regard them with a sentiment of veneration. They appear to me to be fulfiling a holy mission upon earth. I see no ostentation in their peculiar dress, their large and uncomely cap or hood, and the bandages by which the principal part of their faces is concealed. To me they seem to say, "Come unto me, all ye that are weary and heavy-laden, and I will give you rest; buy of me wine and oil, without money and without price." *Revenons à nos moutons.*

I said, that I *saw* these things, but at this early hour (half-past seven A. M.) the streets themselves are hardly visible, much less the interior of a house. By accident I am in the surgical ward of Mons. Blandin. Directing my steps to two or three flickering candles, I traverse the long hall. Stranger, tread with care, lest this waxed oaken floor, which reflects, like a mirror, the little light in the distance, should convert you, on a sudden, from the character of a student into that of a patient of the learned surgeon. Around the bed stand fifty, or perhaps a hundred, students, some with note books, listening to the words of the surgeon, and completely hiding him and his "suite" from view. Anticipating his progress, and taking a position by the side of the next patient, I may perhaps succeed in seeing him.

The idea I had formed of this excellent man, is not disappointed by his personal appearance. He is some fifty years of age, perhaps five feet ten inches in height, erect and well made. His fine open countenance, unhidden by beard, high forehead and sparkling eye, bespeak the man of intellect and decision, quickness of thought, and promptness of execution; characteristics most necessary to a surgeon, who should possess them, combined with perfect coolness under all circumstances, that he may be able to seize upon the proper moment to render useful assistance to the sufferer under his hands. These qualities are evident, as he goes from bed to bed, examining quickly, but carefully and closely, the condition of the patients. The heart of the surgeon is not always callous, and the questions which he puts, though often hasty and loud, are nevertheless always mild and softly spoken. He wears a white linen apron fastened round his waist, attached in part to a button on his coat, which protects his clothes from the lint of the beds, and the numerous soiling articles around a patient. In a button-hole of his coat is seen the narrow red ribbon, worn by all the members of the Medical Society. After him come the students attached to the hospital, some five or six in number, called *internes* or *externes*, as they reside in, or out of the building. Three of them carry books, pens and ink. One records the state of the patient, as described by the surgeon; another, the medical prescriptions; and the third, the diet. Mons. Blandin himself carries another book, containing a summary of the case and treatment. The other three take off the bandages, and assist in such slight operations, as are performed at the bedside. These are surrounded by the crowd of following students. As in such an assembly, it would be impossible to carry the hat in the hand, the custom of wearing it in the wards of the sick, which strikes an American stranger so unpleasantly, is explained.

There is none of that false modesty here, which is so prevalent at home. Perhaps some sneering reader may suggest, that there is less of the real. However that may be, there is certainly no affectation of it. Men and women lose their sex, when sick, and are viewed in the character of patients merely. To understand their cases aright, it is sometimes, and in surgical cases always, necessary to see. All diseased parts of the body are unhesitatingly displayed without a thought of indelicacy. This is as it should be. Mrs. Farrar, in her work on the education of young ladies, amid many pruderies, has good sense on this point. Over-nicety in these cases is almost entirely American. In the hospital of a house of correction, where I attended some time, I have known the most abandoned women object, as strenuously as a young girl, to the necessary examination of her person. The prude perhaps might call this behavior a remnant of her original condition, or a germ of better feelings. She is welcome to the rationale.

Behind the students follow waiters, with bandages, lint, water, and the entire surgical apparatus. At this early hour, it is impossible to see without artificial light. Each of the scribes therefore carries a candle attached to his book, and the surgeon himself another of wax, about the size of a pipe stem, which is curled upon itself in an oblong form. This is placed under the patient's nose, occasionally singeing it, in order to see his tongue, and sometimes a little hot wax falls upon the patient's person.

The visit of the day is finished. The books of diet and medicines, which have been prescribed, being signed by the physician, thus authorizing their dispensation, he follows the students to the lecture room, and delivers a brief, but comprehensive, description of some disease, illustrating it by reference to patients in the house. Not having removed his apron, he is ready to perform any operation, which may be required. The hand of Mons. Blandin is quick and steady, and his operations are done with dexterity and neatness. The first day on which I attended his clinique, there was a case of dislocation of the humerus. He described the many methods employed for its reduction, especially for this form, where the head of the bone was in the axilla. Among them he mentioned the excellent method of Dr. Mott, of New York, of which he spoke in high terms, and finished by saying, that he would attempt the reduction on this occasion by that method; which he accordingly did with perfect success. It gratified me exceedingly to hear him speak of my countryman in language so flattering. I had been in Paris but a short time, and then scarcely knew a soul in the great city. I was lonely. But this public recognition of the merits of an American, though I had never enjoyed the pleasure of seeing him, operated on my spirits like a charm. It electrified me with delight. The glory of our great men may be slighted, or even withered, by detraction, at home, but it is ever very dear to the heart of a countryman in a strange land. It elevates him in the eyes of foreigners, and what is better, it raises him in his own.

A great trouble in attending these cliniques, and, in truth, all the medical lectures in the city, is caused by the little attention paid to the comfort of hearers. The seats are hard and without backs, and there is but scanty room for the feet. This confined position it is very uncomfortable to maintain for such a length of time as the lectures frequently last. Here, too, as in the wards, the students listen with their hats on their heads, if more convenient.

V.

Bal Masque.

I have just returned from the first masked ball of the season, and, as the peculiar manners of a people are apt to be conspicuous in their amusements, I shall attempt to give you a description of it.

These balls are very frequent during the Carnival, and are held at various places. The one which I attended, was at the French Opera House, and, as it was the first, is supposed to have been the best, of the series. Its claims to superiority are founded on the capacity of the building, allowing the entrance of more persons at one time, than any other place of amusement; the number and surpassing excellence of the musicians; the brilliancy of its illumination, and the superiority of the maskers, whose means enable them to appear in richer and more fantastic dresses, than at the other balls, and perhaps selected with more taste. The cost of a ticket, when obtained single at the bureau, is ten francs, (about two dollars,) but they can be bought for half the sum of persons around the door, who purchase them by the hundred, and sell them very low.

The crowded streets, for a circuit of half a mile around the building, are guarded by numerous soldiers, both mounted and foot, who regulate the approach and withdrawal of carriages, which are constantly going and coming. Eleven o'clock, p. m. is the time for commencing, generally on Saturday or Sunday evening, when the world is most at leisure to attend to amusements. Arrived there, all men are admitted, who have tickets and are decently dressed, either plainly or fancifully; and women in any tidy garments, be they petticoats or breeches, if masked. Masks are confined to women, who are compelled to wear them

The first resort of a stranger is to the upper boxes, whence he can obtain a "coup-d'œil" of all that is beneath him. On entering, the intense brilliancy dazzles the unaccustomed eye. A thousand gas-burners emit as many jets of flame, reflected back from numerous mirrors and cut pendants of glass chandeliers, which, agitated by the trembling building, shaken by innumerable dancers, twinkle like the stars of the firmament. Looking, however, below and beyond the blaze, we have a view of the pit, covered with a spring-floor, and enlarged by the addition of the stage to more than double its usual dimensions. It is occupied with *two or three thousand dancers*, decked in habiliments of all kinds and colors, the fashion of every nation and age, and representing animals of various climes. Presently you behold this immense assembly dancing a quadrille with the most uncouth and extravagant gestures; leaping, walking on their hands and feet, like quadrupeds, or on their knees. Sometimes, from being intentionally tripped by one another, and pushed by the crowd, a dozen, perhaps, are lying on the floor, kicking, screaming and rolling, men and women together. The music changes, and a gallopade finishes the figure, which grows every moment quicker and quicker, till it becomes a race around the halls, in which each one disregards both time and tune in the eager attempt to outstrip the rest. This is varied by the polka, a waltz, and the mazourka.

Beyond the dancers, in the back part of the stage, is placed the orchestra, to me the most attractive part of all that is presented before us. Two hundred of the finest musicians, which this city of music can produce, are here collected. In the midst is seen Musard, the conductor, whose vigorous exertions in flourishing his baton and guiding the players rival the polkars before him.

It is altogether impossible to remain longer in the box gazing. If the harp of one man, like Orpheus, could overcome the natural reluctance of oak and granite, and rouse them to a *country dance*, surely the music of two hundred professors, every one doubtless very much his superior, must animate even the wooden legs of the gray-haired pensioners themselves. Mine, at any rate, which do not pretend to be either marble or timber, soon gave way to the delicious epidemic, and I found myself mingling with the enthusiastic multitude. Perhaps we may find among the masks, some which conceal intellect and beauty. With great difficulty at length we get upon "the floor." Four thousand persons are here, and every avenue is clogged. Your path is stopped by many, who seize you by the arm, and forcibly restrain your progress, at the same time whispering some impertinent compliment or merry nonsense. Perfect freedom of speech and action reigns. Nothing is too gross to be said, and very little that is not permitted to be done. Have you ever escaped from the turmoil of the city, and, wandering in the green woods, far from the dwellings of men, where none could hear your voice, have you ever then thrown yourself upon the verdant sward, rolled about in perfect wantonness, shouted and sang and screamed, till the hills reverberated the sound, and the birds flew about astonished at the sudden uproar? If you have, you may obtain a faint conception of the *abandon* of this unparalleled assembly.

The mask worn by the ladies is made of black silk, satin, or velvet. It is so small, that it serves only to cover the eyes, nose and part of the cheeks, leaving the mouth and chin exposed, or but partially concealed by a piece of black lace attached to it.— This exposure is sufficient to enable one to distinguish the comparative age, and to judge pretty correctly of the charms, of the wearer. The domino is merely a mantle of silk with edgings of lace, and serves to hide the form of the person. This is not, as I have remarked, the only female dress, but it is the one worn by such as really desire to conceal their face and figures. The prettier the person, the more of it is generally to be seen.

Among the masks were many, certainly a third, who wore the garments of men, such as those of sailors, Scotch, Swiss, and the dress of pages at court. With this metamorphosis, their characters were also changed, and they were observed to be the roughest and most foolish and even indecent in their behavior. Those, who object to the close contact of the sexes in the "mazes of the giddy waltz," might not think the evil any greater in this, than in other dances, were they to observe the still closer affinity in the quadrilles. Such warm embraces are never seen in America, not even at the parting or re-union of relations or friends.

It is part of the etiquette of the evening, whether in the dance, or out, to embrace all. One, in particular, disguised in the skin of a white bear, went round with open mouth, and, as if partaking the characteristics of the beast he personated, hugged almost as forcibly as the brute himself, all the women, whose appearance pleased his animal taste. Here might be seen a mask, climbing upon the shoulders of a cavalier, and rudely assisted to ascend by the pushes of the passers by. Others were observed sitting in each other's laps, fondling and kissing.—Bare necks indeed were considered public property, and received salutes with as little ceremony, as if they had been left so for the purpose.

With a desire to ascertain, merely as a point of philosophy of course, the real character if possible, of those who were among the principal attractions, I went from one to another, talking, dancing and waltzing. The first object of my examination proved to be a grisette, mourning for the loss of a bracelet; her pleasure for the evening was destroyed. She had waltzed with one, whom she suspected to be the purloiner. She unhesitatingly proffered an assignation with me for the morrow. One I noticed sitting near me, whose flaxen ringlets revealed her to be not only from another country, but of a different taste from those around. She was dressed in one of the most extravagant costumes of the evening, and I had previously seen her dancing with a freedom of manner quite remarkable. Just now she was refusing in pure Castilian the urgent entreaties of a young Spaniard to join in the next quadrille. Not doubting a similar reception myself, still, merely for amusement, I asked the favor of her company in the waltz, which had just commenced. She accepted to my astonishment, and in French so good that I imagined her a Parisian. To a neighbor she afterwards spoke Italian, and with me she conversed in excellent English. Expressing my astonishment at her fluency in so many tongues, she said she was equally so in German. "But which is your vernacular, I would beg to know?" The question met with no satisfactory response. "I have lived in many of the United States," she replied, "in New York, New

Hampshire and others. "What towns in New Hampshire, my wonderful friend?" Among others, she mentioned Peterborough. "The birth-place of Judge Smith," I remarked. "Yes," she responded, "but the silver locks of this good old man are hidden in the tomb."—"Did you know the M. family?"—"Yes," she said immediately, "there are five or six, tall, long-legged sons, I remember John and Nat, Sam and Jim, and—there are several more for aught I know." Was n't she a queer acquaintance for a Paris masked ball? I must not forget to say that she polkaed *à ravir*. The next was pretty enough to be better. Without urging she gave me her address. In the course of the evening she sought for me, with the desire that I should give her some money to pay for her hack, as she was going to retire immediately. Two hours after, I saw her dancing with great animation. A fourth lady, whose superior education was very evident, after much urging for her address, wrote thus: "I am an angel; my home is in Paradise." Nothing farther could I learn. Thus continued this remarkable ball, without the least symptom of flagging, till half-past six in the morning, when the last dance was finished, and I went home, where I arrived in season for my morning visit to the Hospital.

From this sketch of my experience, some conception may be formed perhaps of the appearance and customs, the character of the persons who attend, their occupation while there, and finally the probable tendency, of the Bal Masqué. I shall leave you to draw your own conclusion.

VI.

CONDITION OF WOMEN—HAIR MARKET AT CAEN—BOURGEOIS PARTY—
FUNERALS OF THE RICH AND THE POOR.

I HAD no sooner set my foot upon the soil of France, than the servitude of the women arrested my attention; and this, too, in Havre, the birth-place of Madame de la Fayette. In this land of *politesse* and chivalry, one cannot but notice with wonder the numerous evidences of barbarism in the common walks of life. Women are employed to sweep the streets, transport the heaviest burdens, and in numerous other similar occupations. Often have I seen them, when age and disease had crippled their powers, carrying two pails of water, whose weight would terrify an American damsel of twenty years, upon shoulders already bowed down by the pressure of time, rudely jostled by the crowd, with scanty clothing, and no covering for the head, but a thin cap, which did not restrain their silver locks from playing around their wrinkled foreheads. Would to God, this were a single instance! 'T is but a poor picture drawn from the scenes of every-day life.

At Caen, but a short distance from Rouen, there is a market, whither young girls resort, and stand hour after hour with their flowing hair, rich and glossy, deriving additional lustre from the contrast with their naked shoulders. This is the resort of the merchant barbers, some of whom come even from England. The merchants pass along among them, examine the color, texture, evenness, and other qualities of the beautiful fleece, haggle for a sous, and finally buy. The hair then, after being cut as closely as possible to the head, is weighed and paid for, and the girl goes home to prepare for another shearing, or perhaps to purchase a husband with her money. An American girl prefers to let her hair turn to silver on her own head, or if it must be cut off, to enjoy the crop herself.

Higher up in the social scale is the small shop-keeper with Madame, who contributes to the income by teaching music and Italian, and constructing flowers with worsted. Of the first and last she knows but little; her talents, as a polyglot, I am unable to appreciate. She has her party, as well as those above her, consisting perhaps of thirty persons. Among them was a gentleman, who resided with Joseph Bonaparte at Bordentown for two years. Her apartments are on the second floor, in reality the third, for a vintner occupies the ground floor, as a shop. You go to the door, and knock with a massive ring eight inches in circumference, and so thick, that both hands are well-nigh required to lift it. It makes a tremendous noise. But—don't be alarmed, because the door gives away. It is the *concierge*, who, in his room at a distance of some forty feet, has pulled the cord attached to the spring latch. You shut the door on entering, and grope your way along, stumbling and stubbing against the pavement, towards the glimmer of the stearine candle in the dim distance. The concierge informs you, that Madame D——s rooms are on the second floor, whither you pursue your way in the dark, as before. You are admitted by the hostess herself into a little entry four feet square, deposit your chapeau, and enter the drawing-room. This is a "maid of all work." It answers for eating room, (I know not but kitchen too,) parlor and bed-chamber. In a niche is the bed with festooned curtains. The floor is of tiles, waxed. The walls are decorated with daguerreotype portraits of the family, some wood cuts of guinea pigs, and a horrid daub in oil, called a portrait. The mantle and a case of drawers contain, under a glass shade, specimens of Madame's talents in making flowers, and a metal clock. In a corner stands a miserable piano, shockingly out of tune.

Into this room, thus encumbered with furniture, you are ushered, and make your obeisance, probably to the portrait in oil, the only face that looks at you—no one seems to notice your arrival. The master is engaged in talking, and "it does not pay" to leave his conversation for a mere form. For a full half minute, the longest period that a Frenchman is still at one time, you are permitted to rest. That time is employed in taking a coup-d'œil of the company. It is a collection of ugly women of forty years, and a few girls, who are admitted into society, because their personal attractions expose them to no danger of being led astray. Around is a number of mustaches and beards, but no faces are at all perceptible. The half minute is over. You have no time to scrutinize, what indeed would not pay for the labor, for the hostess advances, seizes you by the hand, and hurries you to the dance. Ten couples commence a quadrille in this small room. At the piano are seated the two children of Madame, from six to ten years of age, who attempt a duet. When one of them hurries the time, after having got sufficiently ahead, she very obligingly waits for the other to "catch up," who, having succeeded, thinks it time to take the lead herself. Thus they proceed in regular alternations. All this time the dancers are performing wonders with their feet, somewhat at the expense of skin and bone, it is true, in so limited a sphere of action. There being two tunes, as we have said, the company have a choice, some preferring one, some the other. A considerable irregularity naturally ensues, till doubts begin to arise, as to what figure they are attempting to execute, when the quadrille becomes a riddle. Suddenly the noise of the piano changes. All ready for a gallopade—away we go, treading on each other's heels, and turning round, overturn some one, who chances to be next. Ah! there is a little more room now. The fat lady has "given in," and sits puffing like a locomotive. We gallop along, the space gradually becomes larger, for that young lady, who apparently has no dress on under that thin muslin cape, has lost a shoe in the race. Hip! away we go, my partner and I, "neck and neck," the gallop becomes a "trot" or "canter." My partner is certainly a Pegasus, and I am on the "rack." Ah! the orchestra has stopped performance. The waltz is now in the ascendant, and away we whirl again with another old lady, who, I perpetually fear, will shake off her curls. Were our habiliments different, we might be taken for the ancient Athletæ contending for the prize of wrestling. No wonder Byron and others have written so touchingly of the waltz. It is shocking. Ladies who waltz, should really abjure the bulbous esculents, and breathe of roses. "No, no—I do not wish to dance any more; I am not a polka man, but prefer to look over these card players." The interest is great, where two sous are at stake.

And so the scene continues from eight o'clock in the evening, to two and a half in the morning, interrupted only by the entrance of a liquid, called grog—Washingtonians need not be alarmed—it tastes of nothing but sugar and water, though, on a close examination, by the olfactories, the presence of a slight homœopathic dose of some kind of spirit is detected.

On inquiry, it is discovered, that at this *réunion*, there is a Portuguese, a German, a Scotchman, and an American. Our hostess is fond of lions, and she has got together a collection of birds, who warble different tongues; the consequence is, that, confined in so small a cage, all are uneasy and ennuyé. I inquired of several the names of their neighbors—none knew. Introductions are not thought of.

You, who live in a city, which has once had its ball-room in a grave-yard, will not be surprised, if you find in this letter, but a single step between my description of a dance and that of a funeral. Such is actual life. The house of feasting is often the very next door to the house of mourning. One cannot have had his eyes open in travelling along through the world, who has failed to observe that painful and startling intermingling of comic and tragical events, so vividly depicted by the master-hand of Shakspeare.

To-day I chanced to be passing the Church of St. Sulpice, just as a funeral procession was leaving its portals. A few days ago I witnessed a similar scene. There is nothing remarkable in either of these events, nothing can be more common than they were. It is this very commonness, which makes them penetrate the thoughtful soul so deeply, and renders them worthy of notice. The pageant, which is now passing before me, is the funeral of a rich man. A long line of black carriages, drawn by black horses, and driven by coachmen in black, followed a hearse in the same sombre color, with numerous curtains, adorned with silver lace and tassels, ostrich plumes, and other bravery. The noble horses, fretting under the bit, tossed their heads, richly decked with feathers, in the air. The sexton, in his long official robe, with cocked hat in hand, opened the coach doors for those who were to follow the honorable dead to the cemetery of Mount Parnassus; and with numerous bows, apparently regardless of crumpling his snowy neckcloth, ushered them in. The portals of the church were concealed by an ample curtain, similarly embellished; and within, immediately before the altar, was erected a temporary mausoleum of black hangings to the memory of the deceased.

The poor man's way to the grave contrasts very sadly with all this pompous marshalling of the opulent to his marble tomb. Nothing, in fact, can differ more, unless it be their several journeys through the perpetual hard toil, and boundless gratifications of their respective lives. It is not enough, it seems, to maintain these distinctions while they live; but they must be thrust as far as possible into the silent mansions of the departed; and, if it were practicable, the humble dead would be left literally "to bury their dead." We shall see in the other funeral occasion, to which I alluded, how nearly, in some places, they have approached the point of requiring the deceased poor to walk to the grave themselves.

It was the obsequies of a—nobody—evidently not "a feather in the cap" of any undertaker. A priest, in his long black robe and cocked hat, hurries along, as fast as possible, with his prayer-book under his arm. He threads the crowded street, dexterously dodges the numerous obstructions in the way, occasionally slipping on the muddy pavement, in his haste to finish the small job, which he has undertaken, of burying a poor man. After him, but scarcely able to keep equal pace with the holy man, encumbered as he was with his burden, came a person with a rough unpainted box upon his shoulder, containing the remains of mortality. This sweating porter was in his shirt-sleeves, which, unfortunately for the credit of the funeral procession, were not clean. No matter. Nobody but myself observed it. Finally, came the mourners. I should speak more correctly in the singular, for there was but one, who strode along, his sabots keeping time with the clinking of the living hearse before.

> "Death cuts down all,
> Both great and small."

as the Primer beautifully saith.

VII.

Musard—Mardi-Gras—Père Goriot—Louis Philippe—Bastringues—Traiteurs—Feasts—Fasts—Clergy—Confession—Order of the "Holy Cross."

The Carnival, with all its pleasures, extravagances and absurdities, is at length finished. The masked balls are suspended. The numerous crowds of joyous beings no longer throng the theatres and other dancing saloons. The reign of "Musard the Great," the distinguished composer of quadrilles and dances, is at an end. At one of the last balls at the Grand Opera, where he officiates as conductor of the two hundred musicians collected there, a number of the giddy dancers, making their way through their midst, penetrated to his throne, and taking him thence, bore him in triumph around the theatre, which rang with the voices of some six thousand persons, shouting *vive Musard, le Roi de la Danse*. The greatest excitement prevailed for some length of time in spite of the efforts of the soldiers and municipal guards, always present in all public assemblies, to prevent disturbance.

Mardi-Gras, or the fourth of February, being the last day of the Carnival, is the great holiday of the season. Into this is crowded more of folly and mirth, than any other day in the year. The whole community are permitted on this occasion to appear masked in the street, and under cover of this license to commit a thousand extravagances, which amuse this easily excited people. On the Boulevards—the fashionable promenade—crowds of people throng the *trottoirs* to witness the maskers, who, dressed in every color and fashion, rode through the streets in open vehicles. One I saw striding a poor old horse, whose every bone was distinctly visible through his shaved skin. The window of a victualer in the vicinity, attracted a large crowd. In it was displayed an immense turkey, apparently of some thirty pounds weight, stuffed with truffles. On it was affixed a label, stating that it was to be sent to the Duke of Wellington at a cost of one hundred dollars.

Mardi-Gras is the gala-day of the butchers; and the principal object of attraction is the procession, which is formed by them. It is but the remnant, however, of a great ceremony of olden times. The progress of modern refinement has gradually been detracting from the interest formerly attached to it, and soon, like others of these customs, it will fall into disuse, and finally be entirely neglected. From the fact of an ox, the largest and fattest that can be found, being led around the city in triumphal procession, and afterwards slaughtered, I have thought, that it might be the remnant of some religious solemnity, and that the ox was sacrificed to Jupiter, or some of the other heathen divinities. As it is, I will attempt a slight description. In order to make the entire circuit of the city, to visit the numerous public slaughter-houses, two days are employed; Mardi-Gras or Shrove Tuesday, and the Sunday preceding. They visit the King, the Ministers of State, and other functionaries. I was present at the Palace of the Tuilleries on the visitation to Louis Philippe. First, sedately marched a detachment of the Municipal Guards, then a band of musicians, each in a different dress of the most fantastic character, playing the popular airs of the day. These were followed by a detachment of young butchers on horseback, whose garbs represented the fashions of the courtiers of by-gone days. Surrounded by six or eight athletic men, bearing axes and other implements of this kind with wreaths upon their heads, who might be called the pall-bearers, came the colossal ox—the renowned *Père Goriot*, as he is styled—having a velvet mantle trimmed with gold lace upon his back, and his silvered horns glistening in the sunbeams. For a wonder the sun shone brightly for the first time during many weeks. In fear that he might be unable to walk two days in this procession, his place was filled on Sunday by one of the five others, who were competitors for the honors of Mardi-Gras. After him came a triumphal car, drawn by four horses in gorgeous trappings, in which were eight or ten of the butchers, apparently representing the mythological divinities. In their midst was a young child of some five years of age, who is called "l'Amour." He was clothed in a white muslin frock, with short sleeves. Around his head was a wreath of roses. I pitied this child, for the day was very cold. On the Sunday previous his little arms were purple, and he trembled involuntarily. Enveloped in a cloak and in my thick clothing, I was uncomfortable on this, one of the coldest days of the season. In the court yard of the palace the procession halted. The King, Queen, and the young Count of Paris, the heir to the throne, came out upon the balcony, and saluted the dense crowd, which filled the place. It grieved me to notice the feeble shouts of the people at the appearance of the King. I longed to hear those old walls ring, and his ears to be regaled with such huzzas as greet Daniel Webster, or any of our great men, when coming before the people. I was sorry to see another proof of the little appreciation the people have for a monarch, the wisest in the world, who consults with great tact the best interests of France.

At a sign from the King, the cortége dismounted, and, while some danced the Polka to the fine music of the band, others at his particular invitation, entered the palace, bearing with them "Love," who probably was not sorry to have an opportunity to warm his chilled members. During this interview, an incident worthy of notice occurred. While the attention of the royal family was otherwise directed, one of the butchers, in the garb of a courtier of the time of Louis XIV, made his appearance in the balcony, which a short time previous had been occupied by the King. He was received by the crowd with great cheering. A liveried menial, authoritatively striking him upon the back, soon brought him to his proper place. The interview finished, they returned to their proper stations, the cortége again commenced its march, the King retired, and shortly after the court-yard was empty. The poor ox too soon finished his journey, and duly killed and dressed, was eaten, a portion by the royal family of France, another portion forwarded to London, formed a part of the Lent dinner of Queen Victoria and her spouse—Marshal Soult and the other ministers shared the remainder—and thus ended the days of the Père Goriot of 1845.

The evening of this day was spent by many of the inhabitants of Paris, in attending the masked balls, of which there were some twenty. The balls at the barriers were also fully attended. These are at the places called *Bastringues*. Outside of the barriers are the houses and gardens of *traiteurs*, a kind of victualler. They are called *guinguettes;* and here the lower classes resort in great numbers to drink and to eat; for the wine and provisions not having paid the tax, which is levied by the government on every article brought within the city walls, can be afforded of a better quality for the same money. For instance, a bottle of Burgundy wine pays eight cents duty, and is worth twenty cents in the city. In these guinguettes it may be obtained for nearly half the money. When a guinguette adds an orchestra and a ball-room to its other attractions, it is called a bastringue. At the barrier St. Martin there are numerous places of this sort, and, for a great number of years, there has existed a custom at the close of the Carnival, after finishing the bal-masqués of the city, for all the maskers to ride to this barrier. This has received the name of "the descent of the masks." In order to see it in the company of my friends, I arrived at the barrier at four o'clock, A. M. It being then too early, the city balls not having finished, we went into one of these bastringues. The price of admission was twenty cents, or one franc each, and entitled us to admission and a bottle of wine a-piece, either white or red Burgundy, and of quite a good quality. See us then entering with a bottle in one hand, a tumbler in the other, with hat askew, endeavoring to have the appearance of "being no better than we should be,"—a very necessary precaution in this quarter of the city, and at this time of night. At tables around the room were seated the men, women and children of the lowest classes of society, some eating, all drinking. The soiled dresses gave a not very pleasant odor to the place. On one side, an orchestra of perhaps a dozen musicians were hard at work, and before them sixty or more dancing with great energy, evidently endeavoring to "get their money's worth." The space for dancing was surrounded by a fence, to keep off the crowd, for the dancers paid for each performance five cents. At the end of the figure the place was vacated, and a man at the gates took his toll on each one, as he entered. Some time was passed here quite pleasantly, but soon, the maskers beginning to arrive, we went into the street to view them. For several hours we stood witnessing the constant succession of carriages passing by, filled with women and men, some having lanterns or torches, laughing and shouting, and at seven in the morning we retired, the current still rolling on.

This custom, like many of the others connected with the observance of the Carnival, is fast wearing away, and now it is observed more as a matter of habit, than one of real interest. Indeed, the observance of the ceremonies connected with the Catholic church, are here very much neglected. Their feast days and fast days pass like all others, and are known only by the sound of the bells, which announce them. If you enter the churches on any of these days, unless perhaps on Christmas, you find but very few worshippers. The marriages are solemnized in the churches, but those that are married are, when there, inattentive to the service, and employed, sometimes in conversing, sometimes in laughing. I have even seen the bridegroom with great difficulty restraining his laughter. The Catholic religion prescribes a peculiar diet for particular seasons, yet few conform to it, and, when asked the reason, and on being charged with not being Catholics, they reply, that they are Catholics, but not "*devotes*." I inquired of several, what they said when they went to confession? They replied, that "they merely answered the questions of the priest." But did you not *confess*, literally speaking, any sin that you had committed? "If he asked me, I did, *sometimes*." Thus, the confessional is merely a dead-letter, a form only. I am afraid that the character of the priests in general, is not such as to raise the standard of religion, or even of morality. Many of the better classes, of both sexes, have said to me, after conversing upon their habits with that freedom, which is done only in France, "I like the religion very much, but I do not like the priests." The grisettes have given me descriptions of their actions and conversation, even in the confessional, which are equal to anything in the book published as the disclosures of Maria Monk. For their truth I cannot vouch. They have, however, been told me by more than one, names mentioned, and even the churches to which they were attached, the description of the person, &c. &c. They are such, that if true, must necessarily sink their reputation in the eyes of every one. Is it strange, that with such a clergy, or at least with the general belief among the community of their character, that the reputation of the church should decline?

His holiness, the Pope,* is in not much better repute. Falsehood, however, is the crime alleged to him. The passion for wearing decorations is here the mania, as that for wearing the title of Major, or General, is in the United States. The order of the Holy Cross, in the gift of the Pope, may be bought, as I am credibly informed, for fifty dollars, from his ambassador, and with it, a statement from the Pope himself, that it was earned by some meritorious deed, which is mentioned with numerous particulars, done in behalf of the church. I question, if the Puseyites in receiving the creed, accept the Pope and his clergy with it. The Protestants of Paris have a much higher reputation. They are styled by the Catholics *devotes*.

* Gregory XVI. Since deceased.

VIII.

WEATHER—FUEL—POOR—GRAND OPERA—VIENNESE DANCING GIRLS—CARLOTTA GRISI—DUCHESS D'AUMALE—PRINCESS AND PRINCE DE JOINVILLE—PERSIANI—MARIO—JULIA GRIZI.

THIS has been an uncomfortable winter. I would not complain, merely because the French *language* is a stranger to the *word* comfort; but the misery is, that comfort is not to be met with *anywhere*, neither in the language, nor the houses, nor the streets. Many of the latter are shockingly muddy and destitute of *trottoirs;* and the sidewalks, where any exist, are so narrow, that it is necessary to step into the gutter, to permit another person to pass. Without being very cold, the weather is often excessively chilly. On the day of the meeting of the Chamber of Deputies in the latter part of December, a fog, as dense as any that float over the river Connecticut in a summer's morning, enveloped the city, completely shrouding the king and the whole military host from view. It lasted all the day and night; the impenetrable darkness of which resisting every effort to disperse it by extra lights at the corners of the streets, occasioned serious accidents. Such is the state of things abroad. The administration of affairs within doors is very little better. In the ordinary sort of residences, a room is separated from the rest of the house by a frame covered with paper. The windows are large, and open with a hinge. These are frail defences against a wintry atmosphere; for snow and ice are not uncommon visitants at Paris. The means of warming these airy dwellings is, perhaps, a *white* China stove; and the heat, evolved by the combustion of green wood, of course takes French leave up the chimney. I believe it impossible to get *dry* wood here, because it is sold by weight.

For several days past, the weather has been cold and warm, wet and dry. The thermometer has fallen to 14° Fahrenheit, and the cold has quite terrified the people, unaccustomed to such severity. The Seine was frozen over a few days, sufficiently to suspend navigation. This, apparently a trivial matter, was of very great importance to the inhabitants, especially the poor; for the suspension of navigation immediately produced an advance in the price of coal of five cents on the hundred pounds. The French custom, which exists among the better classes from inclination, and among the lower from necessity, of living from "hand to mouth," obliges them to purchase fuel every week; so that, in case of obstruction in navigation, the stock on hand is soon exhausted; especially at this time, when the consumption is much more rapid than usual, in consequence of the augmented rigor of the weather. Thus the great evil in this, as in most other cases, in France, falls upon the poor. Several slight showers of snow, which covered the dirty streets with a white coat of some two inches in thickness, has entirely destroyed the equilibrium of the people. Were they half as active in removing the slimy, slippery, filth, which fills most of the thoroughfares, as they are in carting away this cleanly visitor, more might be said of their neatness, which cannot now be included in the catalogue of their virtues. Indeed, the papers are loud in their praises of the department for putting three thousand workmen (half women!) and six hundred carts, in employ to remove the snow, and empty it into the Seine.

Saturday evening I attended the Grand Opera, on the occasion of the benefit of thirty-six young dancing girls from Vienna. These children are between the ages of four and fifteen years, and their astonishing performances have drawn a crowd during six weeks, which has filled the largest theatre in Paris. On this evening, notwithstanding the prices were nearly doubled, (varying from one dollar to four, according to the situation) the house was crammed to its utmost capacity. The play of Molière's *Le Bourgeoise Gentilhomme*, afforded an excellent opportunity for these performers. The Polka and Mazourka were introduced with great effect. The novel and difficult figures, and the extraordinary skill of these little children, brought down thunders of applause. Though viewing them with pleasure, I could not banish the thought, that their lot at present was similar to that of dancing dogs; that their wonderful art and grace were not acquired in the splendid satin robes, which they then wore, but in soiled rags, and at the expense of reproofs and blows. Their sweet countenances, as yet unused to dissimulation, too plainly revealed the fact, that this exhibition, causing transports to others, was a weary labor to them. But when the beholder thinks of their future life, his pleasure is still further diminished. Young and innocent now, very soon they become kept mistresses, and their descent is afterwards rapid to the condition of the common courtezan, the street-sweeper, the inmate of the hospital, the *subject of the dissecting-room!* Here we leave them—the secrets of another world are not, as yet, unfolded.

The "Ball of Gustavus," among others of reputation, introduced Mademoiselle Carlotta Grisi, who, after Ellsler and Cerito, holds the first rank as a dancer; Taglioni's departure from the stage making her the third on the list. According to the opinion of many, sanctioned by the general applause, which she elicited,

"She ne'er danced better,
Every footstep fell as lightly
As the moonbeam on the waters."

In the concluding dance by the Viennese, some one, instead of a bouquet, more wisely threw upon the stage several boxes of sugar-plums, the breaking of which caused more activity than grace among them. Those, who thought them Cupids before, suffered a terrible shock in their feelings by the sudden metamorphosis.

Among the distinguished spectators were the Duchess D'Aumâle, and the Princess and Prince de Joinville. The keenest aspirer for rank and station, unless totally devoid of taste, would hesitate to accept the eminence of the young prince, if he were obliged to take with it the princess also. To be sure, he would possess a princess of Brazil, and a heap of gold and diamonds, but with them must be included a face, whose most prominent characteristic is a long nose, which does not appear less long, or ugly, because it is princely; a skin probably colored by contact with Brazilian gold; and a neck, which, though rivaling the swan's in length, certainly does not in whiteness, or in grace. Her head-dress, of flamingo colors, was deficient in that taste, which belongs to every French woman of the realm. The Duchess D'Aumale, though coming from the extreme south of Italy, has the complexion of a Saxon. Her face, devoid of color, is deformed by a nose, which, sympathising with her neighbor's in length, has apparently received some blow, which renders it somewhat of a pug. This is a term I desire to use with diffidence, because I fear it may not be often heard at court in relation to the nasal organs of royalty. If not, you must pardon me for the sake of the truth which it expresses. A feather of a bluish tint was very well arranged, and dropped gracefully over the left ear. In short, neither they, nor the prince, were adapted to make a favorable impression on one, whose ideas of the beauty of princesses and princes had been drawn from his researches in the Arabian Nights' Entertainments.

Last evening was the benefit of Madame Grisi, at the Italian Opera, and a large company of auditors "assisted," as the French phrase has it, at the representation. The evening performances commenced with the first act of 'La Ssomnambula,' by Bellini, in which Madame Persiani, and Monsieur Mario sung most delightfully. The praises of both of these celebrated actors have been wafted all over the world; it is therefore needless for me to attempt a description. Her voice is not powerful, but sweet and flexible, and lingers on the ear long after its sounds have died away. It is in her graceful execution, that she is most distinguished. All vocalists know the great difficulty of singing softly, and at the same time well. But Persiani executes the most difficult strains upon the lowest and highest keys alike, in the most touching manner, when the least noise in the house would entirely drown her notes. Her shakes and trills, like the motion of the trembling leaves of the silver aspen, which rustle without a breath of wind, are performed without apparent effort. In personal appearance it cannot be denied, that she is rather plain. "I would not hear her enemies say so." The critics, I believe, give her the palm among the artists in Paris.

Mario is by birth a Prince of Italy, but, like many others of that country, was poor. If he is so now, it is his own fault, as his large salary at this theatre, and in London, if saved, would soon enrich him. In point of rank, he stands below the celebrated Rubini, now in St. Petersburg. His voice is a fine tenor, sweet and flexible, and is augmented in compass by a falsetto of very superior excellence. As an actor, he is not distinguished. The second piece, the famous Norma, likewise by Bellini, exhibited Grisi in her best character. The residents in and around New Jersey, are all familiar with the Opera; but were they to witness the "queen of song," in this her best part, I think they would be obliged to confess, that "the half had never been told them!"

Though to Grisi, as a singer, is assigned by the critics a rank inferior to Persiani, and Dorus Gras of the French Opera, her performances are much better liked. This is because she combines beauty with tragic and musical talent. As a beauty, she is not precisely what we should call so in America, where women, thus distinguished, must not very much exceed the age of twenty years. At forty-five, Madame Grisi is not a rose-bud, but the full blown flower. In her, one looks in vain for the delicious tint of youth, but this by gaslight is not much needed. In its place shines out the matured woman. Her face is oval, full, with regular features, Grecian nose, exquisitely beautiful teeth, and black, glossy hair, which, in length and beauty, rivals George Sands' description of the famous *chevelure*, of the Princess Quintilian. Her eyes may be gray, or blue, or black. One can scarcely seize their color, so changeable are they every moment. The expression of the countenance, when at rest, is sad, melancholy; but, when excited by the character which she personates, it vividly reflects her varying emotions. As a tragedian, I have seen no equal in her sex. In the distinct line of tragedy, where plain prose is unencumbered with musical expression, I question, if she does not surpass even Rachel herself. Though laboring under this serious disadvantage, her passages are enunciated with startling impetuosity. Her tones and acts of tenderness, or passion, possess a truthfulness, which find a response in the breast of every hearer. If inferior in talent and cultivation, as a singer, to Persiani, or Dorus Gras, which I am, myself, unwilling to allow, her immensely powerful voice, far superior to either of her rivals, added to her imposing presence, and tragic force, renders her by far the superior artist. This is evident from the fact, that she is engaged for the coming season in London at the Queen's Theatre, while Persiani is rejected.

It is really a pity, that one, so distinguished for talents, should be almost as much so for her gallantry. Her history, as far as I can learn, is substantially this. She was born in a small village near Milan, where she first appeared. Nothing very remarkable distinguished her performances there. For several years she sang unnoticed, till accident brought her to Paris. Following the fortunes of a banished lover, she broke her theatrical engagement, and the next we hear of her is on the French stage, and at the same time the mistress of an English nobleman. Her beauty and talents induced Lord Castlereagh to overlook her character as a woman, and he soon after married her. After a few years, being divorced by law, and once more free, she lived with the celebrated composer Bellini (who wrote for her 'I Puritani,') till his death, when she passed to the great singer Rubini, now at St. Petersburg. On his departure, his place in the affections of this apparently easily pleased woman, was soon supplied by his successor at the opera, Mario. This lady, whose talents and beauty may shade, but cannot conceal her faults, was received on this night of her benefit with boundless plaudits, and pelted with bouquets throughout the evening. At the close of the performance, when called out to receive the homage of the audience, her path was literally on flowers. Wreaths and bouquets almost covered the stage, thrown by the fair hands of the nobility and beauty of France. Her salary for six months in Paris is sixty thousand dollars, and it is the same in London.

IX.

Love of Country—Danger of Assassination—Tapis Francs—Prevalence of Crime—The Morgue—Henri Herz—Concert of Sixteen Pianos and Thirty-two Players—Priests—Midwifery—Artificial Arm.

The reception of letters from home, after a lapse of almost five months without the least tidings, has a very enlivening effect. I am astonished at the avidity with which I seek for news from America, though of persons and things of which I possessed no previous knowledge: every thing is attended with interest. Ah! the ties that bind one to his country are strong indeed. They live in the forest of his recollections. They are bound strongly around the family tree, and run along its numerous branches. They cling to the stumps of old friendships, which seem to have received new life, and wind themselves around the unfading image of schoolboy days, which, like the solitary pine, a scathed and blackened remnant of a noble company, that have passed away forever, still exists, a pleasant vision in the soul, though draped by sorrow and bereavement. They are twisted together with old loves, which, though their verdant tops have been long since dead, remain firmly fixed in the heart.

One may well think of home, when it is so uncertain whether he will ever see again the shores of his native country. Not only does he encounter the chances of a natural death from change of climate, the dangers of the sea, and the accidents of travel by land, but even when quietly at rest in his Paris home, he is subject to one unknown in the United States. The hazard of assassination is by no means slight, and is equally dreaded by the man of courage and the timid. To give you a faint conception, I will mention a few circumstances, which have lately happened in this city, filled as it is with troops constantly on guard in numerous places; with agents of police, and secret spies of government. One can scarcely go ten steps at midday or midnight, without meeting some of these gentry. Notwithstanding this, a young woman walking, a short time ago, through the very heart of the city, was met, near the Italian Opera House, by a well-dressed man, who, after passing her, turned suddenly round, and placed a mask of pitch upon her face, so that she could neither call for assistance, nor even breathe. He bound her fast, and, after robbing her of one dollar and seventy-five cents, left her to her fate. Fortunately, she was soon discovered and her mask removed, before she was entirely suffocated. This was transacted almost under the eyes of the guard, and at only eleven o'clock at night.

Scarcely two weeks ago, the police surrounded the *guinguettes* and *tapis francs*, at the barrier of St. Martin's, which I visited a short time before, and gave you a slight description of, in a recent letter. The readers of Eugene Sue's "Mysteries of Paris," very well know the character of the *tapis franc*. They took from them two hundred and ninety-nine persons, and put them into prison. On a subsequent examination, one hundred and ninety-nine of them, who could give a satisfactory account of their manner of living, were set at liberty. The remaining one hundred are retained for trial. Among them are numerous murderers, thieves, and other felons. An entire band of assassins and thieves, to the number of eighteen, was included in this single draught of the net of the police.

In a part of one of these *tapis francs*, called the Cave, was found the body of a murdered man.

Ten days ago, the chief of a band of murderers and robbers was guillotined. Though but twenty-three years of age, young Fourrier had confessedly killed twenty-four men! I hope that this is not a specimen of the Fourrier system, which my friend Horace Greely so warmly and ably advocates. I saw his body and head in the dissecting-room. His physiognomy would not lead any one to doubt the truth of the charges alleged against him.

A carriage was stopped, a few nights since, in front of Meurice's Hotel—the resort of all American and English travellers—and its occupants plundered at nine in the eve! Coming still nearer, only Monday evening last, in the next street to me, a man was assassinated and robbed of two or three dollars at ten o'clock in the night. In this short street there is a guard-house, and having a friend residing there, I have been accustomed to pass through it at all hours of the night.

Some of my brave Americans may ask me, "Why do you not carry arms, so that when you see a suspicious individual approaching you may be ready?" In answer to this I say, the assassins are not suspicious *looking* individuals. As you are walking in the street, you pass a well-dressed man, who instantly turns, and the first suspicion of your danger is derived from feeling a poniard in the back. 'Tis then too late to stand on the defensive, and draw your dagger. In a moment you are robbed, and thrown over the quay into the Seine. The next morning your friends, seeking for you, find your body in the Morgue.

This structure has been often described. It is a building appropriated for a receptacle of all persons found dead in the city. As I pass by it, on my way to the hospital "Hotel-Dieu," I frequently look in. What tales of suffering those gloomy walls might tell, could they but echo back the groans of the many wretches, that have therein been deposited! The poor seduced girl, who in despair has thrown herself from the quay into the rapid, turbid Seine, is fished up, brought hither, stripped of all her clothing, which is hung up by her side, a soiled cloth placed upon her loins, and exposed for public exhibition. Here, too, is brought the miserable and decrepid man, who has died from cold and hunger at the corner of a street. But no one claims his withered, meagre body, and he is carried to the silent tomb in a coffin of rough boards, without a relative to follow him to the grave, or a friend to shed a tear. Poverty begets no friends.

To change the subject, let me tell you of a concert which I attended on the 20th. It was given by the celebrated Henri Herz, whose music is in the hands of every one in the United States. It was held at half-past one o'clock, P. M., in his saloon. This is one of the most magnificent rooms in Paris. Its lofty walls are supported by numerous richly carved and gilt pillars, and ornamented with portraits in fresco of Weber, Beethoven, and others. The whole interior was radiant with gold, and this morning, with diamonds, bright eyes, and beaming faces. The performances consisted principally of duos, trios, and quartettes upon the piano, by the pupils of Herz, together with some fine solo singing and solos on the violin and bass-viol, or as more fashionably styled, violincello. Herz himself assisted in one piece, but it was not one calculated to exhibit his powers. The most peculiar compositions were the following: "Overture of 'Puits d'Amour,' Balfe, arranged for fifteen pianos by M. Billard, and executed by thirty pupils." "Overture of 'Semiramide,' Rosini, arranged for sixteen pianos and executed by thirty-two pupils. These were produced with very fine effect. Such a number of instruments of this kind played together, is, I think, a novelty, even in Paris. This concert was entirely gratuitous, and intended to exhibit the proficiency of the pupils, many of whom had gained prizes. The pianists were all young girls, whose ages varied from twelve to twenty. The youngest indeed executed as well, if not better, than any of the others. In short, it was a performance which well sustained the reputation of their instructor.

In music and dancing one frequently has a *pot-pourri*. I think, that a similar melange of tittle-tattle, odds-and-ends, and gossip, may well enough serve the turn of bringing this letter to a close. Voila! Two great men honor Paris with their presence, Lord Brougham, and General Tom Thumb. M. Michelet, the celebrated lecturer and writer, has lately issued a work, of which the first edition was almost immediately sold; the second edition being issued in three weeks. It is entitled "The priest, the wife, the family." The attack, commenced in previous works against the clergy, as at present existing, is kept up with great spirit. M. Michelet lectures three times a week at the college of France to a most crowded audience, who come from half-an-hour to an-hour beforehand to obtain a seat. A celebrated Abbé who has attempted to answer his charges, lecturing with more warmth than judgment, has been compelled to discontinue his course by order of government.

The treatise on Midwifery by Chailly, of this city, translated by Dr. Bedford of New York, has passed into a second edition here, much augmented and improved. The medical community await with great impatience a treatise on the same subject by the celebrated Paul Dubois, who is at the head of this branch in France. It is the labor of many years, and besides containing all the previous information in relation to it up to the present time, will be enriched with new matter, derived from the investigation of its talented author. It is said that the work is already in the hands of the publishers.

Another hospital is shortly to be commenced in this city, to be called the Louis Philippe.

M. Magendie read on Monday last, in the name of a committee of the Academy, composed of Messrs Gambey, Velpeau, Rayer and Magendie, a report upon an *artificial arm* presented by M. Van Petersen, a Dutch sculptor. "It is not one of the least prodigies of human industry to be able in some sort to re-construct the work of the Creator by repairing destroyed organs, and even replacing them entirely, by means of mechanical apparatus. The new invention, which M. Magendie has made known to the Academy, the object of which is to replace the entire arm, and even both of them, is certainly one of the boldest of its kind; and the service, which it promises to render to a large number of mutilated unfortunates, accounts for the interest with which the committee are examining it. To replace the arm and hand in all the extent, variety, rapidity and precision, which nature has given to the motion of this member, is doubtless a thing impossible; and the inventor exhibits no such lofty pretensions. He proposes only to give to persons deprived of their arms, the power of performing for themselves actions the most simple and necessary to existence. The committee of the Academy have seen the invention of M. Van Petersen upon five mutilated individuals, and among others upon an invalid, who has been deprived of both arms ever since the wars of the empire, and who, by the aid of two artificial arms, took with his hand a full glass, carried it to his mouth, drank from it without spilling a drop, and then replaced the glass upon the table, from which he had taken it.

This same disabled man can pick up a pin, take hold of a sheet of paper, &c.

The artificial arm of M. Van Petersen, is not adapted indifferently to all, who have lost an arm; those only, who have preserved untouched the superior part of the humerus, are fitted to profit by it, and it can render no service to those who have no stump, and have submitted to an amputation of the shoulder. The invention is composed of three parts, articulated and moveable, which represents the arm, the forearm, and the hand. This last composes a kind of wrist, with fingers of triple phalanges, moveable, and maintained in a firm state of flexion and resistance with the thumb by springs. The whole weighs scarcely five hundred grammes, (equal to about a pound of the standard weight of the mint of Paris.) The stump of the maimed arm is received in a cavity of the machine, and the following is the contrivance, by the aid of which M. Van Petersen has succeeded in making the different parts play upon one another. A corset is fastened over the breast. To this corset are attached catgut strings, some of which are fixed to the forearm, others to the fingers. When the maimed man carries the stump forward, he exerts attraction upon the forearm, and bends it on the arm. When, on the contrary, he moves it backward, the forearm stretches out upon the arm. It is by this double movement, that the hand is carried to, or removed from, the mouth. The movements of the fingers are produced by analogous mechanism; and the committee have been struck with the celerity and precision, to which mutilated persons have arrived in executing them. The idea of employing a corset, as a support necessary to overcome the resistance of mechanical fingers shut by springs, is not new. Quite recently, Grafe had indicated the part, which might be drawn upon for the construction of a mechanical arm; but no one, until now, has been able to execute this project, at least with the success which M. Van Petersen has obtained. The committee think, that the invention of the latter is preferable to any, that has been previously conceived with the same design. They hope, that the author will be able to improve it still further, and especially to reduce its price, so as to render it accessible to the amputated poor and to mutilated soldiers."

X.

FASHIONS—BIRTH-DAY OF WASHINGTON—BALL OF THE AMERICAN MINISTER—EXPENSES OF THE EMBASSY—BALL OF THE CAFE TORTONI.

"WHAT!"—I think I hear the ladies say—"so many wearisome long letters, and not a line about the idol of our hearts! Among dingy princesses with long noses, and splendid actresses with short-comings, the empress herself, who rules them all, has been wholly overlooked. And this, too, in her own metropolis, and in the very seat of her fascinating court. How is it, that you only find time to prose away about women who wear masks and breeches, and poor he-devils too indigent to get either; artistes of good *heels*, or *voices*, rewarded with salaries of one hundred thousand dollars a year, and miserable beings, of good hearts, who starve in the shadow of the theatres and opera houses, where crowds are paying their costly and noisy homage to those frail divinities that reign within? Pray, say no more about a nation who cannot do without a king, and yet don't know when they have got a good one—till you have told us what the fashion is."

Really, I wonder at the oversight myself. Beside a dozen more as good, the intrinsic difficulty of the subject must be an ample apology. The painter could not catch the Protean features of the inimitable Garrick. Which of you can stay the evanescent shapes and tints of the sunset clouds, while you are putting them down upon the canvas? If one passes along the streets of Paris to see the mode, he is, at the very outset, "in a sea of trouble." Two persons can hardly be met with, who agree in dress. Enter into any place, a hat or bonnet shop, for instance, and inquire for their goods in the best style, a half dozen will be shown, all of which the polite tenders assure you, are equally in the fashion, and equally worn. Every body in the the United States knows very well, that the fashions there originate in Paris; but, every body asks, whence do the Parisians get them? This is the important secret, which I am about to tell. It was disclosed to me by the highest possible authority—which you will all acknowledge to be so, too—a *milliner* in the best street in the Latin quarter, where I reside. In the meantime, pray ladies don't allow yourselves to be thinking of caps and bonnets, for if you do, not all the "Brown's and Preston's Inexhaustible Smelling Salts" will prevent a hysterical fit, after you have heard the secret. When I certify, that this accomplished woman has had twenty years' experience in the business, I think you will allow, that I know how fashions are invented without the shadow of a doubt.

Take a stroll in Broadway on any fine day, and you will observe, that every one is dressed alike. The coat is cut the same, the pants' are apparently turned out by a machine, and boots have toes of the same curve, and heels of the same height. I wonder, if those *petit-maitres*, who plume themselves on being *bien chaussé*, know, that stable-boys in Paris sport *French boots.* If they are indeed aware of this surprising fact, is it not strange, that they should worship them, as they do? The freedom existing here in the selection of one's dress allows, it must be obvious, the exercise of taste. If any one is pleased to think, that a particular shape, or combination of color would be becoming, a garment is forthwith constructed according to her fancy. Another is struck with the phenemenon, approves its taste, and straightway orders one like it. Thus many styles have at the same time their respective partizans; but that which obtains the largest suffrage is said to culminate, and is thenceforth pronounced *the* fashion. Thereupon it is forwarded to America, and seized upon in haste by all, each expanding its peculiarities in the most outré manner, in her eagerness to outdo her neighbors, and become the most fashionable. One says, that bustles are the fashion; yet six in Paris might be made of the hair, straw, bran or cotton, that go to the composition of one, which forms the beautiful outline of a Broadway belle. At present, indeed, another texture is said to usurp the throne; but it is not to be expected, that I should know any thing concerning it.

At several recent balls, where I have been present, I observed the different toilets quite critically; but it is a difficult matter to decide what was the rage, silks or satins, muslins or velvets. In one thing all agreed, that diamond tiaras, necklaces, ear-rings, &c. &c., were in good taste, provided the stones were as large as small filberts. The toilet for young men consists of black dress coat and pants, vest of white marseilles embroidered, with a cravat of black satin, or white stamped cotton, only long enough to tie in front; or a vest of cassimere embroidered with silk, with a white cravat, as above. Full toilet requires pumps and silk hose.

Last evening was passed by most of the Americans in Paris in the same manner as they have been accustomed to spend at home the anniversary of the birth of Washington. Mr. King, our excellent minister at the court of France, opened his house on this occasion for the reception of the Americans in Paris, and such others as were interested in the welfare of America. This was the first ball that his health has permitted him to give this winter, and I think, since his arrival in the country. Unfortunately the change, from the dry and warm atmosphere of his own state to this constantly damp and cold city, prevents his seeing his countrymen so often as his natural hospitality would dictate. At this time, however, the Americans in Paris were collected together for the first time. I found several old acquaintances and townsmen, who I imagined to be still at home, where I had left them. It was quite late, near eleven o'clock, when I arrived, having been detained by the breaking down of my hack. As I entered the spacious apartments, and saw the graceful forms in the mazes of the whirling waltz, I did not think the Americans were far behind the French, either in beauty or any other respect. The only ornament to the rooms was a portrait of Washington, a copy by Healy, from the celebrated original, belonging, I believe, but am not sure, to Lord Landsdown. It was, at any rate, a portrait of the incomparable Washington, and that was enough to arouse all our patriotic ardor. It is strange, how little the French know of this great man. One of them, on reading my invitation, which stated that it was in honor of the birth of Washington, very inquisitively asked, *Vashington, Vashington, qui est cet Vashington la?* At the palace of Versailles there is a picture representing a scene in American history, where General Rochambeau is placed in a most conspicuous situation, and Washington is cast quite into the shade by his greatness. Exotics and other flowers embellished, and, at the same time, scattered delightful odors throughout the saloons. Surrounded by those who spoke the same language, and whose breasts were swelled by similar emotions for the first time in this land of strangers, I felt myself at home. Here were fair examples of the grace and beauty of the cities of New York, Philadelphia, Boston, Charleston, New Orleans, as well as specimens of nobility and station in the persons of the Prince and Princess de Joinville, Duke de Montpensier, the Austrian, Prussian, and other repsesentatives at this Court, and many of the nobility of England and other countries. The news of the decease of the brother of the British Ambassador prevented the attendance of Lord Cowley. I had the honor of dancing the Polka several times with a pretty, graceful, and animated grand-daughter of General Lafayette. The present consul, Mr. Walsh, the ex-consul Mr. Draper, and their families, were among the guests. Mons. Guizot, whose health would not allow him to be there in person, sent his regrets, stating his great respect for the memory of the illustrious American patriot.

With such music, as was poured around by Tolbecque, and his celebrated band, which never fails to infuse life and activity into all, who could possibly stand still? Polkas, mazourkas, waltzes, *deux temps et trois*, and quadrilles permitted the taste of every one to be gratified. Moreover, we discovered that "Yankee Doodle" makes a capital quadrille.

An excellent table in an adjoining room, loaded with every delicacy, allowed the guests to refresh themselves as they wished. Behind it the head servant of Mr. King directed his assistants. He is a tall, intelligent negro, and appears devotedly attached to his master. I said to him one day, "I am very glad to see you, it looks to me so much like home." "Ah, yes," said he, "but it is not home; I shall be glad to return." This man, though free, and in a country where the blacks and whites are on an equal footing, and beautiful white women are occasionally seen promenading arm-in-arm with them in the streets, and though gratified here with having numerous white servants under his direction, still prefers his southern home, with all the degradations to which he is there exposed. At four o'clock the ball broke up, the orchestra playing "Hail Columbia," which received the plaudits of the company, when all returned to their temporary homes, to dream, I fancy, of their real ones, so far distant.

The American Minister is about to exchange this house for a smaller. His expenses, though giving few dinner parties and no balls, amount to scarcely less than seventy dollars a day. The wood bill alone for a year is fourteen hundred dollars. I was on the point of exclaiming, increase the salaries of the French and English ambassadors, or else abolish their offices, when a sudden thought quite checked my indignation. How many men have sacrificed, and are perhaps this moment sacrificing their ease, and, I am afraid, in some cases, their consciences too, at home, in order to obtain these same costly, but honorable, offices abroad!

Writing to you of one party reminds me of another, which I attended lately. A slight description of it may give some notion of the difference between the customs of this city and the United States, which, for convenience sake, I hope may some time or other be expressed by a more appropriate name. I would not quarrel with Atlanta or Telluria, Columbia, Yankeedom, or Interoceanos, since I could then inform a questioner who I am, which is not an easy thing to do at present.

The party was given at the café Tortoni, on the Boulevard des Italiens. Who, that has ever been at Paris, has not often heard of the celebrated ices of the café Tortoni? I do not say ice *creams*, because they are composed of neither cream nor milk; but flavored with every article almost that man was ever induced to taste from the beginning of time till now. Raspberry, strawberry, lemon, and such like, of course, are used, and chocolate, coffee, rum, and all sorts of liqueurs. Thinking of these unparalleled manufactures has involuntarily led my pen astray; pardon! we will return to the ball.

Madame, the hostess, unfortunately *knew few gentlemen*, and, as French ladies drink no tea, she justly considered that a party of none but ladies might possibly be quite stupid. I think, myself, she was right. But how could she obtain these desirable gentlemen, namely, those who could dance, and waltz, and polka? You will be surprised to be informed, that half the gentlemen have not these valuable gifts, though we have always thought that Frenchmen brought them with them at their birth. So she asked a friend of hers *to invite six gentlemen to come and dance*, eat her ices, and be agreeable. Unluckily, the male acquaintances of her friend proved to be not more numerous than her own, so she asked *my hostess*—who asked me, and I—asked three American friends. On my accepting, the husband of the friend came to make my acquaintance the evening of the ball. We agreed to meet at the place. Arriving there before him, we intended to wait in the anteroom till his appearance. In this we were prevented by the host, who, *on hearing the name of the person who invited us, insisted on our entering.* When the gentleman and his wife came, he introduced me to her, to whom I introduced *my friends*, after which he introduced us all to the lady of the house.

This is all that etiquette demands. One asks anybody to dance with him, whether an acquaintance or not; and after the dance is finished, it is the lady who says, "I am much obliged to you!" When I heard this first, I was *astonished*. *I thought it was something peculiar and extraordinary*, began to be a little proud, and replied, "Certainly not; it is I that am indebted." I here began *to feel the risings of* a Turkish sentiment, and to question, whether, after all, it is not, in reality, I that do the favor. Such is the effect of custom.

4*

XI.

The Prado—New Year's Day—Greetings in private Life—To Military Officers of the National Guards—To the King by fifteen hundred Drummers!—Champs Élysées—Place Concorde—Obelisk of Luxor—Goat Carriages—Learned Dogs—Punch and Judy.

I gave you, in a former letter, some description of the Masked Balls at the Grand Opera in Paris. Every man is naturally desirous of penetrating the real character of the people among whom he may happen to be residing. One, among the many ways of acquiring this knowledge, and certainly not the least agreeable, is to observe them in their pleasures and amusements. It is owing to this reason, that I have already written to you, and shall probably continue to write, so largely of balls and parties, of public spectacles, and exhibitions of various sorts, and especially of such as tend to show the social condition of the population, and develope the peculiarities of their domestic relations. It is with this view, in conjunction with others, that every stranger is induced to visit such a place as the Prado.

This is a ball-room, situated on one of the islands in the Seine, and nearly opposite to the Palace of Justice. This ball rejoices in the reputation of collecting, beyond a question, the lowest class of the community, who have means sufficient to obtain an entrance. Dancing is absolutely necessary to the very existence of the French, and all indulge in it—the young and old—the rich and poor. The numerous students, who reside in this quarter, and are among the most dissolute and reckless inhabitants of the city, compose the dancers, with their mistresses and the common courtezans of the town. No attention is paid to dress whatever. The men make their appearance in soiled frocks, with heavy, muddy boots, and the women in bonnets and shawls, in cottons, or silks, in petticoats, or breeches. Gloves are rarely seen. The dances are the same, as at other and more respectable places, except that the quadrille, which is the common dance, is modified to suit the loose habits of these people. When executed with this freedom, it receives the appellation of *cancan*. It consists in the cavalier's seizing the dame with both arms around the waist, she often assisting in the embrace; and so they "forward and back, cross over and balance." The other figures, are but modifications of this hugging, with the exception of a kind of balance, in which the opposite couples approach each other, and then rapidly strike out their feet in a sideway direction, accompanied with a wriggling motion of the body. The whole figure is totally devoid of grace, and its difficulty is its principal recommendation. The American waltzer would be amazed to see the waltzing here. Her sensibility would be shocked to witness the gentlemen clasping with both hands the waist of the lady, and she would be astonished at the rapidity with which they turn, and the length of time during which they whirl without fatigue. Considering the class of the community, who frequent these places, their limited means, and the low price for entrance, (twenty-five cents at the Prado, and at many other places ten cents—females admitted gratuitously) one would naturally expect to see a small hall, dimly lighted, and of mean appearance. On the contrary, when recovered from the blaze of light, that blinds him on his entrance, the visitor finds himself in a spacious saloon of one hundred and fifty feet in length, ornamented with numerous mirrors and chandeliers, dependent from its lofty ceiling. A fine orchestra, whose number varies according to the companies expected to be present, being larger on fête and Sunday nights than others, performs the choicest music of the day. The balls are of various kinds, namely, the simple ball, commencing at eight, ending at eleven o'clock—the night ball, beginning at eleven o'clock, P. M. and closing at half-past six A. M.—the masked and the costume fancy balls, both of which are night balls also.

Many of the customs of New Year's Day, (to which I seize this occasion to recur,) do not differ from those which are prevalent in and about New York. As there, so it is here, a time for a general visiting; and the occasion is embraced either to sustain, or drop, a previous acquaintance. Friends make presents to each other of *bon-bons*, or more substantial articles. One, too, is pestered with a crowd of beggars, whose benevolent wishes for your prosperity, are expected to be repaid by silver. Before rising in the morning, I was thus saluted by the woman having the superintendence of my room. She had taken the precaution beside to bring her little offspring in her arms, to stammer out a wish for my future welfare. Whatever influence these aspirations might possess to promote my happiness hereafter, it is certain, that they very much disturbed my present enjoyment. The doorkeeper was particularly attentive throughout the day. At the café, the waiters were uncommonly assiduous in their attendance, and kindly placed before me with my coffee a cornucopia, filled with *bon-bons*, which they expected me to pay for, without taking, at double its value. The military officers of the National Guard, past and present, were honored by, from two to twelve drummers, who beat the tatoo beneath their windows to the annoyance of the whole neighborhood. But the King himself was glorified in a special manner, at twelve o'clock, by all the drummers in Paris, to the number of fifteen hundred! who were collected in terrible array, in front of the palace in the garden of the Tuilleries. The thunder of this tremendous rub-a-dub, can be compared to nothing but Milton's "insufferable noise," when

" ———— confounded chaos roar'd,
And felt tenfold confusion."

The usual beat to quarters every night at seven o'clock, in the Place Vendome, executed by fifty-two drummers, assisted by six trumpeters, produces a din sufficiently deafening. It is, however, nothing but a whisper in comparison. Surely his majesty, however ardent may be his love of music and glory, must have taken care to give this martial host their expected gratuity and dismission without the least possible delay.

On Sundays and féte days, the Champs Elysées presents many

objects of interest and amusement. Independently of its agreeable walks, the gorgeous Place Concorde, glittering with gilded gas-posts and fountains—the magnificent Obelisk of Luxor, brought at an immense expense from Egypt, and the precursor of the celebrated Cleopatra's Needle; numberless vehicles of the wealthy, flashing with gold and silver, and bearing, beside the driver, one or two pampered lackeys, who, from their stand upon the rack behind, look down with scorn and pity upon all they pass; the numerous booths of mountebanks with the never-to-be-forgotten Punch and Judy, and other similar shows; and, in addition to the whole, the crowds of people of all classes and ages, who throng the *trottoirs*, present altogether a rare combination of novelty, fun, and splendor, and make the Champs Elysées the scene of never-failing attraction. Here are little carriages, to which a team of goats is harnessed, whose white coats and graceful appearance, recall the fairy tales, which excited us so much in infancy; and which now cling to our memories with such tenacity, as to cause a doubt, whether they are in reality the recollections of past events, or illusive creations of the imagination. But these pretty animals have another office to perform, beside that of bringing to our mind our youthful days. The young children of the wealthy delight to ride in these vehicles, and their good behavior for the preceding week is thus rewarded. Here are men with learned dogs, who, beside many similar tricks, will tell you the time, according to the watch, by selecting from numbers printed upon cards, and placed before them. This is done in the open air, and all have a right to observe the performance; the owner being compensated by the generosity of the spectators, who throw him a few sous according to their will. I have always felt a strong desire to see the far-famed Punch and Judy, and now for the first time have had my curiosity gratified. Notwithstanding its simplicity and folly, I regarded it for a time with real pleasure. There is something about it, which is exceedingly attractive. I am acquainted with men of science, who would hardly be suspected of a capacity to be thus amused, who have frequently seen it, and always with great satisfaction, though possibly it might be for the five hundreth time. I am sure, that none of them could have laughed more heartily than I did. In a walk of half a mile, I remarked six or eight of these booths, and every one surrounded by a merry crowd. Jugglers, somerset tumblers, "sights," as they are called in New-England, and other similar attractions, may be witnessed for a sous, and everywhere abound.

XII.

FURTHER ACCOUNT OF THE HOTEL DIEU—ROUX—CHOMEL—MAGENDIE—ECOLE PRATIQUE D'ANATOMIE—MUSEUM OF DUPUYTREN—SHOCKING EFFECTS OF SECRET VICE.

THE account of the hospital called Hotel-Dieu, which was the subject of previous letters, will now, after a considerable interval, be resumed. Among the most celebrated of its surgeons, and indeed of the practitioners of Paris, is a little, fat, good-natured looking man, whose gray hairs cover a forehead always wrinkled, either with laughter or anger. For Mons. Roux is one of those coleric individuals, who are frequently in a passion, but soon out of it; while his jovial character renders him a favorite professor among the students. His visits and operations are consequently thronged with crowds, but there is a sad falling off at his lectures. Their prolixity is extremely tedious, and his digressions insupportable. After a discourse of an hour and a half to a larger auditory than usual, attracted by an operation of magnitude, that was expected to follow, he is accustomed to remark, "Gentlemen, I have no time to say more, and will defer the remainder to another day. So much of the morning has been occupied, that the operation must necessarily be postponed." It is not strange, if persons who have patiently sat, till eleven o'clock, without their breakfast, should not always be contented with so impotent a conclusion to his lectures. As an operator, however, there are few better, and, in surgical diseases of the eye, he is particularly distinguished.

Messrs. Chomel and Magendie are the most eminent among the physicians. The clinique of the former is larger, perhaps, than that of any other physician in Paris. In the diagnosis of the diseases of the lungs he stands at the head of the profession. His lectures are perspicuous, and the reports of them, together with the numerous note-books to be seen at their delivery, attest their worth. Mons. Magendie, a translation of whose work on Physiology has been published in the United States, enjoys a greater reputation abroad than at home.

In following the unfortunate patients of the numerous hospitals, who chance to die, to their final resting-place—which here is not the tomb—we come to the *Ecole Pratique d'Anatomie*. This is one of the largest public dissecting rooms of this city. And it is the most commodious to the student, being situated in the centre of the Latin quarter, and near the School of Medicine. At this, and the amphitheatre of Clamart, four thousand subjects are annually used for anatomical purposes. They are daily transported from all the hospitals, and deposited in a small building appropriated to this object. There are to be seen at this receptacle from twenty to forty at a time, of all colors, ages and conditions—a shocking spectacle to an unprofessional observer. Every day, at twelve o'clock, there is a distribution of them among all the classes of students. Every instructor has a small building for his own use, in which are ten or fifteen tables of cast iron. The human body may thus be viewed in every stage of dissection, and, I may add, decomposition. By perambulating the several buildings, the various parts of the human organism, the nerves, muscles and blood-vessels may be easily examined, and studied. Here, the assiduous student may be seen, with his soiled blouse, and his head bedecked with a fantastic cap. In one hand he holds a scalpel, in the other a treatise on anatomy. He carries in his mouth a cigar, whose intoxicating fumes, so hurtful on most occasions, render him insensible to the smell of twenty bodies, decomposing, putrifying around him. So accustomed is he to this horrid scent, that he perceives not, that his garments are impregnated with it to such a degree, that persons in the streets turn round to see, if they have not passed a butcher or a stabler. Here, too, is the learned professor, who thus prepares himself for a difficult operation by refreshing his anatomy; and thus rehearses his part in the tragedy to be acted on the morrow. The blood and pieces of flesh upon the floor, he regards, as the sculptor does the fragments of marble lying round the unfinished statue. The skeleton, dangling in the centre of the room, and the preparations hanging about the walls, possess, in his view, beauties which the world can never see, and he receives more pleasure in their contemplation, than in the masterpieces of Raphael or Titian. But the man, who *feeds with the flesh of human beings the dogs*, who are kept to take their places on the table in their proper turn, is entirely hardened. There lie these dogs, with their feet bound together, exposed in a latticed cage to the inclemencies of the weather, without even straw to keep them warm, and fed on the bodies of men. Is it strange, that they should whine and bark, and groan, day after day, and *snap at their unnatural feeders?*

The cost of dissecting is about six dollars the season, according to the abundance of subjects, and the number of students engaged. This insures a subject nearly all the time during the winter. Instruction is given by a professor appointed by the government, &c. The attempts at cleanliness are made by servants attached to the institution, and paid also by government. In the summer season, dissecting is forbidden; but operative anatomy may be studied to great advantage.

Near this institution is the celebrated Museum of Dupuytren, so called in honor of the distinguished surgeon, who left seventy thousand dollars for the establishment of a professorship of pathological anatomy. It is only since his death, that the medical school of Paris could boast of a cabinet of this sort. The collection is, therefore, not very large. It, however, contains many *objects of interest*, which are arranged along the walls in glass cases. It embraces all the varieties of disease, but is particularly rich in those of osseous structure, and wax casts, and representations of syphilitic diseases. This is open to the public every Thursday. The visitor on that day is often astonished at the number of soldiers, who frequent this museum. I found, on inquiry, that, by order of government, the officers of regiments publicly recommend those under their command to visit the collection, in the hope that the contemplation of the numberless ills which this disorder entails upon mankind, so varied in their form, and so horrid in their manifestations, might be a salutary lesson, and make them cautious of indulging in the vice, which is their prolific cause. It is, indeed, a sight which might well startle a man of the firmest nerve. For myself, accustomed to see suffering and death, and *never* affected at any period of my life with unpleasant sensations, while witnessing, or making operations on the living or the dead, and having had likewise many cases of this disease, in conjunction with others, in my own practice during some years back, let me acknowledge, that the contemplation of these horrors, arranged together, and displaying such a loathsome catalogue of deformities and suffering, for the *first* time sickened and unmanned me. My brain reeled, a cold chill crept over my body, my limbs lost their power, and I sank helpless on a bench

Fathers, parents! why do you so assiduously keep from your children the knowledge of this disease, and also of its cause? Why shun all conversation on the subject? Why not discover to them this vice in all its deformity, and all its lasting and disastrous consequences? In all hospitals ample specimens of this disease may always be seen, with manifestations so horrible as to chill the heart, and make the blood of the young run cold. In the library of almost every physician colored plates may be examined, which will give a lesson that never can fade from the memory; and which, in moments of temptation, will interpose a barrier between them and crime, too powerful for pleasure to surmount. And, while attending to the subject, let not the parent forget to visit the hospitals of the insane, and point out to them the maladies—the more common American diseases—caused by masturbation. Let him there show to his sons, ay, even to his daughters, the disgusting appearances and the wreck of reason, that have followed this description of sensualism. Let neither modesty, nor its counterfeit, prudery, nor any affectation stand in the way of an honest performance of this duty; but faithfully let him explain the cause and consequence, and leave the tender hearts and good common sense of his children to digest the solemn lesson, and reap its fruits. With this advice, coming strangely, you may think, from the metropolis of France, I close this letter.

XIII.

FRENCH POLITENESS—ETIQUTTE—NECESSARY EXPENSES OF LIVING—
COST OF VARIOUS ARTICLES OF DRESS.

The French have long enjoyed the reputation of being the politest people in the world. The consequence has been, that those, who have presumed to teach the art of politeness, have deemed it prudent frequently to call themselves French, whether they were so in reality or not. Most of the works on etiquette in our country are translations from that language. Everything, in short, which is said or done by them, from the cook to the prince, is thought to be spoken, or performed, in the purest taste and most polished manner. And shall I dare to say, in the face of facts like these, that a most egregious blunder has been committed? Would anybody believe me, if I should assert, that they are so deficient in this accomplishment, that it is pure satire to give them the title of polite? Politeness is surely not a mere matter of words, but a product of the heart. A visible symbol of an emotion of the soul, it can no more be expressed by a formula of language, than devotion can be by a posture of the body. It cannot therefore be acquired by a study of forms alone; and those who put themselves under the tuition of persons, who profess to teach it in that manner, will at least succeed in learning, that their instructors are ignorant of its first principles. If politeness consists in taking off the hat gracefully, and bowing profoundly; in telling an ugly woman that she is charming—a perfect angel—then it must be allowed, the French surpass every other nation in this accomplishment. Indeed a French hat, and an American or English one, are made for very different purposes. The latter is designed to be put upon the head, whereas, the former is intended only to be taken off. This is a land of perfect equality, as far as the bow goes. The lady and grisette, the friend and stranger, are greeted with the same salutations. The hat is lifted to a certain height, the head kept uncovered a particular length of time, and the body bent to the attitude prescribed, while he declares, on his *parole d'honneur*, that she is *charmante*, though she may be homelier than the ugliest *balayeuse* in the city. If, however, these do not compose the standard of politeness, but if, on the contrary, the speaking of the honest truth in kindness, and a willingness to sustain some inconvenience for the accommodation of another, be its genuine characteristics, then the most unsophisticated backwoodsman of the Green Mountains far surpasses the refined of the most polished nation of the globe.

In matters of etiquette, however, the case, it may be thought, must certainly be otherwise. Well, let us see. It is necessary, to be sure, that one should wear a straight-bodied dress coat and white kid gloves at a party or a ball. The former, as it was intended to do, is commonly sufficient to absorb all the intellect of the wearer, and the latter all the yellow dirt, while he is perpetually thrusting his digits into his huge snuff-box. At the theatre, where good manners are affected, the lovely Desdemona, or the sweet Andromache, by way of preparation for her coming part, does not hesitate to turn round and spit upon the stage. At the close of a pathetic scene, the sudden application of a thousand snuffy white pocket handkerchiefs to a thousand sonorous noses cannot fail to heighten the tragical effect. One at first imagines, that he hears the trumpet sounding a charge for a troop of horse, and it takes some time to be so "up to snuff," as to understand the cause. In the street, one gives you a sudden push, at the same time taking off his hat, and crying *pardon!* while you unexpectedly find yourself up to your ancles in the mud and water of the gutter. Umbrellas have the same gravitation toward the eyes of passengers in this country, as in our own.

Sometimes this want of politeness is carried to an extent, that borders on brutality. Most of the physicians of Paris have risen by their talents from obscurity and the lowest classes in the community. Among them many are therefore found, as might be expected, whose manners are coarse, and whose movements are ungainly. Mons. Roux is, however, pointed out as possessing an affable deportment, and, in a word, as being a gentleman. This man, a baron of France, a few days ago, operated on a poor fellow for some malady. When the operation was completed, the unfortunate patient requested that some blood, which remained upon his body, might be removed. "Pooh!" says Roux, and spitting upon the man's person, wiped them both off with a piece of dirty cloth. Such an action was too much even for the broken-down spirit of this enfeebled sufferer. Though prostrated by the union of poverty and sickness, though a menial all his life, this indignity and profanation of his person, notwithstanding it was committed by the foremost surgeon of the city of Paris, touched him to the quick. His languid eye flashed with anger, and his cheek, pale with the loss of blood, on a sudden glowed with the bright hue of passion. And he did not feel alone. The outrage was observed by many who stood around, and the wanton violation of the feelings of a fellow-man, sunk deep into their hearts.

There is only one polite person, accurately speaking, in Paris. It is he, who is selling you some article. In order to extract a sous from you, he will bow and cringe, till you have given him the coveted trifle in pity for his meanness.

How money *does* evaporate in Paris! In America, one thus soliloquizes: "I will go to Paris. Deducting travelling expenses, I may see the world, and luxuriate for the same money, and probably less, than would be necessary for me to vegetate upon at home." He arrives, and is not long in discovering the profundity of his financial calculations. He pursues his inquiries under peculiar advantages for information. He dives, of course, to the very bottom of the subject, and the only unpleasant circumstance is, that he has got to the bottom of his purse at the very same time.

The shorter the period during which a person may remain here, the greater will be his expenses comparatively. To be sure, there are those, who live in this metropolis, on nothing almost. This is accomplished by remaining shut up, as it were imprisoned in their rooms. They do not visit public buildings, because there is a gratuity to be given the guide. They go not to the Opera House, or Theatre, for they make calls too on the pocket. Such persons, in short, see very little, if any more of Paris, than if they had never crossed the water. Whence then come the advantages, or even the pleasures of travel? The matter of mere living here in a barely decent manner is expensive. A room can, indeed, be hired for three or four dollars per month, but it will be in the sixth or seventh story of the dirtiest house in the filthiest quarter of the city—a miniature Augean stable. His bed-linen would be changed once in two or three months. His chamber swept once in four weeks. His neighbors, the *balayeuses* and *chiffoniers*. He can put something into his stomach, called bread, with butter of a quality inferior to stearine candles, and a bowl of chicory boiled in water, and call it breakfast. Ragouts of cat's flesh, and beef-steaks of horse, cannot be extravagant. But if one really wishes to see Paris, and at the same time live respectably, he must expect, for he will be obliged, to pay for it. Comfortably, I do not say, for the thing and the word are alike unknown. One will look in vain for the comforts, to which he has been accustomed in America. A room, decently furnished, and "well up," too, will cost from six to ten dollars a month; not including porter's fee neither, nor a trifle for the domestics, &c. &c. which will swell the sum to one or two dollars more. This, though not demanded, is not the less expected. His breakfast at the café, consisting of a cup of coffee, a roll, and piece of butter, will cost a franc, (twenty cents,) a day. If he luxuriously demands an *omelette*,—and they are really very nice,—the consequences to his purse are frightful. A friend told me, that for a long time after his arrival the only way he knew it was Sunday, was, that he ate an *omelette de fins herbes* on that day. A dinner at a *table d'hote* costs about three francs. At a restaurant one never knows, till a large bill is presented. Taking counsel of his feelings, he cannot persuade himself that he has eaten much, but the formidable *carte*, with the prices annexed, reveals the undoubted fact. Frenchmen never have the dyspepsia; their food is not sufficiently solid. Living in this manner, merely respectably, and allowing *nothing* for what is necessarily spent in sight-seeing and amusements, such as the operas, theatres, concerts, public balls, or for books, accompanied with every effort at economy, some six hundred dollars a year will be unavoidably expended.

Clothing, though not dear, costs as much as in many parts of the United States. A comfortable black dress coat costs twenty dollars; pantaloons, seven to eight dollars; vests, from three to eight dollars; according to the material and labor bestowed upon it. Gentlemen's white gloves are sixty cents the pair; colored sixty-five cents, and the number which a gentleman is obliged to wear, makes it a serious item indeed. I know an American resident, an economical man withal, but from necessity, frequenting a great deal of company, whose gloves alone cost him one hundred and twenty-five dollars a year. Gloves, hack hire, and the perquisite of the *concierge*, when one is out after twelve o'clock at night, make the indispensable expenses, attendant on every party, from two to three dollars. Books, mementoes for friends, will inflame the aggregate to any desired extent. In addition to this, if a young fellow is inflated with the very common, but ridiculous vanity, of procuring his coats and hats, and boots, of a man who has arisen to pre-eminence in the manufacture of them, he must, of course, pay tribute to that reputation. If he can derive a pleasure from the silly boast, that a particular article in his possession was purchased in the Palais Royal, he must contribute his proportion of the enormous shop-rent; and ten dollars are thus suddenly augmented to thirteen, in the easiest way imaginable.

This particularity may be out of place in a communication of this sort; but knowing the erroneous views entertained by the American public on the cheapness of Paris life, and the difficulty of obtaining accurate data upon this point, I have adopted the most thorough and expeditious mode of giving that information, which, previous to coming hither, I sought for in vain myself. Figures never deceive.

If one is desirous of going into society as much as possible, let him remember, that the banker Green invites those, who have money in his hands, to dinner or to balls, a certain number of times in exact proportion to the amount of the deposite; while Hottingeur & Co. content themselves with being polite—in their counting-room.

This letter is decidedly French. At the beginning of it, politeness is the only thing that you observe; but after all, there is nothing at the bottom but a calculation about dollars and cents.

XIV.

MEDICAL OFFICERS IN FRENCH HOSPITALS—IN AMERICAN HOSPITALS—REASON OF THE DIFFERENCE IN THEIR CHARACTERS—SYSTEM OF CONCOURS—SKETCH OF VELPEAU'S LIFE AND PERSON.

ON a very cursory examination of the Parisian hospitals, it is immediately apparent, that the medical officers attached to them, are, almost without exception, men of eminence in their profession. The reason of this striking fact, and also of another still more interesting to the United States, namely, that surgeons and physicians of the latter country have not, in proportion to the magnitude of their labors and responsibility, a similar standing in the fields of science, becomes a question for grave investigation. If the scientific character of the medical corps of the numerous governmental and charitable hospitals in the Union be carefully considered, we shall discover many a surgeon possessing a trembling hand, or an uncertain eye, which renders him unfit to operate successfully; and some unfortunately with such a density of intellect, as to make his judgment worse than useless, because it is employed at the expense of his patients. Physicians, too, will be detected, whose diagnosis, prognosis, and treatment of diseases, are the laughing-stock of all who know them. Such are the facts. The cause of this great contrast is not a matter of difficult solution.

A large proportion of the hospital medical officers of the United States are indebted for their situations to rich relations, or powerful friends, and not to their genius. Some of them have failed to obtain practice from their ignorance, or rough and brutal manners; while others possess qualifications not usually enumerated in a medical diploma. I wish that I was not obliged to say, that their professional brethren sometimes lend their charitable, but questionable aid to their advancement, from an *esprit de corps*, and because they are reluctant to see them dragging on a life of poverty, or descending to charlatanry for a livelihood. Thus the man, whom nobody will employ of his own accord, is pronounced to be " plenty good enough " for the inhabitants of a hospital, whose poverty is the crime for which they have been sentenced to be thus treated within its walls.

A far better system prevails in France, where situations of this description are open to the struggles of all. The *Concours*, derived from the verb *concourir*, signifying to run together, to compete, makes talent, not influence, the necessary requisite for promotion. Every medical office in France, whether military or civil, is thus obtainable by merit. This system extends from the dressers and students in pharmacy up to the professors and highest offices; the qualifications of course increasing with the importance of the place contested. The biography of the celebrated Velpeau, surgeon-in-chief to the hospital *La Charité*, is an instance, among many others, of its beneficial effects.

This man, whose name has been wafted by fame into every quarter of the world, was born fifty years ago, about twenty-five miles from the town of Tours, in France. His honest, unambitious parents, destined their son to follow the trade of a blacksmith, the occupation of his father. By some accident his father, though illiterate, possessed all the books of the village, which happened to be, *a Treatise of Hippocrates, The Country Mason, and The Poor Folk's Doctor*. Having learnt these works by heart, Velpeau—the son—was frequently called upon to treat the sick in the neighborhood; some trifling success having given him a reputation. Having prescribed to a patient one day, accidentally however, a large dose of a very powerful medicine, the effects became alarming, and a scientific physician was immediately called. Terrified at the result of his practice, our young Esculapius was shaking in a corner with fear. "What has the patient taken?" shouts the Doctor. Stammering and hesitating, Velpeau explains his disease, the remedy given, and the effect. Some trifling medicine relieves the dangerous symptoms, and the physician turns from the patient to the youthful leech. He is astonished to see so much wisdom in such dirty clothes. The peasantry of France rarely show a knowledge of anything beyond their sphere, and such erudition pleased and astonished him. In this way learning the history of Velpeau, he became interested in him, and encouraged him to a regular course of study. His highest ambition being to attain the distinction, in his view, of *Officier de Santé*, a species of medical police found throughout France. He soon left for Tours. In so limited a sketch as this must be, I cannot follow him through the constant toil in the provincial hospitals, supported by a scanty supply of coarse bread and cheese sent him by his mother, and encouraged to persevere by the praises of his instructors. Time, however, at length brought him to Paris; and in a public *Concour* he gained the situation of *interne*, or house-physician, of the hospital St. Louis. Here he was at least exempted from the necessity of sleeping in a garret, and the poor room allotted to the *interne* was luxurious in comparison to those to which he had been accustomed. He obtained a small sum of money by giving lectures to younger students. In 1823 he took his degree. In 1828 he was chosen Surgeon of the Bureau Central, without a *dissenting vote*, and immediately appointed Surgeon-in-chief ad interim to the hospital St. Antoine.

It was while here, that he began to publish his opinions, which have ever since been so eagerly sought for, and profoundly respected by the medical public. From this he was soon transferred to the hospital La Pitié, where he recommenced his lectures. His last promotion brought him to La Charité. Here many would have been contented to remain, but his ambition was not satisfied with a second place. A professorship merely intervened between him and the consummation of all his hopes and labors. The acquisition of this would elevate him to the top of the ladder, the highest rank of medical honor. He was unsuccessful in his concour for the Chair of External Pathology, and also for the professorship of Physiology. Still undaunted, in 1830, he contested again the Obstetrical chair. This also he lost. His last effort was for the Chair of Clinical Surgery against the celebrated Lisfranc, Panson, the elder—and Blandin. In this attempt with such distinguished rivals, he bore away the palm

The death of Roux, now quite advanced, will undoubtedly be the signal of his removal to the Hotel-Dieu, and then the blacksmith's son will stand on the loftiest pinnacle of his profession.

Velpeau is principally known in America by his Midwifery, which has been translated by Dr. Meigs of Philadelphia. His great work on Surgery, published here in four volumes, with an atlas of plates, has been very recently translated, as I observe by a New York paper, by Dr. Townsend, with an appendix, containing the valuable opinions and experience of Dr. Mott. The *chef-d'œuvre* of the first European surgeon, with notes by the highest surgical authority in America, cannot fail to find numerous readers, and no less numerous admirers.

It would be foolish to attempt the enumeration of works, of which he is the acknowledged author. They are more voluminous than those of any other writer in the profession, and amount to some thirty thousand pages. The difficulty is to comprehend, how he could possibly find time to execute such a Herculean task. So wonderful a fertility, if not unparalleled in the walks of literature and science, can only be the result of great talents, perseverance, and ambition.

Velpeau is rather above the medium height, stoutly built, of erect carriage, and stiff demeanor. His head is bald upon the summit, but about the ears his once black hair bristles in every direction. Not the least vestige of hair is discernible upon his oval face, save his eye-lashes and brows, which are long and shaggy. From his hatred to whiskers and mustaches, one would infer that he is in favor of the Razorian system. But it is his sharp grey eyes that give a character to his face. His dress is peculiar, inasmuch as he wears on all occasions a white cravat, so high and stiff, that his unremitting inflexibility of manner may be almost accounted for from the restraint which it occasions him. Indeed he scarcely ever turns his head, without carrying his whole body with it at the same time. He is not a man of social habits, and is accustomed to give to strangers such a cool reception, that, like me, they generally keep their introductions to him, though coming from men of eminence, snug in their trunks. At his cliniques, he is attended by probably the largest number of students of any lecturer in Paris; and mainly, because of the pains he takes to explain everything in the most distinct and clear manner. As an operator, his hand is steady, his eye good, his judgment excellent, and undismayed by appearances of danger. He is, however, slow, and his operations sometimes apparently prolonged without necessity. This hasty description of this truly great man will close my letter. A subsequent one may, perhaps, embody further particulars in his life, which may serve to point out some of the evils attendant on the system of Concours.

NOTE.—While reading these letters for the press, and again reflecting on the excellence of this system of Concours, the feasibility of its introduction into this city, is, just now, particularly evident. The Common Council are re-modelling the medical department of the Alms House, and appointing to its care some twenty or thirty physicians. Every medical man in the city would gladly accept the situations without emolument in any way, save that obtained incidentally from the reputation his subsequent services may acquire.

Twenty physicians at one appointment!—and all to personal friends or party politicians! Not one to him who, in a Concour, a strife for the mastery, shows himself to be really the first man in the particular department of the profession to which he is elected! No! His appointment is no such honorable testimonial of skill. It is rather by agreement among the Aldermen, that each should have the privilege of appointing his man, making no objection to the appointments of another. Is this an honest method of action? Perhaps so—for no one is so silly as to suppose, that a surgeon to this or that institution, must, from his situation, have extraordinary abilities.

What glorious rewards might this city offer to the man of real talent! Open wide the doors of the Poor House, City, Lunatic, Lying-in Hospitals, the Physicianships to the City, Tombs, Dispensaries, Colored Home, Eye and Ear Infirmary, Asylums for Blind, and others, to the most talented—proved so in a public display, before competent and unbiassed judges—and then, but not till then, will the name of a Hospital or Dispensary physician be elevated to the rank it should hold. Not till this is done, will the houseless and homeless be properly attended when sick, or the city justly acquire the name of a city of charity and benevolence.

XV.

The Grisette—Lorette—Fille Publique—Hospital Lourcine—Mons. Hugier—Hospital du Midi—Ricord—Disgusting Effects of Certain Diseases—American Students.

I have promised, I believe, to give you *the translation of a word*, of which all Americans have heard, but few know the definition of—I mean, Grisette. To do this adequately, requires a long and deliberate *view of the entire French people*; more particularly, however, of the Parisians, to a portion of whom, rather than to the inhabitants of France in general, this appellation *more appropriately applies*. The Parisians, as a general custom, do not marry young; and when they do assume the matrimonial relation, it is seldom from affection, or any feeling akin to that emotion expressed by the obsolete word, love—but for money. Much has been said about the influence of the "almighty dollar," in America; still, *it cannot be affirmed, that* it has yet been often placed in the scale, and made to weigh against a wife. Since money is a requisite for matrimony, it is evident, that *the poor must be unable to marry*. But Nature forbids a life of celibacy.

Existence, however, cannot be supported by love alone; and though governments provide hospitals for the sick, they do not furnish food and raiment for the well, however young and pretty. It is indispensable, then, that *girls should work for a subsistence*. I am almost afraid to mention what they do, lest those whose conscientious scruples will not permit them to eat the sugar made by slaves, *should also be prevented from wearing* the lace, flowers, worked collars and handkerchiefs, wrought by the grisettes. By rising with the dawn, and working till nine or ten o'clock at night *with constant application*, they can earn in general, not more than a franc, or twenty cents, a day. Rarely, when very active and particularly skilful, can they swell the sum to thirty cents per day. Even in the economical and meagre style in which they live, it costs them eighteen cents a day for nourishment. The two remaining sous will not easily discharge their room rent of four dollars, or thereabouts, per month, with not a bit of furniture, nothing but the bare walls; their washing bill; the demand for clothes, and other pressing items of expense. More than this, Sunday is a fête day, and they do not wish to labor, while others are revelling in enjoyments. But how, then, can they live? Whence will come their Sunday's dinner? Ah! it is infinitely more agreeable to be promenading in the Luxembourg gardens; visiting its galleries of paintings and statuary, or the splendid collection in the Louvre; and, in the evening, seeking pleasure at the Chaumière or Prado ball, or at the Vaudeville theatre, with a silk dress, a jaunty hat, and graceful feather; above all, with *un joli garçon*. But this costs money. Who pays it? It is that *joli garçon* aforesaid. It is he who pays her room rent and toilet, takes her to the balls, treats her to *l'eau-de-vie*, or *absinthe*, escorts her to see the paintings, and enables her to indulge in the whole circle of amusements.

Soon, however, this humble-bee of a *joli garçon* is tired of his pretty flower. From affected jealousy, or some other thin pretence, he seeks a quarrel with her, and they part, after months and perhaps years, of acquaintance. If the quarrel is not very bitter, he furnishes her a substitute, but on the neglect of this attention, she frequents the balls the same as ever; yet, as she goes alone, her widowhood is readily known, and she says to her friends, *Maintenant je suis libre, je cherche un amant pour payer mon loyer.* She takes the first she finds; for she says, "He is not pretty, but—he is amiable; and—I want some one to pay my rent." *He* is more particular, for the market is fully supplied.

A higher class of Parisian citizens is the Lorettes. They derive this appellation, strange to say, from the fact, that many of them live near the beautiful church called Notre Dame de Lorette. They are another species of the genus before-mentioned, differing from them in one important particular,—they do not work at all; their expenses being paid entirely by their lovers. Like all the other classes of the great community, they have their pride. To the humbler *grisette* they do not deign to speak a word. On bright days, they may be seen, in great numbers, promenading in the streets, or if their *entreteneur* is rich enough, riding in the Champs Elysées, preceded by duchesses, and followed by countesses, without a perceptible difference from them either in manners or appearance.

The offspring of these classes is the *fille publique*, or the common woman of the town. The glare of day is unpropitious to this unhappy race; but as the shades of night descend, every step discovers some of the sixty thousand women of this description, that throng the city. The delineation of Solomon was not incorrect: "They stand at the corners of the street, and cry after the passers by." "The wages of sin"—forty cents—"will not deter many." These women, in the same manner as the hacks and porters in New-York, are regularly numbered and registered. They are compelled to present themselves weekly before certain physicians, who are paid by the government to watch for the preservation of the public health. When sick, they are sent to the hospital Lourcine, specially appropriated to such of them as are affected with syphilitic disease.

This hospital is closed to the public and to students. As a matter of particular favor I have been allowed not only to see, but to attend it frequently, following the visits of its different physicians and surgeons. Mons. Hugier is the chief surgeon, and through his influence, I have been enabled to enter and enjoy the privilege of seeing his practice, and that of the other physicians attached to it. A letter of this kind is not the place for a particular description. Were the public mind, as I have intimated in a previous letter, divested of much of its affected modesty, and, instead of being diverted from the cause and effects of this disease, were instructed to give the subject that attention it deserves, the three hundred beds of this hospital would be far too numerous, instead of being, as now, much too circumscribed for the wants of the community.

Friends of humanity! turn not away your eyes, sickened at the sight of lovely women, transformed into hideous creatures; of smiling children, whose beautiful faces do not reveal the plague-spot, which has corrupted every organ; of infants, who have prematurely entered the world, covered with disease, which they have innocently contracted, but whom fortunately death will shortly remove from suffering. Is it impossible, that a similar disease, existing at the era of our blessed Saviour, might have prompted the question which was asked him, "Has this man sinned, or his parents, that he was born blind?" Although the first mention of this disorder was in the fifteenth century, it is by no means improbable, that a similar one then existed.

Near this is the Hospital du Midi, or the Venereal Hospital for males. This contains four hundred and fifty beds, always full, and is celebrated for being the dirtiest hospital in Paris. This is attributed to the absence of those real "angels of mercy," the Sisters of Charity, who so unweariedly in the other hospitals watch with the sick and dying. The principal surgeon is the eminent Ricord. This gentleman, at the head of this hospital, is an American, having been born in Baltimore in 1800. He has resided twenty years in this country, and is the author of several works of the highest authority in their peculiar branches. In 1838 he received the order of Chevalier of the Legion of Honor. As a writer—in French—he is not distinguished so much for the beauty of his expression, as for his clearness, a far more important quality in a scientific work. His lectures are frequented by a numerous class, notwithstanding the distance of his hospital, which is situated at the very extremity of the city. I have often attended his visits and lectures, not only for the information to be derived from them, but to see a person of talent without ostentation; one at the same time a man of science and a gentleman, qualifications rarely blended in a Paris physician. On my first visit, on learning that I was an American, he received me most cordially, and when I expressed the use I had made of his work, desired me, if I wished any explanation, to come to his house, and he would endeavor to throw light on any part, which I did not understand. His politeness is not merely a little eloquent breath. His ever smiling, though far from handsome face, portrays the goodness of his heart. He has a French exterior on an American basis. The latter develops itself in a kind of go-a-headitiveness, which never allows him to stand idle a moment. He regards his patients, makes his remarks upon the case, prescribes, and proceeds to the next with wonderful rapidity. Fast as he walks, however, the motion of his tongue is far the quickest. I never heard the tongue of a Frenchman run so glibly. As a private practitioner, his house is beset with patients. A hundred and more are often assembled at a time waiting for their turn. These are principally confined to the disease which has been the subject of his study for many years.

To visit these hospitals, so far from the centre of the city, especially the Lourcine, one must rise at six o'clock in the morning. Think of that, "ye who sleep on beds of ease." The life of an American student in this metropolis is truly fatiguing. He rises early in the morning for his hospital visit. When that is over, he pursues the lions of the town, as the hunter chases the buffalo on the western prairie. The resemblance fails, when evening comes, for it brings no rest to the student. He must spend his nights at theatres or operas, at public or private balls. Some space also must be found to empty his overloaded cranium of the accumulations of his observation, or the consequences might be serious. And this perhaps is the most agreeable occupation of all, and somewhat contributes to reconcile him to those enormous encroachments on his time, that leave him scarcely more than two or three hours for necessary sleep, which but imperfectly refreshes the body, jaded by so much exercise, and destined to re-commence each day the same fatiguing routine.

The good New England farmer once every week winds up his family clock. My hebdomadal to you has a similar effect on me, beside periodically suggesting to my mind the images of you and my country. These insist on mingling with my daily thoughts, however, on a variety of occasions, without the least invitation or prompting, and have taken upon themselves to be especially busy and familiar in the night-work of the soul.

XVI.

GOBELIN MANUFACTORY OF TAPESTRY AND CARPETS—INSANE HOSPITAL "LA SALPETRIERE," FOR AGED AND POOR WOMEN.

A PART of yesterday was devoted to seeing some of the inexhaustible wonders of this city. In the company of several friends, I went to the famous Gobelin Manufactory. This establishment is under the direction of the Government, and, among all the curiosities which the city affords, may with propriety be pronounced unique. Its object is the weaving of carpets and tapestry. Although the descriptions which I had read, prepared me to witness something grand, yet my most extravagant anticipations were far surpassed by the magnificence of the manufactures. The edifices are situated at the very extremity of the city, and the low poor houses of the Rue Mouffetard, the most filthy and dangerous of all the streets of Paris, prepare one well to enjoy the contrast. The external, and even interior appearance of the buildings is not at all attractive. They consist of about half a dozen small houses, some of which are united by bridges.

On entering the first one, immediately on the left, to which we were directed, we noticed on each side of the walls, hung in massive gilded frames, what appeared to be paintings of the highest order. Thinking it very strange to see articles of this kind in a carpet manufactory, I was induced to examine them more closely, and discovered to my astonishment, that they were specimens of the tapestry here made. Among them were three full-length portraits of Louis Philippe, which would be recognized at once without the smallest difficulty. They are copies of portraits executed at different periods of his life, and in various uniforms. Another represents the present Queen holding by the hand the young Count of Paris.

Others are copies of paintings of living artists, whose works are now displayed in the gallery of the palace of Luxembourg. Among them is the celebrated picture of the Destruction of the Janizaries by Horace Vernet, which, for beauty of coloring and nicety of the shade, challenges comparison with the original of this *chef-d'œuvre* of the talented artist. Should those young ladies of my own land, who work sentimental slippers for their dear friends, and strangely delight to see their affectionate gifts trodden under foot, view these specimens of skilful handiwork, I fear that they would scarcely be satisfied in future with the physiognomies, which make up faces at us on their music stools and tabourets. An eye in a Gobelin production is not a black or colored blot with a white streak in it, placed somewhere upon something of a brick color, meant for a face. Nor is it an accurate representation merely, but it speaks and flashes, and the beholder feels the fire of the soul that animates the figure. The largest of these, the Destruction of the Janizaries, is about twenty feet by fifteen, perhaps larger.

Leaving this room, we proceeded through numerous small apartments, in each of which are pieces of tapestry in various stages of progression. Beautiful landscapes, bunches of grapes, peaches, and all kinds of flowers and fruit, are growing under the hand of the workman. One particularly struck my attention. It was a porcelain dish of various fruits, placed upon the corner of a table of variegated marble. By its side lay a handkerchief with a lace border. So finely was the worsted wrought, that the figures in the dish, the stains in the marble, and even the delicate "work," and each thread of the lace, were distinctly visible. The work is called the *haute lisse* from the warp being vertical. The workman stands at the back of the canvas, on which he is employed, with the model behind him, to which he occasionally refers, in order to adjust the color of his woolen or silken thread to that part of the picture he is copying. The object being to present as smooth and delicate a surface as possible, all cuttings and fastenings are performed on the back, which explains the necessity of his operating on the wrong side. A period from two to six years is requisite for the completion of each piece; and the cost often amounts to thirty-five hundred dollars. But even at this rate, the workmen are very meagerly paid; the best of them receiving but three hundred and sixty dollars per year.

This establishment employs about one hundred and thirty operators. None of their productions are sold, being distributed among the various royal palaces, or given away as presents by the king. The wools are dyed in an establishment connected with this; and numerous shades, unknown to commerce, are here produced. Jean Gobelin, in 1450, commenced this manufacture, which was continued by his descendants, till purchased by Louis XIV. in 1662. During his reign, under the administration of Colbert, Alexander's battles, the four seasons, the four elements, and the history of the principal acts of Lous XIV. from his marriage to his conquest of Franche Compte, were wrought at the Gobelins from the design of Le Brun. Louvois caused tapestries to be made during his administrations, after the most beautiful originals in the king's cabinet, of Raphael, Julio Romano, and other famous painters in the schools of Italy, which were first drawn in large dimsenions by the most able French painters, such as La Fosse, the two Coypels, Jouvenet, Person, &c.

To the tapestry manufacture, one of carpets has been attached, which was made a royal establishment in 1604, by Marie de Medicis. Like the former, the carpets are suspended perpendicularly, with this difference, the workman is here placed on the right side. The carpet is of the kind called Persian, having a long plush, but for evenness of surface, fineness and strength, they are said to be superior. These magnificent productions, some of which cost thirty thousand dollars, are, like the tapestries, never sold. The largest ever made was for the Louvre, in seventy-two pieces, and was thirteen hundred feet in length. Nothing can exceed their gorgeousness of color, and the surpassing beauty of the figures.

From the Gobelins we went to the hospital devoted to the aged and poor women, and the female lunatics of Paris. It is one of the most immense of the establishments of the city. The distance around its walls exceeds three miles. Within the enclosure are contained the numerous buildings, which formerly were used in the manufacture of saltpetre; whence it derived its name in common use *La Salpêtrière*. The population of the place is now about seven thousand; but it has comprehended in by-gone years, nearly ten thousand souls. A large church is most worthy of notice among buildings possessing little that is remarkable, except their enormous size. It is built in the form of a star, four angles of which compose as many chapels, which look particularly light and cheerful, when contrasted with the sombre appearance of other churches and cathedrals. Of the inhabitants at present, fifteen hundred are composed of lunatics, idiots and epileptics. These are the materials used by Esquirol, in the formation of his distinguished treatise on the insane. With such opportunies for observation, it is not astonishing, that so talented an individual should have accomplished such valuable results. His successors are indebted for distinction more for their occupancy of his place, than any contributions they have made to science. The multitude of patients allows their classification according to their degree of lunacy, thereby contributing exceedingly to their happiness and probability of cure. This is in a great degree impracticable in the United States, from the limited number collected in one place; which is very much to be regreted, since it is well known, by all who have had the care of this unfortunate class of patients, that one noisy and turbulent individual is almost certain to excite all within the sound of his voice. The most violent are disposed of, in a place far away from all the others. Within the exterior walls, are some twenty small brick houses, each having one, perhaps two apartments, containing a bed. These houses are about thirty feet from one another. Warmth is communicated by means of a stove placed in the walls; the fire being kindled from without. One of these structures is appropriated for an intendant, who has the charge of the patients placed here. In this manner the noisy and quarrelsome are prevented from exerting a detrimental influence on those around them.

This method has been adopted in many of the Insane Hospitals of the United States, in a modified degree. One edifice in particular, at the city pauper establishment at Boston, has recently been erected, which however, I fear, will but partially effect its object, since it is to contain a half dozen patients, or more, who will mutually excite each other; while from its contiguity to the main building, the noise can be easily heard, especially in summer, notwithstanding its arched walls are expected to entirely muffle the sound. The absence of the iron-grating, universally seen on the windows of similar institutions in America, and the unlocked doors, permitting the patients to go out at will, into the inclosure, whose lofty walls forbid escape, comprise the most striking peculiarities. Each of the separate divisions is supplied with a garden, courtyard and work-room, and in fact is a complete establishment in itself, totally unconnected with the others. Here are spots of land belonging to the patients, which, though neglected at this season, bear marks of order and attention. They were collected at our visit in the work-rooms, some of the old being engaged in spinning flax, knitting, &c. The making of clothing seemed the principal employment. In one I noticed a piano. The bed-rooms, arranged for twenty beds or more, were perfectly neat, the floors nicely waxed, and the linen white and clean. I wish some of our Yankee girls would learn to make a bed of the French. The sheets are always smooth, and everything disposed so comfortably, that one really likes to go to bed, which, with your good leave, I will now take the liberty of doing, being very much fatigued in recalling some of the incidents of the day's perambulations. As the perusal of this letter will no doubt have a lulling influence on yourself, another reason is added for my retiring, and giving you an opportunity to enjoy your couch, which, I am persuaded, is an exception from the foregoing insinuation.

XVII.

SUPERSTITION—HOLY RELICS—MICHELET—FELICIEN DAVID—HIS CONCERT—FETE OF LONG CHAMPS—GEN. TOM POUCE—TIME AND PLACE FOR MAKING FASHIONS—CONSERVATOIRE ROYAL DE MUSIQUE—ITS CONCERT—MADAME DORUS-GRAS.

SUPERSTITION has not yet been banished from the civilized world. The high and noble of the land unite with men of intellect in venerating what more properly belongs to an age of barbarism. They still continue to fall down and worship before blocks of wood and stone. This very day I noticed in the journals an account of a mandate of the archbishop of Paris, giving information, that on Sunday next, there will be exhibited in the church of Notre-Dâme, some of the most valuable and sainted relics that now exist. They are enumerated substantially as follows, according to the best of my recollection. The sainted crown of thorns, which was placed on the most holy head of our divine Saviour. A sainted nail, from the cross of our divine Saviour. The sainted reed, which was placed in the hands of our divine Saviour. Some of the most holy blood of our ever-venerated Saviour. Some of the *holy milk* of the divine Virgin Mary. These remains are all guaranteed to be genuine, and represented to have performed at least one miracle by their divine power, namely, that of saving themselves from the destruction, which overwhelmed most objects of a similar character during the Revolution. Mons. Michelet, who loses no opportunity to have a hit at the absurdities of the Catholic religion, will doubtless expatiate upon them. Why are not "The Jesuits," and a still later work of his, "The Priest, The Wife, and The Family," translated and published in the United States? I imagine them to be exactly the works to *sell*. They certainly overflow with genius. This, the excitement, which they cause among the "believers," sufficiently attests.

O, poor Americans, condemned to stay at home, far from the land, where everything is collected, which can disgust or please! Wonderful city! comprising within its bosom whatever can gorge the coarsest taste, or delight the most refined. I am not of that class, who believe, with our friend Othello, that

"He that is robb'd, not wanting what is stolen,
Let him not know 't, and he's not robb'd at all."

On the contrary, it is, in my opinion, a real substantial loss not to hear, whatever the circumstances may be, the delightful music with which this city abounds. In truth, I begin to feel a new liking for Paris, since I listened to the exquisitely fine Concert given this morning at the Italian Opera House. It was the music of a new composer, Felicien David. These compositions have been performed but two or three times this winter. At first, their novel character took the public by surprise. None knew how to judge them. The rules by which the inspirations of Euterpe are ordinarily tested, were here at fault, for these were of a different order. While the critics stood aloof in meditation, the multitude passed sentence, and applauded. Of course, the leaders quickly followed; and nothing is now heard but loud and universal praise. The name of David seems destined to be almost as renowned as that of his royal namesake of Israel, who sang and played upon the harp so well, and danced, too, with all his might, though whether with much grace or not, admits a serious question. However that may be, the modern David has inscribed his name upon the roll of fame with those of Weber and Beethoven.

Every ticket was sold for this his last Concert. The first part consisted of a symphony, Allegro, Andante, and Scherzo. The last movement of the Scherzo was received with loud plaudits. The second, *La Danse des Astres*—a chorus, with solo. *Les Hirondelles* was beautifully sung by Mons. Dupont. This sweet song, which is marked with the peculiar style of the author, though in a less degree than many of the others, is adapted to the capacities of ordinary singers, and will undoubtedly be soon within the reach of all on the other side of the water. *Le Chibouk melodie*, *Le Sommeil de Paris* chorus, with solos, finished the first part. The second was the performance of *Le Desert*, the *chef-d'œuvre* of this great composer. It is the description of the movements and actions of a caravan, with some accidents that befall it. The entree in the desert, orchestral. "Glorification of Allah," grand choir. This is an exquisite passage. The appearance of the caravan is told by a charming march and chorus; but in the midst rises a wild storm, the wind whistles, and the caravan is all confusion. One can feel the hurricane and the clouds of flying sand beating against him, so perfect is the imitation. By and by the tempest lulls, and shortly after the march is re-commenced.

In the second division are the "Hymn to the Night," and the "Evening Revery," two enchanting songs, which I wish that you could hear; I am certain you would then pardon me for filling your page with this description. In the third is the "Rising of the Sun." This to me is one of the miracles performed by music. At first, in the breathless stillness, which reigned throughout the crowded theatre, a slight sound might with difficulty be heard, like the buzzing of a musquito, aroused by the faintest ray of light shed upon the world. This increases imperceptibly, and the solitary insect is joined by another and another. This trill changes to a fifth higher, as the twilight deepens, and increases in force, till the sun bursts with a flood of light from behind the hills, and any of the audience who may have been sleeping, are awakened by shouts of applause. The old walls, accustomed as they are to respond to hearty expressions of delight, shook fearfully with the unwonted fervency of the unanimous and thundering demand for a second performance.

I scarcely remember being more pleased, than at this concert. The orchestra of one hundred and fifty performers, seemed imbued with the spirit of the composer, and played with uncommon precision and taste. The name of David, without any farther works, is immortal. He appears to desire the resuscitation of the neglected instruments, the oboe and bassoon, as most of his solos are composed for them. These excellent instruments will undoubtedly be more used hereafter on this account. "The Desert". is in the market to-day, and selling in great numbers, and also a portrait of the author on stone.

In a former letter I informed you how they made the fashions, but I have not yet enlightened you as to the time and place of their origin. Within the last few days I have been to the great manufactory, the Champs Elysées, to witness their formation. Good Friday, and the two preceding days, are celebrated in Paris as the fête of Long Champs. This fête originated in a custom, among the fashionable and wealthy, of going in Passion week to attend Mass at the Abbey Long Champs, attracted thither by the superiority of the music. After the demolition of the Abbey the drive to the woods of Boulogne was still kept up. On the last of these days, or Good Friday, the Champs Elysées was crowded with vehicles. These were marshalled into two lines, one going, the other returning, by the numerous guards, and not allowed to turn out, or deviate from the path, but were compelled to perform the entire circuit, a distance of three or four miles. Being unable to proceed faster than a walk, this necessarily occupied considerable time. In the centre, circulated more freely the carriages of the nobles, ambassadors, and such others as could obtain permission. A curiously formed vehicle, of large size, lined with white silk, and drawn by four horses of different colors, contained an extremely beautiful young lady in pink satin. By her side sat a dashing buck. The driver, with two lackeys behind, shone in purple coats and scarlet breeches. This remarkable apparition attracted vast attention. The tiny carriage and little horses of Gen. Tom Thumb, or, as here designated, Gen. Tom Pouce, constituted the only representative, that I observed, of the United States. His excellency himself, disliking a crowd, unless of persons with each a dollar in his hand to neutralize its vulgarity, staid at home. Each side of the carriage way was filled with a dense crowd of spectators, amounting in the entire length, by estimation, to two hundred thousand persons.

Usually, the fashions of the coming season are invented, or at least exhibited on this occasion, but this year they were postponed, as eclipses sometimes were by Dean Swift, on account of the weather. The spring is excessively chilly and backward, and has benumbed the creative power of the Parisian brain, as well as the germination of the soil, so that both are equally tardy in bringing forth flowers, and giving birth to new modes. At any rate, few specimens were observed among the fair occupants of the vehicles; I assure, you, however, that the summer straws are really beautiful.

This letter, notwithstanding all that I can do,—for I have, as you see, called on fashion itself, though all in vain—has a violent propensity to music, and insists upon indulgence. It is consequently only a natural fulfilment of its destiny to proceed to give you an account of another concert, which I heard last night. This took place at the Conservatoire Royal de Musique. This Institution was established for the purpose of giving instruction in music gratis, and has attached to it about four hundred and fifty pupils. They give annually eight concerts. The solos are performed by the first artists in the city, and the choruses and instrumental parts by the scholars. These concerts enjoy the deserved reputation of being the best in the world; for in no place is such attention paid to the rehearsals. As might be expected, it is very difficult to obtain admission to them. At the commencement of the season, tickets are taken by subscribers for the whole eight. So great is the desire to obtain them, that a *queue* is formed as early as four o'clock in the morning awaiting the opening of the bureau at eleven.

I was unable to procure a ticket; but going thither about an hour before the commencement, with forty others, I received one entitling me to stand at the door till everybody had passed in, and the concert begun, and then to the further privilege of seeking for a seat, or vacuum rather, which is as rarely found in these exhibitions, as in nature herself, who, you very well know, abhors it. Of course, the privilege did not avail me much. By the side of the stage, however, the boxkeeper for a small gratuity gave me a chair in what she justly denominated a dark closet. I there found three others, whose faces were the only ones visible to me the whole evening, and those only by the flickering ray of a candle about as bright as an American fire-fly. But I heard the music distinctly. What could be desired more? I did not come to *see*; and what lover of the muse, who makes her revelations to the ear, could have ever thought of using his eyes, when such pieces were performed in a style that nobody else could do them, as Haydn's Creation, Overture to Oberon by Weber, (encored) Symphonie in *ut* Minor of Beethoven! The Boston Handel and Haydn Society, and Boston Academy of Music have performed these pieces, and the little world of the Literary Emporium were delighted. Are there not many of those bright-eyed ladies, who were then so enchanted, who would most gladly be thus shut up in a dark closet with me? There is no knowing what they would do—in order to hear the sweet voice of the celebrated Madame Dorus-Gras warbling the beautiful strains of Haydn's most beautiful Oratorio.

Music has carried me through this sheet, which I commit to the mercy of the waves, trusting it will have a better fate than the three American packet ships, whose loss all deplore, especially those who have again to cross the big water, and who found sea-sickness quite sufficient, without going to the bottom. I have a suspicion that this letter is rather stupid; if otherwise, it must be accounted for by the following, which was once said by somebody, and which I leave every one to translate for himself, and apply as he can—*Les bon mots sont des fruits, qui viennent sans etre cultivés. Ils surprennent autant ceux, qui les disent, que ceux qui les écoutent.*

XVIII.

COMMON SCHOOLS—COLLEGES—LIBERTY—M. MICHELET—PRISONS—THE DEPOT DE LA PREFECTURE DE POLICE—THE CONCIERGERIE—MARIE ANTOINETTE.

A TRITE old adage says: "Where there is a will, there is a way." Like many other intellectual heir-looms, which have come down to us from the flood, it has been much oftener on our tongues, than in our practice. But if you ever have the misfortune to be imprisoned in a crowd, I advise you to summon one of these "old saws," to your aid; for you will find, as you shall see I did on a recent occasion, that they are eminently useful instruments to *cut* a passage through. At such a crisis politeness and perseverance are invaluable pioneers; and, if the patient can have the good fortune to summon to his aid the spirit of wisdom, wrapped up in a classic cuticle, such as *Suaviter in modo, fortiter in re*, for example, his speedy delivery is certain. The truth of this I had abundant experience of in going to the College of France to hear a Professor deliver one of his usual lectures, of which I will tell you by and by.

Much as we boast in America of our facilities for general information, our system is by no means perfect. A common education can be acquired, it is true, at least in the Northern States; and so far it is well. But how long are the Common Schools, the legacy of the Puritans, to last? Apostates have long ago been found to disparage the character of an ancestry, of which they are unworthy; and bigots have now appeared in sheep's clothing to disturb, and finally destroy, some of those invaluable institutions, which—and nothing else—have made our country, what it is. The seeds of decay and ruin are being planted in the Common School system, and theological sectarists are laying on it the spoiler's hand, and parting its once seamless robe among them. Alas, for the time, when the glory of New England and New York shall be quenched in total eclipse! God shield me from the sight of our School-grounds turned into cabbage plots! O, may I never live to see the day, that shall witness the treacherous conversion of these sacred nurseries of sound letters and humane manners into arenas of polemic wrangling, or spots for teaching a man-invented catechism, longer or shorter!

But though the Common School—the palladium of the Republic—is certainly menaced with a fearful trial by those large sections of the community, who are accustomed to look upon their party advantages, as superior to the common welfare, yet the strong common sense of the people at large, it is hoped, will warn them of the danger, and cause them to rally for the rescue of an institution, peculiarly their own, and eminently democratic. This is more than can be affirmed of the colleges, which are too exclusive in their action, contribute less to the common stock of science, literature and improvement, than is justly expected of their imposing organization and munificent endowments; and wear an air of stately exclusion, which contrasts unfavorably with the American theory of Government, and with similar institutions in this country. In France the portals of the libraries and literary institutions are thrown wide open, and the rich and poor stand on equal ground. Lectures are daily delivered on every subject, with which man is conversant, by professors of the profoundest learning. Of every language that is spoken in Europe, or Asia, there is a public instuctor. No subject is too abstruse or rare for the public to hear; no experiments too costly for them to see. The people pay, and should they not have an equivalent? Ah! France is indeed a glorious country. No wonder the Frenchman feels so keenly the *amour de patrie*, and, having made a fortune in a foreign land, sighs to return to *la belle France*, and to spend it there. No ties are generally strong enough to bind him permanently to any other soil, or prevent him from coming home to lay his bones in his native earth.

When in my last letter I ventured to assign to France, not only a happy physical position with regard to variety of climate and productions, and an attractive centre for the selectest treasures of other countries, but to designate her capital, as a focus where science, the arts, all sorts of learning, refinement, taste, luxury, and sensuality, if you please, converge, and make her perhaps the most brilliant star in the Universe, I anticipated that the want of freedom might be objected, as casting a deep shade upon an otherwise bright exterior. And what is *American* liberty? Does it not consist in the absence of all restraint in speech and action, except what is necessary for the general welfare? And is the Frenchman a bondman? Certainly not. In many respects indeed he is freer than my countrymen. He is not depressed by the surveillance of public opinion, which, though often a salutary check, is sometimes, it must be confessed, the most vexatious of tyrants. Why, what degree of comfortable liberty can a poor fellow enjoy, even under his own vine and fig tree, if the busy body of a public is taking notes all the while? If every man is a spy, and every old woman an agent of the police, or a bill-sticker to make proclamation of his violation of some of its often arbitrary and foolish rules, his life becomes a perpetual running of the gantlet. Though this odious despotism of the public, which spares not even one's own castle, does not possess the power of actual imprisonment, it notwithstanding, imposes heavy bail, and lays a man under bonds for good behavior, as long as he lives. One may wear a hat in Paris of any form, or a cap of Harvard College notoriety, if he chooses; he may put on a coat of any cut or color; a Dickens' bear-skin, even, and no mob will follow on his trail, no inquisitive stranger ask him the price of his integuments.

I found myself near one of the lecture rooms of the College of France fifteen minutes before the usual hour, and resolved to hear, and see the "agitator," the Dr. Steiger of France, the inflexible persecutor of Jesuitism—Mons. Michelet. But, though so early, not only was the hall filled, but the steps also leading to it; and numbers were going away in despair of effecting an entrance. On the strength, however, of the maxim with which this letter commences, and with the exercise of a little agility, which it inspired, I soon carried the place by escalade, and was finally most comfortably seated directly in front of the speaker. Before the lecture began, I had ample time to inspect two large pictures, representing passages in the history of the college, and to examine the audience, with a view of ascertaining its character. The two front rows were occupied by ladies, without whose patronising presence few lectures of any sort are ever delivered. My scrutiny, however, resulted in nothing satisfactory. The only peculiarity noticed was two negroes of the most polished ebony, which contrasted agreeably with the less highly colored complexions around them.

The stillness of the assembly, and my reflections, were suddenly interrupted by a clapping of hands and other demonstrations of welcome, and I saw entering at a side door, a gentleman of some five feet six or seven inches in height. His form was slightly bent, but not with age, for he appeared not to have seen more than fifty years at the utmost. His dress, with the exception of a white vest, was entirely black. Seating himself behind a table, and waiting a sufficient time for the greetings to subside, he commenced his lecture. The face of Mons. Michelet has little that is remarkable, as the features are quite regular; but his dark eyes are bright and beautiful. His gray hair, parted nearly in the middle, is suffered to grow long, almost encircling his ears. He wears neither beard nor mustache, and his somewhat sunken cheeks are without any other color, than the general yellow tint of his whole face, which indicates an infirm condition of health.

As a speaker, he is forcible rather than elegant. In the tones and modulations of his voice he has a mannerism, reminding one sometimes of a Methodist preacher; at others of a theatrical performer, especially in his cadences, which are drawn out with a slow, tragic intonation. Otherwise, his delivery made no pretension to oratory. Like most of the French professors, he sits, while pronouncing his lecture, in consequence of which his gesticulation is much repressed. It is his clear and logical deduction, which renders his discourses so attractive. Add to this an ever-pleasing power of analysis, a vein of humor and sarcasm, and the excitement which agitates all around, and extends through Europe, I may say, against Jesuitism, and his popularity may be accounted for in some degree. His remarks, which are extemporaneous, with the exception of a few notes before him, were frequently interrupted by applause. Note books and reporters were very numerous; and his distinct, slow utterance made it easy to transfer all he said to paper, word for word.

Michelet, and his colleague Quinet, are causing a great commotion throughout the kingdom. A short time ago a petition came from Marseilles, numerously signed, praying the Chamber of Deputies to stop the lectures of the former. His last work, *Du Prêtre, des Femmes, de la Famille,* has, in the space of a few months, gone through six or seven editions. The priests are doing their utmost to allay an excitement, which, they are very well aware, can be kept up only at their expense. But I have not heard that any of them, as yet, have used any *Brownson knock down* arguments. I trust, before long, to introduce to you Mons. Quinet.

With much difficulty I have succeeded in gaining admittance to the prisons of Paris. Of these there are about a dozen, containing every class and grade of offenders. The government is exceedingly slow in granting permissions to visit them, for various and obvious reasons; and it was only after making great exertions, and explaining that I did not wish to enter them from mere curiosity, but from a desire to study their construction and arrangement, the treatment of the prisoners, their food and accommodations, the character and amount of their labor, and other particulars, for future use, that the privilege was at last granted to me.

The first that I visited, was one of the oldest in the city, the *Conciergerie.* Its rough and gloomy aspect struck me very forcibly, the more, no doubt, because, since my entrance into France, my visits have been principally to see the grand and beautiful, with, now and then, a peep into the fantastical or grotesque. In architecture, noble churches and splendid palaces have been the chief objects of my contemplation. The difference was startling indeed between their waxed floors, walls glittering with gold, and glowing with the handiwork of renowned artists, and the grim, cold stone, grated windows, and iron doors of these dark habitations of crime. The contrast is, notwithstanding, not so great as may be imagined; for both are associated with historic, or redolent with romantic lore; both have been the abodes of kings. In both, subtle statesmen have plotted; sweet maidens, and innocent princesses, sighed. What, then, is the mighty difference? Ah! "Disguise thyself as thou wilt, still Slavery! still thou art a bitter draught! and, though thousands, in all ages, have been made to drink of thee, thou art no less bitter on that account."

I will describe these buildings more or less minutely, commencing as nearly as possible, in the order that the prisoners enter them. The first, then, is the *Dépôt de la Préfecture de Police*. This was erected in 1828 at a cost of sixty thousand dollars, and is situated near the river Seine, at the head quarters of the Prefect of the Police. It is capable of containing three hundred persons; but now has generally one hundred and fifty. Though comparatively a modern structure, it is not built upon a recent model, but resembles the gloomy strongholds of the olden time. Its fastenings and windows have not their strong and massive look, however; and this arises from the circumstance, that the occupants are such as are *yet only accused* of crime. Everybody arrested in Paris is first brought to this place, where they do not remain more than two or three days. The edifice is divided into several apartments, appropriated to the various grades of those who are confined. Those accused of *crime* are separated from such as are arrested for *minor offences*. The young are divided from the old, males from females, those respectably clad from the filthy and drunken, and finally, the sane from the insane. The polite director himself accompanied me round the apartments, obligingly pointed out their peculiarities; explained their uses, and, what was more than all, answered my numerous inquiries. Beside these general divisions, there are subdivisions into private and single rooms, and others for a multitude of twenty or thirty. The former rooms are plain, every one having a grated window, and each containing a bedstead, generally of wood, but sometimes of iron; the sacking of the latter so arranged, however, that its principal advantage—freedom from vermin—is counteracted. On this are placed two or three mattresses, of a mixture of wool and hair, with suitable sheets and blankets, which altogether make up a very comfortable bed; a chair completes the furniture of the dormitory. The arrangements for the toilet are poor. A basin of water permits the indulgence of washing; but when a towel is asked for, the response is the same as was made to the heroine of Mrs. Clavers, "Haint you got a 'andkercher?" One who has money can command such things as he pleases. The large rooms are filled with the commonest people. Extending the entire length of one side of the room is a something, whose use one cannot at first imagine. It resembles the leaf of a table, but is in fact a species of bedstead, constructed without sacking. This is let down at night, and covered with mattresses; here, with all their clothes on, the whole company of twenty or more, as the case may be, sleep together in the same bed. Truly crime, as well as poverty, makes strange bed-fellows. In the day time the mattresses are piled away in a corner, and the bedstead is elevated again to make room for promenading. Such lodging strikes one as rather too bad at first; but after taking a view of the motley crew, who, like the *Chourineur*, never took their clothes off, perhaps in all their lives, to go to bed, the slight deficiency of etiquette almost disappears, and is partially atoned for by its manifest convenience. Many of the company, indeed, it is quite probable, never enjoyed a better lodging. One of the wards is appropriated exclusively to common prostitutes, who have been apprehended for making a noise in the streets, intoxication, or disease. Another is for the insane, found wandering at large. After their examination, which follows the arrest, as soon as possible, these are all either discharged, or sent to other prisons for their trial. All the Courts are held in the Palais de Justice, of which the *Conciergerie* is a dependence, and with which it is united by an internal passage. To this last all prisoners on trial are brought for convenience, and, at its close, are liberated, or conveyed in the space of two days to the places of their sentence.

The *Conciergerie* claims a dreadful pre-eminence among most of the other prisons in its local history. Within its frowning walls have been enacted many of the bloodiest and most horrible tragedies of tyrannical power, and of the no less arbitrary violence of infuriated popular vengeance in the numerous revolutions. The entrance is by an arch in the *Quai de l'Horloge* to a court, and thence through a great gate, guarded by a portcullis. The stern, sombre vestibule subdues the mind to a tone suited to the gloomy apartments to be afterwards seen. From the vestibule one door conducts to the *greffe*, where is the office of the directors; another to the advocate's room, where the counsel of the prisoners are admitted to consultations with them. It is divided from the vestibule by a grated partition; so that it is completely under the inspection of a multitude of jailors, who are constantly seated there. Another door leads to the *parloirs*, or speaking rooms. There are two for the two sexes, and are alike in their construction, which is peculiar. A double grating two feet asunder, divides the room into two parts, into one of which the prisoner is introduced, and the visitor into the other. None but relations, with a few exceptions, are allowed to visit here. From this description, it is apparent, that nothing can be communicated from the visitor to the prisoner, who, in addition to this effectual isolation, is subjected to the incessant vigilance of a jailor. In this prison there are few private apartments, properly speaking, though every one sleeps alone in a small room, which occasionally contains two beds. The furniture is similar to that already spoken of at the Dépôt. At seven in the morning a bell summons all to rise and sweep out their rooms; at eight they are served with their allowance of soup; at ten with their meat, and at twelve with vegetables. They may eat them when they choose, but they have no more till the next morning recommences the same routine. They all enter into a common courtyard together; in the centre of which, a fountain permits to all, who wish, the privilege of washing. In this court-yard, the assassin and thief, the footpad and burglar, assemble together. In bad weather a large room affords them shelter; when cold, the cell of Louvel, the murderer of the Duke de Berri, contains a stove, round which they gather. This is the only place, which is warmed on the men's side. In the Dépôt, on the contrary, each cell is warmed by an iron pipe running through it, heated by steam. The cell of Louvel is circular, and in the top of its arched ceiling is a hook, from which was suspended the iron cage, in which he was confined. The dungeon is wholly destitue of light, but what comes from the grated door.

The side of the females is the same, as that of the men, except that the chauffoir is a common apartment; but, at the same time, it is the most remarkable of rooms. That, now used for the Sacristie, is particularly worthy of notice; for it was here that the unfortunate Queen Marie Antoinette was incarcerated two months and a half; and left it only for the guillotine. The room is now much altered and enlarged by the addition of several smaller ones; but its original dimensions are easily discernible. Allowing for the part, occupied by her bed, a space of ten feet by two was all that remained for a tenant of palaces, and a daughter of the illustrious house of Hapsburgh. Behind, a small room was constantly occupied by an armed guard, who watched every motion. It now contains three excellent pictures, which, from the darkness of the room lighted only by a colored glass window, are scarcely visible. They commemorate portions of the sad history of her checkered life; her parting from her family before going to prison; her prison, as it was, when she was there; her dress with every article truthfully painted; and her absolution by the priest, before she mounted the scaffold. Her sweet face, as there depictured, with the memory of her excellent character, made even the jailor blush for the despicable and unmanly barbarity of his country. This room leads to the chapel, where mass is chanted every Sabbath to the assembled prisoners. The men are stationed below, and the women in a grated gallery above, which screens them effectually from observation.

A large apartment, now unoccupied, is used in times of disturbance, to confine persons under arrest; and is capable of containing two hundred individuals. Still another, much smaller, without any furniture but a stove, is called the Condemned Cell, in which all, on whom judgment of death has been pronounced, are confined, till their removal to the *Prison des Condamnés.*

They are sent hither, as soon as sentenced, a strait jacket put upon them, a mattress laid for them in a corner, and an armed soldier placed on constant guard in the cell. Three days after sentence they are executed, unless they consent to make confessions, in which case forty days are allowed them.

No work is done in the Conciergerie, and its capacity is two hundred and fifty persons, though rarely containing that number.

XIX.

Prisons of Paris—St. Lazare—An Actress off the Stage—Filles-Publiques—Debtors' Prison.

In continuing the particular description of the prisons of this metropolis, we come to that exclusively devoted to females. *St. Lazare,* situated in the *rue du Faubourg St. Denis,* was, at the close of the sixteenth century, a hospital for the leprous. When that loathsome disease was extirpated, it was given to the establishment of Saint Vincent de Paul, and to the congregation, which he founded in 1625. From being a Convent of the Lazarists, it was employed for the confinement of genteel young debauchees and licentious poets, till it has now been converted into a place for the detention of females committed for trial, or condemned to a confinement of less than a year; or for those, awaiting removal to the general prison in the centre of the kingdom at Clermont, whither all are conveyed, who have been sentenced for a long term.

Before proceeding farther, let me remind the reader, that St. Lazare is the thrilling scene of many a chapter of Eugene Sue's Mysteries of Paris. Here are the walls that encompassed the sweet *Fleur de Marie,* the kind-hearted Rigolette, and the bold, fearless Louve. While reading that work, I remember being struck with the achievement of Louve in saving the drowning Marie by plunging into the rapid Seine. My surprise has ceased. This apparently improbable portion of the history is now rendered less remarkable, for I find, that a great many French women are expert swimmers. The river in summer is almost concealed by immense floating buildings in the form of a hollow square. In these buildings are baths; and in the centre, which is covered so as to defy the intrusive eye, is the swimming school. There are many of them of both sexes, and both are well filled during the warm weather. A few days since, at noon-day, a poor girl, in a fit of melancholy at the loss of a lover, threw herself from one of the bridges with the design of putting an end to life and sorrow together. A cry of horror arose from the numerous by-standers, but not a soul moved to her rescue. A splendid carriage suddenly drove up, a young woman in gay attire leaped out, and casting aside her rich cashmere and fine bonnet, plunged fearlessly into the swiftly running current, which foamed in wild eddies twenty feet below. Bravely she buffeted the waves, though encumbered with heavy clothes, reached the miserable unfortunate, and brought her to the river side, where both were assisted out. The girl was saved, and her lover, struck with remorse, returned to her. Her daring rescuer, having played her part brilliantly in the comedy of the morning, was heartily greeted in the evening by the applause of another crowd, assembled to see her enact her part in another comedy at one of the Boulevard theatres, of which she is a member. Were the women of America thus physically educated, the disaster that befell the Swallow, and similar ones, would probably not be attended with so painful a sacrifice of human life.

Hoping by this little episode to have caught your attention, you may be willing to go with me into the prison, and learn its condition, which is the object of my visit. It is divided into *three fundamentally distinct parts*, each of which is the receptacle of different classes of individuals, who are entirely separated from one another. *The first* contains persons committed for trial. *The second* those who are undergoing sentence of imprisonment; and *the third* is for young children under sixteen years of age. I shall say nothing of the *first*, as it is like others of the kind in similar buildings. *The second class* is principally one peculiar to Paris, to understand which requires some preliminary description. The *filles-publiques* of the city are subject to regulations of Government in every respect. To engage in this vocation, it is requisite to have the name and residence recorded at the office of the Prefect of the Police. A license is then granted, as one is in our country to a retailer of ardent spirits; with this exception, that on the certificate are inscribed the rules and regulations for the control of their behavior, which are carried into actual execution, instead of sleeping on the statute-book. These consist principally in limiting the hours and places of their perambulations. They are forbidden for example to enter any of the public gardens, the Palais Royal, and many other places; to address in the streets any one, who has a child or female in company, or any one whatever before the city is lighted in the evening, or after eleven o'clock, &c. &c. This card is frequently required to be shown to any of the numerous police, who may happen to imagine, that a woman has commenced business without a license. The reverse of the card supplies a place for the date of her physician's visit. There are more than two hundred of these physicians, called *officiers de santé*, supported by the government, whose whole duty is to keep an eye upon the health of this class, *ne quid detrimenti respublica capiat*. To effect this object, every *maison des filles* is licensed, and visited weekly. The loose women, who occupy their own apartments, go themselves once a fortnight to the bureau at the Hotel de Ville for a similar purpose. The rules are so rigidly enforced, that if any are detained a day or two beyond the time prescribed, a messenger is despatched at once to inquire the reason. Change of residence can make no difference, for the police know every inhabitant of the city, and every alteration of abode is immediately noted. Disease among them is treated as a crime; such as are thus guilty, are sent to the prison of St. Lazare to stay till cured.

The whole system arises from an opinion, that this mass of moral evil is necessary, and absolutely beyond a cure. Whether this is true or not, I shall not now undertake to discuss; but it is apropos to remark, that we all ought to understand the state of the question. For it is an actual and mighty leprosy of the social body, like intemperance, lotteries and gaming. About these and some other epidemic vices, every man is called upon, and bound most solemnly to act. It is consequently a duty, pressing him with equal force to think, investigate and decide. There are but two ways of treating these disorders of the state—for he is not a good citizen who does not regard them as such—one is extermination ; the other regulation ; and people have arranged themselves into two denominations, espousing respectively these diverging modes. The subject is eminently practical; but still cannot be trusted wholly to experiment. The advantages of control with respect to the *femme publique* are practically shown in the small amount of disease in this city, compared with London, New York, and even moral Boston, where the adverse theory of legal extirpation is strongly practiced on, with all the favorable countenance, which public opinion can lend. *Disease* however is by no means a measure of the mischief, either to society, or this infected portion of it. Other consequences equally hateful flow from this copious fountain, and its very *extent*, however regulated, is itself an evil of alarming magnitude. But I have little time to mention even facts, and none at all to build theories on them. Of this class of persons the prison contains at present upwards of three hundred. They occupy the hospitals principally, which are large and commodious.

The third section contains the *Orphan Children*, who, having nothing to do, are begging in the city, and leading a vagabond life, like Fleur de Marie; or making the first timid experiments in petty thieving. Such are taken from the streets, and placed here, where they often find better accommodations, and are really happier, than ever before at any period of their lives.

In their treatment, conveniences, nourishment, and other particulars, no difference is known among the classes. All are roused at six o'clock from their slumbers, and in half an hour proceed to their respective work-rooms, where they labor under the superintendence of an officer. Needlework of various kinds is their chief employment. There is, however, a manufactory of paper boxes, and another of suspenders. The strict discipline, enforced in the American Houses of Correction, is not observed; but every thing is conducted in a much more lenient way. The prisoners are not prevented from conversing together in the work rooms, if no noise is made to disturb the prevalent tranquillity.

On the entrance of any one, all stop their work to cast a glance, and sometimes a prolonged gaze, at the visitor, which furnishes a striking contrast to the manners of American institutions. No task is allotted, each laboring as she pleases, provided her indolence is not noticed by the superintendent. Work is continued to six o'clock P. M., interrupted only by their meals and hours of recreation. This sounds strangely—recreation in a prison! It is so, notwithstanding. Two hours a day—one in the morning, the other in the afternoon—all are permitted to walk in the court shaded by fine trees; and there they laugh and sing and amuse themselves together, as much as they like, keeping within the limits of good order and decorum. In these courts are fountains, which are the general wash-bowls, but refreshing breezes are the only towels, which the government supplies.

In this prison, as elsewhere, it may be seen, how much better it is to be a great rogue, than a small one: to steal a thousand dollars than to pilfer one; for here, as at St. Pelagie, money will procure every object of desire. Six sous a week will buy the privilege of sharing a room with one or two others, and of working in it instead of the public shop. The ill health of the prostitutes confines most of them to the hospital. This is a long hall with partitions, extending only to the entry, which traverses the whole length of the edifice. This arrangement is attended with the advantage of supplying a number of separate rooms with an improved ventilation, and an easier superintendence. There are a resident physician and apothecary; the physician *en chef* visits the establishment every morning. For punishment of bad behavior, the shower bath, black hole, and such like, are entirely unknown. The sole correction is solitary confinement in her room without change of food for four days at most. On expressing my astonishment at its lightness, my conductor said that "solitary confinement is enough for *women*." In an adjoining chapel, those who are inclined, attend mass on the Sabbath; the number of such amounts to about half of the inmates. The internal management is under the direction of the inestimable Sisters of Charity. These *religieuses* have the care of all the institutions in the city, where females are confined; and their winning ways, and attractive kindness, have been the means of drawing many from the devious paths, into which they had been straying. The work executed here, is of the most perfect description; funds are thus collected, which are remitted to them on their enlargement.

The Prison for Debtors is situated in the Rue de Clichy, a retired quarter, where most of the English population live. To be a candidate for admission to this Retreat, a debt of thirty dollars, in the case of a foreigner, is a necessary qualification. It must be payable to the original creditor; and the candidate must be under seventy years of age. No person can be arrested on a Sunday, or fête day; or in any place of religious worship, or of the constituted authorities; or in any private house, if admittance is refused; or between sunset and sunrise. These popular enactments naturally cause many debtors from England to take refuge in this city. The creditor, who puts a man in prison, must make a monthly advance of his board at the rate of six dollars per month; neglecting which only for a day, the debtor is set at liberty.—The doors are opened to him at a fixed time, in proportion to the amount of the debt; and the creditor has no further power to again confine him, the debt being thus legally cancelled. Imprisonment for a debt, less than one hundred dollars, ceases in two years: in four years for two hundred dollars; and in ten years for all sums above a thousand.

The lot of these individuals is not very unfortunate. They are deprived of liberty indeed; but they pass a life of ease at the cost of others, and, judging from their faces, I imagine they have a merry time of it. Notwithstanding the universal cry of freedom, men in all countries are ever ready enough to sell it; the only question being about the price. The twenty cents a day are given directly to the debtor, with which sum he is to provide himself with food and lodging. The government charges him six cents a day for his room, furnished with a bed, two tables and three chairs. One would think, it would puzzle him to keep house with the small remainder of this sum, even with an allowance of a sufficient length of tether to enable him to do his marketing himself. But most of them have money at command; or friends, who come to see them, laden with provisions. Should no such providential manna be deposited for their gathering, they still can manage to keep the great enemy, hunger, at bay, and even pass the time quite comfortably.

The whole interior administration is vested in a Committee of Ways and Means, elected by the prisoners. A republican government is thus, you observe, already established in the heart of France. This Board have a *table d'hote*, where all, who wish, can take their meals at a stipulated sum per day. They have also a capacious kitchen, and grant every one the privilege of cooking whatever he chooses, for two cents daily, which is ascertained to remunerate them for the charcoal used. They have, beside, some property, which belongs to the prisoners; such as a billiard table, a nine-pin alley, and other things, which they let to those who have money they can spare, at the rate, for instance, of two cents for thirty rolls at the alley. The friends of the prisoners are likewise allowed to spend their time with them from ten o'clock, A. M. to six, P. M. of every day. Each one has his room, which is furnished by himself, or friends, with various degrees of luxury according to his ability or taste. A fine garden, adorned with trees and flowers, affords an agreeable promenade; and no labor is exacted, but every one consumes his time precisely as he pleases. Many individuals might employ themselves as well within these walls, as without; tailors for instance. And so might the poet, the flight of whose fancy is not to be hemmed in by stone partitions. I mean this hint for his particular benefit, for though the poet's corner may be after death, in some grand old Westminster Abbey, it is, notwithstanding, in his life time, apt to be the inglorious debtor's prison. This, the only Institution for the confinement of debtors in the city, is capable of containing four hundred individuals; but, at present, encloses only one hundred men, and eight women, who are kept, of course, in separate apartments.

"We have always a good many of your countrymen," said the guide. What country? "English." I am not English, but

American. "Ah! we have but one now from America; a Protestant clergyman of New York,"—well-known to the residents of West Point. Another was pointed out to me, as the son of a peer of France, who, having spent a fortune in prodigality, was expiating his indiscretion, and receiving, with the approbation of his father, some wholesome instruction in this severe school of economy. The penny postman had left his letters, and I had finished my visit; so we both went out together.

XX.

PLACE DE LA BASTILLE—COLUMN OF JULY—HOTEL DE VILLE—PALM SUNDAY—EDUCATION—LOUVRE—RELICS—HORSE MARKET—THIERS.

IN the company of three friends, Drs. Carey of New York, and King and Davis of South Carolina, I set out to visit the Hotel de Ville; for admittance to which I had written and procured letters of the proper authorities some days previous. By inattention to the time specified in the billet, we arrived there about an hour too early. Unwilling to lose the time, we employed it in going to the Place de la Bastille. This spot is full of interest, having been the scene of many historical events. The Bastille has, however, disappeared, and in its place shoots up the high and beautiful column of July. It is constructed of bronze, rising to an elevation of one hundred and sixty-three feet, and measures twelve feet in diameter. A great deal of taste is displayed in this monument. Its pedestal stands upon a basement of white marble, supported by blocks of granite. Around this is a tesselated pavement of white and black stone, and finally a border of red Flemish marble, surmounted by an iron fence. At the angles of the monument is the cock, which is now an emblem of the French nation, though I do not know the reason; perhaps from that well-known principle in Heraldry, by which arms possess in many instances a certain relation to names. Thus the ancient sovereigns of Dauphiny and Auvergne bore a dolphin on their shield; the city of Lyons a lion; that of Berne a bear. So Gallus, a Gaul or Frenchman, might for a similar reason assume the figure of the polite and gallant leader and champion of our poultry, as emblematic of his nation. The family of Law in Scotland, however, dispute the exclusive claim of the French to this really noble bird. They bear this figure in their arms in allusion to the common method of expressing the cry of that bird among the Scotch "cocky—leery—*Law.*" If it is of ancient adoption among the descendants of the Gauls, I suspect this emblem has become more popular than formerly. The shaft of the pillar contains in large letters of gold the names of the five hundred and four citizens, who were killed during the three memorable days of July, 1830, and now lie buried beneath it. On the top of the monument is a gilt figure, representing the genius of liberty. This image is said to be one of very great excellence. What pleased me more than anything was, to see the numerous wreaths, hung upon the pickets of the iron fence by the hands of affectionate relatives of the "glorious dead." I suppose, there were some twenty, many of them fresh, beside others, which had apparently hung there for a long time. Under the monument runs the canal St. Martin, which is spanned by one stupendous arch of masonry. It was here that Bonaparte intended to erect an immense elephant in bronze, which, with the tower, was to have been seventy-two feet high, from whose trunk a fountain was to play. The project was to construct it of cannon to be taken in Portugal and Spain, but, unfortunately for the plan, these were never captured, and by consequence, the mammoth water-spout was never built. The plaster model, however, is remaining near the column. A monument on this plan is expected to be erected shortly, but in another portion of the city.

Returning from this digression to our primary destination, we entered the Hotel De Ville, or Town House, after lingering to admire its elegant exterior. This, you may imagine, consumed some time, for it is one of the most beautiful buildings in Paris. It is in vain to attempt a description; this must be reserved till my return. I will say, however, that it has turrets and minarets and windows and niches. These niches are filled with statues of the great men of France; among whom I recollect Buffon, Rollin, Descartes, Sully. This edifice was built by Philip Augustus, but, like the jack-knife, which had possessed seven new blades and five new handles, and yet remained the same instrument, the Hotel De Ville has been so thoroughly renewed, that its original founder himself could not possibly recognise it. The repairs are even not yet completed. This is the spot, where all the revolutions have commenced, and which has witnessed most of the great political acts of these times. It was here from a window in the saloon of the throne, that Lafayette, having embraced Louis Philippe, presented him to the people. In this building, too, Robespierre held his council. The rooms, which are shown, with these exceptions, are devoid of peculiar interest, and only distinguished by the richness of their furniture, their painted ceilings, silk and gold curtains, large mirrors, and similar embellishments.

The recent snow and subsequent rain have plunged the streets into a condition by no means unusual to an American. Notwithstanding this, it being Sunday, there were crowds of people in the streets. Being unfavorable for promenading, they directed their steps in greater numbers than usual toward the churches. Another reason beside, which influenced me, also attracted them. It was a fête day, Palm Sunday. Around the church of St. Sulpice, which I attended, and others likewise which I passed, were many old men and women, having piles of a kind of green shrub, principally, if not entirely, box. A branch of this they sold for a sous. Every person who entered, that I saw, bore one of them. The numerous priests also, who assisted at the service, held them in their hands. On a strong box, placed to receive the contributions of the charitable, I noticed a label, stating that it was intended for those who wished to consume milk and butter during Lent. The heinous sin of this indulgence is wholly washed away by a few sous dropped into this receptacle, the number of which is governed, I presume, by the appetite of the contributor. Every day this form of religion becomes more and more disgusting. I do not think, however, that there is much hypocrisy among the people. It is simply, because their organ of faith must be remarkably large. This, I consider, originates in ignorance. The multitude of Paris are unacquainted even with the rudiments of education. If they can read at all, it is with so much difficulty, as to give no pleasure. It is not uncommon for porters, concierges and others, to mention in their advertisements, that they can read and write. When they possess the ability to read, their low wages allow them to buy few books, and their tastes select those of very indifferent character. The churches are therefore filled with the lower orders of men, and the higher classes of women. The latter are unfortunately not so well informed as in the United States. Two things are very rare here, though of perpetual occurrence in America—blue stockings and prudes. The former are *raræ aves*, the latter absolutely unknown.

After church I went to the Louvre. A part of the old pictures has been taken away to make room for a yearly exhibition of the works of modern painters. This was the first day of public exhibition, since they have been placed there; and notwithstanding the rain and "slosh," the crowd was very great. The two sous, which are exacted for the care of umbrellas, must produce quite a sum for Louis Philippe. Speaking of umbrellas, they have an excellent custom at Paris in regard to the care of cloaks and other loose gear at all public places, and also at private balls, which ensures their safety. A number is attached to each article, which is then put away by a servant. A corresponding number is presented to the owner, on the return of which, his property is instantly restored. How much better is this, than the vexatious exchange of garments at an American party or ball! What a confusion of moveables and personal chattels! What a disregard of old landmarks and notions of meum and tuum! It is almost as hazardous to be the last to depart from an American assembly, as to sit down to a dinner table after the guests have risen. What a capital scheme this ticketing would be on steamboats to secure the re-appearance of one's boots! At the masked balls a considerable revenue arises from the ten sous on each bundle. At the museums of Paris and Versailles, where two sous are charged on canes, parasols and umbrellas, which are prohibited from being carried into the galleries, the income is forty thousand dollars a year.

In such a crowd it was quite impossible to observe the pictures. The critics, who have been permitted an entrance for several days, complain that the character of them is not equal to what it has been for several years past. In one thing, however, they are not inferior to the master-pieces of the old painters. They are in general quite their equals in freedom from drapery; not even a fig-leaf is thought necessary. Strange, when the actual men and women of society owe so much of their consequence to the tailor and dressmaker, that the mimic representations of them should dispense so entirely with their services.

I have been to see the relics, of which I lately wrote. There were not so many, as I had heard, consisting only of the true crown of thorns, a piece of the true cross, and some nails which were used in fastening our Saviour upon it. All these I have seen, though at a little distance. They were placed on the altar of the cathedral of Notre Dâme. The crown no longer retained its thorns; they had been broken off, and given to various churches. The remains were enveloped in a box of crystal, so overlaid with gold, that little, if any, of the wood was visible. The nails, which are described as red with the blood of our Saviour, were also enclosed in a case of gold, or gilt, so that they were in a great measure concealed. The piece of the true cross was more exposed, and looked as if it might have been part of the panel of an old oaken door. A multitude of carriages was before the entrance, and the church was thronged with women. Though four or five thousand were probably present, its vast dimensions would have very easily admitted as many more. I heard, or rather saw, a sermon; for on account of the distance of my seat from the priest, I could not hear a word; yet I had the satisfaction of seeing him point frequently to these relics. The priests were allowed to advance and kiss them; but the poor public were only indulged with a look, and the liberty of "lifting up their eyes to Heaven and saying, God be merciful to me a sinner."

Let me say a word of the Horse Market, where I found collected five or six hundred horses of all kinds and conditions, from the immense Norman horses to such as resemble the American and Canadian. In the centre of the market was a course of about five hundred feet in length, where the speed of the animals was tried. Around it stood the jockeys with whips, whose privilege it was to strike every creature that passed. The poor beast in going round this ground would sometimes receive several hundred blows. The students of Paris are frequently "taking courses," on Chemistry, Theory and Practice of Physic, and other sciences;—here were many engaged in "taking a course," on Anatomy; for the skin and bones they bestrode, often could not merit a better name. On one side, a hill called an *essai*, with a steep ascent and descent, afforded an opportunity to test their strength, and this is done by attaching them to a cart with clogged wheels.

Mons. Thier's new work, the "History of the Consulate," a sequel or continuation of his "History of the Revolution," has sold with unprecedented success. The newspapers state, that ten thousand copies were disposed of the first day, and the edition exhausted. The fame, which he acquired by his first work, sells the second. I have seen no report of its character.

The French generally serve up every kind of food separately. But there is one dish in the dessert, which is a mixture, called *les quatre mandiants*—the last word not in the lexicon, meaning, eatables—consisting of filberts, almonds, raisins and figs. The mélange which I have prepared, though it will not compare with the mandiants in relish or adaptation, can boast, you must certainly confess, of a much greater number of ingredients.

XXI.

ENGLISH—WASHING ESTABLISHMENTS—ST. SULPICE—THE "SWISS"—CHAMBER OF PEERS—TRAITS IN FRENCH CHARACTER.

THE twenty-third of last month was a great Fête day, and I went to the church of St. Roch, to hear mass. I am ignorant of the composer, but it was excellently chanted and sung by the first-vocalists of the Italian Opera. It was with no little difficulty, that I effected an entrance into the building. At a very early hour, it was completely filled, and on my arrival, the soldiers extinguished absolutely every hope of admittance. But, accidently I happened to overhear a gentleman remark to two ladies, that he had obtained leave to enter at a back door. On the instant, I followed them, and just as they were going to enter, taking the arm of one of the ladies, I very unblushingly walked in, not forgetting to thank her for thus successfully, though unwittingly, covering my attack. Notwithstanding this skilful manœuvre, I was, after all, under the necessity from the immense press, of remaining in one of the chapels, where, though I could hear perfectly, I was unable to see either singers, priests, or what all were more desirous of doing, the Queen, who regularly attends this church. It is wonderful to meet everywhere so many English men and women. There is scarcely a company into which I go, or a street I pass through, where I do not hear some one speaking my own tongue. And, indeed, without a word, it is easy to recognise them, especially the men, whose shaven faces and haughty strut betray them, accompanied, not unfrequently, with a rawness, which not only bespeaks a want of acquaintance with Paris, but even with good manners. Quite a common sign in the shop windows is—" English spoken here."

From sheer curiosity, just follow my "washing," in its perambulations through the city. A young girl takes it from my room, and carries it to the establishment of her mistress. Here every article is marked with a bit of thread. Thence it travels to the river at the dirtiest portion of it, where the city sewers disembogue their foul contents. At this delightfully selected spot are large houses built on boat-shaped foundations, two hundred feet long or more, two stories in height, and provided with windows, chimneys and other conveniences, like a common dwelling on the land. The lower story floor is nearly even with the water's edge, and open to the air. On this platform are to be seen some hundred or two women in each of these establishments engaged in cleansing the linen. One should never allow himself to imagine, even for a minute, that the chattel is his own, which he observes undergoing the torture of purification; the consequences would assuredly be fatal to his peace of mind. When a man beholds his house burning up, he is in some sort reconciled to his misfortune by witnessing the manly efforts put forth by generous firemen to rescue his property. But he is reduced to positive despair, when he views the wanton exertions made to annihilate his nice shirts, and without any apparent compunctions of conscience. But labor is cheaper than soap, and therefore it is used with greater freedom. Economy is duly attended to; but it is the economy of soap, and not of linen. Fuel, as well as soap, is so dear, that no one ever thinks of boiling the "white things," as in the United States. In the place of the former, they use *l'eau de javelle*, which is nothing more nor less than lie, and so strong, as to flay the hand which touches it. This is applied without mercy. After this corrosive ablution, they are pounded with a wooden hammer, till every button on the shirt is broken, a signal, that they have been beaten enough. The poor victim is yet not entirely despatched; there are still some remains of vigor left. This is soon dissipated, for it is next laid upon a board, and a brush of stiff bristles is energetically applied by a lusty woman. It is then rinsed in the yellow river, conveyed to the room overhead and dried, returned to the first hands to be starched and ironed, and in a few days the bundle of rags is brought home to the unconscious proprietor, who pays six sous for the transformation, and consigns it to the paper-maker. Two sous are charged apiece for a similar conversion of collars, handkerchiefs and hose. The consequence of all this is, that dirty shirts are so excessively numerous, as to become almost distinctive of a gentleman. To mark linen with indelible ink is perfectly useless; after such a process, even Kidder's is invisible.

The 24th was a decidedly musical day with me. I have already given you a sketch of my morning and evening feasts, but, between the two, I was treated by a lucky accident with a capital luncheon. Virginie came running to my room, and said, that I had better go to St. Sulpice—a step only from me—and hear the Hallelujah and Gloria. I was too late for the former, but the latter I heard. The immense church was crammed, the vast multitude uniting in the music with the hired singers and orchestra. Never have I heard such music performed by such a choir. At a Methodist camp-meeting on Cape Cod, I once heard ten thousand people, or thereabouts, singing their humdrum melodies, but at this time the finest music in the world was sung by almost an equal number, led by a large choir of finished performers. I do not know, that I was ever so affected on any similar occasion, as now, when the priest, taking the cross from the altar, and turning to the multitude, presented it in blessing them. With one accord all fell upon their knees, and bowed their heads in adoration; then rising, every mouth was open, and every voice loud with the praise and glory of the Lord. Every voice but mine. I was completely choked. My heart came into my mouth; it was impossible to utter a sound, and cold chills went and came. This strong effect was new and surprising. Yet it was not a religious emotion. Strange to say, I do not remember thinking of the cause of this adoration. It was but an ecstasy of mere social feeling, which I doubt not many mistake for a more holy sentiment. In the midst of all these solemn and impressive influences, I was strongly tempted to laughter. A poor girl, who was standing in the passage, knelt down with all the rest, but the *Swiss*, or servant, who has the charge of preserving order, objected to her obstruction of the avenue, and asked her to remove. She arose, and again kneeled in the same place. He again insisted on her removal, but still again she persisted in occupying nearly the same position, and by the time the controversy was ended, the whole multitude had arisen.

This *Swiss* is quite a prominent person in the church. He is dressed in scarlet, richly trimmed and adorned with gold lace, a chapeau with three corners, a sword by his side, and in his hand a baton of office perhaps five feet long, ornamented with a large gold head. Over one shoulder is thrown a scarf, which crosses the breast to the other side, extending to the knee, and is also highly embellished. This functionary precedes the priest in his short walk from the sacristy to the enclosure of the altar, making way for him by striking the stone floor violently and repeatedly with this truncheon. During the service of mass and other exercises, he marches round among the people, demanding offerings for the church, and followed by two priests with each a bag, one to contain collections for the church, the other those for the poor. At three sous for every chair, the amount so obtained is by no means small.

In the afternoon of the twenty-sixth I went to the Chamber of Peers. To obtain admission a ticket is required, which is given by one of the members. On the point of entering, to my inexpressible chagrin, I discovered, that I was in that agreeable position called a dilemma, and termed by some elegant writers, a fix. My ticket was not to be found! What was to be done? Time pressed; I did not despair of obtaining entrance however. I asked the guard, who declined to admit me without one, where I could get a ticket? He said of the Swiss (or servant) below. I found him easily. On propounding the matter to him, he with solemn mystery and pretended secrecy, conducted me away from all observers, and said he had *one* ticket. On inquiring what he asked, he replied in the obsequious manner, which this class always affect the world over, towards one whom they design to take in, "What you please." I was not born in New-England for nothing, and therefore discovered, that too much *amour-propre* costs very dear in France. Instead of two or three francs, which he probably thought would have been almost urged on him for a ticket, bought in a dark corner, and enveloped in mystery, he got a fifteen sous piece, which happened to be in my pocket. I begin to understand the people, and am no longer to be wheedled by bows, or overawed by bluster. I offer a man half what he asks, without a thought that I am insulting him. And, after all, I often think the purchase might have been made for half the price agreed to. Ah! the French are a sorry people. A remark in the Britannia, a London paper, which I saw this morning, was so striking, that I give it to you with the endorsement of several Americans, to whom I read it—"France is only taking her first footsteps in civilization. This language would probably enrage Frenchmen, who, by some original fantasy of their nature, always regard themselves as the first of mankind. But as they grow wiser, they will comprehend, that civilization does not mean glass and gilding, millinery and bon-bons; but common sense common freedom, common law. In all these things Frenchmen are still but children, and children they will remain, so long as they think that plate glass and palaces, and boasting about France, and bravadoes against the world, are the substantial power of a nation."

This is not telling you of the Chamber of Peers. I got in, as you have seen. It cost twice as much to see Gen. Tom Thumb. The room, where the public session is held, is extremely beautiful. It is in the form of a semicircle. In the middle of the axis are the seats of the President and Secretaries; before them the rostrum, from which all the speeches are made. The chairs in front are for the members. They are lined with green and yellow damask. The carpets are of the same colors. The walls are brilliant with gilding, and the ceiling is painted with allegorical representations of law and justice. Around the walls are numerous busts of the Marshals of France, and pictures of scenes in the lives of Louis XI. and Philippe of Valois. I sat through the speeches of several of the honorable members, which were delivered with very little animation, employing myself in looking at their dresses. They all wore a coat with collar and cuffs embroidered in gold. This uniform, with vests, cravats and pants of all colors and shapes, reminded me of a stable boor, who slips on a white jacket to wait upon the table at dinner, but whose nether integuments reveal very plainly his more legitimate calling. As soon as the clock struck five, they all jumped from their seats with an alacrity unexpected from their gray hairs, and rushed to the doors; and, before the President could say, "session is adjourned," they were half of them in their carriages. Dinner bells have the same effect in French palaces as in the Mississippi River steamboats.

XXII.

ARC DE TRIOMPHE—WALL OF PARIS—DUKE OF ORLEANS—HIS DEATH AND MAUSOLEUM—CONSEQUENCES—SUCCESSOR TO LOUIS PHILIPPE.

On a fine day, a short time ago, Dr. Cary, of Buffalo, New York, accompanied me for a promenade in the Champs Elysées. We soon came to the Arc de Triomphe. Our attention being diverted and engrossed by a great many equipages, which were being shown off by their aristocratic proprietors, the distance of three miles was insensibly passed. I shall not take up the space requisite for a description of this monument of the genius of Bonaparte. I say of Bonaparte, because, though actually erected by Louis Philippe, it was the design of the Emperor. Passing the barrier, we came to the famous wall, which is now being built, and nearly completed, around the city. This evidence of the folly of legislation, though many think of the monarch's sagacity, is a stupendous work. Independently of the cost of the land which it occupies, the expense of its erection alone has been immense. It is constructed of solid stone some twenty feet in height. This is encompassed by a deep trench, capable of being flooded, constituting an impassable moat from twenty to thirty feet wide. Earth is heaped up behind the wall, forming a solid massy rampart. Numerous forts are interspersed along the line. What the eventual cost will be, it is quite impossible even to conjecture. In 1841, thirty millions of dollars were granted for the commencement. A day or two ago, Marshal Soult presented a bill to the Chamber of Deputies, asking an appropriation of three million dollars, and more, for the necessary guns and equipments. A newspaper of the humorous and satirical order, called the

Charivari, which, like the ancient court jesters, with its folly, utters many truths, says, "M. Soult wants three million dollars for the fortifications. Surely, it is the policy of the Government to preserve peace at whatever expense."

A little beyond the fortifications is the spot, where in 1842 the Duke of Orleans, heir to the throne of France, breathed his last. All must recollect, for the tragical catastrophe concerned the world, that his horses, becoming unmanageable from fright, the Prince, in attempting to jump from his carriage, fractured his skull, and died in four hours after. He was borne into the shop of a grocer; and on this spot has been erected by the King a most beautiful chapel, dedicated to St. Ferdinand. It is the most charming object that I have seen in Paris, or indeed anywhere else. The structure is but fifty feet in length, and twenty in height. There is nothing striking in its external appearance, except the cross, which surmounts it, and the windows, which are of a peculiar shape. Little of it can be seen from the street, as it is surrounded by a high wall. The interior is of white marble. Directly opposite the door of entrance is an altar to the Virgin, situated on the exact place, where the unfortunate Prince expired. This is surmounted by a fine statue of the Virgin and child The simple ornaments of the altar, candlesticks, cross, &c., are chased silver. At the right hand is a most touching monument, representing the Prince upon his death-bed, enveloped in a cloak, which however does not conceal the star upon his breast and the epaulet upon his shoulder. At the head of his pillow is an enchanting "Spirit," with expanded wings, in the attitude of supplication. Nothing on earth can be more pathetic than this. I defy any one to look upon it without being affected to tears. The monument is in two parts, but so delicately joined, that an observer does not at first notice the fact. The "Spirit" is the work of his deceased sister, the accomplished Princess Marie, who little imagined it was one day to serve for the mausoleum of her brother. The rest is by Triqueti, from a sketch by Mons. A Scheffer. The windows are of colored glass, depicting the patron saints of the family. The pavement consists of white and black marble. In a small room behind the altar is a painting of great merit, which must have been placed there within a short time, as the date upon it is 1844, but I neglected to take the name of the artist. It is a literal representation of the closing scene in the life of the deceased, who is represented lying on a bed placed upon the floor. His features have already assumed the ashy hue of death. He is dressed in a shirt open at the neck, with the red pantaloons of his uniform. A priest is in the act of applying vinegar to his nostrils. Behind, attentively watching, are his physicians, hastily called, and another priest. At the foot of his bed kneels the king, no longer a king, but a father. The queen and two of his sisters are on their knees by his side. A little behind them stand two of the younger brothers, and at the door Marshal Soult, Guizot, and the aide-de-camp of the dying Prince. It is a very impressive tableau indeed, and, aside from the fine execution and excellent likenesses of the piece, the interest of the scene is very great.

The death of the Duc D'Orleans was not merely a domestic bereavement to the reigning family. It was a momentous loss to France and to the world. The consequences are yet to come. The throne, on the death of the present tenant, will descend to the son of the deceased, the youthful Count of Paris, who is not more than eight or nine years of age. During his minority the administration of affairs will devolve on the Duc de Nemours, who is by far the most unpopular of the princes. There are besides two competitors for the succession, who have numerous and ardent adherents, and who are all prepared for a desperate contest for the supreme power. The claims of the House of Bourbon are strongly advocated in private. Many seize every opportunity to decry the present king. By a base artifice, practised by lying politicians on the everlasting gullibility of the common people on both sides of the water, and meant to rouse the slumbering fires of national jealousy, they say, that he has submitted to be dictated to by England. That he has allowed the Great Nation to be humbled, in consequence of which the eye of Europe is no longer fixed on France, to inquire what step she shall next presume to take. These angry declamations they universally finish by adding, to my unutterable astonishment, "that it was not so under the Bourbon dynasty." My surprise is owing to the circumstance, that, though not old enough myself to have a personal or contemporary knowledge of that portion of the world's history, yet I have a feeble remembrance of hearing my father say, that the Bourbon dynasty of our times was fed, clothed, housed, and nursed by England; and, when it was not able to walk alone, from sheer debility, was taken in her brawny arms, carried back to Paris, and made to sit upright on the French throne. She also put a sceptre into the hands of this remnant of the Bourbons, and tried to make the monarch hold it, but it dropped almost immediately from his puny grasp. Louis Philippe picked it up, and has held it ever since, and will continue to wear it, till death shall dissolve his hold, and mingle his ashes with those of his lamented son. To him he would doubtless have bequeathed it, "but destiny denied."

Again there are many, who are dazzled by the glorious monuments of Napoleon. These sigh for a return of that stirring and brilliant epoch, when the French Empire was the fear and wonder of the universe. Of course they aim at the restoration of his power. They do not want a niggardly prince, they say, who seeks to fill his coffers, and provide a magnificent revenue for each of his many sons.

But in the meantime Louis Philippe is no fool. His gray hairs cover no empty caput. He sees as far into the dark as most men, his enemies not excepted. Wrecked in his early hopes and fortunes, expelled from his country, and abandoned to wander, like Ulysses, over the face of the earth in grief and want, he did not return without bringing back with him to his native land some of the wisdom and experience, which marked that acute Greek. When the world beholds upon the throne, a man, who has gone to school, like him, to poverty and misfortune, and been taught by them to contend with hardships and vanquish difficulties, they may be sure they see a constitutional master, as Government ought ever to be, of a free people, and not the miserable pageant of a palace; one, who is "every inch a king," and neither the organ nor contemptible tool of a mob. He is as profoundly sensible, as any one, that waves of trouble may ere long break upon his house, and is anxiously preparing for the possible event. The bit of red ribbon worn in the button-hole, which catches the eye so frequently in the street, costs nothing, and gains a man. His sons, whom he has pushed forward in the army and navy to the highest posts, reflect upon his family some portion of the glory won by the conquests in Algeria, and cause the names of Orleans and victory to be sometimes mentioned together. These redound not only to the honor of France, but illustrate the name also of Louis Philippe. Numerous cheap portraits of the Royal Family are framed and hung up in the apartments of the peasant and mechanic—will they avail nothing? The large picture of one of the battles of Algeria, now exhibiting in the Louvre, the largest painting in the world, and by the first master of the age, representing the victory of the French arms, and a son of Louis Philippe, surrounded by fugitives imploring safety—will this have no effect? Ah! the forty thousand dollars paid for it to the great Horace Vernet were not badly invested; and the hundred thousand dollars to be paid for the battle of Isly to the same illustrious master, who has already gone to Algiers to view the localities, when viewed in connection with the mild beneficence and uninterrupted prosperity of the present reign, must also contribute its mite in promoting the tranquillity of the succession of his family.

While he thus captivates the popular mind, the king does not neglect the opposite class. With all the irreligion existing in the kingdom, there is an abundant mixture of piety, and this is the more active, because it is obliged to struggle with difficulty. He therefore does not overlook this conservative spirit. His wife and daughters are assiduous in their attendance on divine worship. So bigoted is the queen, indeed, that she ascribes the death of her son to the fact of his being a protestant, and is said even to persecute his widow, almost unceasingly, for her adherence to this faith.

I saw, a few days ago, a tall, fine-looking woman in the street, who was evidently shopping, as she stood a long time regarding the goods exhibited in the *Magazin de Grand Condé*, immediately opposite my apartments. My " know-everything," Virginie told me it was a cousin of the Empress Josephine. I took my hat and went out to see her, but she looked to me just like—a cousin of anybody else.

XXIII.

EXHIBITION OF FLOWERS AND FRUIT—LOVE OF FLOWERS—FLOWER GIRLS—HORSE RACES—AUBER—WAR BETWEEN ENGLAND AND AMERICA.

To-day I have been to see—and I know how you would have rejoiced to accompany me—the show of flowers and fruits, which, I think, is held annually at the palace of Luxembourg. This is not the exhibition of a society, but individuals are induced to present their productions in the hope of obtaining rewards or commendation from the committee. This committee is appointed, I believe, by the Government, and the money for the prizes is contributed by public-spirited individuals. In addition to the former usage, this year medals were offered by the Duchesses D'Aumale and Nemours. The prizes had been awarded previously to my visit, and in the various collections were placed the owners' names, and notices like the following: "The medal of the Duchess de Nemours;" "First prize-medal of the ladies;" "Honorable mention, third prize," &c. The flowers were arranged on the lower floor of the palace, a situation far from favorable; first, because of its darkness, and next, from its contracted space. One would suppose that a palace could afford a suitable apartment for an appropriate display. It is certain, that, if there is one, it was not used on the present occasion. The windows were obscured with curtains, lest the sun might injure the flowers placed near them. While I gazed upon these plants, a comparison spontaneously arose in my mind with those exhibited every Saturday at the Horticultural Room in Boston, where, you know, I was a regular attendant. After a slight description, you shall have the effect which they had upon me.

The show was to continue four days, and this was the morning of the third. As there were few or no *cut* flowers, their appearance was little, if any, inferior to that of the first day. You know the species, which bloom at this season in the United States. Here were very few, if any, different sorts. There were Rhododendrons, Azalias, and Heaths of numerous descriptions in very fine condition. The latter were in great variety, and superior to anything of the kind that I ever saw at home. As they are indigenous here, growing spontaneously in the country, the soil and climate necessarily cause this superiority. The next largest family was the Camellias. These were very few in number, and the varieties quite limited. I was sadly disappointed at their paucity. A few white, and some red, were very good. The Roses white, yellow, tea and common monthly, were very poor. No Tulips were to be seen, but Hyacinths bloomed in large variety, and were very excellent; also a few Pionies. And here the list must close, with the exception of a few strangers, such as Cacti, Magnolias, &c., perhaps a dozen of each. As to fruit, little could be expected at this period of the year, and therefore no disappointment was felt on beholding two or three dozen apples and pears, a few green figs, grapes from Mons. S. Rothschild's green-house, and strawberries of the same cultivation in pots, of course not numerous. They also reckoned one cauliflower, one cucumber, a few cherries and such like, all growing in pots. In short, take it altogether, don't you think it rather meagre ?

In an adjoining room were tools of every description for tilling, grafting, &c., but all on the small garden scale. I did not see a plow or pitch-fork; nothing but little implements for Countesses to scratch the dirt with, and to help Duchesses cut bouquets. The apartment contained plenty of books on the cultivation of Pansies, (which I neglected to state, formed a conspicuous part of the display) also on flower gardening; in short, everything of the nice, pretty order—altogether French—nothing on farming, the method of growing good fruit, or vegetables—nothing American. There were *pictures* of flowers, much handsomer than the originals, and *artificial* ones, exquisitely natural, though possessing the same fault as the pictures; for the French flatter even nature herself. So far, indeed, as the texture was concerned, I hesitated, whether they were real or not. I considered, that they might be extremely fine specimens of the work of nature in a happy moment. They are made, however, from something like the rice paper of the Chinese. I never beheld better imitations of Camellias and Carnations.

If they go on at this rate, the time may come, it is not at all improbable, when nature will give up the trouble of producing flowers to the ingenuity of the French, while she herself shall confine her whole attention to the growing of the more substantial, but coarser esculents, such as corn, cabbages and potatoes, in which department she encounters no competition from them at present. It is to be hoped, however, that she will never go so far as to desert the regular and time-honored way of propagating men and women, the latter especially, and so permit the tailor and dressmaker to fabricate them entirely—as they already do to a startling degree, of "wood, hay, stubble," and any kind of bone, except their own. Should such a revolution ever happen, I pray that it may be postponed beyond my day; else my long, laborious attendance on hospitals of *maternity*, and kindred institutions, will avail me nothing in my anticipated practice among the fair portion of the community of New York.

Among the plants, that might be termed rare, were one or two specimens of a shrub, which grows wild throughout New England, called Lamb's kill, or Lamb's bane. It made me almost sigh, again to behold it growing on its native hills, where I have so often viewed its showy blossoms in the company of some, alas, whose faces I shall see no more forever.

Another room contained, among other things, stands of wirework, and ornamental flower pots. Out of doors were hand pumps for watering. A great curiosity was a piece of Guano, which is just begun to be imported.

This exhibition on the whole disappointed me extremely. The flowers were quite handsome; yet their number was small, and their varieties very limited. But France has long been behindhand in the horticultural art, and it is not to be expected, that enthusiasm and consequent improvement will revive immediately.

But the same guardian hand, which has for fourteen years done so much to increase the general prosperity of the State, will undoubtedly continue the noble work so auspiciously commenced. Should life be spared him, we may look with confidence for better things.

The habits of the people encourage the cultivation of flowers. I never saw a population, who seemed so passionately fond of them. Shut up and imprisoned, as they are, among these old gray walls, the sight of blossoms of the earth have to them a peculiar charm. Rigolette of Eugene Sue memory exemplifies this taste. Every body almost has them, from the rich and noble, whose wealth supplies them with green-houses and gardens, to the grisette in the garret, who feels more pleasure in spending four or five sous—a quarter of her day's labor—in the purchase of her little pot of violets, or lady's delight, than her wealthy neighbor does with his superb bouquets of choicest exotics. This *petit pot* shares the window seat with a sweet rose bush, and they equally divide the attention of their mistress. Ah! she is quite happy, when the returning Sunday allows her to promenade with her simple bouquet in her bosom, composed of the two flowers grown on her own little plants at home.

You remember how the flower girl has been depicted. Such beauty, as has been given her, must have been seen in some vagary of the imagination. Go over the whole of Paris, and I challenge a person to find one who is passably pretty. The actual, bona-fide flower girls, are old women, who sit near the bridges or in the crowded streets, engaged in making ugly bouquets, composed of about ten little violets, placed in a ring round an *artificial* rosebush, (now when roses are so rare,) two green leaves outside, and an envelope of white paper; all which with a most shocking voice they entreat you to purchase for one sous. This little violet (like the double violet we used to have in our garden at Roxbury) is a very favorite flower, and vast numbers are sold to all classes of people in this one sous form. You may frequently see the workman in his blouse, and the fine lady, purchasing at the same stand together; and the exquisite promenading with one in his buttonhole but at a little distance from the poor girl with a huge pack on her back, and the omnipresent bouquet in her bosom. Grisi at her benefit had one thrown to her as large as a cabbage. As this was in the dead of winter, it was very expensive, costing about twenty dollars.

Sunday, 20th. I have been quite unwell all day with a most violent colic. I was awakened at five in the morning, and till eleven was in great pain. At one I arose and dressed; since then I have suffered only occasional touches. Every body cooks in copper vessels, which however are usually tinned. This wears off gradually, and the first notice of the event, as to-day, comes in the shape of an excruciating colic to all the members of the family.

Since one o'clock I have been to see the horse races, which commenced to-day. Yes, it *is* Sunday, but we must economise in Paris. It costs nothing to go to the race, but the English churches cost a franc. Then, too, one wishes to see the races, and Sunday is the day. The Dukes D'Aumale and De Nemours were there. M. Rothschild was there, and one of his horses beat. More than 30,000 other people were there, *and the day was Sunday.* O land of the puritans, that condemns lotteries and horse races! what think you of the nation, where one is run upon the Sabbath, and the other managed by the church? No one cares, whether the horse Prince, this or that, Duke B. or C. were victors; or whether two or three men were thrown off in jumping the fences in the hurdle race. Nobody cares, so I turn my back on the whole matter, and as the fashion goes, condemn the fault, which I have no longer a desire to practise.

Auber has written a new opera called Barcarolle, which is said not to equal his former ones. Nobody wants to hear it, for they have not yet heard his old ones. There is great talk between the English and Americans in regard to the bellique threats between the two nations. It seems to be the general conclusion, that it is a battle of words, conducted on the principles of Brag. One thing looks squally though, if it is true, as has been affirmed, that Gen. Thomas Thumb has been sent for by Mr. Polk, and requested to hasten home with his war-horses, uniform and sword. The moment I hear that the General has left the country, I shall hurry after him with a new set of surgical instruments, because I am certain, there will be *something to pay* whithersoever he shall go.

The Fête of the King will take up one day, and then on Saturday I go to Versailles, intending to view the Museums and the celebrated Water Works, which are played very rarely, on account of the immense expense of nearly two thousand dollars a day, as it is asserted.

XXIV.

Prisons of Paris—St. Pelagie—La Force—Nouvelle Force—Its Singular Construction—Maison Centrale d'Education Correctionnelle—Remarkable Form and Peculiar Discipline.

Having a convenient opportunity, I send you another of my letters on the prisons of Paris, to which I some time ago referred. One of them is *St. Pelagie,* in the Rue de la Clef, and was formerly a convent of nuns, which, among the convulsions of that terrible epoch, was suppressed with so many others. It has since served as a prison for debtors, till very lately, when it has been used for the confinement of those condemned for a period not exceeding a year, and for political offenders committed for trial, or sentenced for a short time. The latter have distinct apartments from the others, and are not compelled to labor. This old and badly-contrived building is capable of containing five hundred and fifty persons, and generally has its complement. The prisoners are all male, and employed in making list shoes, brushes, friction matches, and other things. The food does not differ materially from that in other prisons. Six ounces of meat twice a week are each man's allowance. They perform their ablutions at the fountain in the great court, which also supplies them with abundance of healthy beverage; and time, that dries the wet eye everywhere, is here the only napkin after washing.

I advise every one who steals in France to take something of value; for money makes a wide distinction in the condition of the prisoner. With silver in his pocket, he can, even when condemned, feed on chickens and the fat of the land; clothe himself in silks and velvet; repose upon a couch of down in a private room, furnished with the finest linen sheets, changed as often as once in twenty days at least, and live like a gentleman, that is, do no work, unless he wishes, which a gentleman never does, of course. The pitiful sum of six sous a day confers these precious privileges. Indeed, those who have the good fortune to be masters of a nice trade, may earn sufficient by it to purchase these luxuries, and at the same time avoid the severe labors of the penitentiary, which others must undergo.

There is not such discipline as I expected to find. When I entered with the intendant, all the prisoners were talking together in the hall, with no one to oversee their labor. Every person turned to gaze at the stranger, and most of them touched their hats to me. What a striking contrast to the manners in American prisons, where none dares to turn his eyes, or raise them from his work! There is nothing distinguishing in their dress; each one retains the clothes he had on entering. When his term of punishment is completed, if the convict has no dress of his own, he is supplied by the government with a suit of clothes, and forthwith consigned to the House of Correction at St. Denis, to work there, till he shall have earned sixty francs to pay for it.

The only punishment is the dungeon. There are two, composed of large rooms with the windows of one partially blinded, but still admitting light enough to read with ease. An inclined plane of boards serves as a bed for the refractory. Bread and water only are granted for the first fifteen days; afterwards the usual allowance is made. A less offence is expiated by confinement in the other cell, which is not so dark as this, where a more nutritious diet, than bread and water are said to be, is prescribed. By special permission, the wives of the prisoners are indulged with visits to their husbands in their cells twice a week for several hours. Another order grants the liberty of *conversation* once or twice a week, according to its terms, in a public room with an officer on guard. Still another certificate confers the privilege to converse in the grated *parloirs*.

The prison, called *La Force*, is made up of buildings part of which formerly composed the hotel of the Duke de la Force, and, like all structures which have been diverted from their original design, are more or less inconvenient. In 1780 they were converted into a prison for prostitutes; and about the same time another was erected by its side for a similar purpose. These were united in 1830, the females removed to St. Lazare, and the whole devoted to persons committed for trial. The inmates are classified as follows. Old offenders form one class; those committed for acts of violence, another; old men above sixty, and boys under eighteen, are respectively kept by themselves. The rest are divided into the peaceable and quiet, and turbulent and quarrelsome. In this prison there are no single cells, but the dormitories contain from four to thirty each. No work is required, except of the young boys, to whom a life of idleness would be eminently injurious. All may labor, however, who wish; the work principally done being the manufacture of list shoes. The sleeping room of the boys is divided into dormitories with a bed for each, which are separated from each other by their partitions. The front is latticed, and open on the passage way. The whole structure possesses very little interest;—old and inconvenient, it will soon be superseded by *La Nouvelle Force*, a cellular prison, which is now being erected in the same faubourg de St. Antoine.

This structure is now in the process of erection upon an entirely new plan, at a cost of more than eight hundred thousand dollars. Though three years of labor have been bestowed upon it, still it is not sufficiently advanced to convey an adequate notion of its future character. It is to resemble a fan, each stick of which, to the number of seven, will be a wing, and the corridors of all will terminate at a central point, commanding the entire establishment. The structure is to be three stories in height, and is intended to contain twelve hundred prisoners. Between the wings are to be open courts for the due exercise of the inmates. The point of junction of the united wings on the first floor, is to be used as a place for stripping the prisoners, as they enter, to ascertain that they have no arms or prohibited articles on them. Above will be a chapel, and the doors of each cell will be so adjusted, that the tenants can look upon the priest without being visible to each other. The handle of the fan will comprise the apartments of the superintendent and officers, and the entrance will be at its extremity.

This, when completed, will be the second cellular prison in Paris. The other can scarcely be called a prison, indeed, for though the persons detained there are kept apart in cells, it is rather a house of correction. This is situated in the *rue de la Roquette*, and has the name of *Maison Centrale D'Education Correctionelle*, but sometimes spoken of as the *Prison des Jeunes Détenus*. The form of the building is remarkable, and has, I think, on a hasty reflection, a great many advantages over the numerous other plans on which these institutions have been built. This structure, enclosed within two massive stone walls of immense height, is a regular hexagon, with circular turrets at each corner, and four stories high. The apparently diminutive size of the windows, though in reality they are sufficiently large, the circular turrets of ponderous stone, of which material all the building is constructed, and the frequent groups of soldiers around, altogether give it the air of a feudal castle, as it lives in our imagination, rather than a stronghold for convicts. Its internal form cannot be better described, perhaps, than by comparing it to a wheel, the rim of which is formed by the hexagon, the spokes by piles of buildings, which rise from the turreted corners, and converging, though not meeting, but abruptly breaking off, are united with a circular building in the centre by means of iron bridges in each story. Six courts are thus produced of the same shape and size, which, being planted with trees, still young, supply a place of exercise for the prisoners. The building in the centre is now used for a chapel; the rest of the structure is divided into cells. The stairs are all placed in the turrets.

The convicts are young boys under sixteen, who have been sentenced for petty thefts or vagabondism; the term of confinement being of unequal length, but never extending beyond twenty-one years of their age. Within the last six years, an entire revolution has taken place in the government of this institution. Before that time, the youths were classified according to age and size; and, as much as possible, with reference to the turpitude of their offences. These classes were kept so scrupulously distinct, as not to be suffered to see each other: but still, all those of the same class wrought, ate, and played together. It was by and by conceived, for many reasons; more particularly from the astounding discovery, that, of one hundred who were liberated at the completion of their term, eighty returned hither, or were sentenced to a similar place; that the seeds of vice, instead of dying, were only planted in a hot-bed, to germinate and bear a fearfully increased harvest of crime. As a matter of experiment, and in the confidence that no worse consequences could possibly ensue, another plan of treatment was adopted, which, at the very outset, was adapted to strike one as excessively cruel, and, in all probability, productive of effects no less injurious than the former, though of a different nature. Entire seclusion—solitary confinement, for hardened criminals, convicted of the most horrible outrages against the laws of God, humanity, and their country —has encountered the opposition of many and most powerful antagonists. They have pronounced it cruel in every view, and worse than death; and there are not a few, who deny that the human mind possesses a capacity to bear up against the awful monotony and oppressive load of perpetual isolation and silence. If such views are held in relation to minds of hardened maturity, how much more plausibly may it be urged against a similar imprisonment of the young, whose feebleness, want of cultivation, and ignorance, combine to disqualify them for supporting the utter forlornness of such complete desertion!

Looking at such facts, and their alleged consequences, government has thought to remove these unhappy effects by employing the mind; thus obtaining all the benefits, without the opposing evils, of solitary confinement. The youth have therefore been placed in a private cell, and detained there not unfrequently four or five years, without a sight of any human face, except occasionally that of a visitor, or his own officers; never hearing for all that long period the sound of the voice, or witnessing a single feature of his next neighbor, separated from him merely by a distance of little more than a foot. The only circumstance, that can ever vary the wearisome monotony of such a life, is his labor. In his little cell are placed his bed, a chair or two, his work bench and tools. The youthful convict, on entering, is indulged with the choice of one of the twelve trades carried on in the establishment. The different divisions are now merely the different trades, to each of which a master workman is attached, who is styled the teacher, whose duty is to instruct the youth in his particular branch. Another teaches reading, writing, and arithmetic, and some have a professor in drawing, or rather, in design. The trades are turning, cabinet work, wood carving, various kinds of iron work, etc.

The order of the day is somewhat as follows: Rising at seven o'clock, two hours are given to labor before the first meal at nine. The nourishment is much better than in any other prison, as youth, on its passage to manhood, is thought to require a more nutritious diet than a person at maturity. All the bread is white. After breakfast, a space of an hour or two is devoted to study. I saw writing books in some of the cells, which contained very creditable specimens of their accomplishment in that neglected and undervalued branch of the fine arts. A translation of the Penny Magazine was one of their reading books; this indicates a considerable advance; for when they enter, scarce a single boy can read a word. An hour in the forenoon, and an equal length of time in the afternoon, are given up to recreation. One would suppose this almost impossible in the case of these solitary beings; but on the contrary, I remarked that those occasions were enjoyed in the true spirit of the grant, and in real earnest. Each boy is sent by himself, for the purpose, into one of the courts; and there, alone, he engages at once with the elastic alacrity of youth in some spirited juvenile sport, as trundling hoop, and rolling ball. These pastimes are prosecuted with an ardor, which indicates a delight scarcely, if any, less than persons of a similar age experience in mingling with their mates and companions in the diversions on the green, free common of a village school. It is a strange sight to observe pleasure and punishment, which in the progress of vice are cast into scenes far asunder, brought here side by side into a single picture. Labor fills up the rest of the day.

XXV.

Methods of getting a Living among the Poor—Bread—Chiffoniers—Dogs.

There are many ways of getting a livelihood in Paris. This is not difficult—for those who have education; but the ignorant and poor are reduced to all sorts of expedients. One, who has ten or fifteen dollars at command, purchases a vehicle mounted on two wheels, with the body suspended on springs. His credit will fill this with commodities of various kinds. Another procures fruits, which he divides into piles, according to the quality, and sells at different prices. A third gets a supply of paper, blank books, ink, sealing wax, and the "everything" necessary to make one an accomplished writer. A fourth collects glass ware, crockery for the table and kitchen, spoons, knives and forks, and a dozen other articles, starts on a pilgrimage, and offers everything he has at the same price. Being blessed with fine lungs, all these make themselves heard at an immense distance, the high shrill tones of the women making full compensation for any want of force. A slight nasality proves very attractive to customers. *Tous les articles du bureau pour huit sous! Tout qu'il faut pour la cuisine pour dix sous! Voyez mesdames!* And so they go, making a confounded, everlasting clatter under one's windows all day long. With the aid of a candle enveloped in red paper, the same clamorous traffic is continued till ten o'clock at night. But what is the commotion, yonder? Look! The ambulatory shop, which has been besieged for a long time at the corner of the street by spectators and purchasers—none are too proud to buy of them—is suddenly darting away at a speed, which threatens destruction to its fragile commodities. What is the mighty cause? Do you see two men in black dresses and white buttons, with cocked hat and sword, just entering the street? With what a self-important gait they walk! Those are gentlemen of the police. The law forbids these perambulating merchants to *stop*, and these are the officers to enforce its sanctions. The penalty is fine, and confiscation of the goods.

Begging is another method. This being prohibited, innumerable artifices are in use to evade the law. In the portals of the churches, old men and women sit with a brush wet with holy water, and expect a sous or two for their trouble. On the bridge called Pont des Arts, sits a blind old woman with a roll or two of pencils before her. Give her a sous, and take or leave a pencil, as you please. She prefers the latter. Sometimes one is accosted a dozen times an hour by persons, who have a paper-cutter, on a quarter-quire of paper, which they pray you to buy for the love of Heaven, and in mercy for many starving wives and children at home. Hand-organs, wonderful infantine prodigies, who play marvellously on wretched fiddles and harps, accompanying their instrumentation with voices, calling on the spirits of the high notes of a song, but which refuse to come when called. A few days ago, in the court of a respectable house, I heard a strange noise, which no fancy in fine frenzy rolling on my part was able to manufacture into music. On examination, I found it was a man who owned good lungs, if he had no ear. Unable to procure a crank-going instrument, and lacking skill to perform on any other, he had got a French horn, and through this he was blowing a hurricane, till the occupants of the chambers should be willing to capitulate.

Connected with the musical line of business is the Block-tin cock seller. This branch of trade is much greater here than in America, arising principally, as I judge, from the fact, that all the water drunk, comes from the river Seine, which, being turbid, requires filtration. Every family is therefore provided with an instrument for the purpose, whose cocks are frequently getting out of repair. This itinerant carries on his shoulders a sort of monument-shaped contrivance, composed of an odd mixture of bright tin, and red or some other showy colored velvet. This contains numerous perforations, into which is thrust his merchandise. To draw attention to his wares, he carries a trumpet, which he blows with very little cessation. A handsome young merchant passes by my apartments almost daily, who plays several tunes, and really quite skilfully.

Another of the sounding brass and tinkling cymbal race are the water carriers on a large scale. These have hogsheads mounted on wheels, and drawn by a horse. They go round the streets with a metallic pail on their heads. A loud noise is easily made with the iron bale. The small merchants have two pails, which they fill from the aqueducts at the corners of the streets, and empty into the filters for a sous apiece; no charge made for the mud deposited by their sabots on the entries and floors.

An interesting man is he, who is met at every step, making known by loud cries, that he is a *marchand-d'habit.* A much more appropriate term is old-clothes-man. He buys and sells every article of dress. At night he carries the remains to the "Temple," where his wife patches them up, makes them as good as new, and sells them herself, while he is abroad seeking for more. One of them has just passed my window. Behind is an old lame woman bearing a long pole, from which silken cords are suspended. Not the cords of Hymen, ladies, but equally *near to your bosoms*. They are stay-lacings. Immediately in the rear comes a porter, who, with a frame and basket, applied with straps to his shoulders, is lugging some four or five hundred pounds of wood and coal into the fifth story of the opposite house. How dexterously that young woman balances the basket, containing perhaps a gross of eggs, upon her head! She threads her way through the crowd quite calmly. I'll watch and see how she will contrive to give the nod of recognition to her acquaintance, for she will not be lacking in politeness. So, she is gone—but here comes a woman with lamp shades. Mercy! what a screeching! O, "cease rude Boreas!" To what base uses are the limbs of woman, by nature delicate, applied! There is one, for example, coming yonder, bending under the weight of an omnibus wheel of the largest size! Why, the women of my own country would not put their fingers to a *spinning-wheel* even, though they knew that they could thereby spin out a longer thread of life;. which would be the result, if they had the good sense to revive some of the obsolete habits of their grandmothers. Besides, women are not made Venuses by idleness in America, any more than by excessive labor in France.

At the corner of a street one sees a box, on the top of which is a raised block of the size of the foot, having about the same resemblance to that member in man, as the print did, which Robinson Crusoe discovered in the sand. That worthy, if I recollect aright, was so astonished at the curiosity, that he put his foot into it. It is altogether probable, when you notice this singular appearance in the street, that you will be tempted to follow his laudable example. If you should, the moment you place your foot upon the stand, you will find an astonishing brilliancy come over it, and what is more, that you have three sous to pay.

Perhaps one of the most perfect luxuries yet discovered, is to be found at the operas and ball-rooms. Many a man prefers walking to these places to riding at twenty-five cents the trip. I shall not stop to account for a freak of taste; *de gustibus non*. He does not, however, wish to enter with unpolished boots. And he need not, but on the contrary, his embarrassment is converted into a novel source of positive pleasure. In a small room attached to the establishment, he is directed to mount a step or two, place himself in a velvet-covered seat, and put his feet on two stands—a position of sweet repose—and a newspaper is then handed him to read. Two persons, one for each boot, soon obliterate the spots, and put him on an *equal footing* with those who have come in a vehicle. Thus he has escaped a perplexity, and enjoyed a Turkish luxury beside—this is a clear gain. The two females, who once performed this agreeable office for me, as I was giving to Madame, the proprietress of the brushes and blacking, my gratuity of three sous, anxiously hoped, that I would not forget the *garçon*. Connected with this are the *Cabinets d'aisance*, equally cheap.

In the United States, every body makes more or less bread. In

Paris, and, I believe in France generally, this devolves on the bakers entirely. Hot biscuits are unknown. Bread is of different qualities, and the price is fixed twice a month by the government. This depends on the price of grain, and is of course exceedingly variable. The regulation is undoubtedly introduced for the benefit of the poorer classes, that they may not be compelled by avaricious dealers to pay an exorbitant sum. Every baker in Paris is obliged to keep constantly deposited in the *Grenier de Reserve* twenty full sized sacks of flour. This storehouse is of immense size, and was built by order of Napoleon to contain sufficient grain for four months' consumption of the city. In addition to this quantity, the bakers have frequently a good deal more deposited there, for the storage of which they pay a moderate charge. The cellars contain wine. This vast granary is much smaller than it was at first intended to be. The original plan of building it five stories high, beside the ground floor, was abandoned in 1816. Being then in an unfinished state—the ground floor only completed—it was roofed, and divided into three stories. It is two thousand one hundred and sixty feet long by sixty four wide, and thirty-two high.

Bread is baked in loaves of two and four pounds, and also in the form of rolls for breakfast. It is of various degrees of consistence and character, but always good. The loaves have a peculiar shape. A two pound loaf is nearly two and a half feet long. The four pound loaf is twice this length, but doubled on itself. One eats by long measure—a foot and a half sufficing most for breakfast. A nobleman might require two of the large loaves, making a complete heroic metre; while for the Royal Family, the *needful* Alexandrine must

"—— drag its slow length along."

The loaves are placed upon a frame, similar to that which is used to transport wood, and borne on the backs of women to the regular customers, where it is deposited in chairs, on the floor, like a cane in the corner, or elsewhere, as may be most convenient; it being the general opinion that it cannot, by any possibility, be soiled. At meals, it is circulated from one to another, each cutting off a piece as large as may be desired.

A class of inhabitants peculiar to Paris, as a distinct and numerous body, is the *Chiffonier*, or rag collector. It is composed of both sexes; their business, as their name imports, is the collection of small pieces of cloth, metal, and other matters, possessing the least value. The streets are swept every morning before six o'clock, and the citizens are prohibited from placing ashes, or any dirt, in them, between this hour and eight in the evening. The chiffonier collects his stores from this refuse; it is, therefore, necessarily done in the night. His appearance is singular. Clad in the dirtiest of dirty garments, with a basket on his back, and a lantern in his hand, he reminds me strongly of Diogenes seeking an honest man; with the addition, however, of a basket to put him in, which the philosopher did not take, because he had no expectation of finding one. In the other hand he grasps a stick, equipped at its farther extremity with a crooked nail; thus he wanders about the streets. He regards not the passers by. He never deviates from his path. In fact, he is a sort of prince, for all turn out for him. With downcast eyes, (not from humility, for however lowly his lot, he is not wanting in self-respect, and even pride,) he seeks for hidden treasures. Every heap of filth is a mine of unknown riches, which he is to open and work. He pokes it over with his stick, catches with his hook every piece of paper—it may be a bill of the Bank of France, he says—every rag, of however small dimensions, and tosses it over his shoulder. See him, now. He has found a prize in the heap just at the corner of the street. He picks it up, and rubs it on his coat sleeve, that he may the better observe its value. What is it? From my window I cannot easily see, but I think it is an old broken trunk lock that I threw away this morning, or a fragment of a shovel. No matter—it is too valuable to be contemptuously consigned to his basket; so he slips it into a bag at his side—the receptacle of articles of worth. His business ending with the night, he retires to rest with the man of fashion at the break of dawn. His dreams, however, are not disturbed by the indigestion of *pâtés*, or the fever of champagne, which trouble the young fashionable. O, no! He fancies himself the favorite of fortune, which has transmuted his trunk lock into a golden lantern, and his old shovel into a silver rag-hook. In his dream, he is transported, not to any voluptuous palace on the lake of Como, such as Claude Melnotte so beautifully describes—far pleasanter visions soothe his slumber. Imagination takes him to the side of some extensive dirt heap, pregnant with the rich sweepings of a tailor's shop.

I must, though with sorrow, leave this poetical picture for the humble walks of prose, though not forgetting, that from the stained contents of the chiffonier's basket comes the smooth billet, *qui me prie de faire l'honneur de venir passer la soirée*, where wit sparkles and beauty enchants.

The receipts of this interesting personage amount to about twenty cents a day. Occasionally an article of real value is found, for which he rarely seeks the owner, preferring to pocket the entire proceeds, arising from its sale, to the small fraction thereof offered as a reward. Some days ago, a student in medicine, discovering one of this calling sitting on the *trottoir* with his face bound up, and evidently in pain, inquired the cause. He was answered very gruffly, that it was the tooth-ache, which occasioned this suspension of his labors. He told the man, that, if he would come to his apartments the next (Sunday) morning, he would extract it gratis. At the appointed hour a stranger was ushered in, clothed in a suit of black, a fresh-looking hat, gloves, and well polished boots, whom he did not once mistrust to be the crabbed chiffonier, whom he encountered the previous evening. It was, notwithstanding, the veritable man, who, when making an appointment that morning with *another gentleman* of his own class to visit the Louvre, and inspect the new paintings, placed there recently, observed, that he had a previous engagement with *his dentist*.

The stranger, especially if he has lived where mad dogs are in vogue, and the race is heavily taxed, is astonished at their frequency in this capital. Paris contains more puppies, reckoning *all descriptions*, than any other city, perhaps, in the world. Every body has a dog of some kind. The fashionable lady rarely walks, or rides abroad, without her favorite to accompany her. The rich have a leveret, a small animal of the greyhound species, originating in Italy. The poor have such as they can get. I have seen several, that equalled in size the ponies of Gen. Tom Pouce, the distinguished representative of American dignity at the foreign courts, who is reported to be kissed so much, by this kissible and kissing nation, as to be compelled to protect his cheeks and lips with a mask of goldbeater's skin, graciously sent him by her Majesty Queen Victoria. This mark of her anxious interest in the health of this renowned warrior is the more valuable, since, according to rumor, it has been shown at the expense of incurring the jealousy of the hero of Waterloo. I trust, that no one will imagine by the accidental mention of this distinguished Yankee, in connection with puppydom, that I dream of classifying him with these pets. Certainly not. Private opinions must yield to circumstances. That which, at home, I might incline to censure, is here, with ardent nationality, upheld and praised. In Paris, every American pronounces Gen. Jackson a hero, greater in every respect than Napoleon, or any other person who ever lived. If they say any thing regarding cotton bags, we immediately retort, that he differs but little from the French themselves—that if he used breast-works, French women do the same—the difference being, that he *fought* behind them, whereas they *surrender*—" at discretion." No; Tyler is a man of probity and consistency; Bobby, the greatest living poet, not excepting Prince Albert himself; and Polk a Cincinnatus, called from the plough-tail, to tell a tale to old Europe, now in her second childhood, which makes all its members tremble. We insist, and satisfactorily prove too, that the republic is our *mother* country: for within three months, she has brought into the world two states at a birth, and is already far gone with two more.

But *revenons à nos moutons*—the phrase is good, since dogs are frequently served up for muttons. These dogs are generally muffled, when large, and all are confined by a cord around the neck, which, as one is walking, is often also found around his legs. If a man wishes to insult another, or wreak his spite against him, he kicks his dog. If you desire to speak to a pretty woman, whom you do not know, stumble over the dog, attempt to soothe his barking, take off yourhat, bow three times to the snarling, ugly brute, and the heart of the lady is won. Wind the cord adroitly around your legs—do it quickly, while she is gazing at the goods in the shop window—and you can be as long as you desire in " getting out of the scrape." If he quarrels with another dog, and is thrown down into the gutter, take him up carefully—never mind the white kids—and wipe him with your cambric. This last was never known to fail. " Love me, love my dog," is of French origin. This is part of what is called the dog exercise, and is almost as curious an art, as that of the fan in Madrid. Poets may talk of the beauty of women, when "floating in the mazes of the giddy waltz," or at the domestic fireside darning stockings, the dear creatures never appear so interesting, as when exhibiting the sublime virtues of " patience, loving-kindness, and tender mercy," while they stand awaiting the pleasure of this sweet animal busily occupied at the the side of a house, or by a lamp-post.

The end of the sheet admonishes me to conclude this doggerel description of some of the peculiarities of Parisians and their habits. In a future letter I may resume the thread of my narrative, unless you find the subjects are already worn thread-bare.

XXVI.

HOSPITAL LA CHARITE—GERDY—ANDRAL—RAYER—CRUVEILHIER—FOU-
QUIER—BOUILLARD—COURSE OF MEDICAL STUDY IN PARIS AND AMERI-
CA COMPARED—IMPORTANCE OF A SPECIAL ATTENTION TO A SINGLE
BRANCH—DIFFICULTIES OF AMERICAN PHYSICIANS—THE FRENCH AND
AMERICAN PRACTITIONER CONTRASTED—AMERICAN STUDENTS AT PARIS.

WHEN speaking of Velpeau in a former letter, I incidentally mentioned the hospital La Charité. This is one of the most important of these institutions, and at the same time one of the oldest. This its time-worn and dilapidated appearance fully attest. The same renovating hand, which is employed on many of the other public buildings, is also engaged in re-constructing and modifying this. There is little in its history worthy of mention, except that it was founded by Marie de Medicis, in 1613, for a community of Monks, who discharged the double duties of physicians and priests. It contains 530 beds, which are appropriated to all sorts of disease, the class of patients differing not much from those received at the Hotel-Dieu. Mons. Gerdy assists Velpeau in the care of the surgical patients. Being wholly independent of his profession, he is not obliged to seek for practice, which perhaps he might not obtain, if he did; his bluff, sarcastic manners creating many enemies. His personal appearance is not more prepossessing. His continually contracted forehead, and heavy, lowering eye-brows, add not to the beauty of a dark-skinned, hard-featured countenance. As a writer, he occupies a fair position, possessing the merit of good arrangement and perspicuity. His judgment, one would be apt to consider faulty, had he witnessed some operations lately performed by him, which many present considered not only useless, but as hurrying his patients out of the world. The physicians are Andral, Rayer,

Cruveilhier, Fouquier, and Bouillard. The first three are well known in the United States by their numerous works, which have been there translated.

Without exception, these same three gentlemen are much less followed in the wards, than the other two. Fouquier is the private physician of the King, and his class is much the largest. This is very much owing to his gentlemanly manners, in addition to his acuteness in detecting the nature of disease. His grey hairs, or rather white locks, have brought wisdom with them. Mons. Bouillard, in personal appearance, resembles Benjamin Pierce, the distinguished mathematician of Cambridge University. When I saw him first, I was struck with the similitude, and followed him, from curiosity to ascertain, if their intellectual developments corresponded. Although pursuing a different branch of science, I found that Bouillard was not deficient in the good judgment, fine reasoning, and correct deduction, which distinguish so highly my old instructor in mathematics. His bedside remarks are exceedingly interesting and improving, and I strongly urge every student to follow him. His number of pupils, not being so large as many of the other general physicians, enables one to see the patient, and sometimes to examine the disease in person. Mons. Rayer, author of a work on the diseases of the skin, with his lofty, bulky person, will clear his own way in the world. He needs no trumpeter. The stentorian voice, with which he interrogates his patients, and prescribes for their wants, will speak for him, and will leave a record of himself, ringing in the ears of the poor sick, which will perpetuate his memory to the end of their lives.

The method of studying medicine in Paris is very different from that pursued in America. In some respects it is better, and inferior in others. There is none, or next to none, of what is called office study; and indeed very little study of books anywhere. Many students finish their entire course with scarcely ever having looked at a medical work. The cost is also far less, and the opportunity for deception in regard to the time employed, almost impossible. In the United States, a certificate of three years' study is not unfrequently obtained, by a novitiate, for a few dollars. No such certificates are here required. The Government regulates that matter most admirably. Each student is required to inscribe his name with the secretary, and his time commences at that period. During his term of four years, he is obliged to pass five examinations, and to pay a small sum to the Government, I think about ten dollars for each, the whole expenses for four years' study and degree, being nearly two hundred dollars. Every branch of study has a particular examination. The student previously applies himself solely to this, and without difficulty, of course, can make himself master of it. In the United States, on the contrary, there is but one examination, and that at the end of three years' study in *every* branch at the same time. The preparation for this is extremely difficult. The overloaded brain is distracted with the vain attempt to recall the *minutiæ* of every department of the science.

This reminds me of an advantage, which is not connected with the study, so much as the practice of medicine and surgery in the large cities of Europe, suggesting one reason why the European physicians are more profound scholars than the American. It is because the immense number of the inhabitants of their cities allows the study and practice of *specialties*. The science of medicine is so very comprehensive, as to prohibit one from understanding the whole of it perfectly in all its branches and details. The possibility of taking one branch, that to which the taste of the man is most disposed, and pursuing this to the comparative neglect of the others, allows an approach to perfection in it. Do you ask, why Roux and Velpeau and Lisfranc are such distinguished surgeons? Why Dubois is the first accoucheur in Paris? Why Louis and Chomel and Fouquier are at the head of the physicians? The answer is easy. They have each taken one branch and pursued it, aiming at perfection and attaining an approximation to it. Look at the poor man in America, at the same time, physician, surgeon, accoucheur, attempting to be skilful in operations on the eyes and ears, percussion and auscultation, the diseases of women and infants. The intellect of a

Solomon is not sufficiently comprehensive to grasp the whole circle, even with the years of Methuselah. How much less an inferior mind and a feeble memory!

Arguing in this manner, I have assumed myself, according to my own taste and powers, a special branch of study, and have striven to avail myself of all that France can furnish on that particular subject; I trust not without some success. Whether the new world will give encouragement to such a procedure, time will determine. Be it remembered, that no man can attain to great knowledge on one division with ignorance upon the others. The whole science of medicine and surgery is so intimately woven together, that he, who is not well versed in the principles of each branch, must necessarily be deficient in some fundamental and all-important particular in his own specialty. The study of a specialty does not therefore imply a *less* degree of information; on the contrary, it requires more, far more. But I am wandering far from the subject that I commenced. Pardon this digression.

Although there is but little book study, it does not follow, that there is less real attention paid. There is more *practical* information obtained, than by the office student of the United States. The knowledge is obtained at the bedside on the morning visit to the hospitals of the first physicians of the country. The clinique upon the cases, points out to the student the peculiarities of the disease, the resemblances it has to others, its cause, probable termination, and treatment. These are very often written down, and many thus make for themselves manuscript books of theory, comprising information derived from the very highest sources. This is far better than a treatise on the subject, inasmuch as the student can compare his own observation of the disease with the opinion and description of one, whose judgment he esteems and venerates. However imperfect may be his notes, having seen the patient himself, his ideas of the disease are much clearer than any description, minute and perfect though it may be, of the same disease, which he had not actually seen. The man who has read an ever so good delineation of Swiss scenery, has an idea, more or less vague, of its extent, color, beauty and grandeur. But the traveler, who has seen himself these majestic peaks, though half obscured with clouds, and with eyes almost blinded with falling snow or chilling winds, when reading, after the lapse of many years, his own imperfect notes, written with benumbed fingers by the dim light of a cottage fire, and half asleep, has a far more vivid conception of that splendid panorama. This imperfect simile but faintly illustrates, how little the uneducated student observes even of the prominent characteristics of disease. Yet this little is worth more than whole pages of description. Would that the American physician were adequately encouraged in his toil! Some few are, it is true, but ah! how many, after years consumed at college in laying a basis, and years more afterwards in building the superstructure, live but to see some ignorant blacksmith rolling in wealth, derived from the sale of a nostrum! Yes, so long as the world seizes with such eagerness every new pill, which professes to raise the dead; as long as homœopathy, magnetism, hydropathy, "laces," are in vogue; so long as the laws of the country suffer quacks and charlatans of every description to live in a state of piracy against the world, robbing and killing all, who come in their way, or are allured by a false flag; so long as these ignoramuses, or something worse, are sustained, and allowed to collect their exorbitant exactions for poisons sold under the protection and by the help of the law's strong arm—while these exist, it cannot be expected, that American physicians will devote their energies to such an extent, as to rival the French in their attainments, who are not protected merely, but spurred on, and animated, by the "powers that be."

Apart from this, the American physician, with all the good will he may enjoy, labors under insuperable embarrassments, which, in the present condition of the social state, it is impossible to surmount. Theory is excellent, and not only excellent, but necessary. Still, without practice, it is nothing. This is the reason, why the young physician is inferior to the old, though his head is stuffed with book information to the crown of his hat. The hospital is the place for supplying this deficiency. But the small institutions of the United States are greatly inferior to the

Parisian, not only in their numbers, but in the character of the people who resort to them, and the difference of their respective sensibilities. This inferiority, which attaches to the American, as a patient, exalts him however as a human being. In the United States it is not the poor and miserable generally, who come thither; such as have not, and never had a penny in their purses. But it is those, who have the ability to pay three dollars a week for their board. Such persons say, they are willing to describe their complaints, show their tongues, and allow their pulses to be felt by the physicians, but not by twenty or thirty inquisitive, ignorant students. "I pay my board, and do not wish my privacy to be intruded on." For three years I was living in different hospitals of the United States, and well know the feeling which prevails. The women of America of the lowest classes, even those whose lives, one would suppose, must have extinguished this feeling entirely, have a delicacy and repugnance, quite unknown to *any* class of Parisians. Their description of many diseases is imperfect, and many prefer even death itself to allowing a physician worthy of confidence to examine ocularly the nature of their malady. The French woman, on the contrary, knows nothing at all of this queasy sensibility. She has no hesitation, not only to describe, but to permit her physician to see every complaint. This is particularly to be observed at the midwifery hospitals, a description of which I reserve for another letter. In this respect, therefore, the Paris educated physician enjoys superior advantages to the homebred man.

Every patient who enters a hospital is, in a certain degree, Government property, and, not only through life, but even after death, is subject, in some sense, to the control of the physician. Thus science is benefited by the post-mortem examination, which is made of every disease that is marked with anything peculiar, whether objected to by friends, or not. Among American citizens, extraordinary horror is felt on this subject, and great opposition made by the friends of a deceased person to such an examination. Fortunately this squeamishness is every year less strong, and gradually wearing away. The community are beginning to see the advantages flowing from an inquisition after death, not only as it concerns the physician, but because it sheds light on the peculiar constitution of a family. This knowledge serves to put the descendants on their guard against the special causes, which may excite the latent germ of a similar complaint, that may be slumbering in their systems; or, what is equally needed, to dispel fears, and quiet apprehensions, which, if allowed to be cherished, might of themselves awaken the very evils that were apprehended.

The hospitals furnish so large a supply of subjects, that the chirurgeon has the facilities to make himself perfectly familiar with surgery and operative anatomy.

These are the advantages, not trivial, which the Paris School affords; but it is not without its defects and disadvantages. Having such opportunities to witness diseases in all their forms and modifications, and such facilities after death of ascertaining the correctness of their conjectures, the medical body in this country generally have fallen into an error, and a serious one. They have directed their attention and energies to discovering the nature of disease, and that at the expense of the treatment. The English and American have equally erred upon the opposite side. They have directed their zeal to the treatment, neglecting the diagnosis. To any reasonable person it must be apparent, that to discover the character of the disease, without knowing how to treat it is useless; and also that treating a patient without knowing what the malady is, is a kind of charlatanry. It is a combination of the two acquisitions which makes the accomplished practitioner. This is not to be attained by any one who allows himself to become a partizan of either school. Indeed, the advice which the celebrated Marshal Hall, the most distinguished physician of London, and perhaps of England, gave to a countryman of mine, is full of sound sense, and shows that the opinion, which I have advanced, is that of the highest authorities in medical topics. "Go to France, to Paris," said he, "and study diagnosis, and *then* come back to England and learn practice." This is the advice that all candid men of real information will give.

Indeed, the names of fifty American physicians, which I have, who are here for the purpose of perfecting themselves in their science, coming from every State almost in the Union, is conclusive evidence of American opinion. Those who imagine that the obtaining of a degree denotes the end of study, of course will say that it is useless; but those who consider that they have then but entered the threshold only, will look upon it in a far different light.

These fifty young Americans may be seen wherever anything, which appertains to the science, is to be learned. The best seats in Velpeau's amphitheatre have the name of *American* seats, as they are always filled by the Yankees, who have gone and occupied them long before the lecture commences, in order to secure them. The skilful and intelligent instructors, who have what are called "private courses," are mainly paid by Americans, whose generally short stay prevents their attending to the courses given by the faculty, as they are extended through too great a length of time; some of them indeed last several years. From sunrise to sunset, literally speaking, they are engaged in the close and arduous study of their profession. The evening recreations of operas and visits, are very often given up to continue their scientific pursuits. Where they have studied one hour in America, they study two here. The few hours that are given for recreation, are no more than exhausted nature, and the fatigued brain, demand.

The physicians of the hospitals give the American superior advantages to other students, even to their own. They reason upon this principle. The "United States is more than three thousand miles distant. These young men have come this great distance to a country, whose manners, customs, and language are different from their own. They visit us at a great expense. Why have they put themselves to such peril and inconvenience, placed themselves in such a disagreeable position, often without the power of speaking and comprehending in a foreign country; and subjected themselves to the necessity of expending so largely for their indispensable wants? It is because they are resolved to investigate the science, which they have commenced, under the best advantages, and to make themselves thorough masters of it. I will second such devotion. The doors of my hospital shall be open to them, and they shall have encouragement in prosecuting their investigations." The standing of those who have been here before us, warrant such a belief, and such conduct on their part. May the future show, that the present generation have not "fallen from their high estate," and are not inferior to their predecessors.

XXVII.

CELEBRATION OF THE KING'S BIRTH-DAY.

The tumult is over; the hubbub has ceased; the last rocket has long since exploded; the falling rain has undoubtedly extinguished the only remaining lamp, which illuminated the gardens, and the populace have returned to their labor. In short, the *Fête de Roi*, the anniversary of the birth of Louis Philippe is past. Like the calm that succeeds the storm, an unusual stillness reigns throughout the city. This very natural effect is no doubt deepened by the gloomy weather, which has followed, as a shadow, the brilliant sunshine, which yesterday shone so propitiously.

The fêtes in France are more quiet and orderly than formerly. The disorder of preceding years is attributable to the fact, that food of various kinds, and wine, used to be served to the public by the king. Hogsheads of the latter were placed in the public squares, with dippers attached, and any one who was athirst, might go, and drink as much, and as often as he desired. At the coronation of Napoleon, it is related, that the Fountain of the Innocents, in one of the market places, ran wine throughout the day. Such freedom could not but be abused, and excess with all the natural consequences, was universal. Louis Philippe, seeing the hazardous results, wisely put a stop to the practice. Provisions, no longer distributed promiscuously, are given to the poor at their rooms. The effects of this are very evident. Now, even on the days of fêtes, a person intoxicated is rarely seen. Drunkenness, indeed, is not near so common, as in any of the cities of the United States, even where the teetotal societies are prevalent. Those societies are not known here. Everybody drinks, not only their light wines, but brandies and stronger liquors, and usually with discretion.

Deputations from all classes of people waited yesterday upon the king to wish him health and happiness, and many joyous returns of this his natal day. Fêtes are not for the rich and powerful, but the poor; we will therefore leave the palace behind us, and accompany the crowd to the great square of the Champs Elysées. The way conducts us through the gardens of the Tuilleries, and as the immense multitude obstruct rapid locomotion, we linger beside the basins of water, and admire the jet, which glitters in the sunbeams, the numerous gold and silver fish which sport in the ripples, and the merry faces of the children, who stand around, feeding the pretty sparkling finny creatures with bread and cake crumbs. When fatigued with this, we turn to another scene, where the graceful swan floats lightly, as a snowflake on the blue water, arching his long neck to collect the donations cast to him. Before us a most magnificent prospect opens. Round us, and before us, far as the eye can reach, a double row of trees line the long avenue;—the elm with pendent limbs, and the horse-chestnut, now in the pride of its beauty. By constant pruning and attention, their symmetry is rendered perfect. The branches, which, when bare and leafless in winter, have such an air of prudery, now clothed in gay attire, and adorned with their finely contrasted blossoms, present a rare object of elegance. At the extremity of this grand avenue, two or three miles before us, relieved by a back ground of remote blue hills, stands the pride of art, the proud *Arc de Triomphe de l'Etoile*, one hundred and fifty-two feet in height, seeming even at this distance, still more immense. Nearer to us, surrounded by golden lamps, rises the obelisk of Luxor, appearing to pierce the great arch of the Arc de Triomphe. The remainder of the way to the great *porte* of the palace is embellished by a host of marble statues of great value. It is the sight of such beauties and objects of splendid luxury, as these, which surround and grace the palaces of monarchs, that can alone awaken in my bosom any love for royalty.

But, while we loiter here, the amusements of the day are commencing. In the *Place Concorde*, the tritons and sea-nymphs—

altogether too handsome for fishwomen—still hold fast their bronze dolphins, from whose mouths a jet of water is thrown into a basin above, to fall again into a thousand pellucid sparkles below. Not all of it, however, thus escapes. Not a little goes to fill the tin vessels borne about upon the backs of many a man and woman, which, half-boiled by the sun, and sweetened with *radix glycyrrhizae*, or liquorice root, is drunk by any one that chooses—not I—for a sou the glass. A little bell, incessantly tinkling, like that borne on the neck of a grazing cow, keeps you perpetually aware of the presence of these sweet itinerant pedlars. This is the best proof I have at command, of the fact, that the French are a liquorish people.

As we proceed up the Champs Elysées, the crowd increasing at every step, we find its sides lined with booths of every description. Here one plays *rouge et noir* for macaroons, or swings a ring suspended from a cross tree, ten feet perhaps in height, attempting to catch it on some hooks placed in front; his success is to be rewarded in the same coin, differing in amount from the number placed upon the hook. If fond of sporting, take a gun, whose crooked barrel one would imagine was intended to shoot around a corner, and fire little rockets at a bird, hanging from the top of a pole twenty feet high. If of a warlike, destructive disposition, near at hand is a stuffed man with a wooden heart; hit it, if you can, at three feet distance, with a pop-gun crossbow. If you are not content with an exhibition of your skill, without doing any damage, advance to the next. The scene before you represents, in a moment, an army of Moors, each man a foot distant from his neighbor. "Pick off the officers" was Gen. Putnam's order at the battle of Bunker Hill; so you aim at the captain. Ah! you have knocked him over, and in his fall he touched a spring, and out runs an old woman with a long red nose, and a pail in her hand. Kill the corporal, and another rushes into the scene, mounted on a pig, whose tail looks as if it had not yet done curling, to such an intensity is it twisted. When you have thus done it effectually for Abd-el Kader and all the hostile Arabs in Africa, behold no dead are to be found. The attendant woman sets them up, and they are quite as sound again as ever. Like many other warriors, victorious without results, let us go to the next, where the damage we may do, cannot be so easily repaired. Rough and fragile images of crockery are here, pieces of glass with figures painted on them. Now give the organ of destructiveness the rein. The fragments jingle as they fall into the basket below. Isn't it delicious? And all for two or three sous; a good investment. Novelties thicken, as we proceed. What keeps them laughing so perpetually in this quarter? Why, at one extremity of the circle, perhaps I should say, one of the foci of the ellipse, there is a post, to which a tin pot is attached. At the other focus fifteen feet off, we see a young man give a sou to the proprietor, who in return presents him with a stick. He places on the youth's head, concealing it entirely, a horrid looking mask, the eyes of which look crosswise. With this he can see nothing. Confident of success, where so many others have failed, he advances, thus blindfolded, to strike the pot with his cane. He proceeds very cautiously in a direct line, as he supposes, but following, as the bystanders well know, each eye of his mask by turns, till getting near the object by his computation, with deliberate care he deals the blow, which he is confident will make the old pot ring like a church bell. But the only sound which reaches his ear, is the universal merriment of all around. The mask is removed, and he is astonished to perceive that he has "missed the wrong house" by a long distance. Notwithstanding the shortness of the space, and the apparent ease of the performance, I saw but one hit the pot, among several essays made during my stay. Do you wish to know your temperament? A man is ready to give you the information with a hand thermometer. This has two glass globes united by a hollow tube, and filled with spirits of wine. The warmth of the hand causes the fluid to run from one ball to the other, and the height to which it ascends, indicates the temperament. Changing hands, he counts in a loud voice, five, ten, fifteen, twenty, as long as the liquid rises, and this shows the degree. Men are content to spend five sous in order to learn that they are ten degrees of "sanguinity" or *something else.*

Arrived, at length, at the Grand Square, maugre the innumerable obstacles, which impede, or attractions, that divert; in the midst of an ocean of heads in constant motion to catch a glimpse, but always interposing before, behind, around, every where, one may possibly succeed in seeing the stage of one of the temporary theatres, erected only for the day. In these are enacted battles, fights, and other diverting pastimes; guns and cannon are fired; drums beaten; prisoners are taken and miraculously escape, and the French come out always victorious, the enemy retiring in a laudable and regular manner, after discharging their muskets at, and dangerously frightening sundry peaceable and thoughtless crows, which are innocently flying over the unroofed stage. The spectators are very numerous—and very quiet—when they can see—but, when the view is obstructed by any one taller than themselves, they are easily amused by throwing small stones at his hat, and often with an accuracy not altogether pleasant to the wearer. Short people are decidedly below par in such a place. I did not see the stage perfectly but twice, once when lifted from the ground by the pressure of the crowd, and thus elevated above the world. But I could not turn my good fortune to much account, for unfortunately my attention was very much distracted by the instant necessity of inventing some new method of breathing, as my chest was so wedged in and compressed, that the old one would not answer. My hat too, obstructing the prospect of those behind, was vigorously saluted with a copious shower of the aforesaid gravel. The second time, just at the climax, when the savage Bedouin was about to destroy his captive, a French girl of birth, I felt a hand at my coat pocket. The fellow was disappointed, however, for previous to leaving home, I took the precaution to leave there watch, pocket book, and every thing else of value. But the incident drew off my observation of the stage, and, after all, I have therefore lost the pleasure of informing you, what became of the beautiful heroine.

In the centre of this place was erected the *mât de Cocagne*. This is a pole of as great a length as can be obtained, and perfectly straight, resembling in this respect the lofty hickory and ash poles, planted during the late election throughout the United

States. This is entirely denuded of bark and branches, and made as smooth as possible. To render it still more slippery, it is plentifully besmeared with soft soap and other unctuous matters. To the top of this a large wreath is drawn up, to which is attached prizes of various sorts. On this occasion there were a gold watch, a cup of silver, a *couvert*, or silver fork and spoon, and a silver mounted pipe. The first ascension is the only difficult one; those coming afterwards mount with comparative facility. The first essay was made by an athletic man, who stripped himself almost to the state of nature; entirely, save a piece of cloth around his loins. He carried with him, suspended on each side, a bag filled with a kind of powder, or dust, with which he covered the slippery pole, as far up as he could reach. Then hitching up as far as he had dusted, he held by his feet and one hand, while with the other he renewed his anti-lubricating process. He ascended not more than fifteen feet, when his bags were exhausted; and, casting a longing look at the glittering prizes far above, he slid down again. The second climbed some thirty feet, when his strength was exhausted, and his ammunition failing, and, projecting also a Fox-and-Grapes-Tantalus-looking regard at all that was dear, he too "declined the honor." The third was a dexterous climber, and was also fortified by a double supply of the "all in all," without which it would be as vain to think of rising, as to get up in the world without that other yellow dust, called gold. His cap too, served to wipe the path before him. After a struggle of nearly half an hour, he attained the summit, seized the flag placed there, exultingly waved it round his head, helped himself to the gold watch, and descended very quickly. The track once prepared, it was easy to follow; so the other prizes were taken without difficulty, and on that account were of far inferior value. This sport attracted a large crowd, who divided their regards between it, and the neighboring theatres. A young American physician, extremely agile and muscular, who now resides in Boston, is said to have gained this prize some years ago. This is a real example of genius overcoming difficulties, and of talent elevated above the crowd.

After the accomplishment of this exploit, another scene soon opened upon us of the grand comedy of the day. Wandering about, I accidentally came in among a throng, surrounding a flashy four-wheeled vehicle, of a form peculiar to France, and drawn by two horses. On the front stood a man, engaged in haranguing the multitude. His appearance was very remarkable. He was tricked out in a strange style. His pantaloons were of black velvet, with a waistcoat of blue cloth, having tight sleeves. His coat was of green velvet, with large flowing sleeves, shorter above than below, where they hung, coming to a point, and exposing the blue sleeves of the waistcoat underneath. All his clothes were decorated with a profusion of gold lace. By his sides were watches—two on each—with other jewelry. His head was surmounted by a crimson velvet cap, encircled with a gold lace band with a long flowing silk tassel depending from the top, which he frequently removed, thereby exposing a bald head. What hair he had was gray, and so was his beard, which was cut close except on the chin, and under the jaw, and this was left some six inches long. On his nose he wore a large pair of spectacles, whose immense glasses were intended to intimate research, and, in connection with his venerable beard and gray hairs, wisdom. From the first expression which struck my ear, I thought he was a democrat. He was proclaiming himself a friend of the working class, and professing to be a worker himself; but he explained by stating that he was that moment at work—addressing the people. As he advanced in his oration, he put me more and more in doubt about his object. He came at last to inform us that he was a Portuguese, (he spoke without a perceptible accent) that France contained many charlatans of all kinds, that even his native city, Lisbon, harbored them, but that he was a truly educated man, that he was versed in the noble science of medicine, and could cure diseases in an incredibly short space of time, especially those of the muscular system; and finally requested such as were afflicted to come upon the carriage, and he would examine their complaints before the multitude. Immediately a young man of respectable appearance jumped up, stripped off his coat, rolled up his sleeve, and exhibited his arm, which he declared to be the seat of much pain. Our hero turned his head, and nodded to some men seated behind him on the top of the vehicle. Then I noticed, that these four fantastically dressed individuals were musicians, who immediately began a tune with horns, clarionet, trumpet, drum and cymbals, completely drowning the sage questions asked by the learned man. After a suitable lapse of time he rang a little bell by his side, and the music ceasing, he announced that the patient had a species of rheumatism. He had, however, a never-failing specific for it, an unguent of great power, which was always sure to cure in twenty-four hours. Again he turned and winked, after remarking that he would show the method of its proper application. I involuntarily rubbed my eyes, for I began to suspect that I was at a theatre, and that one of the ludicrous comedies of Moliere was being acted, where tailors tried on coats, countrymen learned wisdom and manners, physicians felt the pulse, and nurses gave *lavements*, all to the sound of martial music; for, as the sage rubbed the grease in the arm, his movements were in unison with the slow-measured notes of the artists behind; and when the tune changed to a polka, he continued the friction with a polka rhythm. The scene was inexpressibly ludicrous. So this "learned Jenkinson" of the inimitable Vicar went on prescribing for numerous complaints, feigned by an accomplice, which were all to be well in twenty-four hours after his treatment. Any number of boxes of similar medicines were constantly on hand; but, from their peculiar efficacy, the price was of course necessarily very high.

Before the *Pavillon des Horloge* was erected a stage, covered with crimson velvet, where, at seven and a half, P. M., by forcing through a crowd of artisans in dirty blouses, smelling vehemently of cheese and garlic, one could hear a band play the *Marseillaise* or the *Parisienne*, and, by walking towards the Seine, have a view, in one of the upper stories of the palace, of the Indians from Oregon now visiting here with Mr. Catlin. By order of the King, they had been placed in the vacant apartments of one of the absent princes, commanding a view of the gardens, the *quai de Tuilleries*, the *Pont Royal*, and the immense assemblage that thronged every avenue in this quarter. From this point, also, a favorable view of the fireworks was to be had. The adjoining room was devoted to the accommodation of Gen. Tom Thumb. It was amusing to hear the speculations of the multitude in regard to these red skins, who, in all the pride and pomp of paint and feathers, were very conspicuous at the windows, and arrested the gaping notice of vast numbers. The lower classes of the community are as ignorant of geography, as the aborigines of America, when discovered by Columbus. One imagined they were Patagonians; another surmised that they were Chinese; a third Egyptians, and, when informed they were from the backwoods of the United States, from Oregon, they innocently replied, that " they thought all the Africans were black."

As the shades of night descended, the lamps, arranged in triangular groups of thirty-six on lofty stands, and placed at intervals of forty feet perhaps along the green fringed walks, were lighted up. This exhibition, extending even to the Arc de l' Etoile, and to every little avenue around, was almost magical. At such a moment it was easy to have any quantity of poetical imaginings of diamonds and such like, that could be wished. Poetry is a description of fancy. This is the reason, as I take it, why calling red hair, golden; oil lamp lights, diamonds; and talking of silver moon and pearly teeth, is being poetical. To those who live in the garret, gold and silver, diamonds and pearls, exist but in the imagination. When the twilight had entirely melted away, there commenced from the Quai d'Orsay a shower of rockets, which with their bright light of various colors illuminated all around. Being of large size, the noise of their explosion was very great, as they burst high in the air, pouring a deluge of brilliant sparkles on every side. At the moment, when the first rocket shot up, commenced the discharge of the great guns at the battlements surrounding the Hotel des Invalides. Had this captive Prussian and Austrian ordnance been as faithfully served in times gone by, as they were this evening, they might have changed the destinies of nations, and not been left, as now, to illustrate the prowess of French arms. At every report, I beheld in imagination the veterans, who now served them, at the battles of Lodi and Wagram and Austerlitz, their hearts burning with a fire scarcely less vehement than the flame which consumed their powder. Those heroes, who then protected the body of the Great Warrior, now, surround and guard his mouldering ashes.

Near this quai, high in the air was a beautiful cross of variegated lamps of large size, which was the object of universal admiration. On the Pont de la Concorde rose two lofty monuments of fire, while from their base flashed Roman Candles and flames of every description. For half an hour an unbroken succession of rockets, wheels and other productions of pyrotechny were played off without the least intermission. No delay in the preparation of the pieces fatigued the spectator, and there was no parsimonious apprehension of burning too many at a time. The air was in a continual blaze with sheets of fire in inexhaustible profusion. The final piece was an immense bouquet, extending the entire length of the bridge, of every hue and of surpassing lustre; thus closing an exhibition exceeding in magnificence anything of a similar kind, which it has been my fortune ever to behold.

No report has been made of any accident happening during the day, notwithstanding the vast number assembled. Three or four hundred thousand persons were undoubtedly spectators of these fireworks. Indeed, there were fifteen thousand troops of the line in active service in or near the garden, besides numerous other grades of "guardians of the peace." The crowd was of the most orderly character; though they were required to rest five or ten minutes in the midst of a "squeeze,"—a trying moment,—near the outlet and the Pont Royal, I did not hear a complaint escape. Thus ended the day, and I close this description with my best wishes for the health, long life, and prosperity of Louis Philippe, the wisest of modern kings. In addition, I think I shall communicate pleasure to all by sending herewith a translation of the principal speeches made by the heads of the various delegations sent to wait upon him, together with his responses. A translation cannot possibly retain the force and beauty, so strikingly expressed in the originals. The *tournure de phrase* is very expressive and beautiful, but of so extremely delicate a texture, as often to become gross in the version, and in its bluntness wholly to lose its force. Notwithstanding this disadvantage, I think that no one can read the address of the President of the Deputies—or the lower house—without being touched with the simple beauty, that pervades it. The response of the king shows, that he was deeply impressed with its sincerity, and his words have less of that stereotype style, which necessarily distinguishes the others.

XXVIII.

VERSAILLES—THE PALACE—ITS COST—DESECRATION IN 1792—ITS RESTORATION BY LOUIS PHILIPPE—ITS EMBELLISHMENTS, PICTURES AND STATUES—NAPOLEON AS HE LIVES ON THE CANVAS—EFFECTS OF THESE PAINTINGS ON A SPECTATOR.

YESTERDAY and to-day I spent at Versailles, with Dr. Potter of Augusta, Me., and when I say at Versailles, I mean at the palace, for the town itself can boast of few attractions. It owes all its consequence to this single building, one of the most remarkable, considered in itself, and also on account of its contents, which the world contains. It is situated at a distance of twelve miles from Paris, toward the south-west, and though it possesses few inhabitants and no commerce, two railroads connect it with the great world. Before the Revolution, 100,000 people were numbered among its citizens, and all the great and noble of the land spent a large portion of their time here. It is now comparatively deserted, her lordly mansions are vacant, and her spacious, but dreary streets, no longer echo with the equipages of rank and wealth and fashion. Her once flourishing and voluptuous population have dwindled now to thirty thousand persons.

In the 16th century, Versailles was but an inconsiderable village environed entirely with forests, whither the King of Navarre, afterwards the renowned Henry IV., resorted to hunt. In 1624 Louis XIII. purchased the land around, and erected a small chateau, the germ of the present immense pile. It is of red brick, and occupies the centre of the present structure. Louis XIV., in 1664, commenced the construction of the palace, as it now exists, with the intention of making it the seat of his court. The most celebrated architect of the day was entrusted with the execution of the kingly design. The many difficulties to be surmounted, from the nature of the situation, served only to stimulate the monarch; and the work was prosecuted with such vigor, that a proud habitation for a proud monarch soon arose under their hands. Le Notre arranged the gardens and grounds. Excavations were dug, terraces raised, and the immense park, measuring twenty leagues, was protected by a wall. Two or three other walls divided the land into extensive gardens, parks and other enclosures of luxury or utility. For the water required to fill the reservoirs and fountains, a plan was conceived, and actually begun to be executed, of turning the river Eure from its course. Nothing, in short, deterred that magnificent monarch from the accomplishment of his grand designs; not money, for though no accurate accounts can be obtained of the expenditures, the estimates exceeded two hundred millions of dollars; not labor, for the entire army of thirty thousand men during the peace were not unfrequently all employed at once upon the works. The palace itself, with all its richness, cost less than the works around it. These statistics may serve to communicate, perhaps, some idea of its grandeur.

Every effort was made to people the town; every encouragement held out, to all who wished to build; so that ere long an elegant city and a numerous population surrounded the royal residence. In 1681 the Court removed thither from St Germain; since that time the works have been in continual progress, each successive monarch adding something to improve his splendid inheritance on his accession to the throne. In 1792, with the vandalism, which disgraced the age, its furniture of the richest quality was sent to market. Its invaluable paintings, together with every thing else that was moveable, shared the same fate.

Napoleon's influence alone saved the entire royal property from the hammer of the auctioneer *in lots to suit*. The estimated cost of ten million dollars, for its restoration, was the only hinderance to his residing here. Louis XVIII. limited his expenses to one million and twenty thousand dollars, which were laid out principally in repairs. Charles X., in the contracted spirit of his reign, did nothing. Louis Philippe has given to the place a destination,

"Time had produced its revolution in opinions, and Versailles could not longer exist under the conditions of the monarchy of Louis XIV.—it could no longer be the abode of a population of courtiers, or the Olympus of a monarch. To become the concentration of all the illustrious of France, to collect the inheritance of all her glories, and, without being despoiled of the type of grandeur now passed away, to be clothed with other grandeur new and national, was a destiny not less splendid and august, than that at first assigned it." Louis Philippe has done this with equal felicity in design, and promptitude of execution. He has effaced the disfigurements of time; restored the grand conceptions of its great originator; reproduced the painted ceilings and gildings, formed new saloons and galleries; improved and harmonized the whole, and finally embellished it with an immense collection of paintings and sculptures, which illustrate every period and, event that have reflected lustre on the French name. Three million dollars have already been expended, and the disbursements are still going on. The Royal Family no longer make their abode in the palace, now converted into one vast museum, but the Trianon, originally a dependency merely, now receives the King and his interesting household into its quiet retreat.

On approaching from the railway dépôt, two enormous buildings appear immediately in front of the palace, the size of which, as well as their somewhat aristocratic air, distinguish them as residences of nobility. Great then is the astonishment on learning that they are merely stables, though at present vacant. They supply accommodation for a thousand horses. The great court-yard of the palace is adorned with sixteen colossal statues of the ministers, generals and great men of the country, exquisitely chiseled in white marble; and, in their centre, an excellent equestrian statue in bronze of Louis XIV, of gigantic dimensions. I noticed several good-sized men engaged in some cleansing operation, standing under the horse with their hats in their hands. On the wings of the structure is an inscription which announces the present destination of the palace, A TOUTES LES GLOIRES DE LA FRANCE. The views of the palace from the town, and also from the Park, are of the most beautiful description. The same boasting spirit, that pervades the French nation not less than her neighbors, and which has always characterized every people, that have performed anything which would sustain a vaunt, has caused to be placed on each side of the grand entrance of the courtyard two emblematic sculptures in stone, one representing France victorious over Austria, with a statue of Peace by its side; the other, France triumphant over Spain, and at its side a statue of Abundance, the former by Marcy, the latter by Giradon.

Leaving the exterior, and entering the building, we find it consists of two large apartments, richly gilded and otherwise ornamented, formerly the abode of different officers of the court. The furniture, I have already mentioned, was disposed of many years ago, and the whole interior has been remodeled to suit its present design. The partitions have been removed, and large halls thus formed, to the whole of which has been assigned the name of "The Historical Museum." Each part has likewise a distinguishing title. The American, who has never been accustomed to see more than four or five hundred pictures at a time, is bewildered with the immense multitude all around him. For hours and hours he walks through continuous galleries and smaller rooms; he mounts to the garret, descends almost to the cellar, and still he beholds paintings on paintings, busts and statues, "a multitude which no man can number." The very immensity of the collection to be seen, prevents his properly observing any. If he can grasp the general scope, and penetrate one or two of the striking characters in some of them, he does well; but the slighter and less observable points, which so often indicate the consummate artist, are not visible to his rapid glance. Although I have spent hours in these galleries, and feasted on their treasures, I am scarcely willing to assert, that I have seen them, because I have not been able to look upon them calmly. Independently of the little time which I could devote to each, the agitation excited by their contemplation kept me in a state little favorable for criticism, or close examination. As a person on reading in intensely interesting tale, or beholding the tragic creations of a great author, represented on the stage, is wrought up to such a delirium of feeling, as to pass over with slight notice the beauties of description, the nice shades of expression and the poetical imagery, so one is equally transported on witnessing similar scenes start out before him on the canvas—the breathing lip, the eloquent eye, and the countenance dissolved in grief, as portrayed by the hand of the great master. Never before did I feel the real power of the pencil, never had I, till now, acknowledged in my soul the mighty intellect of the man, who was the *fons et origo* of wonderful imaginations, like some of these.

But my object is description; and first of the historical pictures, which are principally representations of the great battles, in which France has acquired unfading renown, and which illustrate her prowess from the earliest period. Passing by the old paintings, which treat of events in the earlier periods of the national annals—the times of Charlemagne, the Crusades, of the Louises XIV, XV, XVI,—we come to an epoch, more interesting at present to most persons, as the events have occurred in the presence, as it were, of many now alive, and are fresh in the minds of all; the time of the great Napoleon. Here are vivid pictures of the principal battles where he triumphed. Wagram, Austerlitz, Marengo, and Moscow, are exhibited with a power and faithfulness, which, while they chill the blood at the sight of so much suffering and carnage, exalt the consummate general who achieved them, and stands out the most conspicuous object in the groups. The effect of these paintings is wonderful. In the great city, almost everything is stamped with his genius; his comprehensive intellect, surveying all things with a glance, is there seen to penetrate into the depths of futurity. The voice of that city is full of the praise of the soldier and the sage. The grey-haired veteran limps about on crutches, with both arms gone, yet, having his hat attached to an iron hook on a wooden arm, waves it about his head, and with feeble shouts hails the memory of the departed hero. Full of these emotions, I enter these halls, and am still surrounded by the same master spirit. I contemplate those fields of his and the nation's glory, fight over again those battles, already engraven on my soul by the pen of the historic muse, and, unconsciously to myself, a feeling of hatred creeps gradually over my heart toward that nation, who, profiting by an accident, brutally triumphed over the greatest mind that ever lived, and insulted and enslaved the man, whom they still feared, but could not humble nor subdue. I can, I do feel deeply for the French; my heart goes with them, and I can sympathize with that party, who are disgusted with the peaceful aims of the present ruler, and desire once more to stand in the imminent deadly breach, again to strike for France, to fight once more, though but with the memory of Napoleon for a leader. I defy the greatest advocate of peace that lives, to look upon these paintings calmly; to view with cool composure the brown coat, the cocked hat, the white horse, the calm features of the man of destiny, who subdued all—even himself and his own feelings,—for ambition—for glory—for France. Had I lived in those tempestuous times, my heart tells me, how easily I could have shouldered the musket, and drawn the trigger, under the auspices of that glorious commander. Were I now engaged in actually doing what has now an existence only in the fancy, my heart could not beat more tumultuously, than it does at this moment, while recalling what I have seen, and recounting an oft-repeated tale. If this is human nature, how long will it be before the epoch shall arrive, when our swords shall be beat into permanent ploughshares, and our spears into lasting pruning-hooks, and men shall learn war no more?

These pictures are not to be enumerated by fives and tens, but by fifties and hundreds; many are of the size of life, where each face is a portrait, and each action represented, a real event. In some, every eye is turned upon the general; in others, the poor sufferer lies mortally wounded near him, and, as the last life drop is oozing from his veins, with his latest strength and dying breath, he hails the presence of his general, *king*, EMPEROR. The return from Elba, the parting from the troops at Fontainbleau, the presentation of the cross of the Legion of Honor to a Russian enemy, distinguished as the bravest in the army, and many other scenes of his eventful life, have employed the pencils of the greatest artists of France, how well, I have attempted to express, not by critical analysis, but by a simple account of their influence over an unprejudiced beholder.

To avoid the prolixity of my last two communications, I will defer what I have further to say of these pictures to the next letter.

XXIX.

PICTURES, COINS AND MEDALS IN THE PALACE AT VERSAILLES—CHAPEL—
LOUIS XIV—OPERA ROOM—GRAND GALLERY OF GLASS—FOUNTAINS—
PARTERRE D'EAU—ANCIENT ORANGE TREE—BASSIN DE NEPTUNE—
FOUNTAIN OF LATONA—CHARIOT OF THE SUN—BASSIN D' ENCELADE—
BOSQUET DES BASSINS D'APOLLON—BASSIN DES ENFANS—AMERICA AND
HER ARTISTS.

Leaving the reign of Napoleon, we come to that of Louis XVIII. One or two pictures represent his flight from the Tuilleries, and serve only to exhibit his portrait and his fat dumpy figure. Charles X. succeeds. Few incidents occurred in his short sway, though much too long for the good of his country. Pictures of his reviewing the troops in the Champ de Mars are the principal, and possess but little interest. In addition to his own portrait, that of Louis Philippe, as Lieutenant General, appears in them. Next follow the numerous paintings commemorating most of the political occurrences in the chequered career of the present sovereign. We see him, the favorite of the people, leaving his residence in the Palais Royal on horseback to go to the Hotel de Ville; while the honors of the three days of 1830 are showered along his path. The excited populace, with arms in their hands, surround him, but not with hostile intent; for hats are waved, and the very walls quiver with their cheers. Again the deputies by delegation announce to him the honor the country had conferred upon him. His family are around him, and participate in the thrilling event. The portraits of Lafayette, Soult, and many others, are striking. A similar scene is presented by a deputation from the Chamber of Peers. In another he refuses the crown of Belgium offered to his son. The number of such representations is very great. Few preceding kings have had so many incidents in their reigns illustrated by the pencil. It is exceedingly interesting to look upon the portraits of all the kings from Pharamond to the present day, the Grand Admirals—among whom those of the discoverers, the unfortunate La Perouse and others, are particularly deserving of attention—the Constables, Marshals, and great Warriors and distinguished men of France. Beside these, there are coins and medals, which illustrate the different ages. Many of these are marked with much rudeness of execution, and exhibit such distortion of faces, that one cannot entertain a very favorable opinion of the vaunted beauty of the originals. They are interesting too for the variety of styles displayed in their costume. One, celebrating the court of some queen and the company dancing, arrayed in hoops and high heeled shoes, was especially ludicrous.

The busts and statues are very numerous; some in plaster, but very many in marble; among the most observable of which are Richelieu, Mazarin, the brave Gaston de Foix and Bayard, the ever-venerated Fenelon, Blanche of Navarre, and the beautiful statue of one of the most remarkable heroines, that we have any knowledge of, the famous Joan d'Arc—the work of the Princess Marie, deceased daughter of Louis Philippe. In giving some account of the chapel of St. Ferdinand, in a former letter, I mentioned a beautiful angel, also the work of the same talented Duchess of Wirtemberg. To this succeeds the Hall, where are some very large pictures, representing still later events than any yet mentioned, in which figure the different sons of the king. The siege and capture of Constantine shows the Duc d'Orleans and a younger brother; while, near it, is a sea-fight to the glory of Prince de Joinville. These paintings are all by Horace Vernet, the great painter of the present day, and are gems of art. The sea-scene is exceedingly fine. The light shines through the sail, and the splinters in the ship's side, which a cannon ball had struck, are nature itself. A large picture now in the exhibition of the works of modern artists in the Louvre, which, I believe, I have heretofore alluded to, will shortly be placed here. It is saying much to affirm, that it is worthy of the immense space, which it will occupy. Many other works of this great master are in various galleries of this palace.

An interesting part of the building is the Chapel, which has lately been restored to all the splendor for which it was remarkable in the age of Louis XIV. Whatever else this overrated monarch did, or omitted,—and none comprehend his quantum of merit more accurately than many of his countrymen—he resembled many a solemn American in a punctilious attendance at church. He went *daily* to mass, but not content with securing his own salvation, he required his courtiers to bear him company. *Quam prope ad pietatem sine pietate.* On this portion of the palace extraordinary taste and grandeur are lavished. The pavement is of the richest marbles, wrought into Mosaic, and the walls and ceiling, supported by a superb architrave and cornice above lofty Corinthian columns, are magnificently painted by the distinguished A. Coypel, Lafosse and Jouvenet. Statues, basso-relievos and pictures are not wanting to complete the garniture of this exquisite apartment.

The Opera Room is secluded from the public view, but on presentation of the talismanic *ticket*,

"———— It opens wide
Its ever-pleasant gates, harmonious sound,
On golden hinges turning,"

and the beauty and lustre, which then break in upon you, well repay the trouble requisite to obtain it. The ornaments are crimson and gold, accompanied with a profusion of mirrors and chandeliers. The first grand representation here was given in honor of the marriage of Louis XVI., and the last on the inauguration of the Historical Museum, the 17th of May, 1837. On the first of these occasions, it was illuminated with ten thousand wax candles. Now gas is introduced. The expenses of a Grand Opera, given at this place, are not less than twenty thousand dollars.

Among the noble apartments which are decorated with regal splendor, is the king's, with its marbles, rich gilding, and painted ceilings; the queen's, less richly, but not less agreeably embellished with white and gold; but the Grand Gallery of Glass excels them all, and is one of the most magnificent rooms in the universe. It is two hundred and forty-two feet in length, thirty-five feet wide, and forty-three feet high. As its name implies, it possesses numerous mirrors, one entire side being wholly filled by them, set in arcades, which reflect the light let in through seventeen immense windows opposite. Between the arcades and the windows are sixty composite pilasters of red marble, having bases and capitals of gilt bronze, and the entrances are adorned with similar columns. The ceiling is vaulted, and painted by Le Brun with allegorical representations of the leading events in the career of Louis XIV. In the sleeping apartment of that king is the famous "Titans" of Paul Veronese, which was brought from Italy by Napoleon, and now ornaments the ceiling. Here, also, is the richly decorated bed on which Louis XIV. breathed his last. The coverlet and curtains are satin, worked with superb embroidery by the ladies of St. Cyr. In the private apartments are some evidences of the mechanical talents of Louis XVI., such as a long brass meridian line running across the floor, placed there by that king himself. The locks still upon the doors are of royal workmanship.

Here I shall conclude this running sketch of the exterior and interior of this celebrated and wonderful palace; one that never has been equalled in ages past, and is not likely to have a parallel for centuries to come. This prediction is based on the altered character of the times. Kings have so often been made and unmade within the last half century, general information and the spirit of liberty have been so widely diffused, that generations on generations must rise and fade away, and some unforeseen revulsion of the social state, or eclipse of learning intervene, before any people will ever again suffer so vast an expenditure of public money to be wrung from their own starving industry, merely to gratify the whim, or promote the aggrandisement of one, who, if called King, is no longer the sacred vicegerent of heaven which he pretended to be at former periods. *Afflavit Deus, et dissipantur.* Still the future is unfathomable. The taste of some future Roman emperor may attempt a similar work of splendid extravagance. His power is despotic enough, and his subjects sufficiently enslaved and ignorant.

But an account, sketch though it be, which should stop with a description of the palace, would transfer a very imperfect impression indeed of this extraordinary spot. It would be painting the head of Venus only, forgetting all the other unapproachable beauties of the goddess of beauty. The gardens, parks and fountains of Versailles equally deserve the best efforts of the pencil and pen, as well from the immense sums, that have been unsparingly lavished on their construction, as for the sculptural beauties, which are every where scattered around. The fountains are among the most celebrated artificial water-works in the world, and are visited by every stranger, who comes to the metropolis. From the palace, following the great avenue on the terrace, is the *Parterre d'eau*, which contains two oblong basins, on whose borders are twenty-four groups in bronze, eight nymphs, eight groups of children, and the four principal rivers of France, with their tributaries. A *jet d'eau*, in the form of a basket, is in the centre of each. At both ends of the terrace are fountains with bronze animals, the water gushing from their open mouths. Descending from the terrace, on the south side of the palace, after passing over a hundred marble steps, and more, we come to the *Orangerie*. This is simply intended for the preservation of the oranges and pomegranates during winter. One of these orange trees the antiquarian will view with gusto, as it has lived and flourished in its vegetable kingdom, while dynasties and governments of men have risen and crumbled repeatedly around it, and in its very presence. The pedigree of this venerable patriarch is not completely known, but its seed was sown in 1421—before the discovery of America;—it has prospered during twelve reigns, and is still in good health and the enjoyment of a green old age. It is called the *Grand Bourbon*, from its being part of the confiscated property of the Constable de Bourbon. This is the legend, but I cannot stop to investigate its foundation, and if I could, *le jeu n'en vaut pas la chandelle*. " I say the tale as it was said to me."

What an inestimable privilege is this! A beautiful garden ever open to the pent up resident of the city, who, tired by labor all the week, and heated by the intolerable rays of a many times reflected sun, can hither resort, and lie in the shade of the green trees on the soft sward, and listen to the sweet melody of sylvan songsters, and the rippling of the water-falls. Or, if he pleases, he may enter the beautiful palace, and stroll from one elegant object to another, and drink deep draughts of rapture at the sight of master-pieces of painting and sculpture. When the United States have a king, they may expect to have picture galleries and public gardens. Till the advent of such a personage, or his "counterfeit presentment" in a Pericles or a Medicis, greedy of gold, and avaricious of every spot of ground, where a blade of grass can grow, or tulip bulb be planted, they will speculate on the possibility of making a carrot or a cabbage usurp its place. The elegant must give way to the useful—utile *sine* dulci—and the reins of fancy are held in check by the rough hands of the money-getter. Is it a wonder that the old world produces the poets, the painters, the sculptors and artists of all kinds, when schools, such as these, are always open, free as air, to every comer? These halls during week days are filled with painters, who have come to study and copy the striking beauties of the great masters. So it is in every large gallery of pictures in the realm, and there are very many of them. In the United States, the government can boast of owning some half a dozen paintings, which have been thriftily hawked about the country for exhibition at twenty-five cents a head. In France, besides the opportunities thus afforded for study, there is a public school held in the palace of fine arts, where the best one hundred of the competitors are every six months received for gratuitous instruction; two-thirds in painting, the rest in sculpture. The competitors number about five hundred. Every year the best three scholars are sent to Rome at the government's expense, to study among the *chef-d'œuvres* of the world. Thus France is the vigilant foster-mother of genius; so the United States should be; but on the contrary, she not only neglects the instruction, but withholds the rewards of genius. Even when an artist has shed lustre by his talents on his native land, he is left to starve for want of employment. If by a strange accident the government happen to order a work of art, with skinflint meanness it cuts down the price—to lavish it on a partizan contractor—till its encouragement becomes an ignis fatuus. Witness the last work of Greenough. And Power, the gifted Power, shall he not find work in his own land? Must genius expatriate itself to find bread? I call on you, President Polk, to attend to this. Instead of despicable live office beggars, let the court-yard of the Capitol be filled with the statues of the dead signers of the immortal Declaration. Not with paltry busts, but bid the greatest of our own land to rival one another in the perpetuation of the lineaments of the great men of our common country. Do this, and hope to receive the honor of a statue yourself—twin glory with the laurel among the Ancients in the next collection—that of the Presidents of America. The National Gallery of Painting and Sculpture! Where is it? Let not a future generation repeat the demand. Let a commencement be made now, if only with an engraving and a plaster bust. Let every State pay these pure honors to her great men. Warren, Hancock, Adams, and many others should stand before the Capitol at Boston. Let New York surround her City Hall with the images of Hamilton, Fulton, Clinton, and similar worthies; and Jersey illuminate the heights of Trenton with those of her Stocktons and her illustrious military heroes. Which of the old Thirteen cannot claim numbers deserving this high reward? And the new States, if any of them cannot yet point to their great men, have the same blood running in their veins, and will soon create them.

The fountains, which have been running and shooting up their spray and foaming bubbles, have now subsided. My pen too is still; its airy architecture has vanished, and nothing remains, but hopes, strong anticipations—are they baseless?—of the future artists and glory of America.

XXX.

GRAND TRIANON—LITTLE TRIANON—PRIVATE APARTMENTS—FRENCH GARDENS—COOPER, THE PIONEER AMERICAN NOVELIST—FREEDOM OF THE PRESS.

EVEN from my inadequate description of the royal residence at Versailles, a person might be ready to imagine, that little could be added to increase the magnificence of the condition of kings; and that any other buildings and gardens, placed near this miracle of art, would not only be superfluous, but wanting in judgment and taste. Though these might be rich and elegant in themselves, that a direct comparison must necessarily be the result, and everything else less imperial, must become dim, if not entirely lost, in the shadow of the mighty palace. Such is the first impression; yet, when that person comes to see the Grand Trianon, and the Little Trianon, his opinion will be entirely changed. The difference in the architecture, and the whole external appearance, render comparison as impossible, as one between a ship of the line and a pleasure yacht. The Trianons do not enter into competition with their proud neighbor. They have no extended court-yard, adorned with colossal statuary, no towering walls and pointed turrets, no gaudy Corinthian pillars, nor lofty balconies, which so strongly characterize the majesty of the larger structure; but, simple, modest, and unassuming, the Grand Trianon bears away, without the least arrogance, the palm of beauty.

The Grand Trianon was built by Louis XIV. for Madame de Maintenon. It is in the Italian style, and of a single story in height. At the extremity of the Park of Versailles, its situation is retired and enchanting. It consists of two wings united by a gallery, pierced with arcades and fronted with magnificent Ionic columns, and coupled pilasters in Languedoc marble. The grand palace, as already observed, is no longer the abode of the royal line, having yielded that honor to this less imposing building, which possesses a simple beauty charming to every eye. Louis XIV., XV., and XVI. were fond of retiring hither from the pomp and bustle which oppressed them at the more lordly mansion. Napoleon spent much of his time here, and, to facilitate his approach, constructed a direct road from the palace of St. Cloud, his still more favorite habitation. It is now occupied by Louis Philippe for some months every autumn. In the left wing are the apartments of the Queen, those in the right belong to the King. The Grand Gallery, one hundred and sixty feet long, is filled with objects of art. Among them are some executed by royalty, statues and other works. "Here," says the guide, "the King dresses." Cataracts, earthquakes, and even the deluge itself have been converted into music, why then should not a dinner be? And it is;—for, "here," continues the guide, in a little anteroom, "are placed the band, who play while he eats." This is the last refinement of cookery, and must prove, it is not doubted, a substantial help to royal mastication, and contribute very much to keep the kingly organ of digestion in proper tune.

At any rate, it must effectually drown conversation, and so leave greater leisure to play with the knife and fork.— "Here their majesties sleep," pointing to a bedstead, so overlaid with gold, that the wood could nowhere be seen. The hangings are of crimson satin, embroidered with gold, and bordered with a fringe of gold lace. The coverlet is white satin damask. The bed, like those of all the royal family, consists of but one mattress, which fact was particulary remarked by the guide, probably to show the hardships endured by royalty. This is not so shocking as the floors, which do really seem to be uncomfortable. They are similar to those in all the palaces, constructed of oak, and waxed. The private bed-chambers and bath rooms are all finished in this manner. I have not seen a carpet on any room, with but a single exception, in the royal palaces. I wonder if kings and queens have cold feet, like ordinary humanity. The little prince and princesses of England were said—it might be a scandalous rumor—to have had the whooping-cough last spring. "This," quoth the guide, again, "is the bed-chamber of the princess, this of the maids of honor, and this of the valet," et cetera.

The little Trianon is a two story edifice, seventy-two feet square, with four fluted Corinthian columns in front. It is situated at a little distance from the Grand Trianon, and is at present occupied by the mother of the Count de Paris. The Empress Marie Louise formerly resided here, and the bed room remains just as she left it. It is hung with blue silk, and the bed with a drapery of muslin and gold. The whole interior without having anything remarkable, is light and pleasing. The garden is laid out in English style, and is particularly fine. A garden in France would scarcely pass for one in America. It is not necessarily filled with flowers. Indeed, it is far more often a portion of land, divided by box-fringed walks into regular compartments, with here and there a few flowers. The trees which shade it are cut and trimmed, till they assume a square, precise, and quaker-like appearance, which is far from pleasing. The main difference between a French garden, and one *a l'Anglaise* is, that in the latter the tailoring is carried on to a less extent, and consequently the trees have more the look of nature. The beds, too, have not the regular square and diamond form, which characterizes the former. As far as relates to flowers, there is but little difference. I fear, if you should attempt to cut a sizeable bouquet from either, that they would be missed, and, as happened in another garden, some time ago, when Eve plucked the forbidden apple, they

"Would feel the wound, and show forth signs of woe
That all was lost."

In one part, on the banks of a piece of water, is the "Swiss Village." These peculiarly shaped houses, with their thatched roofs, were erected by Marie Antoinette. They have a charming picturesque effect, surrounded and enclosed as they are completely, with verdant foliage. They serve for the residence of domestics. A short distance from the Trianon itself is the temple *d'Amour*, situated on an island, and built of white marble. It is simply a roof upheld by numerous pillars. The floor is tesselated marble. In the centre, on a pedestal, is a beautiful statue of the wily god.

> Here lovers may resort, and breathe sweet sighs
> Beneath the cold pale moon and silent skies;
> While wanton zephyrs play upon the trees—
> Those forest harps of wond'rous harmonies—
> Wild strains, that bathe the soul in ecstasies.

But I am straying from my path. Is it strange? Kings and nobles have done so before me.

While describing the pictures in these palaces, I am reminded of some fine engravings, that I have lately seen. They are recently executed, and are illustrations of portions of the works of Cooper. Among them is the scene, where Leatherstocking kills the cougar, which menaces the destruction of the two girls. Another is taken from the Last of the Mohegans, where the Indians are retreating into the cave, concealed imperfectly by branches of trees. The gallant officer is standing ready to defend the two trembling girls behind him. It is not on account of the extraordinary beauty of these engravings that I mention them, so much as for the sake of the author of the works from which these scenes are borrowed. This man, whose writings, translated into every tongue of Europe, shed lustre on his country, praised as he is, and respected abroad, is abused and persecuted in his own native land with a virulence almost without a parallel. The family of a great man, though partial enough in many respects, are not the first to discover, and pay extraordinary deference to his merits. The housekeeper of the eminent mathematician, D'Alembert, during the whole forty years they lived together, saw nothing but poor St. John le Rond, the foundling, in the man who was all that time making Europe resound with his name. And the United States, ever ready to pay a kind of colonial homage to foreign blood and stamps and imprimaturs, have been slow to perceive the excellence of anything of domestic origin:

> "Slow rises worth by *cold neglect* oppressed."

With regard to Cooper, the wrong is inflicted not by public opinion, but private animosity. The licentiousness of the American press is assuredly a very different thing from what our fathers sought. They never contended for the freedom of blackening the fair fame of private individuals, and had not the remotest intention of transforming a telegraph of public events into a tremendous vehicle for the outpouring and diffusion of private hatred. Say what they will, Cooper will live as long as letters shall survive. His works are grafted into the literature of all nations; and, till that shall be destroyed, long after the red man, driven from hill to valley, and flying before the steps of civilization,—that is, rum and bloodhounds, shall have ceased to exist,— so long will Cooper be remembered, like Leatherstocking, the first to penetrate, and the first to gain a settlement in the unknown wilderness of American literature.

Something I wished to add on a more entertaining topic, but the steam-ship will not wait, and the wanton nerve of a defective tooth is just now amusing me with its gambols. The poor thing is not an unapt emblem of many a man we meet with in the world, always fretful and disagreeable, often offensive to the public taste, and sometimes even outraging private feeling, he is yet flattered, coaxed and borne with, merely for the gold which he possesses.

XXXI.

PRISON DES JEUNES DÉTENUS—RESULTS OF THE SOLITARY SYSTEM—DEPOT DE CONDAMNÉS—PERSONAL APPEARANCE OF THE CONVICTS—THE FACE AN INDEX OF CHARACTER—EMPLOYMENTS, PRIVILEGES, AND MANNERS OF THE PRISONERS—THE SYMPATHISING TURNKEY.

My last letter concluded with a description of that prison in Paris, called *Maison Centrale D' Education Correctionelle,* or the *Prison des Jeunes Détenus*; but I was under the necessity of bringing it to a close, before any adequate account of this remarkable institution could be completed. This extraordinary structure has been mentioned; its tenants; their diversions, and some of their employments. In addition to those already alluded to, I saw specimens of carving, in oak and mahogany, executed by the prisoners, of great elegance. The carvers are also skilful in design. This is not acquired by means of plates or engravings, but by the presentation of the object itself, or a plaster cast to the pupil for study. As practical usefulness is the end of all this application, their attention is directed principally to the copying of carvings or casts, representing old wood sculpture. The proceeds of their industry are laid aside, and given them, when they go out, that they may not, by the temptations of want, be drawn to the commission of crime to supply themselves with the absolute necessaries of life. Two small holes in the door enable the person, who has the care of them, to inspect their proceedings with facility; and at the same time furnish the tenants with the means of calling either the teacher or officer by placing in them a small stick.

The prisoners no longer go to the chapel to attend mass, but are present there by a theological fiction, notwithstanding they are, during the whole service, personally in their cells. The value of this fiction every one, who is conversant with the frequent occurrence and efficacy of similar ones in the venerable science of the law, will be able to appreciate. The ingenuity of the invention cannot be too highly esteemed, which is indeed susceptible of very extensive application, as it enables the priest to say prayers and preach without any immediate visible audience, who may in the meantime stay at home, and receive as much benefit, as if they had been physically present. There is little, if any, appearance of gloom in the faces of these juvenile offenders. One, who had been there four years, told me, "it was very comfortable, though sometimes, he regretted, rather sober." "Ah!" says the guide, laughing with the young fellow, "they sometimes fret a little for the first week after entrance, but soon get accustomed to the place."

But the principal question is not yet noticed, which is, the effect of this mode of treatment compared with its opposite; and this is the agreeable ingredient in this investigation. Notwithstanding all the fine reasoning, that has been employed with so much power; the mind cannot yet be entirely divested of the first deep sentiment of horror, created by the silent cell with its perpetual lonely tenant. There is something so dreary and distressing at such a sight, and even in the bare imagination of it, that a benevolent man hastens to turn to its results for the purpose of reconciling himself to such a plan. And if, by the operation of the *silent system*, eighty out of every hundred convicts return to their wallowing in the mire, but by the *solitary principle*, the tables are turned, and eighty prisoners out of every hundred are redeemed, and "sin no more," as is the fact, do not such inestimable consequences compensate for what, I really think, is only an apparent inhumanity of the scheme? Does it not seem almost a miracle to restore to the community, ignorant, wretched, destitute and vicious beings, converted, after a temporary seclusion only, into educated and virtuous citizens, having money at their disposal, the earnings of their industry, and a trade, which will almost insure them the easy acquisition of more? When the public safety has been secured, all punishment afterwards degenerates into vengeance, and the law, whose single aim should be the public good, becomes a mere *lex talionis*. But *justitia* should be *regina virtutum*, and it ought not to be forgotten, that among the hecatombs, which are continually offered on her altar, are victims for whose real welfare, as well as that of the state, those sacrifices are made. The number here confined is four hundred and twelve.

The spacious structure opposite, is the *Dépôt de Condamnés*, to which all convicts, sentenced to imprisonment for hard labor during any considerable length of time, are sent; those however condemned for any period beyond a year remain there, only till they can be transported to the galleys in the various parts of the kingdom. Such also, as are sentenced to death, are kept here, till their execution. To these last two prisons the home-sounding name of *The Tombs* might be appropriately applied. Their situation, too, in close proximity to Père la Chaise, would seem to favor the nomination.

This building was erected on the plan of M. Gau, in the short space of eighteen months, at a cost of one hundred and fifty thousand dollars nearly. It lies in the form of a hollow quadrangle, making the contained court one hundred and eighty feet in length by one hundred and fifty feet in breadth. It is three stories high, the lower of which is occupied by workshops, and the upper by the cells of the prisoners. Each one, on arrival, is immersed in a bath, and assumes a suit of gray cloth instead of his own. He enjoys the liberty however of wearing such shoes, linen and hat, as he wishes, if he can procure them himself. From a number of trades, which are constantly prosecuted, one is found which he either knows already, or which is thought to be most adapted to his talents. This he is obliged to pursue, whether it be the last, the needle, iron work, or any other craft. If he refuses to labor, as it sometimes happens, the rebel is introduced into the dungeon—the only punishment in use—where he is left to chew the quid of reflection, sometimes for six or more weeks, on the antiphlogistic diet of bread and water, till his reverence for law and order has got the master of his contumacy. Submission to wholesome authority is almost the only growth, to which the dark, damp atmosphere of a dungeon is at all favorable; but this is in general quite certain to succeed with the help of the beforementioned regimen. This *cachot*, as it is called, is a room about ten feet square, without furniture of any sort. Its hard oaken and polished floor suffices for chair, bed and table, having neither straw nor any other substance to mollify its surface of flint for the repose of weary bones. A small grated hole in the door, some three inches square, is the only aperture for light.

A most sorry sight are these convicts, especially as I saw them on entering the court, where they were all together, spending their hour of recreation in promenading. As confinement here—with hard labor, and, in many cases for life—is the highest punishment, next to death, pronounced by the law; I was of course surrounded with a very choice collection of miserable wretches. All persons are aware of the endless variety in human faces, though few rarely think of the cause; or perhaps, without troubling themselves much about it, carelessly take it for granted, that they are such as nature gave them. A grievous mistake, as it appears to me—for I look upon it in a more transcendental light—if it is not heresy to write the word. I deem the face to be the window, through which the spark of divinity shines out, that animates the man. The idiot is senseless, and accordingly his inexpressive features hang down with gross stupidity, giving notice to all, that the ethereal tenant is no longer there. More particularly still, a man's character may be very well read in his countenance; and all the better for its being strongly marked. This is vastly preferable to feeling for it, like the phrenologists, through thick masses of hair lying unequally over the cranium. It is also much more convenient, natural, and useful. It might with good reason be expected, that men should be endowed with the ability to judge in some way of the qualities of one another, for self-defence, if for no other reason. Through what avenue so natural and easy could this important knowledge be transmitted, as that of sight, the channel of so large a proportion of our other information? But if the precious intelligence must be derived—or not at all—by first making oneself master of another man's caput, how obviously may the revelation be withheld by merely defending the citadel from capture. In that case, the excellent direction in the cook-book for boiling a turbot, is in point, "first catch the fish!" On the contrary, if we have need in our intercourse with the world to know the real characters of those we meet, it is philosophical to infer, that the means afforded us to obtain the information will be adequate to that end. They must therefore be susceptible of rapid application, because the occasions for their use are sudden, unexpected, and often transitory. They will neither admit delay, nor submit to machinery, which would be quite as much out of place, as a slate, and book of arithmetic to help one's reckoning in the market.

But the muscles of the face, we know, are common to all, and give it its expression. Every man possessing similar muscles can express the same emotions, though nature seems in many instances to have been in a merry humor, when she put together some features that I wot of. These may be so frequently called into action by particular passions and emotions, as finally to stiffen into their permanent expression, like the corporal members of a Hindoo devotee. The cunning rogue and daring cut-throat cannot help hanging out upon their fronts infallible signals of what they are; but yet they try to wear a mask, as natural as possible, to render that equivocal at least, which they cannot entirely conceal. Under these dubious colors multitudes in all the professions and crafts of life continue to sail along the stream, better in the fog than in the broad sun-light; their actions contradicting their pretensions; and both belieing their real characters and deceiving their patients, their flock, and their clients. But such "wolves in sheepskins" are not often very dangerous beyond a limited gullible circumference; they are "known and read of all men" in the world outside of that charmed circle. We see in the wild Indian, who is uncontaminated by his fatal scourge—the white man—unequivocal traits of his real disposition playing on his copper countenance.

The intention of this digression is to add a feature or two to the picture of the vicious men, who thronged around us in the court, in number about five hundred. Here were housebreakers, burglars, murderers, assassins, specimens in short of every shade of crime, that darkens the face of society. While the jailor left me alone to search for a key, I amused myself with the comfortable reflection, that if one of these miscreants should happen to desire the diversion of striking me on the head, or stabbing me to the heart, what was there to restrain him from such an indulgence? Not fear certainly, if some people may be believed, whose humanity to the convict is cruelty to the victim; for he is now condemned to the worst species and highest grade of punishment, in their opinion, within the rightful power of man to inflict —exclusion for life. I could read robber and cut-throat engraved on the countenances of nearly all, as they passed me with scowls of anger or hatred, because I was free, and they themselves were irrevocably chained.

In the middle of the court was a fountain, where they were permitted to wash themselves; and on one side a shop, where any, who had money, might buy better food, more comfortable shoes than the heavy wooden sabots given them by government, and even wine to drink; but this is a limited quantity per diem. This money is the donation of friends allowed to visit them in the *parloir*, and bring with them such things as are not deemed injurious. The bread thus given is always cut up and thoroughly examined, to see if it is really what it seems, lest any instrument be introduced with it to facilitate escape—an event here entirely unknown.

The lower story is divided into several shops, where work of various sorts is done; as shoemaking, tailoring, and such like. No labor is imposed so arduous as cutting stone, which is, however, a very common one in American prisons. One branch of industry is particularly applicable to the *Maîtres d'Ecole*, who may chance to find themselves *scholars here*, and that is, penmaking. A quill is cut into a pen, which is then separated from the stock, and a new pen made as before and cut off, till the quill is exhausted. These are nearly in the shape of steel pens, are intended to be fixed in handles as those are, and are much used by book-keepers and others.

The food is similar to that in other prisons. The rooms are large, accommodating often twenty or thirty individuals. The linen is as clean as can be expected, when used by laboring men some thirty days. All who wish to attend church on the Sabbath, are allowed to do so; but few, as you may suppose, avail themselves of the privilege.

Fights and quarrels are not unfrequent among the prisoners; and even the officers occasionally get a blow over the head with a wooden sabot. The jailor informed me that several murders were committed but a short time ago. In one case, a man stabbed another with a shoe knife in the side, and death ensued in two or three days. He was taken again to court, and tried; but, it being proved that he was first attacked, he was left to work out his former sentence without addition. In another instance, where the same extenuation could not be alleged, a term of twenty years was extended for life.

Prisoners are conveyed from here to the Navy Yards, in vehicles like omnibusses, to work out their terms, and, from what I have learnt, they have there nearly the same arrangements as in the prison. To stimulate them to more zealous activity, a quarter part of what they earn is given to them. Those who leave the institution have thus the means of commencing an honest life: and those who are confined for life, receive their wages in commodities to ameliorate the hardships of their condition, as linen, and similar comforts. This prison is said to support itself; the labor of the convicts being sufficient to pay the expenses.

It is here that those condemned to suffer death upon the guillotine are placed. I saw one such sitting in a court, separated from the rest. On one side of him was the guard; on the other a jailor, who was reading to him a book. His arms were placed in a strait jacket, that he might not commit suicide. The jailor expressed considerable feeling in regard to this individual, remarking, that they deem it an awful thing to hold a fellow-being awaiting a certain and ignominious death! This is truly an amiable thought, especially considering its source. And there is not a bit of affectation in it, said I to myself, is there? The philanthropic jailor further told me, "that the convict in question was a very *clever fellow*," although then under sentence, as I learnt, for killing his wife and two children!

XXXII.

The Clinique—Nelaton—Midwifery—Paul Dubois—Hospital for Orphans—Sisters of Charity—Private Lecturers—Chassaignac—Cazeaux—Longet—Chailly—Breschet—Lamartine—His speech on the removal of Napoleon's body—Rumor of his visit to this country—Manner of treating foreigners of distinction.

Among the most remarkable of the Paris Hospitals is the *Clinique*. This is divided between two branches, one of surgery, under the care of M. Nelaton, a man of talent as a lecturer, and an excellent surgeon; the other of midwifery. It is this latter which I call remarkable, but only because it is of a different character from anything, that can be found in our own country. It is under the care of the most skilful accoucheur in Paris, Paul Dubois. He has taken the responsible place which his father held before him, and has proved himself fully competent to fill it. He is a man of forty-five or fifty years of age, of medium height, and gentlemanly appearance. His mild blue eye is his most marked feature, and one that gives an expression of gentleness and kindness of heart, which his real character does not belie. His voice is soft and pleasing, and all his actions indicate a man not ostentatiously proud of a position, which he has attained by superior talents—a great contrast to the majority of the Paris medical men of eminence. In short, he is, to give him the highest compliment that can be paid to any one in his station in France,—a gentleman; and this implies more than wearing fine clothes—the definition of the word here. He speaks English with facility, which makes his communications with Americans and English the more agreeable. To strangers he is extremely kind and obliging. To me, in an especial manner, he has been particularly attentive. Though coming hither a stranger, without any letters or introduction to him, on merely stating, that my great object in visiting Paris was to devote myself to the branch, at the head of which he was, he immediately interested himself in my behalf, and gave me every advantage, which his large institution would afford. His great kindness I shall ever remember with the warmest gratitude.

It is in this building, more than in any other in the city, that the great difference between the American and French woman is made apparent. Modesty is scarcely known to the women here. They speak of, and do, actions in public, which the Yankee girl, on oath, would scarcely allow that she had ever heard of. For this reason, among others, the midwifery hospitals in Paris are full. All students, who have studied a sufficient number of years, are admitted to the lying-in room. Whenever a female is in labor, a signal is placed at the door indicating the fact. All, who see the notice, enter. The first comer is the *accoucheur* under the direction of the resident *sage-femme*. Around the bed a railing keeps off the multitude, who often number fifty or more. I have seen the room crowded during the performance of such operations as are necessary. The patient is uncovered, as the labor advances, for the benefit of those around. How many of the very lowest classes in the United States would be thus willingly exposed? Yet hither quite decent women are frequently brought. At the end of the usual time after delivery the woman leaves the hospital. Sometimes she takes her infant with her, but much more commonly she leaves it. The pitiful wages she can receive by her constant labor, do not suffice to support more than herself, and that very meagrely, with bread and water. She has no time to spend therefore in the care of an infant. These children are sent to the *Hospital des Enfants Trouvés*; the healthy are put out to nurse, but the weakly are protected as long as necessary. Women from the country apply at this institution for children to nurse, and receive from four to eight francs per month, in proportion to the age of the infant. The average number received annually at this establishment is about four thousand, some two hundred of whom are legitimate. The mortality is very great, one in three and a third dying.

Connected with this is the Hospital for Orphans, one of the finest institutions in the city. They are taken, educated in the common branches, and, at a proper age, apprenticed to different callings. Here also are received the children of the poor, who, taken sick, resort to a hospital; during their illness their little ones are here protected, to be restored, when health shall again permit. Both these institutions are under the care of those most excellent women, the Sisters of Charity. I have already spoken of them, but it was then from a slight knowledge of their character. A more thorough acquaintance with them and their duties has given me new reason to pronounce most decidedly in their favor. Their incessant vigilance and tenderness for the sick and suffering, their utter disregard of themselves and their own comfort, are worthy of exalted praise. They have left all, that the world regards, behind them; they have discarded the forms of dress, and devoted their fortunes, talents, their all, to the care of these unfortunates. The world is always loud in the praise of a daughter, who, disregarding self, watches devotedly at the bedside of a sick mother. But these sisters have no ties of blood which draw them to the dying pillows of these poor creatures. Their characters are beyond praise, their lives above reproach. The contrast of their black robes with the snowy whiteness of their uncouth caps is not more striking, than the opposition of their lives to those of the world around them. With their beads and cross hanging from one side of their waist, and their bunches of keys on the other, they go from bed to bed, on their silent errand of mercy, moistening the parched lips of one, whispering words of peace to another, always calm and composed, ever ready, ever present; with a gentleness that awes the quarrelsome, and persuades the peevish and fretful; asking, looking for nothing from man, and seeking only a crown of immortality in a world beyond the grave. A memorable confession of their excellence is recorded in the fact, that during the horrors of the revolution, which enveloped all classes with unsparing impartiality, this society alone remained untouched. The brutal mob acknowledged its celestial agency, and bowed with reverence. Napoleon, who swept away the various religious orders, and broke open the convents and nunneries, forbore to lay his regenerating hand on this alone. Had the society of Jesus been composed of such materials, they would have been more worthy of the divine name, which they assumed. Men would have respected and venerated them, confessed the justice of their designation, and hailed their order as one of heaven's best gifts to man. Instead of this, they are universally despised and condemned, even their sacred patronymic is turned into a by-word; and Jesuitism now expresses that dangerous compound of priestly hypocrisy, political craft and Machiavelism, that wanted a name, till the followers of Loyola invested it with their own.

In attending these hospitals and the lectures delivered at the School of Medicine consists the study of the French student. But the American and foreigners generally, have not time to avail themselves of these public lectures; for the course on one branch alone is often protracted through three or four years. These are also delivered with a particularity and verbosity quite unnecessary to him who is generally well advanced in his medical education. He comes hither with all that the schools of the United States can give him, or at least is expected to be thus prepared. He does not therefore wish to commence with elementary principles, but to continue, and push still further his investigations of his favorite science. A class of men have consequently sprung up to satisfy this want, to whom they resort. These are persons who are not professors in the school, but are waiting for a vacancy in the expectation of becoming so. They are generally individuals, who have devoted themselves to one branch of study, and when perfect masters of it, give lectures to private classes. This they do for several reasons—to acquire reputation among medical men, and with the public, who see their notices posted at the corners of streets, and are apprized of their pretensions in other ways. Not unfrequently, the gratuity received from every pupil is a considerable motive. This varies with the expense of the experiments introduced, the reputation of the man, and other disturbing considerations, but, as a general thing, five dollars constitute the fee for each pupil for one course of three lessons a week during six weeks. Several deliver public lectures with a view to facilitate the sale of works, which they have published. These men are often quite distinguished. Chassaignac and Cazeaux are *Agrégés* to the Faculty—a situation of no easy attainment. The latter is author of a work on Midwifery of standard worth. His lectures are thronged with American, English and German scholars. Chassaignac, who is eminent as a surgeon, gives a course on surgical operations, in which he requires his pupils to perform every operation several times. Chailly, whose work from a translation the American well knows, gives a public course on Midwifery, which I have heard with great profit. His hall is always crowded. Though enthusiastic, he is not so pleasant a lecturer, as his rival just mentioned.

Among the most interesting lectures at present are those by Longet, member of the Royal Academy of Physicians, on the functions of the brain and nerves, especially his course with vivisections. In these he gives his scholars ocular demonstration of the various functions, with a minuteness not dreamt of a few years ago. However satisfactory to the student, the fact cannot be disguised, that operations on live animals are cruel in the extreme; but, after Alfort, one gets to bearing them without much sentimentality, especially when re-assured by the reflection, that science is thereby advancing. Beside these, there are many others, who in this way are at the same time getting money and a name, and fitting themselves for public lecturers in the School of Medicine.

Within a few days the distinguished Breschet, the professor of Anatomy, has died. His funeral was attended by many friends, and by delegations from various societies, of which he was a member. His place will be strongly contended for in public concours, of which I have already given an account. His death too leaves an arm chair vacant in the Institute. The winner of the professorship will make sworn enemies of all his competitors; and the successful candidate for the arm chair will realize his own brilliant hopes, but cause those of many others to be suddenly blighted. Speaking of this society, it is rumored, that one of its shining members is shortly to make a visit to the United States;

I mean Lamartine, the great poet and orator of France, now a member of the Chamber of Deputies. This eminent man is no mercenary reporter, travelling beyond his vocation—*sutor ultra crepidam*—to procure materials from kindness abused, and attentions misplaced, for the purpose of manufacturing a book on his return to pay the expenses of an egotistical tour, and make a small dividend among uneasy creditors at home. A very different personage from this, he possesses a well earned fame and lofty station. Is it too much to hope, that the sovereign people will succeed for once in governing themselves, and obtain as much credit far the treatment of a noble friend, who shall come among them, as they would be sure to do for that of an enemy, who should land upon their shores? An individual of real worth and dignity likes very well *laudari a viro laudato*; but every man is not a caricaturist, and would not be flattered by monkey tricks and exhibitions, whose apparent design was quite as much to gratify the vanity of the host, as to honor the guest, and sometimes, if there indeed has been any honor at all, it has not been easy to see, which party has received the most of it. My countrymen are quite too serious a race, and are charged with duties pressing much too heavily to allow them time to run after opera dancers, Vespuccis no better than they should be, or penny-a-line writers.

We bespeak for Lamartine a warm reception, kind feelings, and no absurdities. Republican in his principles, he is a friend of the people. An ardent admirer of Washington and Lafayette, one of his noblest speeches had their praises for its object. Read a portion of his speech on the disinterment of Napoleon, which filled the chamber of deputies with astonishment at its beauty, when delivered. "If this great general had been a great man, an irreproachable citizen, if he had been the Washington of Europe; if, after having defended the country, intimidated the contra revolution without, he had regulated, moderated, and organized the liberal institutions and the advancement of democracy in France, &c. &c.;—if he had retired, like Solon, or as the legislator of America; if he had withdrawn, in his disinterestedness and glory, to leave his place to liberty; who knows, if all that homage of the multitude, who adore that, which oppressed them, would be rendered to him. Who knows, if he would not have slept more tranquilly, and perhaps more neglected, in his tomb?

"Lafayette, who recalled to you in 1830 the opinions of '89, as fresh, as untouched, as disinterested, as ineffaceable, as when he first drew them from the fountain-head in the soul of his friend Washington; Lafayette reposes under the humble cross of a family tomb, and the man of the 18th Brumaire; the man to whom France owes all, except her liberty, the revolution triumphant goes to seek beyond the seas—to make for him an imperial tomb! The revolution triumphant! I ask, if upon the soil of France she has a monument sufficiently grand, sufficiently holy, sufficiently national to contain him?

"Where then place him? At the *Arc de triomphe de l'Etoile?* It is too heathen. The dead is sacred, and his asylum should be religious. And besides, what think you! if in the future, as we ought to hope, new triumphs shall await us, what *triumpheur*, what general would ever dare to pass by that spot? This would be to interdict the Arch of Triumph; this would be to close this door of national glory, which ought ever to remain open to our future destinies!

"But be it, that you choose St. Denis, or the Pantheon, or the Invalides, remember to inscribe on the monument, where he ought to be at the same time, soldier, consul, legislator, emperor. Remember to write there the only inscription which responds, at the same time, to your enthusiasm and your prudence, the only inscription which ought to be made for this unique man, and for the difficult epoch in which you live: A NAPOLEON—SEUL.

"These three words, attesting that his military genius has not an equal; attest, at the same time, to France, Europe and the world, that if this generous nation knows how to honor great men, she knows also how to judge them; she knows also how to distinguish their varieties, and those who threaten her in their name; and that in erecting this monument, and there embalming this great recollection, she does not wish from these ashes to resuscitate either war, or tyranny, or legitimacy, or pretenders, or even imitators."

The chamber was carried away with enthusiasm on hearing with what happiness he distinguished the part of glory and that of liberty. This is the sort of man, who is to visit a free country. One, whose principles are "Liberty for all, and in all things. A Government strong, but liberal. The people, the origin and end of all political action. Opinion coming from them and returning to them." No longer young, he goes to America with a mind strengthened, a vision corrected, a judgment matured by years and experience. Born in 1790, he has lived through scenes which tried men's souls. A traveller in his own country, Asia and Africa, he has learnt that each nation has its good qualities, and therefore does not condemn, as vile and uncivilized, everything which differs from the habits and customs of his own. No fear but he will have a welcome in the country where his friend Lafayette's memory will ever live; but in his reception, it is desirable, that no ridiculous extravagance should make the world imagine, that men of intellect are *raræ aves in terris*, and that the appearance of a great man in the United States is as an extraordinary an event, as that of Gulliver among the natives of Lilliput; let them rather show they are accustomed to them, and know how to practise the rites of hospitality with decorum and respect.

XXXIII.

Spring—French Mothers and Children—Squares in Paris—Their great Utility—Thalberg—His Concert—Motion not Music—Spontini, the Composer.

This letter, though bearing a recent date, was begun, you perceive, a long while ago, and runs through a considerable space of time. In truth, it was a kind of receptacle—Chiffonier's bag, if you please—like some others which I have sent you, into which odds and ends were thrown for private use, or the amusement of friends.

When I wrote to you in March, all was cold, uncomfortable, cheerless. If the sun ever showed his face, we took it as a particular favor, just as we do, when a beauty puts aside her veil for the express purpose of imparting those delicious smiles and glances, which are of no sort of use whatever to their possessor, but are known to yield great comfort to quite a large proportion of mankind. Now, O delightful spring, thou art come in thy beauty, and never hast thou been more welcome! Not a cloud has dimmed the heavens for several days; all is bright and gay and animating. One can feel with the poet:—

> Oh! qu'après de rudes tempêtes
> Il est agréable de voir,
> Que les aquilons sans pouvoir
> N'osent plus gronder sur nos têtes!
> Que le repos est doux après de longs travaux!
> Qu'on aime le plaisir, qui suit beaucoup de maux!
> Qu' après un long hiver le printemps a de charmes!

Ladies—beautiful birds—begin to promenade the streets. But one swallow doth not make a summer. The trees and shrubbery in the gardens are evidently thinking of putting on their green dresses, and their swollen buds foretell new charms.

Louis Philippe's revenue, derived from the letting of chairs in the public gardens, is just commencing.—Yesterday (April 2,) as I passed through the Tuilleries, I noticed that they were nearly all full. Into this garden all persons in soiled garbs, or carrying packages, are prevented from intruding, and in their places are nurses and mothers with their infants and young children. Here they drive hoop and play with the ball, battledore and shuttlecock, and stretch their little limbs in other pleasant pastimes. The French are much more sensible in this matter, than the Yankees, as all Americans are designated. They are not afraid to give their children a breath of fresh air:—

Il n'est rien de si doux que l'air qu'on y respire.

Instead of putting the lively wee creatures into a cradle, and packing them up like mummies in thick cloth, which compels them to breathe a second time the air contaminated by the first inspiration, they take them into the gardens and promenade with them. If sleepy, they repose sweetly in their arms, and respire an atmosphere, as pure and uncontaminated, as can be found within the limits of a city. It is far from easy to rouse a community to an adequate comprehension of the inestimable value of anything so very common, as air or water. The city of Boston, among others, is an example of the latter. New-York, to her imperishable honor, has proved, that this *vis inertiæ* is not invincible. *Dum alii verba incassum fundebant, opus est actum.* If the cost has been more than was predicted, the utility will not be less; and the money, after having circulated through the arteries of the State, will be returned by its thousand veins to the heart again in proper time, after giving growth in its progress, to the noble Croton Aqueduct. But, in Paris, the very *air* itself is a matter of deep concern; the government, with that wise, paternal care, which is exerted generally for the benefit of the whole, constructs public gardens, and lays out squares and places in the very heart of the city. This is not, as one at first would be apt to imagine, to add to its beauty merely, and form convenient resorts for promenade or business. Whatever attention may be bestowed on the embelishment of the city with monuments and fountains in the centre of these hundred squares, the *main* design of their construction is never out of sight. Ventilation is the principal aim—health the first object to be attained. After this, the beautifying of the city, and giving objects to be viewed by the people, adapted to excite feelings of bravery and pride in the deeds of the past, and hopeful sentiments of patriotism and courage in the future, are not neglected; for these help to agitate and purify the atmosphere of the soul.

Since this was written, I have been to a concert of no ordinary character. The first in his profession! What a magical phrase! I feel an involuntary reverence for any one, to whom these words can be justly applied. I went yesterday with a friend to the shop of a cobbler. "This man," said he, "is the first cobbler in Paris. He is an artist of great fame, and will incorporate a patch with a boot so ingeniously, as to be invisible almost to the eye; he is a man of genius." Do you suppose I passed by this individual as an ordinary man, because his vocation happened to be patching old boots and shoes? By no means truly. I studied his appearance, his features, his character. I meditated whether his talents and perseverance, if turned into another direction, might not have produced another Raphael or Michael Angelo. With impressions akin to these I saw *Thalberg*—the great composer—the greater performer—the prince of the piano; and never prince had more absolute sway. What shall I say of him? What words can express the pleasure I enjoyed? To be sure, I did not in the manner of many around me, go into a hysteric fit—jump up—sit down—writhe with ecstasy—laugh—cry—*scream*, all at once. No, I sat still, behaving decently, but for all that, not the less pleased, excited, transported. I begin to believe the fable of the old ages, when a musician made nothing of drawing after him rocks and trees. Thalberg's talent is little less; for he draws houses. The pieces, which he played this evening, were all his late productions, and have not as yet, I presume, been published in the United States. They were two fantasias from movements in the operas *La Muette de Portice* and *Don Pasquale*—a funeral march with variations—a barcarolle, both his compositions, and a *capricio* of his on several airs in the *Barbier de Seville*. Of these pieces I will say nothing, except that they are very beautiful and very difficult, two qualities which many know, are by no means novelties in his compositions. It is the man I wish to set before you. 'Twas an evening concert, commencing at half-past eight o'clock; the doors opening an hour before. The tickets were all sold more than a week beforehand. At seven o'clock I was waiting at the door for entrance. Being determined to secure an eligible seat in the pit—it costs a small fortune to a constant frequenter always to sit elsewhere; and the high prices, even there, guarantying its respectability.—I was there in good season, and took a position near the head of the *queue*. In a very short time after, there were a hundred behind me. But the guards preserved the utmost order, as usual. For one half hour I stood there, and then waited an hour in the house, before the performance commenced. But without counting six francs for the ticket, it costs something, you perceive, to go to a concert, or theatre. Every seat in the beautiful *salle* of the Italian Opera House was occupied. On the stage also were placed in chairs some hundred and fifty. The orchestra was partly boarded over, and here the grand piano was placed.

Has the king deigned to enter, that such enthusiastic applauses are ringing around the theatre? Yes, it is the king—but not of the French. It is the great descendant of Apollo. And, along with his powers of music, he inherits a portion of his beauty. He is a person of good size and figure, but not large. His appearance is modest and extremely prepossessing. Owing to the distance at which I sat, I would not wish to describe his air and person minutely. It is, however, perfectly apparent, that his complexion is light, his hair brown, his nose aquiline—without whiskers or mustache—and that he has probably completed, so far as a judgment could be formed by fallacious gas-light, his fifth climacteric. After numerous bows in return for the plaudits that welcomed his approach, he sat down at the piano, and ran his fingers carelessly over the keys—surely that is no common instrument! The tones, which follow his negligent touch, are not like any sounds that I have ever heard before. The subject is far beyond my pen. Mrs. Child must hear him, and, shutting her eyes to the gross creation about her, open them on the celestial world and the thousand harpers. The wildest frenzy of an imaginative mind would not, however, approximate the reality, which was here to be actually seen and heard. I have examined with infinite delight a great variety of machines, from the tiniest horologe through all the gradations of grace and strength up to the mighty engines, which propel the Atlantic steamers through a stormy ocean, and fill the beholder with wonder and awe—and some of them seem almost to have borrowed inspiration from above—yet I feel that nothing, among all the highest works of man, can be brought into comparison for a moment with the creations of the Almighty. Man originates no power, and in his grandest operations simply avails himself of the latent energies of water and the electric fluid. "The greatest piece of mechanism is the human hand," which, actuated by the propelling agency of the will, regulated by persevering practice and directed by genius, far surpasses all human inventions. This remark never appeared so striking, as while I listened to the astonishing exemplification of its power, which was going on in my presence this evening.

With Thalberg every thing is calm, collected—no grimaces, no writhings of the body. A *furor* was excited some two years ago in the United States by a second or third rate artist, called Miss S——. Every body was in raptures. Her houses were crowded—old men and women put on their spectacles—what for? To *see* music? Not exactly—but to see her *efforts*, the movements of her body, forward and back, sidewise, otherwise, and rotatory. To see the smiles, which opened so many dimples in her face, as to resemble small-pox marks; to see the self-complacent air, with which she threw up her white and well-formed " pieces of mechanism," and turned upon her music stool to receive the overwhelming plaudits of the first and second childhoods present, who exclaimed,—" Only *see* how she plays!" But Thalberg is quiet and still. Not a muscle in his countenance is disturbed —not an unnecessary motion of his body occurs. Nothing escapes to show the difficulties he is surmounting. A person, ignorant of music, might imagine, that all is simple and easy, as a game of the Graces.

At the close of the concert, the call for him was unanimous; and, in obedience to it, he came forward, while the room was ringing with cries for his celebrated fantasia on a movement in Moses in Egypt—the funeral march, and other pieces—each one asking for his own favorite. He played one of them, and his first and last concert in Paris this season was ended.

There was a very ugly man present. He had a pug nose stuck upon the front of his face, an immense mouth, black hair, black eyes, sunk deeply in his head, and a head deeply sunk in a white cravat. He is gazing at everybody in the house through the medium of a large opera glass. Who is he, do you ask?— Why it is Spontini, the great composer, He has recently received the order of —— conferred upon him and Mendelsohn—I think the name is spelt so—by the king of Belgium.

XXXIV.

COSTE ON EMBRYOLOGY—PARTY AT MR. D.'s—DONNE's LECTURES ON THE CIRCULATION OF THE BLOOD—OXYGEN AND HYDROGEN MICROSCOPE—PHOTO-ELECTRIC MICROSCOPE—ENGLISH EPISCOPAL CHURCH—PALAIS ROYAL—HEALY, THE PAINTER—VETERINARY SCHOOL—SCIENTIFIC CRUELTY TO HORSES.

YESTERDAY I commenced attending a course of lectures on Embryology, by M. Coste, which was begun a day or two ago. Notwithstanding a violent rain, among the company assembled in the lecture room in the College of France, was quite a number of women. This college enrols among its professors some of the most eminent men; among them, Guizot, the present minister, and Villemain, till very lately, minister of public instruction. Villemain is at the head of the anti-jesuit party, and has been troubled of late with a disease which has paralyzed, if not destroyed, his faculties. The Jesuits have seized the occasion in their instructions to their young children, to declare that "God was angry with this party, and had stricken their head with a grievous malady."

The evening when the preceding letter was written, I went to a party at Mr. D——r's. It was a small assembly of Americans, with the exception of one or two English, and I have not enjoyed myself less, I am sure, at any one this winter. The unsocial habits of the Yankees cling to them like purse-pride to a rich man, and are almost as disagreeable. How preposterous to allow a previous unacquaintance to fasten a padlock on every mouth! Have they not been requested to come together for the very purpose of making that acquaintance? But he has not been introduced. Is it so? Did not Mr. D., for example, give a general introduction and certificate of good character to all his company, when he issued his letters of invitation, and admitted them to his drawing-room? Had the company been French, I should have been certain to pass a charming evening. Away with this frigid reserve, by which hearts can never be united, unless by freezing together. It is neither Christian, politic, nor polite. These icy manners not only impair the happiness of all within their atmosphere, but induce a reaction—ay, they recoil and congeal the heart's blood of the cold formalist who fosters them. I have no desire to mingle in American circles, and probably shall not hereafter, as my sojourn here is drawing to a close, and the visiting season is over. There is no lack of business to occupy all my time. My daily augmenting knowledge of the advantages of Paris suggests a thousand things to be performed. My days are occupied with lectures of various kinds, my nights with study, writing, and visiting my French friends.

Among the lectures, there was one given by Mons. Donné, at the College of France. It was rather a supplementary lecture, illustrating some previous ones, which he delivers in the day. The experiments he made, were intended to *show* the circulation of the blood, and they succeeded capitally. The object was accomplished by means of an instrument, called the oxy-hydrogen microscope. It is a species of magic-lantern. The light, which is intense, is produced by the ignition of a piece of charcoal, and directing upon it jets of oxygen and hydrogen. The objects to be viewed are then placed in a proper situation, and their reflection, highly magnified with a powerful microscope, is thrown upon a white field. The disc was nearly three feet in diameter. The tongue of a frog, exposed in this manner, was shown so perfectly, that every vein and artery were distinctly visible, and also the minute follicles upon it. Another exhibition was the tongue of a *live* frog. The blood could be plainly seen rushing through the veins with great rapidity, and a great deal swifter in the arteries. This, too, proved conclusively, that the blood is formed of minute globules; for in the large veins, they could be observed rolling over one another, and tumbling along like the waves of a river. Many of the veins were of so small a size, that one of these globules was too large to pass with ease, and for two at a time, a passage was utterly impossible. The feet of flies, their proboscēs, wings and other parts, lice and similar insects, were shown in this way. The colors of a butterfly's wing were perfectly displayed, and with exquisite beauty. He has just begun his course, and I intend to follow him regularly in future.

The Photo Electric Microscope is a new instrument, at least to me. It is somewhat on the same plan, as the oxy-hydrogen microscope, a description of the action of which has been just given. In this instrument light is produced not by two gases, but by burning a piece of charcoal with a galvanic battery, composed of alternate plates of zinc and charcoal, which is much more powerful, than the usual battery of zinc and copper.

I went to another of Coste's lectures to-day, and wish that you could hear him. Modesty must never stand in the way of science, and, for the sake of listening to this celebrated man, one might be excused for overlooking the many natural and unavoidable indelicacies, connected with the subject of his investigations. It does seem queer though, even in France, to see women attending his lectures with remarkable regularity.

Sunday evening. For the first time, since I have been in Paris, I have been to church, that is, a *dissenting* church; and I think most probably, that it will be the last. This church is the English Episcopal, and the bishop of Paris is the officiating clergyman. On arriving there, I found, in order to obtain admittance, that it was necessary to *buy a ticket*. This I thought was strange. However I paid my franc—the price nearly of a seat in the pit of a theatre—and gave my ticket to a door-keeper sort of person, who pointed me to a seat. Were I to live in Paris, and had no other choice, I should certainly worship with the Catholic in preference to the Episcopalian, for more reasons than one. They get but few converts, I think, at that price. I heard prayers read with a languishment most efficacious in putting half the audience to sleep. The sermon, which, if a "boughten one," must have been cheap, succeeded in procuring repose for the remaining portion of the assembly, with the exception of many impenetrable people, who were continually going out, during the whole service of two hours and a half, to the number, I suppose, of forty at least. This I should have done myself, but, in the spirit of yankeedom, I was resolved to get the value of the consideration stipulated in the bargain at the door.

After this unpleasant episode, I was fain, in order to recover my good humor, to go to the Palais Royal, which is opened on Sundays only, for the inspection of strangers with passports, and natives with billets or tickets. This edifice is remarkable more for the events that have occurred within its walls, than for any thing it now contains. It possesses however some fine pictures, which amply repay examination. The most curious article is a table—about the size of our card-tables, when shut—the top of which, on a careless observation, would seem to be of marble. A deliberate inquisition discovers it to be formed of petrified wood.

The Louvre, in addition to many of the works of the old masters, contains, as is well known, those of living artists, deposited for inspection. A similar exhibition is made during two or three months every year. Among them is an excellent portrait of our minister to this court, Mr. King of Alabama, painted by Healy, of Boston, Massachusetts. The likeness is admirable; no one can see it without being struck with its fidelity. Mr. Healy's reputation has extended to the throne, and the king pays a delicate compliment, at once to our countrymen and our country, in commissioning him to present to him on canvas the features of some of our most distinguished citizens.

From time to time I have remarked upon some of the valuable public institutions with which France abounds. One of them is the Veterinary School at Alfort. There are two others at Lyons and Toulouse. Though this one at Alfort has less land and smaller accommodations than the others, it is their equal in the number of pupils and patients. The former are limited to three hundred between the ages of sixteen and twenty-five. The fee is three hundred and sixty francs per annum. Forty are placed there by the minister of war, and are destined for the department of cavalry. Qualifications for entrance consist in a knowledge of reading, writing, arithmetic, grammar, and smith's work. The regulations are rigid in the extreme; indeed the pupils are almost under military discipline. They are compelled to rise at five o'clock—six in winter—go to bed at nine, wear a regular uniform, &c. Permission to leave the yard is obtained but seldom; one detected in scaling the walls and going to the city, or elsewhere, is punished by expulsion. A common penalty is solitary confinement for two or more days. The young man who conducted us round the premises, showed us the swine that were fed on the flesh of the dead horses, that had been killed there; and complained, that the government was trying an experiment upon them; to me, the experiment appeared to be tried upon the pupils. For these creatures, after being fattened thus on animals diseased, were afterwards served up for the dinners of the students. As yet, he stated, no ill result had followed, the stomach having proved to be an alembic, where the gastric juices removed infectious qualities. I forbore some remarks, which were rising to my tongue, from a tender respect to the dinner, on which he was to regale that day.

The appearance of these young men was very prepossessing; infinitely superior to that of the French students, who frequent the Paris hospitals. When they enter the army, they become under-officers, and the chief veterinary surgeon ranks with lieutenants. The last is a recent advantage obtained with very great difficulty, having been most strenuously opposed in the House of Peers. The course of study requires a period of four years for its completion. The patients are horses, dogs, and horned animals. These are visited every morning by the physician attended by the students. The stables are perfectly clean, neat, and ornamented with bright brass. In one of them I saw a case of pneumonia. At the indication of the physician, we ausculted the beast, and heard distinctly the *subcrepitant râle*. It was the first time I ever thought of thus examining a horse. Everything is on the same scientific plan. The anatomy of that animal has almost the same nomenclature, as the human. Twelve pupils serve as night-watchers of these creatures, and receive all that may come, having fractures, colics, or any other disease. Among other curiosities there was a dog afflicted with chorea, or St. Vitus's dance, and a cow with phthisis. Dogs pay ten cents a day, and horses fifty, for medical attendance and nourishment. In the operation of "nicking" horses, instead of making numerous sections of the muscle on the inside of the tail, as is practised by the English and Americans, the French remove the muscle entirely.

There is a fine Anatomical Cabinet, which well repays a lover of Comparative Anatomy; beside one of Pathological Anatomy, exhibiting specimens of *calculi, ostea-sarcoma* and other maladies.

Thus far I have mentioned portions of the establishment, which may be considered interesting and agreeable to all. But there is another department, which does not possess this recommendation, and though a very useful feature in the institution certainly, I can scarcely dare to say, that it is necessary. I refer to the operations, that are made upon the living animals. I will give you some description of them, and if it shocks your feelings, and makes your blood run cold, my justification is, that such things are, and should be told and known. Let the authors of fictitious cruelties answer for their loathsome delineations, whose immediate tendency is to harrow up the sensibilities of the soul, make the reader wretched for the time, and afterwards callous to real suffering, and all for what? Would you believe it?—for amusement!

The government provides poor old worn out horses for the use of the students, to accustom them to operate, and give them facility of execution. The unhappy creature is led in, snorting and trembling, at the sight of and smell of blood around. Before he has time to recover from his amazement, his legs are drawn firmly together, and he is thrown to the ground. A rope is twisted with a stick around his upper lip, so that his head is perfectly commanded. He lies prostrate and powerless. A dozen pupils leap upon him, and begin their horrid operations. With red hot iron his skin is cauterized in every part of the body, where the cautery is ever applied. One cuts off two inches of the tail, a second two more, another takes out the muscle, and a fourth a bone, till that member is entirely gone. Every variety of shoe is put upon him, his hoofs are cut to the quick, experimental nails are driven in, as if they were accidental, and dug out again.

Imaginary wounds are probed. The ears are then cut out, the eyes extracted. Every artery in the body is "taken up," operations for tenotomy performed, beside many other acts of refined scientific torture. In the meantime, the poor helpless animal struggles and flounders, sighs, weeps, groans, *screams*. He cannot move. The blood oozes from a hundred orifices, "those poor dumb mouths," till finally death, the angel of mercy to the miserable among men and beasts, comes to his relief:—

"And th' o'erloaded slave flings down his burden
From his gall'd shoulders, and, when the cruel tyrant,
With all his imps, and tools of torture round him,
Is meditating new, unheard-of hardships;
Mocks his short arm—and, quick as thought, escapes,
Where tyrants vex not, where the weary are at rest."

Who would be an omnibus horse? A fair retort is, who would be a man? Ay, there have been men, remember that! and thousands of them too, who have inflicted worse torments than these even on their fellow men. Is it possible? And what for? For religious and political creeds—*because they differed in opinion, that's all!*

In this way a dozen horses are sacrificed twice a week;—yes, for years—twice a week—from five in the morning till five in the evening, this dreadful butchery is going on. What think you of the "Chourineur" in the Mysteries of Paris? "Truth is stranger than fiction"—no news to me, I assure you. Horses with glanders are more fortunate. They are killed immediately. No operations are performed upon them now from fear, one of the pupils having died last year of this as yet incurable disease, contracted in his experiments.

XXXV.

COMPARISON OF THE PARISIAN AND AMERICAN PRISONS—SOCIETY FOR THE AID OF BOYS QUITTING THE HOUSES OF CORRECTION—SOCIETY FOR THE AID OF ABANDONED GIRLS LEAVING THE HOUSE OF CORRECTION.

HAVING completed my intended description of the various prisons of the city where vice is prevalent to such an extent, though the account has been already too minute perhaps, you must allow me to make a comparison, in a few particulars at least, between them and those in my own country. In a new region, where multitudes of institutions are yet to be erected, the most minute and apparently insignificant points of information may have a value; and on this account a review, however superficial, of a few circumstances connected with this great subject, may not be out of place.

The well-being of society demands, that means shall be adopted to separate its good elements from the bad; but humanity at the same time requires that the measures resorted to should be as lenient as possible, consistent with security. Another thing is not to be neglected. All the bitter dregs must not be strained out of the cup of the delinquent; his condition must not be rendered almost if not quite enviable to the destitute innocent man, who has not qualified himself by crime to taste the comforts, which sometimes surround the convict. Yet this has taken place, where charity has mistaken her vocation, and left her proper sphere to feed the criminal with luxuries beyond the power of the honest laborer.

In point of *strength* there can be little difference between the prisons of Paris and our own. The former are universally constructed of stone, but ours have the advantage of them in firmness of material, as nothing is quite equal to the everlasting granite, of which the American structures are principally composed. The security of prisoners is perfectly well guarantied by numerous doors and intricate passages, by walls surrounding many of them, and by numberless sentinels, which the vast military force, now idle, enables the French Government to maintain. Escape is absolutely impossible without corruption on the part of the sentinels or jailers. The walls are much loftier than those of similar institutions in the United States, and a long ladder would be requisite to scale them; ours, on the contrary, may be surmounted by the help of two or three barrels placed on one another, or any similar contrivance. A great defect noticed in the general construction of the buildings here lies in the manner of fastening the cells; each one requiring to be separately locked. They are fastened by a bolt and a lock: and in some of them, for example, in the *Maison Centrale d'Education Correctionelle*, a long entry traverses its entire length; and into this all the doors open. To fasten them is the duty of three men. One shoves the bolt; another arranges a bolt connected with the lock, which consists of another bolt, a part of which enters into the door lock, like the hasp of the lock of a trunk. The third man turns the key. The means of securing the cell doors employed in the United States are much preferable, consisting of a single bar of iron running through the whole range of cells, which it fastens by one operation. Beside the superior expedition of this process, the security too is greater, because this bolt cannot be moved, unless every door is shut. But here, in the hurry of locking up, a door might be accidentally omitted. The long bar therefore might supersede with advantage the use of separate bolts, which however are generally sufficient to secure the prisoner with all necessary safety.

Less regard to *neatness* and *ventilation* is seen within the prisons here than in America. The entry walls and floors, being of brown stone, easily conceal the dust and cobwebs, that adhere to them; these would only be brought *into relief* by the whitewashed apartments of an American penitentiary. Neither is sufficient attention paid to the cleanliness of the convicts. All wash in an open fountain, and wipe themselves on a handkerchief, or coat sleeve. All wear their beards entirely *a la patriarche*, and therefore require no barber. In opposition to Sterne, I am constrained to say "they do *not* manage these things better in France."

In the *government* of the inmates of French prisons a degree of *lenity* is shown unknown in ours, and I think, fortunately so for us, as excessive indulgence must very seriously impair the utility of imprisonment. The conversation, which is permitted among the prisoners by the rules, while they are at work, as well as in the hours of recreation, when all are together without restraint, foments disturbances; produces quarrels among themselves not unfrequently ending in death; insurrections against the authorities and occasionally a general meeting. The labor imposed in American prisons is more severe, and does not therefore render special seasons for exercise at all necessary. The government indeed begins to think better of the solitary principle, and attempts in the construction of recent buildings to conform to it as much as possible. Considerable difficulty is felt in the introduction of trades, which will admit the employment of strength sufficient to authorize the suspension of the established seasons of recreation. Stone-cutting is impracticable, because that operation is performed here after the material is placed in the walls of edifices. This practice has obtained in consequence of its tender texture, which exposes it to be marred or spoiled in handling. Even the friction of the rope, employed to elevate it to its proper position, would inflict a serious injury.

In the *punishment of misbehavior*, I think the French are not severe enough. One thorough correction, it seems to me, is more effective than many slight ones. My own experience when at school adds force to this opinion. The lower animals afford illustrations of the same principle. A horse soon becomes insensible to perpetual slight cuts of the whip, especially when administered with the characteristic gentleness of lady equestrians, whose most efficient *lashes* are those of their *eyes*. Thus according to the old doggerel,

> At first he starts and winces,
> Then presently he minces,
> Till fast asleep and dreaming,
> He thinks all drivers women.

I dislike exceedingly to see an unruly criminal put into a place of solitary confinement for twelve or twenty-four or even forty-eight hours. Let him stay there, till it becomes decidedly disagreeable and irksome, and really a punishment; till the culprit feels a little hungry on his stinted allowance of bread and water, and his bones begin to ache with reposing on the soft side of a pine board; till the penalty shall be sufficient to hinder at least, if not prevent, the recurrence of a similar offence. The kind-hearted directors have forbidden the master of the Boston House of Correction from keeping any of his turbulent subjects in solitary confinement longer than a definite period without a special order from them; and what is the consequence? Why, all the prisoners know very well this restriction of his powers, and, though the same efficient person remains at the helm,—whose place could not be easily supplied—there is not the same good order as before. At the end of the period prescribed, he is obliged to release the stubborn spirit, that has offended his authority, and now defies and laughs at his limited punishment. The infliction of the cat is not known in these prisons; and I question if it is used in similar establishments in the United States at the present time, though it was not abolished in the Massachusetts prison, when I visited it several years ago. A degradation is attached to it, which has compelled reflecting men to seek some other instrument of equal power to subdue a rebellious nature. The shower-bath, so efficacious, especially in the case of women, is not employed here.

The *frequent visits* of friends seems to me to be an evil. Such often repeated communication promotes the continuance of old plans of action, and the maturation of new ones to be executed after their release. Instead of repentance, a feeling of anger, and perhaps revenge, is cherished both against the laws and the witnesses of the government. This permission ought surely to be cautiously and rarely granted.

The *food of the convicts*, though good, is inferior to that in the American penitentiaries, which I have visited. The bread is generally black, but well risen and wholesome. The quantity of meat is very limited, and given much more rarely than with us.

Nothing but water is used for drink, if a light soup is excepted, which may answer the purpose of a beverage. Few objections however of any great importance can be alleged against their general treatment, except the extraordinary distinction made between the rich and poor convict. Strong encouragement is held out to the thief to do a large business, provided he succeeds in retaining the property stolen by concealment, or making a deposit of it in the hands of a comrade. The horrors of a prison retire before him into the apartments of the small felons, who have committed petty larcenies perhaps to save themselves or families from starvation. The music of his gold summons around him many of the comforts of a private mansion; and very likely he finds little difference between them, except the superior size, more numerous attendants, and greater amount and variety of company in his new home. The brown bread of government is not for his consumption, as he prefers a nice white roll with good sweet butter. In many of the prisons he is not obliged to labor, if he will pay a small daily sum, which the genteel criminal will of course prefer to do; if he works at all, it must be for exercise, as a substitute for his customary diurnal promenade in the Broadway of Paris—the Boulevards. He disdains to wear the coarse shirts and other garments of the ordinary convict, and can by no means think of divesting himself of the principal and most envied marks of a gentleman—*the superfine broadcloth.* Without these accustomed luxuries he would be unhappy perhaps, and the pursuit of happiness he considers to be not only his inalienable privilege, but positive duty. It is not very common indeed to witness an extent of luxury, like this; but it is common to see a vast distinction made between the poor and wealthy criminal here and elsewhere. Even in the galleys, those who are sentenced for life, and possess rich friends, are much better off, than they who are destitute of their commanding influence. The sentence of the highest offenders, such as assassins for example, are thus virtually modified in their favor, if they are fortunate in the possession of powerful connections, while others under adverse circumstances, are punished with unrelenting severity.

Two Societies are connected with the prisons, whose object is indeed benevolent, but whose success, as well as that of many similar associations, with which I have been acquainted, falls far below their excellent intentions and deserts. If the good seed, which has been wasted on stony places and among thorns and briars, had been scattered always upon good ground, there would have been sheaves enough produced to banish all inevitable want from the world. If we have the poor always with us, we have their counterfeits in equal numbers, who are, it must be acknowledged, the greatest orators of the two. And, these " counterfeit presentments " play their parts with far superior success. For everybody knows, that no real misery ever levied such enormous contributions on a sympathising community, as the nightly actors of fictitious distress. A certain style of acting among the poor, as well as rich, seems to hit the public taste ; and money is often given outside the theatre, as well as within, to the *performance*, rather than the *player*. Unquestionably the benevolent are frequently deceived, for they cannot prevent their ears *from standing open* to every cry, and the most importunate, though least deserving, is apt to drown the rest. As one is also able to hear, where he cannot see, he is in danger from such impulses of making many blunders in the dark.

This morning, in reading a report of the trials, I noticed the sentence of two women committed to the House of Correction for thus abusing the tender feelings of their sex. The first solicited alms for herself and suffering babe, which she carried wrapt up in her bosom. But the helpless little innocent was discovered on examination to be only a child of worn out cloth and straw. —Was not this a case of a person literally reduced to rags ? The other, whose appearance denoted her to be on the point of confinement, frequented the public streets, and as often as a well dressed woman passed, more especially if she was in a similar condition, she became suddenly overtaken with labor pains. Unable to proceed, and too destitute to hire a vehicle, she was kindly provided with money for that purpose, as well as to purchase the commodities which her situation and poverty required. Her case being investigated, the interesting protuberance was found to be produced by a frame of wicker basket work, which very nicely imitated the delicate peculiarity of women. Yet notwithstanding these, and a multitude of similar instances, I am convinced, that with a moiety of the caution exercised in a man's ordinary business, he may bestow all the charity he has a heart to give, at an exceedingly slight hazard of deception. And in the two anecdotes just related, it is abundantly apparent, with what wonderful ease the mystery was unraveled. To tell the truth, the examples of imposition are in exact proportion to the indolence of the giver, and the direct consequences of his laziness and culpable want of caution. Such a state of things is exceedingly favorable to the parsimonious, who commonly are most eloquent about impostors, as their number is just large enough to serve them with an everlasting argument against alms-giving.

The two Societies which I was about to mention, are *La Société de Patronage des Jeunes Libérés de la Seine,* and *La Société de Patronage pour les Jeunes Filles libérées et délaissées.* The former has the care of the boys from the House of Correction, just mentioned, after exit; and the latter the poor abandoned girls, when released from confinement. Mons. de Lamartine is president of the latter, that of the former is Mons. Beranger, peer of France. Of the Society for girls I possess no information: but the other was founded in 1833 to watch over the youth in prison, and aid and encourage them after their enlargement. Every member is an active one, and has always one or two under his care, toward whom he acts as guardian, procuring him labor, overseeing his behavior, assisting him with advice, and if necessary with money. This is bestowed by government, and the benevolence of members. To this Society it is in a great measure owing, that the number of committals has diminished to the extent which I have in a former letter described. Prizes are every year awarded for good behavior, and a report of the Society published. Connected with the department of the Seine are two other Houses of Correction for small offences, and for the suppression of mendicity; but they are in the adjoining towns, beyond the limits of Paris.

XXXVI.

CHURCH AT ST. DENIS—THE SEPULCHRE OF THE FRENCH SOVEREIGNS—
TOMB OF LAFAYETTE—PERE-LA'CHAISE.

A FEW days ago, leaving the dust and tumult of the city behind me, by help of the great locomotive principle of the day—not steam—but omnibus power, I soon passed walls, boulevards, barriers and fortifications, and found myself in the town of St. Denis, two leagues north of Paris. The celebrity of this little place, which has not more than five thousand inhabitants, is entirely owing to a Benedictine Abbey, founded in 250, and to the selection of this church as the burial-place of the French kings. The original edifice, which contained the ashes of the first king known to be buried here, Dagobert, son of Chilperic, was supplanted by another, built by Dagobert I., and by still another, erected by Pepin, father of Charlemagne. All these have foundations. It was then rebuilt by Suger, the abbot of the monastery, in 1144. Two towers of this structure still remain. The rest, as it now exists, was added by St. Louis and his successor between the years 1250 and 1281. This venerable church suffered severely during the revolution. The bodies of the royal line, which had down to that period been there interred, were in 1793, by order of the barbarous Convention, disinterred, and thrown into two large trenches dug near. In 1795, the leaden roof was stripped off, and another decree passed to raze to the ground this the most beautiful monument of the architecture of the time. Fortunately this order was not obeyed. Napoleon in 1806 gave directions for the restoration of the buildings; since that time the work has been going on, and though more than three millions of dollars have been expended, it is yet unfinished. The monuments of the kings have been renovated, new glass has supplied the place of the old, which had been destroyed, and it now asserts its claim to be one of the most elegant edifices in an architectural view, and the most sumptuous in its decorations, in the kingdom. The walls and ceilings are literally encrusted in gold. The ornaments are intended to be as near fac-similes of the originals, as possible, some specimens of which, accidentally found, serving as models. There are very few pictures to be seen, but the various shrines are enriched with old sculptures in oak and statues in stone. Many of the crosses are of great antiquity, and the avant-altars are composed of beautiful mosaic. Around the church are numerous monuments of the most magnificent description. Any account of them would be unprofitable; first, because they have so often been well described; secondly, because the most perfect description would be useless. They must be seen to be understood. The sacristy is embellished with many pictures by the best living painters, which represent the most important events in the history of the church. It contains, likewise, a bronze chair of King Dagobert. The vaults are extremely curious, for there are the ashes of the French monarchs, and the monuments erected to their memory, most of them with statues, and many of them taken from life. Among them is a tomb, closed with bronze doors, made by Napoleon for himself. Death is certain, but the sepulchre is the sport of fortune, and in this monument now repose the ashes of Louis XVI. and XVIII., Marie Antoinette, and some others of the elder branch of this family. The inscription on one monument in the nave of the church particularly attracted my notice. It stated that there lay John, son of Ludovicus, who *migrated* to Christ in the year 1247. Man is truly a bird of passage.

The vespers gave me an opportunity to hear the new organ lately erected. It is the largest, and, since the loss of that in St. Eustache by fire, the best in France. The power is immense, and, when played in full force, shook the whole edifice. The echoes around the vaults, and through the lofty aisles, were extremely fine. The reed notes I noticed to be particularly excellent, the hautboy and clarionet stops imitating those instruments with surprising exactness. Among the priests who officiated, one of the bishops, a fine looking man, was pointed out to me, as a natural son of Louis XVIII.

After this hasty description of the final resting place of royalty, the lustre of whose fame, too often dimmed by bad actions, cannot be heightened by marble monuments, or golden inscriptions, come with me, and view the tomb of one, whose character was so spotless, and life so pure, that even his enemies are unable to find any thing for blame. Leave behind the ideas of greatness derived from the contemplation of overshadowing gothic buildings, gilded walls, painted windows, and monuments of marble. Forget the name of king, and remember only, that "an honest man is the noblest work of God." Divest yourself of the impressions produced at St. Denis, or—if you must take them with you,—bring them for contrast only, as the painter introduces the dark background into his work, merely to project with greater strength the peculiar features of his picture. To see the remains of the greatest man, that France has produced in modern times, and the purest of public characters; of one who preserved his integrity untarnished, notwithstanding the corruption around him,

"——————— Faithful found
Among the faithless, faithful only he;
Among innumerable false, unmov'd;"

one of the very few, who figured during the scenes of the Revolution, whose name is venerated by the people of France, esteemed by Britons, and embalmed in the hearts of Americans; whither shall we go? He reposes not by the side of the kings at St. Denis. Shall we seek him at the *Hôtel des Invalides* under the grand dome, where sleep the ashes of Napoleon? Shall we look for him in the magnificent Cemetery of *Père la Chaise?* Simple in his habits, and unostentatious to a remarkable degree in his manners during life, it is not in such places that he would desire to lay his bones in death. Accompany me then to the *Rue de Picpus*, in a retired quarter of the city. Here at No. 15, in the private cemetery connected formerly with a convent of the order of St. Augustine, but now a boarding school conducted by the same order, you will be shown a tomb covered with a double slab of black stone, such as is used for a similar purpose in the United States. These two slabs are united by a cross, and on each an inscription is cut. No white marble—no golden letters. Contrast this with the monument of Spurzheim at Mount Auburn, so renowned as a model of simplicity. Compare its scrolls and carving, the golden letters, with the one before you of ordinary stone, absolutely denied the least ornament whatever. Read its plain inscription, in harmony with the rest, with moistened eyes and beating heart:—

M. J. P. R. Y. G. B.
LAFAYETTE,
Lieutenant-General, Membre de la Chambre des Deputés
né à Chavaniae Haute Loire
De VI Sept. MDCCVII.
Marié Le XI. Avril MDCCLXXIV.

A

M. A. F. de NOAILLES

Decédé à Paris le XX Mai
MDCCCXXXIV.

REQUIESCAT IN PACE.

On the other slab a similar inscription records the decease of his wife, who died December 24, 1807.

Now read a description of the royal vaults at St. Denis. "The walls of the royal vaults are cased with black marble, and ornamented with stone pilasters; the pavement is of white and black marble, the coffins, some of which are covered with black or violet-colored velvet with ornaments of gold or silver, are placed on iron bars." The tomb of Francis I., and Claude of France, erected in 1550 after the designs of Philibert Delorme, is most sumptuous. The effigies of F. and C. repose on a superb cenotaph, ornamented with a frieze representing the battles of Marignan and Cerisolles. Here the cenotaph rises a grand arch, enriched with arabesques and basso relievos. Sixteen fluted columns support the entablature, above which are placed five statues of white marble in a kneeling posture, viz. Francis I., Claude his queen, the Dauphin and duke of Orleans, his sons and Charlotte, the daughter. Now, what think you of a black stone with an honest name upon it; and a lustrous white marble, enriched with gold and statuary, with names like these inscribed? One, exposed to the elements, but looking up through the pure air into the deep sky, and clasped by the bending and merciful heavens; the other protected by a fretted canopy of gold, the atmosphere loaded with incense, and the sacred *oriflamme* waving overhead.

In connection with this subject, it may be in place to give some notice of the feelings inspired by a view of that cemetery, of which all have heard, and which is one of the first places visited by a stranger. A particular description I shall not attempt, for it is familiar to every one. The great interest, that has been taken during the last few years through the United States in the formation of cemeteries, has caused it to be frequently sketched, and the works of every tourist will give a more or less accurate notion of it. As a whole I was greatly disappointed. Every thing solemn loses in the hands of the French its grave character. The churches with their gilding and pictures resemble the theatres far more than places for divine worship. This is particularly predicable of those of recent construction, such as L'église St Vincent de Paule, and Le Notre Dame de Lorette, which are shown to strangers, as worthy of high approbation. So with the cemeteries, and that of Père La Chaise, of which I am new writing. The street leading to it from the "Place de la Bastille" is well calculated to prepare the mind for a visit. This avenue is occupied by dealers in tomb stones and funereal garlands, and so large a quantity of sepulchral architecture is spread along the sides of the way, though generally without inscriptions, as almost to make one think, he has already entered the precincts of the consecrated ground. A large gateway, however, marks the entrance. The gate posts are of stone, plain, with the exception of the carved torches, which form the corners, and the inscriptions on one of "*Spes illorum immortalitate plena est, Sapient III. IV.;*" and on the other, "*Qui credit in me, etiam si mortuus fuerit, vivet, Jean II.*" The gates are of oak. One soon loses the solemn feelings, which he experienced in his walk hither. He finds himself in a cemetery, where rest the merchants of Paris, whose tombs subserve the double purpose of displaying the wealth of the family of the deceased, and as an advertisement, or sign, for his successor in business. One for instance bore an inscription like the following:—" Here lies —— butcher in —— street, number ——, &c. This tomb is erected by his affectionate son and successor in business at the old stand." The multitude of monuments at first fill one with astonishment, and are put into the ground without any form or regularity. Some are even, others uneven ; they are set sidewise, cornerwise, in any wise, that they can be packed. An oblong of eight feet by three with a railing round and a monument within is succeeded by another oblong, another rail, another monument, and thus the entire cemetery is densely stowed, unvaried, except in the variety of the sepulchral architecture, and now and then a union of two, three, or four of these *mètres*, when some rich skeleton would not be contented without a larger space to lie in. Between the tombs a narrow pass of six inches, or one foot wide, leaves room for a few stunted trees, and so the cedar and spruce have contrived to secure a foothold.

If little taste is discovered in the general plan of Père la Chaise, it is to be found in the tombs themselves separately. The monuments, when isolated, present beauties, which are hidden by their unfavorable situation. They are of all sorts. The most remarkable, such as that of Heloise and Abelard, have been often described. Some of later erection, and those, which for their elegance or peculiarities, struck my attention, I shall venture to sketch, trusting, that I have selected such, as have escaped general notice.

It is astonishing to see, how man regards his last resting-place. He, who was all his days content to live in poverty in a garret, when dead, seeks for a mausoleum of marble, to the erection of which the niggard savings of years are to furnish the means. He, who was satisfied to pass a lifetime in obscurity, desires a posthumous immortality. Thus a poor *épicier*, who lived in a retired street, unknowing and unknown, upon his marble monument has placed his portrait, painted upon canvas, and protected from the winds and storms by a bell glass. Others have casts in plaster of Paris, some painted, these may be found in different states of decay in all parts of the grounds. Others, who wish to live longer in the eyes of the world, have them in bronze and marble of all kinds.

As in all other places of a similar character, many of the monuments serve to show respect for the memory of the illustrious personage, who there lies interred. Among these that of Casimir Périer, erected not many years ago by the city of Paris, is one of the most remarkable. This monument, situated very conspicuously in the centre of a large enclosure, was built by a public subscription, to record their veneration for the great statesman and orator, who for many years, in the highest situations of the government, and as prime minister in 1832, reflected honor upon his native city. On a lofty pedestal, on three sides of which are allegories of Justice, Eloquence and Firmness, in *basso reliévo*, and on the fourth an inscription worthy of his memory, stands his statue in bronze. It is a noble work of art. One, who officiates as guide around the cemetery, relates to Americans the following anecdote: "A few years since I accompanied a party of Americans through the grounds. On coming to this I remarked, that this statue is said by Americans to bear a very strong likeness to one of your most distinguished men, Daniel Webster. There were few remarks made, but, as we proceeded, one of the ladies informed me, that D. W. was one of the party then present." I do not see any resemblance myself. Another of more simplicity, raised by private subscription, is to the memory of the celebrated painter Gericault. The front of the tomb is ornamented by a cast in bronze of one of his best pictures, which represents a party of wrecked sailors on a raft. The sides have sketches, cut in the free stone, of others of his works, and behind, —which struck me as in exceedingly bad taste,—the names of those, who contributed to its erection, are carefully preserved. Another, erected within a few years, records the death of a soldier. It is ornamented with castings of helmets, swords, cannon, spear heads, &c., and bears the inscription, "*Decorum est pro patria mori.*"

Others have inscriptions dictated by family pride. One records the death of Robertson, an aerostat; upon the side of whose lofty monument of white marble are *basso reliévos*, representing a crowd witnessing a balloon ascension, boys climbing upon a fence, and old men looking over their spectacles. Some English tombs record the death of people of high birth; but as they themselves, during life, never did any deed worthy of even the short perpetuity of a tomb-stone, the names of all the distinguished in the family since its existence are emblazoned thereon. Molière, so long denied a Christian burial, lies tranquilly at last under a beautiful sarcophagus of white marble, supported by four columns, and surmounted by a vase. Near him La Fontaine, whose marble cenotaph, crowned by a fox in black marble, is ornamented with two *basso reliévos* in bronze of the fable of the "Wolf and Stork," and the "Wolf and Lamb."

Far more of the monuments record expressions of feeling and sentiment, in which this nation so far excel all others. It is not then surprising, that we find numerous tombs of the most beautiful, lovely, virtuous good of the earth; each of whom their friends fondly imagined to be the best. Many plain slabs, united by clasped hands, whose arms spring from the summit, perpetuate the virtues of a husband and wife, whom "death had severed, and death had united." Another bears upon it under a bell glass, a piece of embroidery, forming a wreath of flowers, in the centre of which is the inscription, "To my sister," which would look much like a lamp-stand, if one did not see therein the beatings of a warm heart. For the tomb of a dissenting minister a pillar of some ten feet of marble is elevated, surmounted by a cushion, on which is lying an open Bible. The effect is very good. The monuments are mostly hollow with iron doors, and variously adorned with windows of colored glass in cruciform, and other shapes. About the walls are inscriptions of the various members of the family deceased. Some contain busts; others, small shrines with cross, flowers, &c., and all, of every class and kind almost, have numerous wreaths of artificial flowers, hanging upon the iron fences, or placed in glass cases. Some are quite filled with them, and little statues of saints and praying children, in plaster. To many are attached small pots of roses, pansies and other sentimental plants.

Thus far I have described the graves of the rich, among whom, on neat slabs of white marble with true simplicity I found two, which particularly interested me. They, like me, had perhaps left kindred and friends behind, and tended by the hands of strangers, had died in a foreign land. The inscriptions are as follows:

H—— E——
W————n
Born in New York, June 21, 1824.
Died in Paris, April 2, 1840.

J—— J——
T————n
Né à New York, le 14 Août, 1814.
Mort à Paris, le 16 Janvier, 1845.

Around them pots of fresh flowers and garlands showed, that, though far remote from home, they still had friends to watch over their remains. From the slab of the first I took the shell of a snail, which I found thereunto adhering, and shall bear it to the United States, as a memorial of this visit.

These are the wealthy, and their tombs are the "perpetual graves," where their bones will remain undisturbed forever. Those, who are not sufficiently rich to buy this right, are deposited in a quarter assigned them for the space of five years, when, being entirely decomposed, they are disinterred to make room for others. The third sort to be provided for, are the poor, who are allowed the charity, shall I say luxury, of a grave for five years also. This class, however, have not a portion of land allotted them. A large trench is dug some four feet deep. I witnessed several funerals of this kind. The bodies, (those which I saw, were infants) were borne, enclosed in a coffin of unpainted boards, and wrapped in black, upon the shoulders of a sexton; behind whom followed the mourners. As he let the coffin down from his shoulders to the ground, the body slid from one end to the other with a most unpleasant sound. The black cloth was rudely pulled away, and the coffin slipped down to the man below, who placed it in juxtaposition with those already there. The mould of preceding generations was then scattered two or three inches thick upon the top, barely hiding it from sight. The uncovered side was immediately concealed from view by the next comer. Having filled up some distance, the dust was heaped upon them, the wooden cross painted black, having an inscription, was then fixed as near as could be computed, to the spot, where the body to which it belonged was laid, the wreaths put upon it, and all was finished.

For five years the mourner can come to the sacred place, which contains the ashes of her departed relative, and bewail her loss. Beyond this time, affection cannot find the spot, where the son or daughter, all that is dear in life, is placed. The poor mother cannot hope to lie after death by the side of her child. No inscription can perpetuate the memory of either. "*Hic et ubique,*" is written all over the ground, and obliterates all others. Death does not make all men equal. All men are not born, neither do they die, equal. A life of suffering, toil and privation is not enough. When death comes at a hospital the poor patient, destitute of friends sufficiently rich to bear the expense of a burial, looks foward in his last moments to no other grave, but the dissecting room; at best, he cannot expect a rest of more than a few years in Christian ground. Is he the only, or greatest monster, who cuts the rich man's throat to save himself, by wealth thus acquired, from abandonment to so cruel a fate? Such thoughts chill the blood, and gladly have I arrived near the end of my sheet, so that I may be relieved for a while from reflection on the misfortunes of the poor. God grant, in his great mercy, that a similar condition of things may never obtain in our own country; and yet, from some things I have heard, I fear, that the public grounds in New-York are not much better conducted. In Boston even, philanthropic, moral Boston, the dead man cannot rest in peace. Yet she too has her wealthy citizens, who have the courage, as they possess the money, to build in their lifetimes their own sepulchral monuments of Italian marble, or some other costly material, or else have in their wills more modestly directed their executors to do it for them. And while these palaces for skeletons are being erected, not only are those, whom misfortune sends to the city poor house, buried without a prayer, but they are placed in tombs, where they remain in quiet for a year at most. Every spring this is opened, the coffin rudely knocked to pieces, and burnt with the linen winding sheet, when they are so fortunate as to get any, which is rarely the case, and the the bodies tossed together into a trench, and covered up. Boston has now a mayor, whose human sympathies the weight of riches has not crushed. Let him look to this. If economy is the order of the day, and a piece of beach land, or hill of sand, is too expensive, let the patients be deprived of a meal a week, and a fund of thirty pieces of silver will soon accumulate to buy a Pottersfield, where the dead poor may no longer be disturbed in their last, and, in some cases, their first repose. In this respect, in the boasted land of liberty, let all be equal

Many have endeavored to institute a comparison between Père la Chaise and Mount Auburn, the beautiful cemetery in the vicinity of Boston, Mass. Scarcely anything can be more absurd. If one should essay to compare St. Peter's church at Rome with the Falls of Niagara, all would cry out at the obvious incongruity. Yet a similar parallel is attempted to be drawn in the former case. The beauties and grandeurs of art and nature can very seldom be brought into competition. It is easy, however, to point out the difference between them. In the case before us, one is distinguished by possessing beauty in the whole; the other in particular parts. The general beauty of Mount Auburn strikes every beholder. Nature has done much, ay all, for her. Her varieties of hill and dale, of foliage, of ponds and rivulets, make her *coup d'œil* most exquisite. Père la Chaise says, I grant you all this advantage, and that you appear charming at a distance; but the ornaments you wear, though superbly mounted, I confess, and seeming on a casual glance to be rich and costly, are poor things after all. I do not, myself, make any pretension on the score of glittering gauds, and simulated gems. Indeed, my general appearance must be allowed to be somewhat unprepossessing; but if you will take the trouble to examine me closely, you will find me decked in jewels of great intrinsic value, with cameos of rare workmanship, mosaics, and antiques.

The money, that has been lavished on the monuments is enormous. Twenty-five millions of dollars is the estimate of an expense which cannot be accurately ascertained. For this great sum, you would look for something beautiful and sumptuous, and you will find it. This computation will cease to appear extravagant, when it is remembered, that many of the monuments are works of the first sculptors of the country.

14*

XXXVII.

Royal Institution of the Deaf and Dumb—Abbe de L'Épée—Sicard—Royal Institution for the Blind—Artesian Well at Grenelle—Comparison of the Royal Institution for the Blind, and the Asylum for the Blind, at South Boston—Thomas Handasyd Perkins.

No matter what a man's taste or character may be, he can be gratified in Paris with admirable ease. Aspirations of the highest order, and propensities of the lowest, meet alike with their appropriate aliment. All sorts of desires may be removed with a promptness that will suit the temper of the impatient, and an elegance, surpassing the conceptions of the fastidious. The most perfect articles, of every description, are constantly within the reach of one's hand, provided always that there is plenty of money in it; for the wants of a voluptuous city have caused the globe to be ransacked for the choicest productions of every country; the most *recherché* gems of nature and art are poured into her lap with luxurious profusion. Napoleon brought from his conquered cities the most celebrated works of the best masters, and made the Louvre a depot of *chef-d'œuvres*. While the senses are thus catered for to an extent and perfection unknown elsewhere, while the man of science and art, the lover of painting and poetry, sculpture and statuary, the gourmand and sensualist, realize all which their hearts can possibly desire, whether lofty or low; the votary of religion, the man of large heart, and expansive affections, of high and correct feelings also, finds the institutions of religion and charity, that kindle his ardent sympathies, and fill his soul with benevolent transport. None among them possess more interest for a philanthropist, than they which have for their object the care and education of those poor unfortunates, who have been deprived of any of the senses, so indispensable to the performance of the duties and labors of life, and, without which, man is in danger of forfeiting his rank, as lord of this lower world.

The Royal Institution for the Deaf and Dumb is one of the noble triumphs of modern times, and the Christian spirit, over a portion of the numerous ills "that flesh is heir to." I returned from a visit to it with great satisfaction, and augmented respect for my fellow-man. It is not in human power to impart the "gift of tongues," or the means of hearing the harmonious voices of creation, to those who have been denied the appropriate organs; but, as the water is made to run from the brazen hands of the giant of the fountains at Versailles, so words of happiness and comfort, peace and love, as well as the language of poetry and wit, brilliant and sparkling as their spray in the sun's rays, can be taught to flow from the fingers of the dumb. The tympanum of the closed ear may refuse to respond to sound;—no matter—the same blessed art conducts the bright electric current of thought along the opaque nerves to illuminate the darkness of the imprisoned intellect, and cause the heart to vibrate with the sharp alternations of grief and joy. Through these portals, thus opened, a communication is established between them and the outer world, and no longer, as in the case of the immortal bard of Paradise—

"Is wisdom at one entrance quite shut out."

This institution is one of the earliest, if not the very first of its kind, that ever existed. It originated in the capacious heart of the Abbé de L'Epée, a man without note, or wealth, or patronage. Like John Kryle, whose name is in danger of being eclipsed and forgotten, by the immortal splendors of the great poet's "Man of Ross," he did more with his narrow patrimony, than others have accomplished with their millions.

"Oh, say, what sums that generous hand supply?
What mines to swell that boundless charity?
Of debts and taxes, wife and children clear,
This man possessed—five hundred pounds a year.
Blush, grandeur, blush! proud courts, withdraw your blaze!
Ye little stars! hide your diminished rays."

This was the actual revenue of John Kryle; it was also very nearly that of this whole-souled Abbé. He was not indeed the inventor of the language of the mutes. That honor belongs to Pedro de Ponce, a benedictine monk. Even the system, he made use of, was soon superseded by his pupil Sicard. But the glory will always be his, of having given prominence to this particular expression of philanthropy, and, by his singular devotion to it of himself, and all that he possessed, of having caused it to become, what it now is, one of the most favored and interesting channels through which good men may pour their love, their intellect, and wealth. From his limited income of about five hundred pounds a year, he reserved one-seventh to himself, the rest he considered the patrimony of the deaf and dumb, to whom he so sacredly applied it, that in the rigorous winter of 1788, when he was in his seventy-fifth year, he denied himself fuel, rather than intrench on the fund he had destined them. His housekeeper seeing this, led into his apartment forty of his pupils, who besought him with tears to preserve himself for their sakes; but he would afterwards say in playing with his scholars, "I have wronged my children out of a hundred crowns." With these humble means he undertook, at the outset, to maintain forty deaf and dumb pupils, and educate them in reading, writing, grammar, and the reduction of the most metaphysical ideas to words. From this feeble commencement, generations since have almost literally *learnt to speak* his praise, and one hundred and fifty scholars, now belonging to the institution, bless his memory.

In 1785 this charity, attracting the royal attention, was, by the influence of Marie Antoinette, made a dependence of the government; whereupon the establishment was transferred to the Convent of Celestines, which had been suppressed. In 1790 the good Abbé died, and the Abbé Sicard succeeded him, and introduced an improved system of instruction. During the Revolution the Institution was removed to its present situation in the Rue St. Jacques. At present it contains one hundred and six male, and forty-eight female pupils; the number of gratuitous scholars is limited to eighty. The only requisites for reception into this class are satisfactory evidence of inability to pay for education, and certificates of age, baptism, vaccination, and the fact of being really deaf and dumb. None are admitted, but those between the ages of ten and fifteen. The sexes are separated, and all are taught during the prescribed period of six years, reading, writing, arithmetic, drawing, engraving, or some other art. Boarders pay nine hundred francs, or one hundred and eighty dollars nearly, a year.

The entire institution wears a most comfortable aspect. The buildings, if not new, are fresh in their appearance, and scrupulously neat. The chapel, a small, plain room, was the first apartment into which I was conducted. Behind the altar is a fine painting by Garnier, of Christ causing "the blind to see, the deaf to hear, and the dumb to speak." It is in reality a speaking picture. In this room was a painting, apparently placed there temporarily, representing the death of the Abbé L'Epée, surrounded by his unfortunate pupils. In the same edifice are a great many work-shops of various kinds, school-rooms, and other conveniences. In an upper story are the beds of the children, arranged around a large hall, neat, clean and comfortable. At the side is the wash-room, encircled by a kind of sink, with several cocks for drawing water. Each pupil has his towel hanging upon a nail, his glass and other accommodations, each his station at this species of wash-stand. This arrangement is vastly superior to that generally seen in the large boarding-schools.

In the first story are the dining-rooms. Long tables run the length of the room with benches on each side. The tables are formed of slabs of magnificent colored marble, supported on iron frames. Underneath a shelf, divided into partitions, contains the napkin and other furniture of each pupil. At the time of my visit, the children were at their sports; the girls in the beautiful garden in the rear, and the boys in various ways amusing themselves in the spacious court-yard.

Almost simultaneously with the foundation of the establishment for the deaf and dumb, the *Institution Royale des Aveugles* was erected. Seventeen hundred and ninety-one is the date of its origin through the benevolent exertions of M. Hauy, who obtained the royal approbation of Louis XVI. In 1843 the establishment was removed, from its former confined quarters, to the present convenient and splendid edifice, erected for its use. Over the grand entrance is a *bas-relief*, representing on one side Valentin Hauy, the first instructor, teaching his pupils; and on the other, a woman giving lessons to girls—Religion, in the centre, encourages both. The building is divided so as to accommodate the two sexes, and watered from the Artesian Well, heated by pipes, containing hot water, and lighted with a mixture of water, and a liquid extracted from wood. I trust that no one will suppose the water from the Artesian Well to be sufficiently hot to warm the house. The heat, even at the well itself, will always admit the contact of the hand to the metallic conductor. I make this explanation, because I saw a communication in a Boston print, proposing to water that city by a similar well, which, besides other objects of importance, was expected to furnish hot-baths, —a paper, which is calculated to mislead the public.

The well at Grenelle is seventeen hundred feet in depth, and was constructed, at immense cost, by constant labor, for seven years and two months. A proposition has been made to dig another in the Jardin des Plantes, three thousand feet deep. At this vast depth the water is computed to be *warm* enough for warm-baths, and for heating the wards of the hospitals in the *neighborhood*, being at from ninety-seven degrees to a hundred and four degrees Fahrenheit. The Bostonians will not be so foolish as to go to the immense expense of procuring water of a doubtful character, and of a temperature not sufficiently high for *hot*-baths, or even for warming the wards of the only hospital in the city proper, in that cold climate, while Spot or Long ponds are so near and so commodious. The *quantity* of water thus produced is worthy of attention. The orifice of the well is twenty-one and a half inches nearly, and seven inches nearly at the bottom, and yields, at the mouth, six hundred and sixty gallons per minute; at an elevation of one hundred and twelve feet—a height sufficient to carry the water into the highest story of the loftiest house in the city, the quantity is three hundred and sixteen gallons—scarcely sufficient for Boston, as it will be.

To return to the Blind Asylum, from which we have strayed, not from a want of eyes, but from turning them upon the future. The gardens, attached to the asylum, are very prettily arranged, so that the lot of the inmates seems still more unfortunate, when we reflect that they cannot see and admire them. Arrangements are there made for gymnastic exercises. Eighty boys and forty girls are constantly maintained in this institution at the public expense, whose education is completed in eight years. Boarders of all nations are also admitted into this philanthropic seminary, which is capable of containing three hundred pupils, who must be between the ages of eight and fifteen, and are required to produce certificates of birth, parents, good conduct and indigence, and their own freedom from idiocy and contagious diseases. M. Dufau is the director.

The dining, sleeping, and wash-rooms are similar to those in the institution for the Deaf and Dumb. One room is filled with seats, placed at regular intervals, and numbering in all perhaps thirty, and before each is put a tub, capable of containing two gallons, or more, pierced with a hole in the bottom. My curiosity was excited by this arrangement, and I was informed that the whole apparatus was designed to secure a regular and thorough washing of the feet.

It was the last of the month, when I visited the institution; it was then opened to the public, as usual, and I made the tour of the building, finding, however, but little difference between it and the admirable one at South Boston, Mass., under the excellent care of Dr. Howe. I inquired of some of the pupils, if they knew the Doctor, who has recently visited the European institutions. They replied, that they had not *seen*, but had heard of him. There are numerous school-rooms and work-shops; in the former of which are taught reading, writing, arithmetic, geography, &c. The advancement was not near so great as at South Boston. One said that he studied geometry, which is the highest branch. When I mentioned my friend Mr. Joseph Smith, and told them that he was in college with me, that he knew Latin, Greek, French, Geometry, Trigonometry, and was also a *Bachelier ès Lettres*, they were absolutely astonished. They never had heard of a blind person so well instructed, and made many interrogatories in regard to it.

The reading is the same as in the United States. The writing I thought different, but am not confident. Their letters are made by means of a tin frame, pierced with holes at regular distances, and in these they write; but not, as I think, at South Boston, by forming them in a shape, similar to the common ones in general use. Here they are made by mere pricks in the paper, the order and number of which constitue the letters. In this manner the writing is unintelligible to one not initiated in this species of hieroglyphics. I was told, that few of the pupils could write, so that the world could read, although they occasionally attempted to correspond thus with their friends. A good idea of geography was obtained by means of raised maps, and of arithmetic, by moveable figures in a frame.

The workshops afford employment for those who are educated, and teach the ignorant a method of gaining a livelihood. The younger scholars were employed in making a species of shoe from strips of the list of woolen cloth, wicker baskets of various sizes and shapes, carpeting of coarse straw, straw hats, and in seating chairs with the same material. Others were occupied in printing, and binding books, when made. Some of the more advanced were engaged in cabinet manufacture; and numerous articles of highly polished mahogany and oak attested their proficiency in this art. In another department are turning lathes, with which they formed boxes, cups, and vases, of wood and ivory, of great beauty. It was astonishing to see with what ability they use these sharp instruments, guiding them with perfect precision to the desired portion of the swift-revolving block before them, which, rough and shapeless at first, soon came forth smooth and graceful, as the marble from the sculptor's hands.

Hair brushes, mats, and rugs, worked in various colors, silk scarfs, and other similar articles, were displayed, as specimens of the skill of the female portion, who, though chattering and laughing, did not neglect all the while to keep their fingers also busy upon the work before them.

The most interesting portion of the exercises was a Concert, which was given in the early part of the afternoon. It commenced with a fragment of a symphony of Haydn, played by an orchestra of twenty-five instruments, directed by M. Gauthier. The most wonderful part of the performance was the exact time and precision, in which it was played. The leader, blind himself as the others, has lately published a treatise on the varieties of music, which is dedicated to Caraffa, and is said to have some merit. He certainly had drilled his pupils exceedingly well. There were solos for the flute and clarinet. A young girl sang several songs with good taste and execution. A girl of about eighteen played a fantasia on movements in the Domino Noir of Auber, and the overture of the Marquess of Brinvilliers by Caraffa finished the performance.

Any comparison between them and the orchestras that one hears in the various theatres and ball-rooms of this city, is out of the question. No competition with these finished performers, can of course be sustained; but a parallel may, with perfect propriety, be run between their exhibitions and the concerts given by the same class of persons at the Blind Asylum at South Boston. It is to be expected, however, that the pupils in a city, where the best music in the world is to be daily heard, and the most scientific and skilful masters exist in multitudes; where the airs which are heard in the streets, sung by the boor and the peasant, (for the French do not whistle,) are gems from the works of the great masters; and the morceaus from the operas of *Lucie de Lammermoor, I Puritani*, and a thousand other similar productions, are as common as Lucy Long, and others of that dingy class of songs in the United States, would surpass the American pupils, who are strangers to all these rare advantages. And so we find it, speaking in the general. The orchestral pieces would well compare with those, which lacerate the nice ear at the American theatres. The instruments are *always* in tune, the time is always correct. The chief deficiency is a deadness, which characterizes the whole. With the same caution that they walk, the blind also play. It seems, as if they had always a fear of going wrong. Our orchestras, on the contrary, take half of Crockett's motto only, go ahead without regarding whether they are right or not.

I have not a particular remembrance of the orchestra at South Boston, as it is some years ago since I visited the school, and do not even remember whether they have any. In the solo performances one can institute a parallel, at least, as far as the piano goes. Those on the flute and clarinet, the former an air from Berbiguer, with variations, were tolerably played. The fantasia on the piano, was, as I understood, by the best player of the school, and was a piece exhibiting some powers of execution. This I found to be much inferior to several of the piano-players at South Boston, especially Mr. J. Smith. Mistakes in striking wrong notes, loss of time, and the imperfect manner in which the runs were made, formed a striking contrast with the comparatively perfect style, in which the former has played to me much more difficult pieces. The organ playing in another room was not worth the comparison with that of Harvard University. In the songs, and a trio by three of the girls, they undoubtedly bore away the palm. The native taste of the country conspires against us. Two songs were exceedingly well done, and met with universal approbation. The young men were extravagantly delighted, especially Mons. Le Premier Violin, whose pleasure oozed out to the surface in the most expressive contortions of face and body.

From this hasty, but correct, account of this noble charity, one cannot fail to have a very high opinion of the management of a similar one at home. A rivalry with the old institutions of Europe, sustained and encouraged, as they are, by the patronage of government, and the influence of general local circumstances, is a great thing of itself. But when we are seen to come out of so severe an ordeal with honor, if not with laurels, we have a right to look with complacency on our plain republican establishments, and feel some pride in being compatriots with those generous men, who devote their wealth to the prevention and relief of human suffering. It may be, though I cannot think it, that no basso-relievos will perpetuate the lineaments of the benevolent individual, who gave a princely asylum to the unfortunate of his race, and that no rich-framed picture will preserve for the contemplation of posterity the celestial serenity of the closing scene, in

"The chamber, where the good man meets his fate;"

yet thousands of poor blind children, whose mental eyes have been opened by his bounty, will for ages to come, read the engraving on their hearts of the name of THOMAS HANDASYD PERKINS.

Who says the wealthy are not to be envied ? Such glorious examples of the proper use of the gifts of heaven, create every day a greater "lust for riches." To be the "Almoners of God" is the delightful prerogative of the opulent, and all must long for such a lot. Boston can proudly point to her Tuckerman and Channing, her Parker and Lawrences, with a score beside, who are creating for their beloved city, that sitteth on her triple hill, a name, *monumentum ære perennius*, which shall outlive her sumptuous palaces, and the granite shaft on Bunker Hill. My sheet is nearly finished; were it twice as large, I could fill it with recollections of the deeds of her citizens, not only on the battle-field, but in the widow's cottage, and the garret of the sick laborer, often performed with such secresy, that the beneficiaries, ignorant who their earthly benefactors are, can only pay their gratitude to the invisible Parent of all good, whom in this they resemble. Such being the character of my countrymen, there is no need of kings and princes to build hospitals for us, for they are the indigenous and spontaneous growth of the soil.

XXXVIII.

RACHEL—HER PERFORMANCE IN VIRGINIUS—EXECUTION BY THE GUILLOTINE—JARDIN DES PLANTES—GOVERNOR OF CONEY ISLAND—MILITARY MUSIC—THE KING—COUNT DE PARIS.

THE great tragic actress was a short time ago, when I saw her, the only performer of any eminence on the French stage. The close of her engagement was fast approaching, and it was necessary to go immediately, in order to witness a display of her great powers, before her departure for the provinces. With difficulty I obtained a ticket, four days previous to her appearance in the new tragedy of Virginius, written expressly for her, and which has created a furor, which seems unsusceptible of abatement. The fame, which she enjoys, I am convinced, now that I have seen her, is richly deserved, for Mademoiselle Rachel is a woman of no ordinary character. In person she is of medium height, well formed, but slight. Her face, though not homely, is neither a pleasant one, nor marked by any evident traces of uncommon genius. Her eyes are small and black, nose Jewish, mouth small and possessing that disagreeable expression, very often seen in the company of projecting chins. Her teeth, like those of most of the French, are white and regular, hair dark, complexion light, and extremely pallid. This was ascribed by an old gentleman near me to two causes; a disease of the lungs, under which it is feared she is laboring, and to an imperfect recovery from a late sickness, attendant on childbirth—a frequent accident among young French misses. Nature has not been lavish to her exterior, but she has made up for this parsimony by showering upon her most liberally the choicest gems of intellect.

The play of Virginius is very well written. The old hackneyed portions of the literal history are avoided, as much as possible, and new and natural incidents are with much felicity introduced. In the second act Appius, accused by the sister of the assassination of Icilius, declares it a falsehood The words *je le crois* pronounced by Virginie, is one of the best points in the whole play. This act closes with the interest so highly excited, that I had great fear of its flagging before the consummation. On the contrary, it constantly increased, and I sat half breathing, till exhausted, I gladly saw the fatal stroke, which finished the matter, and gave me an opportunity again to respire without restraint. Refraining from a critical analysis of her acting, I have merely mentioned, how I felt. The piece is of a very superior order, though possessing the ever recurring rhyme, so disagreeable to a foreign ear. I say nothing against this, because I consider the poetry, as well as the particular religious development of a nation, a sacred thing, to be respected by a stranger, who is unable, for obvious reasons, to appreciate the merits of either. Beside the great part of Virginie, those of Virginius, Appius and Fabius, a Roman senator, afford scope for the display of consummate genius.

From the distress of dramatic fiction, and the emotions caused by the "counterfeit presentment" of the Roman girl, let us turn to the world's actual tragedy,—a spectacle of terrible reality, where the emotions, if calmer, were yet stronger, and where a vastly larger company assembled to witness the awful catastrophe. It was an expiation made for the violation of the majesty of law, where the retributive death of the guilty closed the affecting scene, and the criminal suffered instead of the innocent. Having a great desire to see the far-famed guillotine, I had taken considerable pains to be forewarned of the first occasion, when it was expected "to perform." Great efforts are used to hinder the publicity of an execution, while, at the same time, those who desire to witness it, are not prevented. The criminal, when sentenced to death, is left in ignorance of the day of his dreadful doom. The public are also uninformed. His sentence is made known in the gazettes of the day, but he generally suffers three days afterwards. It is said, that neither the jailer, nor hangman, know the precise time, till the previous night, when they suddenly receive orders to erect the scaffold. The prisoner is sometimes reprieved, and this is for one month only. I had engaged a workman, who labors near the barrier St. Jaques—an unfrequented part of the city—to send me word, when he observed preparations going on in the square. The guillotine is always erected between eleven and twelve o'clock on the night previous to the execution.

I was therefore aroused by his messenger at six o'clock A. M. I made such good haste, that I was dressed and on the spot at twenty minutes past six—having arrived there by running all the way, about two miles. I found quite a crowd already assembled, but it being some time before the fatal hour, I had leisure to inspect the instrument minutely. On a platform erected four or five feet above the ground, supported by legs and surrounded by a railing, was a frame work rising to the height of between eight and ten feet. Those, who have witnessed the operation of a spiledriver, will conceive a very good idea of its action and appearance. The whole was painted red. The cutting instrument resembled a yankee hay-cutter, except that it was much larger. One corner, being placed lower down than the other, facilitated its operation. The axe, or knife, was fixed into a heavy block of metal, and drawn up nearly to the top of the frame. There it remained dull and sullen, like revenge awaiting its opportunity. Two companies of mounted municipal guards, and one of foot, with some twenty *Sergents de ville* kept the square open till eight o'clock, the fixed hour. In the meantime the crowd augmented, and the women began to be quite numerous. One old woman was peddling a biography of the victim, and another endeavoring to let her stands and chairs, both screaming their merchandize at the top of their voices.

At eight o'clock precisely came the guard of cavalry at a fast trot, surrounding the covered cart, which contained the prisoner and a priest. The vehicle was backed up to the scaffold, the door behind was opened, the priest descended, and after him the criminal. The latter mounted the scaffold, accompanied by two officers, with a firm step. He was clothed in his usual dress, a blouse of blue cloth, but without a hat. The hair was cut short, that it might form no impediment to his speedy exit from the world. The officers quickly drew the blouse over his head, and he stood exposed with naked shoulders. He then began to scream with the intention of making himself heard by the crowd, as I thought, but like many unaccustomed orators, ignorant how to use his voice. It might have been an ebullition of either anger or fear. In France the liberty of speech is not permitted, and he was interrupted by the officers, bending his neck, and placing his head in the groove, destined to receive it. The collar, which was intended to check the least movement, was adjusted, and like the weight in the spile-driver on our wharves, the axe was drawn up to the top by the officers. It was instantly disengaged, and dropped; the head, dissevered completely, fell into a basket, and this officer's duty being finished, he descended. Two minutes did not elapse from the time he arrived, till his head was detached from his body. Without the smallest loss of time it was tumbled into a vehicle, similar to a hay-cart, his body tipped in after it, a small guard escorted it beyond the barrier, and in five minutes from the entrance of the prisoner he was borne away, and the place left nearly vacant. The body was conveyed away for interment without the city for some hour or two, to be dug up again, and carried to the dissecting room for anatomical purposes.

There are many methods of leaving the world, but I cannot imagine one, which could be less painful and more agreeable, than this—if any method of dying may be styled so;—with the single, but rather unpleasant exception of the scaffold, none certainly could be more expeditious. How much superior to hanging, where the criminal struggles long and hard often from the ignorance or carelessness of the hangman! From the guillotine, no pain can possibly be experienced.

Amateurs can see the operation of this celebrated instrument on a dog for twenty francs, on giving notice of their desire to the officer a week in advance. Jack Ketches of other countries have free admittance.

In regard to the victim on this occasion, he most richly merited his doom. It is true, as you will surmise, he was sentenced for an *attempt* to murder. The French law is in this respect much better than our own, which does not hang, unless the homicide is actually committed. In this case, I think it best "to take the will for the deed." The deceased was a species of pedlar, and had a *boutique ambulant.* He had several times attempted his wife's life, by hanging cords with nooses attached in blind passages, and for many months daily threatened her with death, beating her cruelly when alone, and kicking her legs under the table, when any one was present. He frequently boasted of having killed a mistress some time previously. In short, his whole history, which I read upon the spot, so much incensed me against him, that, when I saw his wicked looking countenance, I forgot that a man was to be executed, and remembered only the horrid cruelty of the miscreant. I saw him beating the head of his defenceless wife with a hammer. I saw her skull fractured in two or three places. I saw her delirious at the Hotel Dieu.— I fancied her restored to health, to be sure, but with a debilitated constitution and an imperfect mind, and I looked forward impatiently for the time, when he should receive his just recompense. When his head and body were carelessly tumbled into a common cart, I thought not of the deed of horror, of which I had just been a spectator, and was scarcely conscious for several hours, that human life had been deliberately taken; even then, if I must confess it, without evidencing that tenderness of heart, and delicacy of sensibility, so beautiful, it is said, in a young man.

An individual, it is agreed, by all people of sense, may take life in necessary self-defence. What may be thus done by one may be done by another, and so society becomes invested with the same high prerogative, as a *dernier resource.* I do not acknowledge myself under any obligation to incur the trouble, expense and risk, of chaining a wild beast of a man, to keep him from preying on his fellow-men. The virtuous portion of the community is not bound, and sometimes is not able, to waste the fruits of its hard and honest labor, in building penitentiaries, in which the worthless, ay, and still dangerous existence of a demon, may be carefully prolonged, and his body clothed and fed—often much better than the poor, who are taxed to pay for it—till the culprit shall be pardoned by an impotent or corrupt executive, to vex the country again with his murders and conflagrations; or till a natural death shall do for the people, what they had not the firmness to do for themselves—rid them of an enormous and perilous burden, not imposed by any dictate of natural law.

I have been to-day for the twentieth time, to the Garden of Plants. I beg you will not think I intend to give a dry biographical sketch of every monkey, and bear and lion, that are to be seen there, to tell you how much the big elephant weighs, or how high is the cameleopard. No. The live specimens of almost every animal in the world, birds of every clime, and plants and shrubs of every temperature, I had often seen, but, to-day, I went into the cabinets. There I saw the same animals dead, but much better stuffed, than the living; fishes swimming in alcohol; some thousands of birds standing on one leg, and looking very sharply at one another, with glass eyes; among them looking equally sharp, a representative of the American Eagle—the "Governor of Coney Island," who says "I am the Governor of Coney Island—probably as well known, as any man in New-York. I've been to Europe fifteen times, Spain five, Russia six, England nine times, and traveled more in France, than any man, that ever lived. Poh! these things are nothing; in Rome they are twice as fine; I have just come from there; I am a wine merchant, that's why I travel so much. The Bible don't forbid selling wine, I am very temperate myself. Scarcely ever drink myself. The Bible forbids gluttony just as much, as it does wine bibbing;" and thus he went on without interruption, occasionally deigning to look over his spectacles, especially at some stones of different colors, which had papers attached to them, on which were written great long names with gold and silver after them. Really interesting were those names. Glass cases, with iron railings around, containing bits of paper with "Diamonds," "Topaz," "Emeralds," written on them, all in large letters, and by them little bits of glass of different colors.—I had written so far, when I received your letter, saying, that you "trusted, that I would give some description of the Garden of Plants." I read this deliberately over, and concluded, that, what is just said, would scarcely answer after such a requisition from another hemisphere. In a future letter, therefore, I must endeavor to give a more precise account. Rely upon having the statistics of the length of every monkey's tail, &c. &c.

Military music, though of an ordinary quality, as it generally is in America, still almost always inspires a degree of enthusiasm, even in hearts not particularly liable to melt. I think by this time you must have begun to suspect me of not a little fondness for "the heavenly maid." So far from denying the charge, I proceed to confess a most delightful flirtation, on a late occasion. It happened thus. The National Guard, and the troops of the line, went to the chateau of the Tuilleries to salute the king on his birth-day. The clergy had finished their errand, and the deputation marched out. The great court was then filled with all the drummers in Paris, who, together, some five hundred, made a tremendous *tapage* for some time. When they had finished, the band of each regiment marched up, one at a time, and played a piece of music of some minutes in length. This concert lasted nearly two hours, the king, queen, count de Paris, and others of the royal family, being all the time at the open windows, listening. The king wore the uniform of the National Guard. Each of the above mentioned bands consists of about thirty performers, and the music is very excellent. It is not wonderful that his majesty was seen to applaud. Such military music is not to be heard in every city of Europe. At sunset the cannon at the *Hôtel des Invalides* fired a royal salute for the monarch. The little applause which he received from the crowd was heart-sickening. I believe I felt more loyalty myself, than most of the persons there. The little count de Paris was more favorably regarded; and quite a perceptible murmur ran among the multitude on his appearance. Indeed, he did look very pretty with his little white glazed cap, velvet spencer, and white pants. I was standing near the entrance when he arrived. It is a curious sight for a republican to notice the parade made for a little child, whose name is a great deal longer than his body. First came a domestic in red and gold livery on horseback to announce his approach, and prepare the route. A carriage, drawn by four horses, and guided by two postilions in a livery of blue and silver, followed. Behind the carriage were two lackeys also in blue. After these came another servant in blue, too, whose duty it would, perhaps, be difficult to tell. The trumpets sounded, the guard saluted, the crowd made way, the carriage stopped at the door, the domestic opened it, and "parvus Iulus" and his mother, alighted;—"Parturiunt montes, nascitur,"—but my newborn loyalty blotted out the rest.

NOTE.—*From the guillotine no pain can be experienced.* The *Boston Daily Journal*, on publishing a considerable extract from this letter, soon after it appeared in the *Newark Daily*, discoursed in the following pleasant way:—

"Doctors differ—and in no case more widely than in this. While some learned physiologists are of opinion, that death by beheading is attended with less actual pain than any other manner of death, and is, therefore, the most *humane* mode of disembarrassing society of a villain; others contend, and adduce an equally formidable array of facts, to show that intense agony is experienced, after decollation, in both the head and the body; and death by the guillotine, so far from being easier than hanging, *is one of the most painful known!* No one has yet been able to describe the peculiar sensations, which attend the separation of the head from the body; but many curious facts have been collected, which may serve to throw some little, and but a little, light on the subject.

"It is related, that a professor of Physiology, at Genoa, who has made this interesting subject his particular study, states that 'having exposed two heads, a quarter of an hour after decollation, to a strong light, the eyelids closed suddenly. The tongue, which protruded from the lips, being pricked with a needle, was drawn back into the mouth, and the countenance expressed sudden pain.' The head of a criminal, named Tillier, being submitted to examination after the guillotine, the eyes turned in every direction, from whence he was called by name.

"Fontenelle declares, that he has frequently seen the heads of guillotined persons move their lips, as if they were uttering remonstrances against their cruel treatment. If this be so, there is nothing very incredible in the report, sometimes treated as fabulous, that when the executioner gave a blow on the face to Charlotte Corday, after the head was severed from the body, *the countenance expressed violent indignation!*

"In addition to the above facts—it may not be improper to add, that we have seen it stated, and *it may be true*, although, we must confess, we have not hitherto *altogether* credited it, that some galvanic experiments were once tried on the body of an habitual snuff-taker, after he had undergone the operation of being guillotined. On receiving the first shock, the headless trunk joined its thumb and fore-finger, and deliberately raised its right arm, as if in the act of taking its customary *pinch*—and seemed mush astonished and perplexed at finding *no nose* to receive its wonted tribute!

"But the most marvelous tale is told of Sir Kenelm Digby, who was beheaded for high treason, in 1606. After the head was struck off, the executioner proceeded, according to the barbarous usages of the day, to pluck the heart from his body, and, when he had done so, he held it up in full view of the numerous assemblages of people, who had gathered round the scaffold to witness the exhibition—and shouted with a loud voice, *This is the heart of a traitor!* Upon which the *head*, which was quietly resting on the scaffold, at the distance of a few feet, showed sundry signs of indignation, and, opening its mouth, audibly exclaimed, '*That is a lie!*'

"These anecdotes, however, do not prove that there is any thing very painful in undergoing the operation of beheading; and, if they can be credited, they show that the pain is not so intense as to affect the reasoning faculties. And fortunately for criminals condemned to decapitation, although unfortunately for some of the theorists, a case occurred some years ago, in Ticonderoga, N. Y., which settles the question, as far as the body is concerned, and proves that no sensations whatever can exist in the *body*, after its connection with the brain is dissolved. The case is a curious one, and we give it as related in the Boston Medical and Surgical Journal at the time:

"'E. D., aged fifty, a man of hale constitution and robust, in making an effort to scale a board fence, was suddenly precipitated backwards to the ground; striking first upon the superior and anterior portion of the head, which luxated the dentatus anteriorly on the third cervical vertebra. He was at length discovered, and taken in (as the patient said) after he had lain nearly an hour, in a condition perfectly bereft of voluntary motion; but, being present, I did not even suspect, that the power of sensation was also gone, until the patient (whose speech remained almost, or quite, perfect, and who was uncommonly loquacious at that time) said, did he not know to the contrary, he should think that he had no body. His flesh was then punctured, and sometimes deeply, even from the feet to the neck; but the patient gave no evidence of feeling, and, when interrogated, answered, that he felt nothing; "and," added he, "I never was more perfectly free from pain in my life;" but he remarked that he could not live, and accordingly sent for his family, twelve miles distant, and arranged all his various concerns in a perfectly sane manner.

"'The head was thrown back in such a position as to forbid his seeing his body. The pulse was much more sluggish, than natural. Respiration and speech but slightly affected, were gradually failing; but he could articulate distinctly, until within a few minutes of his death. All the senses of the head remained quite perfect to the last. He died forty-eight hours after the fall.

"'Repeated attempts were made to reduce the dislocation, but the transverse processes had become so interlocked, that every effort proved abortive. There was undoubtedly in this case, a perfect compression of the spinal marrow, which prevented the egress of nervous influence from the brain, while the pneumogastric nerve remained unembarrassed.'"

To this article, a correspondent of the Newark Daily replied in this strain.

"In quoting from the Paris letter the account of an execution by the guillotine, the Boston Journal appends a number of striking cases, not so much indeed to prove that pain accompanies the mode of execution mentioned, as to convey an impression, that sensation, and even intelligence, have, in several instances, survived the separation of the head from the body. They are all very much in point, as the lawyers say, but that of Sir Kenelm (Sir Everard?) Digby, who was beheaded in 1606 for being concerned in the famous, or rather infamous, Gunpowder Plot, is very remarkable, and I take leave to transcribe it. 'After the head was struck off, the executioner proceeded, according to the barbarous usages of the day, to pluck the heart from his body, and, when he had done so, he held it up in full view of the numerous assemblage of people, who had gathered around the scaffold to witness the exhibition—and shouted with a loud voice, *this is the heart of a traitor!* Upon which, the *head*, which was quietly resting on a scaffold at a distance of a few feet, showed sundry signs of indignation, and, opening its mouth, audibly exclaimed, ' *That is a lie!*'"

This piece of history shows conclusively the superiority of this mode of capital punishment, as it leaves the culprit afterwards perfectly free to take care of his posthumous reputation, which would be very convenient in all cases, but, more especially, when a man suffers by judgment of law. No other kind of death, by public execution or otherwise, secures this inestimable privilege.

But what I had in view in citing the case of Sir Everard, was this, that a great many years ago, alas! I am afraid to tell how many, I read a portion of history, corroborating in a remarkable manner the anecdote of the English knight. I do not now allude to that singular people, who are in the habit of carrying their heads under their arms, but to the conjuror in the Arabian Nights, who, in consequence of a failure, I don't recollect what, in some of his necromancy, was decollated by order, and in the very presence of the sultan. The head of the sorcerer, after separation from his body, sat up erect upon the floor, and with a mysterious expression of countenance, informed his highness, that, as he rather thought, he should have no further occasion for his books of magic, he would make a present of them to him; and, since he could not very well go to fetch them himself, if his highness would take the trouble to send for them, he would instruct him in their use. On being brought he told the sultan, it was first necessary for him to turn over every leaf in the books from the beginning to the end. But he found it was impossible to do this, as they stuck together, without often wetting his fingers at his mouth. This infused into the monarch's veins a subtle and virulent venom, as the books were poisoned, in consequence of which he died very soon in torture, overwhelmed with the taunts and curses of the decapitated head.

In this instance, the loss of a head seems so far from having been attended with pain, that, on the contrary, the insulted member enjoyed the pleasure of revenge, which it probably never would have done, if it had been suffered to remain upon the magician's shoulders. This is probably the most eligible situation for a head, but as it would appear from the authorities in the Journal, and elsewhere, the next best disposition that can be made of it, is to slice it off skilfully with the guillotine.

XXXIX.

THE GARDEN OF PLANTS—SCHOOL OF BOTANY—MENAGERIE—MEN AND MONKEYS—BENEFICIAL EFFECTS FROM ALCOHOL.

Of all the celebrated wonders, which adorn this capital, none are more worthy of attention and combine more beauty with real utility, than the far-famed *Jardin des Plantes.* Agreeably to your request, I proceed to give a cursory account of it, for a minute one could only be done with a statistical account of bird and beast. The name would lead one to suppose, that it was merely a large garden, as it indeed imports, remarkable for the taste displayed in the arrangement and great variety of trees, shrubs, and flowers, that adorn it. The botanist, who regards this portion only, will tell you so. The comparative anatomist will however show you its cabinets devoted to his favorite department, rich in the dry bones of this and past ages; in skulls and skeletons of all animals, and men of all nations. The geologist will expatiate with rapture on the collections of stones arranged in glass cases under glittering walls, which have not the least interest perhaps to you. The little child will point you to the big elephant and the roaring tigers. In short, every taste finds gratification here, and it is now my task to present such a camera obscura view, as you can obtain from a distance, with as little dullness as possible.

Such a collection of various rare and beautiful objects cannot be the work of a day; in fact, for ages since 1635, the world has been constantly contributing to make these cabinets perfect. In this year, at the solicitation of Herouard and Guy de la Brosse, the physicians of Louis XIII., this monarch founded this garden. In 1739 the immortal Buffon was appointed superintendent, who devoted himself with great energy to the advancement of its prosperity, till his death in 1788. The list of others of inferior reputation, but who by their zeal have aided in its advancement, is too long for this communication. The revolutionary spirit, which ravaged almost all the universities and public institutions, for various reasons respected this, and passed it by untouched. It suffered however very much from neglect, and deteriorated from the want of funds. Bonaparte with the same zeal, with which he gave himself to the embellishment of the city in general, and enhancing the beauty of its numerous galleries and public places, strove to repair the faults of the reign of Terror, and by the fruits of conquest filled it with most valuable objects. At his fall, some of these were returned, but many being retained, the garden on the whole was much the gainer. The magnificent cabinet of the Stadtholder was claimed, but its equivalent in duplicates only was returned. Several valuable jewels were reclaimed by the Pope, and books and objects of natural history returned to individuals, who were the original owners. The institution now flourishes with unaccustomed vigor. It is a favorite object of government, and large sums are annually devoted to increasing and beautifying its cabinets, and paying for the support of the numerous professors of various sciences attached to it. Many courses of lectures are delivered between the months of April and October, to which all have free admission.

The garden is situated in the extreme eastern part of the city on the banks of the Seine, separated from the river by the Quai Bernard. It is in close proximity to the immense hospice or almshouse *la Salpêtrière* spoken of in another letter. Several entrances give inlet from different directions to the student, the laborer, the curious, and the lover of pleasure. Its spacious walks are always thronged. Its different portions formed into divisions and appropriated to particular purposes. On the right is the menagerie; on the left specimens of noble forest trees. Before are the beds for small plants and the nurseries which contain the different varieties of medicinal, perennial, exotic and indigenous plants, shoots and flowers. A portion of this is separated from what is called the *school of botany,* to which is attached a small green-house. Near this is a green-house of large extent, built of cast iron, and warmed by steam. Its high walls are lofty enough to contain the largest tropical plants, of which there is a great variety. Every tree and plant within the *conservatoires* and in the open air has either the name attached to it, or a number; so that the curious can easily learn the character of every specimen. Among the most remarkable of the contents of the garden is a cedar of Lebanon, which was presented in 1734 by Collinson, an Englishman. It is now eleven feet in circumference at the base; also two Sicilian palms, twenty-five feet in height, which were given to Louis XIV. The total number of plants is twelve thousand.

The menagerie attracts the most attention; but it has suffered much from the prevalence of cold during the last winter, and many of the animals have died. The first public menagerie was formed at Versailles by Louis XIV. at the instigation of the Academy of Sciences, which increased in value till the revolution, when many of the animals were starved to death. In 1794 the remnant were removed to this place. Since the present reign this portion of the garden has been greatly extended, and constant additions are being made. It now forms a most picturesque appearance. The ground is divided by winding walks and light fences into enclosures, in which are the tame animals; such as various kinds of deer, the American bison, sheep, goats, zebras, camels, &c. These parks are of considerable extent, allowing exercise and pasturage upon the green grass, that carpets them. The animals are generally in pairs; and at this season their young offspring are often gamboling with them. In another place, are specimens of the ostrich from South America and Africa, whose fine plumage resembles more the feathers in the ladies' hats, than those on the meagre birds seen in our traveling menageries. In a still larger enclosure, in the form of a circle, with a pond in the centre, are the tropical and aquatic birds, whose shrill cries remind one of the descriptions of Robinson Crusoe. Here are the graceful swans, many varieties of ducks and geese, and the fish-eating birds of the warm latitudes. The empire of this enclosure has many claimants. The vain bird of Paradise spreads out its broad title, whenever he can find any one to pay him attention;

the strutting turkey-cock thinks his pretensions indisputable; and the valiant little bantam dares any one to doubt his superior claims. In spacious cages separated from the walk by an iron fence, which keeps the multitude from approaching within a distance of four feet, are confined lions, hyenas, leopards, anacondas of monstrous length, lizards and others. The *volerie* contains vultures, eagles, buzzards, hawks, in numerous varieties; singing birds and others of the gay plumage of foreign climes. A crowd is always collected round the large space, in which are kept the monkeys. The whole is covered with a wire roof, which keeps them from escaping; and in this spacious cage, almost free from restraint, they gambol, running from "pillar to post," now mounting to the summit, and a moment after sliding to the bottom by means of a pendent rope. Thus they sport day after day, screaming and quarreling, without wearying either themselves or the delighted spectators, who stand for hours together under the rays of a broiling sun in this unsheltered place. The *embryo man* is a decided and universal favorite among the Parisians, who have doubtless been recently more gratified with the reported discovery of a new family of monkeys, than if it had been another planet, or the northwest passage. In a building, denominated from its shape, the Rotunda, are confined a great many kinds of the more bulky animals, among which the lofty giraffe, and the ponderous elephant, are most conspicuous. Both these are extremely tame, and receive liberal donations of bread, with which the visitants are generally well supplied. In the company of the largest elephant are two tapirs, who share with her the muddy pond in the centre of the ground. The king is desirous of adding the American Indians, now on exhibition here by Mr. Catlin, to this collection; but the price is probably too high. The large Siberian and American bears are in sunken courts with cells, and afford much amusement to the public in climbing the dead tree, placed in the middle, catching the bread thrown to them, and playing with one another. Comprehensive as the menagerie is at present, additional room has been appropriated for its extension, and it will soon comprise a specimen of almost every rare creature in the world. Sea captains and travellers make frequent contributions; and it receives ample accessions from the gifts of foreign princes, and the munificence of the government.

In connection with the living animals we must not forget the dead, which are still more numerous, and form a Cabinet of Zoology, the most complete perhaps in the world, reckoning one hundred and fifty thousand specimens. The edifice appropriated to it is simple in its construction, three stories in height, and three hundred and ninety feet in length. At every step I perceive memorials of the renowned Baron Cuvier, according to whose system, the splendid contents are arranged. The collection of mammalia, representing five hundred species, is upwards of fifteen hundred in number. This receives constant additions from the death of members of the menagerie, as well as contributions from abroad. So perfectly are the animals preserved, that their appearance is equally fine with the live ones in the adjoining yard. The collection of birds, numbering over six thousand, is a sight that gratifies universally. Independently of any scientific view, their rich gaudy colors have a charm, which the most uneducated can appreciate. There they sit, day after day, a row of black, a row of blue, or any other color; their sleepless glass eyes always open and brilliant; their limbs never weary, though standing incessantly on one leg by the month together. From the ceiling are suspended turtles of every description, from individuals that weigh seven or eight hundred pounds, to the minutest samples, which squat on planks, floating on the sides of any of our muddy ponds. Lizards of every hue; frogs, professors of the art of natation, and snakes, whose method of progression, more wonderful than the locomotive, puzzled the wise Solomon to discover, are congregated here in infinite variety. Alcohol, which destroys the living man, preserves the defunct animals, to which use it is most properly applied. The department of fishes comprises duplicate specimens of twenty-five hundred species. Of the smaller, one is preserved in spirits, and the other dried and varnished.

Twenty-five thousand specimens compose the cabinet of articulated animals without vertebræ, and very numerous samples form that of the inarticulated animals. These two classes comprise all the insects and shells; among them are the varieties of the nautilus, tridachna, also the corals and sponge.

The whole collection is in the most perfect condition, enclosed in glass cases, and arranged in systematic order: so that one can distinctly trace the progressive grades in animated nature. Beginning with the sponge, the lowest order of animal organization, and proceeding from one specimen to another, link by link, we see the great chain of nature running through the monkey, baboon, hottentot, African, Asian, American Indian, and ending in the European, the noblest specimen of man. Does the chain stop there? On the contrary, must we not believe, with the Bible and Locke, that it traverses the shining order of spiritual beings, rank above rank, through the seraphic host, up to the Divinity himself!

The Cabinet of Comparative Anatomy is one of the most interesting, and, like the former, is infinitely indebted to the incessant exertions of Cuvier. The edifice, which contains it, is of older construction, than the others. At the great door of entrance are deposited two immense jaw bones of a whale. Many other specimens may be seen within, including the skeleton of a sea cow, brought by Capt. Parry from the North Pole. Skeletons of the human species from almost every nation in the world allow comparisons to be instituted between the varieties of the human animal; among the most curious of which is Bebe, the celebrated Polish dwarf, who lived to the age of eighty years. The valiant Gen. Tom Thumb, beats him, I hear, in littleness.

There are various anatomical preparations of muscles, brains, eyes, viscera, &c. of animals, disposed in such order, as makes comparison easy. An extensive collection of casts of the heads of many distinguished individuals possesses a rare interest to the craniologist. This Cabinet is the richest in existence, and deserves a particular description, without which nothing but a very feeble idea indeed can be imparted; but this is not the place for so minute an account, as would be necessary to make a sketch useful, or even intelligible.

To the illiterate, the universe seems full of mineral, vegetable, and animal creations, scattered abroad in fortuitous fragments, and involved in inextricable confusion. Such was once the condition of all knowledge, or rather ignorance, before science—at first the offspring, afterwards the guide of man—pronounced the mighty mandate, "Let there be light," and at once these *disjecta membra* hastened to arrange themselves in their natural and beautiful order, and a consistent whole sprang forth in just and grand proportions. The possibility of calling order out of all this chaos, and combining its confused elements into a system, must have appeared one of the absurdest of dreams. At this epoch of science, a sudden introduction to such a universe, though but in miniature, as the Garden of Plants presents, would have disclosed an absolutely new creation; in a revised edition it is true, and much amended and improved in accordance with the laws of science. And this microcosm cannot be viewed even now, without experiencing, as it were, a new revelation of the Creator, in the unexpected lights, that burst upon the spectator, of the relations and design of his omnipotent productions. What was before imagined to be a chaos of chance is proved to be the symmetry of a fixed purpose; and the infinite wisdom and power, which the infant or barbarous man could always behold and adore in the stellar and planetary worlds, are now found to pervade the whole, even the minutest, and, if I may say so, the most neglected portions of the works of God.

I pass over the superb collection of casts of the heads of distinguished and extraordinary persons, and other objects very reluctantly, with a simple mention, because there really seems no middle course between such a notice and a volume, which would be required for a description of any one of them.—To continue my sketch.

In a new building, which is not wanting in pretensions to architectural beauty, erected for the express purpose, is the *Mineralogical and Geological Gallery*, containing more than sixty thousand specimens. These are arranged in a long hall, running nearly the entire length of the structure, in cases on the walls, and in tables along the sides and in the centre, also upon the galleries which surround it. The specimens are all under glass, and labeled scientifically and popularly. The principal ornament of the room is an exquisitely chiseled statue of the immortal Cuvier, by David. He is represented in an erect position, clothed in the rich robes of the Royal Council of the University; his head is slightly bent, his face noble and full of thought. He holds a spheroid, in which is a considerable opening, emblematical of his profound researches into the bosom of the earth. By his side, on a slab, is the most eloquent of all inscriptions,—the titles of his literary and scientific works. Before this *chef d'œuvre* are two marble tables, inlaid with florentine mosaic, most beautifully executed—and a table, of which the top is a specimen of every marble of Spain, cut in a square, and forming an exquisite *patchwork*. This was a present from one of the kings of that country many years since to this museum. The galleries on one side contain all the known rocks and earths, geologically arranged; and on the other, the fossils which are found in them.

The mineralogical collection is divided into four grand classes, viz; earths, containing an acid; earthy substances or stones; inflammable materials, and metals. There are various kinds of spar; precious stones of all sorts, including diamonds of every color, without mentioning inferior ones, called rubies and emeralds, which are quite cast into the shade by the unrivalled brilliancy of the choicest of gems. Vases and crystals of colorless quartz, agate, chalcedony, lapis lazuli, &c., attract the unskilled eye. A large piece of native gold in nearly a pure state is displayed, which weighs sixteen and a quarter ounces. This cabinet was much improved by a donation made in 1825 by Charles X., of a fine collection, bought by the civil list for sixty thousand dollars. Additions are constantly made. Every encouragement is given to the student by the professors, who are assiduous in their efforts to explain and aid the stranger. In one of the galleries are specimens of the skeleton of the mammoth, found in the caves of Ohio, but much inferior to those to be seen at home; also of the elephants found in Siberia.

This is a very meagre account of the minerals, I confess; and, if there were room, which there is not, to draw even an outline of them, it would ill become me to attempt such a thing—me, who regard earths as good for nothing, but the nutrition of grain, cotton and grass; rock not as a chronometer to tell how old the world is, but, merely as furnishing a missile to throw at a dog, who disturbs my night's repose with baying at the moon, or a weapon to extinguish the caterwauling gentry, against whom I would willingly with all my might cast the choicest piece of granite in the whole cabinet, even if I knew that its felspar and mica had been coupled in their everlasting union more than one hundred thousand years ago. Cats however—and it is a remarkable fact—are never heard of in Paris, any more than fires. The reason of this must be left to the decision of the *Epicurean* philosopher, simply remarking, that this scarcity accounts for the leanness of the collection in that branch of natural history.

At one end of this last mentioned gallery, and in a manner continuous with it, is the *Botanical Gallery*, founded by Vaillant. The general herbal contains more than fifty thousand species. There are besides separate ones of New Holland, India, Egypt, and many more, which served as models for various works, as that of Humboldt and others. Here, too, are specimens of the woods, barks, roots and foliage of the trees of every climate. With this collection and the living specimen in the green houses, one, well studied, would never be at a loss to know the name of a plant, or its nature, if wandering alone in the forests of the tropics. Every wood is here found cut in different directions, thus showing its various appearances. The most curious of the whole are two cabinets, representing the fungus family, made in wax, and presented to the museum, one by Charles X., and the other by the Emperor of Austria. The former was executed by De Pinson, and is estimated at the value of four thousand dollars. Each specimen is exhibited in two views; one whole, the other cut lengthwise, showing its interior construction. The number of dried plants is more than three hundred and fifty thousand, and of grains, woods, and fruit, five thousand. The marble statue of Jussieu is of great beauty. The illustrious botanist is sculptured in the act of examining a flower, which he holds in his hand. It is a whole length, executed by Heral.

The library numbers thirty thousand volumes, and fifteen thousand pamphlets; but its most remarkable portion is its portfolios, ninety in number, which contain six thousand drawings, original designs, mostly upon vellum, figuring fruit and flowers. Nothing can exceed the wonderful beauty of this unrivalled collection, commenced in 1635, and valued now at more than four hundred thousand dollars.

I have thus run through the enumeration of a small part of what to *see alone* requires days, and many years to *know*. Sufficient has been said, perhaps, to give some idea of its greatness, its excellence and beauty.

XL.

HOPITAL DE LA PITIE—LISFRANC—VELPEAU—LOUIS—BOURGEOIS MARRIAGE AND WEDDING FESTIVITIES—THE TWO MILLINERS—A TENDER-HEARTED LAWYER.

BEHIND the *Jardin des Plantes* is the *Hôpital de la Pitié*, founded in 1612, formerly an asylum for orphan children; but since 1809 attached to the *Hotel Dieu*, and containing patients of all classes. It is most noticeable for being the one to which Lisfranc is attached. This great man, if talent can make one so, and one of the most skilful surgeons, not only in Paris, but the world, is now advanced in years. His fine head is crowned, like Mount Blanc, by the snows of many winters, his locks being perfectly blanched. His face is expanded and noble; his eyes black and gleaming; his nose slightly Roman; his mouth large. As a man he is said to be very rough and jockeyish, and as a public character, in which light only have I seen him, he is evidently a person of extremely high and irritable feelings. He is abundantly skilful in his operations, possessing at the same time an unerring judgment. In his lectures his tones of voice are most remarkable. After going on in a very low strain for a considerable time, so subdued indeed, that great effort is required to hear him at all, he bursts out all of a sudden, at the top of a most sonorous voice, making the walls ring again, waking all his sleepy listeners, and that too on a word, often the most unimportant of the whole sentence. With Velpeau he has often come into collision, in the Concours, and the battle has been desperately contested, victory sometimes bestowing her laurel on one, sometimes on the other. The consequence is, that a deadly animosity burns between them; and they give it vent, at the same time adding new fuel to the flame, by calling each other hard names with the rough side of their tongues. Velpeau, speaking of him in his public lectures, calls him "that man, more remarkable for the sound of his voice, than any thing he ever said." Lisfranc, who hears the remark from some kind friendly gossip, seizes the first occasion, that presents itself, to throw the arrow back. He almost shrieks with excitement; his arms are lifted above his head, or dashed upon the table before him; he takes huge pinches of snuff in rapid succession, while his countenance is contorted with anger; but

> "The foe invulnerable still
> Foils his wild rage by steady skill."

Rarely does Lisfranc begin a lecture without abusing his competitor; styling him, in revenge, "the little butcher of la Charité." This hatred, so virulent between these distinguished men, is not an uncommon occurrence in the city. It is one of the evils resulting from the system of Concours, to which I referred in one of my communications on the hospitals. A similar ill-will existed between the celebrated Dupuytren and Roux, which ceased only with the life of the former. They however restrained their bitter feelings more within their own bosoms, and never allowed an entire lecture to be polluted with such railing, as disgraces the two competitors of the present day. It is a melancholy sight to see two old people quarreling, and Time standing near, ready to cut the victor down. Gray hairs should exhibit the mellowness along with the decay of age; and can never hope to command respect, unless the fruit, as well as frost of time, is seen in their company.

I was delighted, as you may suppose, to see cousin Ellen and her husband here. "What! come for your health? it is perfectly ridiculous;" and I succeeded so well in convincing her of her *bonne santé*, that she had half a mind to forego the object of her journey, which was to consult the great Louis. His charge, however, is so moderate—only two dollars—that an interview with him was considered by us all to be advisable; for his decision is a *fiat*. Accordingly I called on him at his residence, *Rue de Ménars*, No. 8. While waiting for him in a handsomely furnished parlor, I turned over the books upon the table. Without exception, they were works of caricature. His intention must be, it would seem, to remove the trepidation and constraint, so natural to a patient, when approaching a person who is about to pronounce judgment, as it were, upon his chances of life. Thus restored to a balance in his feelings, the man of science can form a better opinion of his case. Will this fact account for the gayety of many celebrated medical men? With a similar design the celebrated painter, Stuart, was accustomed to interest his sitters with the enchantment of his varied conversation. This brought into action the distinctive lineaments of the face, and displayed their characters, if they had any. If they happened to possess none, which was often unfortunately the case, *tant pis* for the portrait,—no one could be more negligent of his work; but on the contrary, if they were men of rank, or women of beauty, the qualities, for which they were known, were certain to live and breathe upon the canvas.

"He would wait," he said, "upon the lady to-morrow morning, at half-past nine o'clock; or if she would prefer it, she might call upon him; the charge would be the same." An American would demand at least ten dollars for the same examination at his own office. Is the high price of medical knowledge in America, the consequence, as that of corn in Europe is, of the badness of the crop; or is it natural for the advice of the faculty to rise, like a balloon, in proportion to its want of weight?

Louis is the most eminent living physician, who attends to diseases of the chest, and his works are translated into every tongue. He has held various situations in the hospitals of the city; where his lectures attracted crowds of students. Now, however, he is placed at so great a distance from the Latin Quarter, that fewer attend his cliniques. Nevertheless, none consider that they have done all they ought to do, until they have availed themselves of the advantage of the *Hôpital Beaujon*.

Louis is tall and commanding in person, though somewhat stooping. His face, formerly quite full, is now rather thin, and deeply marked with thought; an expression which is increased by his use of spectacles—quite uncommon among the Paris physicians. His hair, formerly light, is now silvered over. His whole appearance is German—I do not know his country—and calculated to induce one to repose confidence in him at a glance.

The meeting took place; the important examination which had been sought at such a distance, so long, so anxiously, was over. "Madam, there is no disease of the lungs." Was it not worth the labor and expense of a voyage across the Atlantic? More than two years, that have elapsed since that day, have set the seal of truth on *our* opinion; pardon me the "our," if only to gratify my vanity in a momentary association of the two names.

The French woman trips through the gravities and even solemnities of life with the same flourish, and amount of forecast, that she would show in going through a waltz or polka. There are two sisters, young women, as they are called in Paris, of the ages of thirty-six and thirty-eight, whom their father at his death, some twenty years ago, left almost destitute. They have been industrious milliners all this time, and now possess five thousand dollars, it may be, between them. This, with the income of their business, enables them to live quite comfortably. They have their shop, and over it three or four other rooms, including a kitchen. Two of the apartments are let, and if the tenant is a foreigner, and can persuade the ladies to suffer him to take his dinner with them, it is accounted an enviable privilege; for it is not easy for a visitor from another country to get domiciliated in a French family.

One day the oldest of these girls discovered, that she had money enough to buy a husband, a luxury never to be had without a dowry. Matrimony here is commenced with the rule of Barter and Exchange, and ended with that of Tare and *Fret*. She selected an *avocat* by profession, but by practice a teacher, of about fifty years of age. On the second of this month they were legally married by a justice, and on the sixth remarried in the church of St. Sulpice. I saw the whole performance with all its fudge and mummery, and as such events are sure to fill a church, I don't see why it should not one of my pages. Each falling on both knees held a huge candle. This, to keep the white kid gloves from being soiled, had a band of velvet round it, the groom's of red color, the bride's of white. On the side of the candle towards the audience is stuck a coin given by the bridegroom for the purpose. This being visible to the company, a piece of gold, I think, will be often substituted for the five franc piece given on this occasion. The cunning originators of the rite were undoubtedly aware of our infirmity of ostentation. This money as well as five or ten francs for saying mass, as much more for the poor, the pay for chairs, and many other items, drops into the coffers of the church, which, like the crocodile's mouth, is always open. So exorbitant are these demands, extracted for a rapacious hierarchy by sacerdotal leeches, that the patience and pockets of the poor husband are pretty well exhausted.

After the ceremony was over, at half-past one o'clock, the invited guests numbering thirty-five, proceeded to the apartments of the bridegroom to discuss a breakfast. Infinite delays occasioned by losing the key to the wines, and other accidents, put it off to half-past four o'clock. It was almost time to dine, so we were not offended to remark, that it differed in other respects very little from a dinner. This done, all separated to make preparation for the evening ball. For this, the entire house of the two sisters was put in requisition, the lodger's rooms and all. Two rooms were used for dancing, the tenants' for card-playing, and so on. Most French floors are uncarpeted; as a compensation they are beautifully waxed, and therefore always in prime order for a dance. All furniture was removed, benches covered with velvet ranged along the sides, and mirrors, which are adored all over the kingdom, covered the walls.

At half-past nine o'clock the company began to assemble, and eighty or ninety were soon squeezed together, dancing, waltzing, and amusing themselves. If M. were here with her fastidious notions about waltzing, she would find herself in a minority of one; which is quite too small to transact business, and barely enough even in Congress to make a report. Frenchmen, so far from deeming one arm around the waist objectionable, find it easier to waltz with both hands of the cavalier clasped behind her. When I shall teach you on my return the polka, deux temps waltz and the French quadrilles, we will have famous dancing.

During the evening, some comic songs were sung; but,

whether I am not yet sufficiently a proficient in the idiom to enjoy the jokes, or whether there were none, I am not able to determine ; it is my suspicion, that the French laugh easily, especially at marriages. Refreshments of hot grog—a very weak beverage, and disagreeable to me—orgeats, orange and other waters, were passed around. Beside these, there were fruits, and nuts *glacé*, that is, covered with sugar, cakes of the most fragile character, very dry, and having the texture of the pith of a cornstalk. They use no such cake as ours.

Thus we went on till half after four, when the company dispersed ; some of whom had come from Rouen, ninety miles. The house being exceedingly discomposed, a few, who remained, sought repose till morning *a la mode Arabique*, with very slight regard to rank or sex, which are never spared by balls, in peace or war.

So merrily went the marriage bell. But when Virginie began to realize, in the solitary stillness of the succeeding evening, that Julie, the partner of her bed and business for so many happy years, had gone away, and left her companionless in her home, she could no longer support the thought, and fell into violent hysterics. It was then that Monsieur Dumas, to comfort her, used the memorable words, afterwards so laughed at among their connexions, " *Croyez bien, ma chere Virginie*," said he, wringing his hands, and crying aloud, with streaming eyes, "*Si vous êtes malade, je serais toujours a votre chevet.*" This little speech was reiterated by him so often and so dramatically, as to become a standing joke, which Virginie is no doubt cracking at this very hour. What gave it point was, that the moon, which lighted the guests to the marriage ball, was scarcely in the wane, before he persecuted her with a lawsuit—next to the inquisition, you know, in cruelty—about his wife's share of the partnership effects. This scandal should have been prevented, if possible, by Madame Dumas, since Virginie was the one whom Monsieur first addressed ; and she kindly passed him over to her sister, because she thought that, being the oldest, it was her birth-right to be married first.

It cannot be disguised that my little milliners were extravagant, especially the capricious Virginie. They had their apartments for retreat on Sundays, from the heats of summer, at Auteuil. I must admit, that their situation was delightful, near the Bois de Boulogne. Then, was it not extravagant for Virginie to pay a hundred dollars for a shawl, which she sometimes wore on such warm days, as to be obliged to carry it on her arm? What vanity! Worse still, she was the cause of the same folly in her sister. Become a madame now, the latter was not by any means to be outshone in dress. She therefore teazed her husband, till she got a shawl, of course more splendid still, which cost monsieur one hundred and twenty-five dollars. Ah! these milliners have a charming taste; and persuade their husbands that they prove it, in selecting them to pay their bills.

My letters lately, I perceive, are tending to excessive length. This propensity must, if possible, be checked. I shall, therefore, nip off the runners, as the vine-dressers do, when I can, and now give you an earnest of my sincerity.

XLI.

How do you like Paris?—Style of the buildings—Fires—Fire Department—Water—Common Sewers.

Questions can be asked in Europe as well as America; in France, as well as New England. We hear, very frequently, "How do you like France?" "How do you like Paris?" One must be pretty adroit to reply without nourishing or wounding national vanity. This is a very sensitive plant, but I suspect, it was not altogether unknown before the discovery of America; though from the figure it makes in some of the late collections, it might be thought never to have been met with in European soils. Ten to one, it was imported along with the wearers of French silks, or English broadcloths, lurking beneath them, like the original cotton seed among tea. Our own indigenous botany is very well known to consist of a more rugged and substantial growth, such as potatoes and Indian corn, which, especially the former, must be admitted to be quite an awkward emblem of our imputed national trait. For further information, the works of Mr. Dickens may be consulted, *passim*. He has treated this subject, as well as others, in such a natural and unexaggerated way, as to excite a wish, that he would devote his strikingly veracious talents to the *exact* sciences, or to an auto-biography, where of course the author would be precisely on a level with his subject, and like two distorting mirrors, would faithfully reflect each other.

Having been some time now in this metropolis, I am better able to answer these queries, than at first. A person should not be in a hurry to break silence on arriving in a country, whose manners and customs are different from his own. It is necessary to see correctly, before he can judge properly. I do not mean to assert, that knowledge of the world comes to a man like nutrition to the air plant—by absorption; but, if it is a fact, as it doubtless is, that all information reaches us, as Locke says, through the avenues of the senses, they ought to be kept in the very best repair, in order to transmit intelligence with accurate promptness without any special act of the will, as the iron rod constantly and quietly attracts the electric fluid from the surrounding atmosphere. The remembrance of home is apt to give a traveller the *mal de patrie*, and distemper his vision. Another thing—we know that *time* alters the focus of the eye; what is not so clearly perceived is, that *space* does the same. I do not now allude to the existence of a bias on the mind: because a person, warped by prejudice or interest, cannot possibly see things as they are, nor report them truly, if he could. A third matter to be mentioned,—though deemed quite superfluous by many—is, that the masculine property of common sense is useful to any observer. One may be versed in logic, a master of science, and of many tongues; but if easily deceived and cajoled, cheated in every article he buys, even at his own door at home; run away with by every pegasus, that some scheming adventurer and admirable rider causes to caracole before him, whether it be homœopathy, animal magnetism, or any other nag, he is not a man of common sense. It it is this Ithuriel attribute, that identifies the gross credulity of the Catholic with the like facility of implicit faith in other denominations; and which is not surprised to detect, beneath the coat and surplice, some of the same impurities, that stain the scapulary. A man who lacks the intuitions of common sense, cannot properly answer the question, What do you think of Paris? All have heard of the tourist in America, to whom a young farmer remarked in conversation, "my poor father is dead, and I am going to pull up stakes, and be off to the West." The traveler whipped out his memorandum, and noted for the information of his countrymen at home, that "when a father dies in the United States, they do not put down a grave stone as in England, but—they pull up stakes!" To regard a country as it deserves, all the senses of the best endowed have enough to do. When a blind person therefore talks of what he sees; a deaf one, like Miss Martineau, of what she hears, "*risum teneatis amici?*"

Let me begin an answer, then, to this Monsieur Tonson of a question—and it will very likely be deemed an apt illustration of the incompetency described. The city of Paris, properly speaking, referring by this to the buildings, is not adapted to strike an American visitor with pleasure. The gray stone, of which they are almost universally composed, has a sad air, even when new, that calls up two very disagreeable images, old age and decay. A few edifices are constructed of brick, as is part of the palace of Versailles. This is wanting, however, in that bright red color, which gives a look of cheerfulness to an American city. The prevailing hue is brown and sombre, with scarce a tinge of red. This circumstance may be owing to imperfect burning, but more probably to the character of its constituent clay. The *Place Royale*, where Henry II. was wounded in the eye by the Count de Montgommeri, is surrounded by structures of red brick, faced with stone copings, which is the only instance of the style in Paris, that I remember to have seen. Wooden buildings are so very rare, that I do not recollect a single specimen. The number of houses in the city is estimated at forty-five thousand.

Constructed of such materials, with walls and floors of some earthy substance, and roofs of tile or slate, fires kindle with great difficulty, and spread with much greater. Notwithstanding the close proximity of the buildings, one rarely or never communicates fire to another. The best proof of their rarity is the state of the fire-department. A distinct set of men, called *sapeurs pompiers* are devoted to the sole business of extinguishing fires; and no one else lends a hand, for he says, "it is none of my business." They are an extremely fine corps, and are educated in gymastics to prepare them for duty. Subjected to military discipline, and having a uniform, they are in truth but an order of soldiers, who, under this guise, are a formidable body, always prepared for an emergency. When a fire occurs, they hasten to the spot with pails, occasionally with an engine. They form a line and pass water from the nearest fountain, and throw it on the flames, or into the engine, which is unprovided with hose for suction. This is not its only deficiency; its power enables it to project water to a very inconsiderable height only. This feeble and inefficient machine resembles those used in America twenty or thirty years ago. The laws relating to fires are very good. If a man accidentally and carelessly sets his room on fire—for scarcely any body has an entire house to himself, if so, the law is the same—he not only suffers by losing his own property, but must pay all the damage it may do his neighbors, to whatever extent it may spread; rarely or never very far, indeed, as I have said, but sometimes a room or two. There is no accounting for tastes; for in America they burn over their prairies and cities, once every few years, in order to give them a fresh and lively growth. Thus they preserve their title to the name of the *New* World. Of this attribute of newness, they are so very fond, as to maintain it with proud tenacity in the names of some of their oldest States; and propagate the darling syllable, wherever a squatter has effected a lodgment, or a hunter spread his blanket for a night. But they cannot have antiquities in such a country, and the spires of their churches will never have time to grow so high, nor their houses so large, as in the Old World. This novelty is an expensive luxury.

I have observed, that I do not like Paris very well for its buildings of snuff color, so closely compacted, and its generally narrow and dirty streets. There are splendid exceptions; some buildings and some streets are as magnificent as can be. I am not speaking, however, of the aristocratic portion of the city, but of the *tout ensemble*.

Moreover, I do not love the water. When I set my foot upon the shore of Havre for the first time, after drinking the stale, stagnant water of the ship for thirty-six days, I longed for a draught of the sparkling element, the literal mountain dew. My first demand of the servant at the hotel was for this delicious beverage, which had played before my fancy for many a long day and night. I tasted it with eagerness, but so unsatisfactory was the result, that, concluding there was a mistake, I ordered him to get some more, and to be sure that it was fresh. The glass was brought again, but the fate of Tantalus was mine, with variations; I could not drink it. I did not know, till afterwards, that it had come from an aqueduct, and been strained and filtered, till the charcoal had deprived it of every particle of taste. Paris water is the same. The nature of the soil, consisting of rocky strata of great depth, has few springs, so that the inhabitants are driven to the Seine, or distant sources, made available by aqueducts. At the beginning of the fifteenth century there were but twelve public fountains, and a century later, in the reign of Francis I., only sixteen, supplying but one inch of water to a population of one hundred thousand. Allowing a quart a day to each inhabitant, an inch will supply about one thousand persons. What must have been the distress, when this quantity was distributed among three hundred times that number! Under Louis XIV. and XV., the city was principally supplied by a pump on the Pont Neuf, denominated the Samaritan, which yielded from thirty to eighty inches, according to the height of the river. The population was then, (1775,) six hundred thousand.

Government has, of late years, taken the matter in hand ; and the city now enjoys an abundant supply of this inestimable element from the Artesian Well at Grenelle, and numerous aqueducts, and from reservoirs filled with water, pumped up by steam engines from the Seine. This serves not only for drink and other necessary purposes, but supplies the numerous ornamental fountains, which are scattered over Paris, and feeds the *fontaines bornés*, or short fountains, at the corners of most of the streets, to the number of sixteen hundred, whose beneficent office it is to cleanse the gutters, and purify the city. Men appointed for the purpose daily turn the cocks attached to them. All the fountain water is purified by a large filter at the reservoirs; but, as it is not after all perfectly free from sediment, every house is commonly provided with another to complete the process. A few houses have water conducted to them by small pipes connected with the larger ones, but generally they depend on the water-carriers, of whom I have before spoken. It is stated, that five millions of francs are paid to these carriers annually.

The spare water flows off by the *Common Sewers*. These are now substantial and capacious. In former times, the city suffered very much for want of them; and, in 1370, the first was built. This was, from time to time, stopped up, and thus engendered many formidable diseases, from the odors and vapors which it emitted. Since 1829, they have attracted extraordinary attention, and are now about sixty miles in length, constructed in vaulted masonry, at a cost of eighteen millions of francs. Thus the purity of the city is accomplished, as far as possible; for the contents of the sewers are emptied into the Seine, and soon borne away by the rapid waves.

It will take another letter, I perceive, to finish a reply to the interrogatory, "How do you like Paris?"

XLII.

ANSWER TO "HOW DO YOU LIKE PARIS?" CONCLUDED—RELIGION—COOKERY—UTILITY OF A TEMPORARY RESIDENCE IN PARIS.

A CHILD can invent a question or objection in a few seconds, that will take a philosopher as many days to solve, and it is likely not complete it then. The embarrassment springs often from the magnitude, more than the intricacy of the subject. A ship of the line will answer the helm with the same certainty, as a Baltimore clipper, but demands more time and space to do it in. A replication to the interrogatory, "How do you like Paris," is the easiest thing in the world; but requires a little world of space and patience too. And so the danger is, that amid the rattle of words the answer may be lost, like conversation in a cotton mill. Many a speech has been spoilt, like the old continental money, because there was too much of it; and a sermon, that, in the first half hour, wound up the audience to the highest pitch, almost always in the last half one snaps the spring of patience, when they all run down again. But the failings of others will never teach us caution, though their success is pretty sure to tempt indiscretion.

When I say, as in my last letter, that I do not like the streets, houses and water of Paris, I have said all I am disposed to do in its disfavor. The condition of the edifices and streets is owing to their antiquity, and the habits of the country. Many of the latter are so very narrow, that a carriage can scarcely pass, and then there is great danger to the pedestrian, who is obliged to save himself by entering under the large *portes cochères*, which are on the side. The trouble and rush are greatly aggravated, when country vehicles attempt a passage. These are extremely large and cumbersome machines with wheels so immense, that one is ready to imagine them relics of a former age, when they were drawn by oxen, now called mastodons, and driven by giants.

Trivial matters there are, no doubt, to disturb the habits formed by early nurture in another world, which sometimes vex us. These must, of necessity, occur whithersoever we may go, even to a country much superior to our own. I have already in various letters described the streets and amusements of this city, and need not therefore say, that I have found the one very gratifying and diverting, and the other exceedingly beneficial and instructive. No one, who knows anything of the matter, questions the advantages of Paris to the student; and by common accord, the world proclaims her the Cyprus of the moderns.

The religion of the Parisians has been variously spoken of. Some indeed have even denied them any at all. But this is the disingenuous view of a bigot or enthusiast. To be rational we must discriminate. I should be sorry to believe, that the amiableness, civilization, refinement, beneficence and good nature, that are conspicuous in this vast population, were not to be put down to the credit of religion. Because such a supposition would deprive Christianity of its distinguishing criterion—" by its fruits ye shall know it;"—and rob it of the pre-eminent glory of being the parent of celestial charity with all its clustering virtues. The manner in which religion here may strike an inquirer, depends— and what does not?—on his *point de vue*. After being disgusted by the harsh dissensions, and useless, and often hurtful, discussions or rather wrangling, of which the fountain of truth in my own country is unhappily the subject, I will not say, the cause; after witnessing the minister-making and unmaking, church-member making and proselyting, that have been systematized into a branch of business there, the general tranquility, which pervades society in matters of this nature in Paris, is soothing to the feelings. I know the purity of the clergy has been called in question—yes, flippantly denied—but who shall place the foibles and transgressions of the various orders of the priesthood in Christendom in the scales, and nicely trim the balance? Those who administer at the holy altar are immaculate nowhere. The highest of them have fallen sadly, by means too of the old temptations, which assail our common nature, "the world, the flesh, and the devil." Is there any principle in the religious institution in France, which strengthens the power of the tempter, or weakens the motives to resistance? Perhaps there is, but it is difficult to decide. Indiscriminate surmise is easy; but the real truth is not obvious to a sojourner for a year; nor, I apprehend, even to a "native to the manner born," without a particular and thorough investigation. One thing is to be expected, that the branches of the mighty tree of religious organization, which overshadows Christendom, should bear the fruits of the original stock; degenerating, as it grows older, till a new one shall spring up from the true seed of the divine and blessed Sower.

Errors there doubtless are in the Roman Catholic code of morals and religion. Upon these it is not my present design—though it is my privilege as well as that of every freeman,—to touch. It will be time however to exert this unquestionable right, when we Protestants can better agree among ourselves, what those errors are. Yet I will venture to select one or two of so odious a character and dangerous a tendency, as to call for rebuke and opposition, wherever they appear. They are exclusiveness, and intolerance, or religious despotism; twins in their birth, and the inseparable Castor and Pollux of every hierarchy. Commencing by making men slaves to the church, they prepare them well for servitude to the civil power. Such a development of religion has been in different ages, now a tool, and now a master of the state; and will play the same parts again, whenever the tragedies, that have in times past dissolved whole countries in tears, shall be acted anew. A discouraging feature in the future prospect is, that, should this malignant power decline, or be extinguished, of which there is no symptom as I can see, it has provided for the preservation of its exclusiveness and infallibility by grafting those usurped prerogatives on offsets from itself, transplanted in all portions of the Christian soil.

Far be it from me to assert, that the people of Paris are less religious than those of America; but I can safely affirm, I believe, that they have vastly less hypocrisy. This base vice has been often said to pay an involuntary homage to the *value* of religion. Such precisely is my own opinion; and it is a tribute paid too by those, who are eminently competent to calculate its *advantage* to them exactly to a dollar. The *devote* in France, on the other hand, is sincere, and unremitted in the performance of the duties prescribed by her faith, not from popularity or fashion, but a feeling of its solemn obligation. There is certainly more freedom of opinion here; and the Christian can repose his confidence in any creed or dogma, without encountering the frown or stigma of his fellow-mortal. Uncharitable judgment and vehement denunciation are nevertheless a considerable mitigation of the inquisition and *auto da fé*; and matters, it is hoped, will grow better instead of worse. But all these favorable omens may possibly prove fallacious. The Church may be temporizing now, but only because it is weak. The time may come, when this still formidable power, confessedly militant, though often military, may claim its original temper with its strength. Then, becoming weary with her long dalliance with the infirmities of men, it is feared she will arise, like Achilles from the distaff, and put on her terrible armor again to conquer and avenge. There are no present indications of the advent of such an epoch, which can never come, till the sects and governments, which chequer and beautify the Christian world, and secure the independence of each other, shall succumb to the famous principle of unity, so dear to despotic power, civil and ecclesiastic.

The transition is natural and easy from the clergy to *good livings*, and so to cookery, the most agreeable of all the sciences, whose pleasant province it is to provide for a table, round which all communions and denominations agree to sit in peace, with liberty for each to indulge in whatever suits its respective taste. Its articles are swallowed with wonderfully less reserve than those of the Council of Trent, or even the far-famed Thirty-Nine themselves. And what shall I say of the *cuisine* of this nation, renowned as a frog-eating, ragout-making, wine-drinking race? Why, I must even re-echo the universal acclamation, and acknowledge for once, that the *vox populi* is also mine. One cannot always expect to masticate with a different taste, though he may see things in a different light from everybody else. I therefore cheerfully consent to the elevation of French cookery among the fine arts, and of French cooks to the dignity of professors. We pronounce the imitation in paste, which rivals the brilliancy of the diamond of Golconda, a splendid invention; but what honors are due to him, who extracts turtle soup from a calf's head, and converts, by his curious alchemy, a tough old ram, the *pater-familias* of many generations, into a delicate, plump saddle of venison!

> "Magister artis, ingeniique largitor
> Venter,"

O, worthy disciple of the matchless Careme! receive the thanks of the innumerable admirers of thy gastronomic skill, now living, and of multitudes yet unborn! And, thou long-necked, broad-backed, fin-flapping, amphibious cosmopolite! tumble about at thy ease in the briny floods, and sleep without anxiety on the sandy beaches. No Robinson Crusoes—at least from France—shall trip thy heels up, while perambulating the sea-shore, nor rob thee of thy precious body to pamper their own. The unsuspecting calf has usurped thy place of dignity at the head of the table; and thou livest but in name at——the head of the *restaurant* bills of fare. But is not that, seriously, a valuable art, which is able to transmute a very indifferent thing—as Lord Peter could a brown loaf into a leg of mutton—into an article of pleasure to the palate? There are those who affect to say, they feel not the slightest preference of one thing over another, provided only, the taste is the same—By stopping the nose, this identity of taste will be accomplished; for then all meats will have the same flavor, all oils the same delicacy, all wines the same *gout*. Even in such a case, the cook will not be useless; for his miraculous skill in overcoming difficulties will enable us to dispense with the fatiguing process of holding on to one's nasal extremity during a dinner of spoiled meat, and a withered salad dressed with whale oil. Glory, then, to the noble cook, the only true agrarian! He repudiates the maxim *Ex nihilo nihil fit*. The grand distinctive among men has ever been the difficulty or ease of obtaining a dinner. He has abolished this odious distinction, and proclaimed to our hunger-tormented race, that all mankind have leave to *dine*. The chiffonier may henceforth come to the table, and when that is the case, we know for a certainty that all men must really be free and equal.

Think of the immense productions of the earth, its millions of bushels, its millions of pounds; and the incredible magnitude and worth of the large portion of the whole, that must pass through the hands of the cook on their way to the millions of mouths, that stand perpetually open, like those of young birds, in expectation of receiving the customary dole. Two mighty processes are thus going on in the world without ceasing. Nature is exhausting her energies in producing; man his life in consuming; while the cook stands between them, the great organ of communication from one to the other.

What an important officer is he in the general dissemination of pleasure, and the protection of so much wealth from waste! Surely such an *artiste* must be welcomed with eagerness among my countrymen in the New World, where his drastic agency is so much needed. There—in the country, I mean,—at one season of the year, nothing appears upon the table from day to day but veal; at another, pork, honest and unaffected pork; while a third larger fraction of the twelvemonth is regaled with sheep and lamb, and lamb and sheep, till a considerable fleece is said to shoot out on the surface of the consumer's skin. What a metamorphosis would follow the advent of a Parisian *artiste* among these grand realities; one, who can erect a superstructure where there is no foundation, and of whose works the remark is as true, as it is of matter, that no particle of them is ever lost! The water, that boils his meats or vegetables, with the addition of a little maccaroni or vermicelli and proper spices, becomes good soup, such as—I shall be very happy to eat, when once more in New York. Health, too, is commonly the result of such cookery as this; for during my residence in this city, all the time in constant attendance on the sick, I have noticed extremely few cases of trouble arising from the food. The various dishes are so well prepared and cooked, that the digestive organs have not been overtaxed in their duty of assimilating them to the body. I have a strong inclination to say more on this subject, thus but slightly touched, and shall do so perhaps hereafter, in comparison with the modes of life in England.

"I hope your brother has not brought home any French puppyisms," wrote one lady to another. A thousand similar remarks are heard, insinuating the kind of importation, which is thought to be usually made by travelers from foreign parts. Are they true? I answer, they are true; and they are false.

They are *true* of those who, at home, are coxcombs, and only go abroad to gad, and gape, and gossip. When one of these is asked, "Have you visited the Coliseum?" he replies, "Don't remember, my good fellow; Frank pays the bills—is it a hotel in Paris?" The Forty Bale theory of South Carolina is quite as applicable to this case as to the tariff; for what a man brings home bears an exact proportion to the outfit. Thus, if the export is an American dandy, depend upon it the import will be a European fop.

"Cœlum non animum mutant, qui trans mare currunt."

These absurdities, more or less, apply to all who roam over Europe, without any earthly purpose whatever. Their clothes, their manners, their principles, their loyalty to their country even, hang very loosely on them, and they are ever ready to exchange them all at any time for those they become acquainted with on other soils. Persons of weak minds, or in the gristle of youth, are particularly liable to the novel influences that surround, and will be apt to overpower them, in strange but refined communities. A famous country, for the first time seen, is ever invested with the halo of romance; every object seems enlarged by the mist of ages, with which it is enveloped. The outside of old polished nations, which is sure to be the best, maintains, in the immature and inexperienced judgment of such people, an unequal comparison with the plainness, sometimes even coarseness of their birth-place. Beside, the mind is first drawn, like a child's eye, to the bright points, overlooking the imperfections, of all the rest of the prospect.

It is painful to observe how many good Americans have been converted into Europeans by being placed, when children, in a

French or German school, for education. At maturity, on returning to their natal soil, they feel themselves to be foreigners in every thing but the name, amid a population to which they are unable to assimilate themselves; and, till death, continue to be attached to ideas which first occupied their youthful minds. Their usefulness and honor have, in this way, been impaired by the mistaken means employed by their parents to increase them. The young American should be educated, and grow up in the midst of his countrymen, on whose generous fellow-feeling he is to repose for his happiness and future fame. Will parents weigh the acquisition of two or three modern tongues, and a few literary and scientific advantages, perhaps, of foreign institutions, against the morals, principles, felicity, and reputation of their offspring? Instead of this, all classes should receive their nurture, as much as possible, in the company of each other; and the glory of the New-England Common School arises from its tendency to prolong the literary and cordial fellowship of youth among all ranks in life. The farther this idea is carried, the better for the country.

But there are travelers, against whom the charge of coming back from a temporary residence in foreign society worse than they went, is *false*. These are such as have high and useful aims in visiting the old world; and go thither with some acquaintance with their own, and an understanding not so vacant as to admit the entrance of every novel notion. These will be likely to return laden with new acquisitions from the European market, and an intellectual capital augmented by foreign traffic. The utility of travel depends upon the traveler—

> "Some minds improve by travel; others, rather
> Resemble copper wire or brass,
> Which gets the narrower by going farther."

XLIII.

FLOWER MARKETS—THE PANTHEON—PAINTING BY GROS—TOMBS OF
VOLTAIRE, ROUSSEAU, LAGRANGE, AND OTHERS.

My malady proceeded from a wisdom tooth, which was filled in Boston, but still the work of decay went on. "You did not know I had been sick?" I suppose, it is because I did not tell you, then. How shockingly one bears sickness, whom Heaven has always blest with health! Compare him with the hopeless invalid. Uneasy, impatient, fretful, he fills the house with uproar, like a spoiled child, who bellows, if a handsome blue bottle does but just buzz near his thin ear. I have an excellent relative, who, good soul, is a little plethoric. Occasionally after trifling exercise in the sun of a New England summer, a slight *nose bleed* ensues. The entire household is up in arms. On the instant, men are mounted and on the road to the physician's dwelling. The horses need no guiding, for they know the way, and the doctor needs no message, when he sees the foaming steeds. The female portion of the household have a trying time. One seeks cold water; another a rusty *key* to thrust along his back, as if it was a case of *lock-jaw*. Red yarn is tied around his neck and wrists, and an amulet of blood stones sheds its selectest influence —and all this—because a man once died of epistaxis. The poor *invalid*, on the other hand, accustomed to lie upon a bed of suffering, for days, and months, and years, utters no complaint, though racked by pain. No ripple agitates the tranquillity of his home. A smile, though faint, must sometimes try to animate that pale face, like moonlight on sepulchral marble, so that cheerfulness shall not be entirely banished from the household.

But the sickest of all men, that have but a slight derangement, is the physician himself. His complaints always augur badly; he he is quick to perceive symptoms of organic disease. His accelerated pulse indicates a fever; a slight cold is sure to be an embryo consumption. He treats himself with trepidation. His constitution is peculiar; half the doses for other persons he deems sufficient for himself. He is then greatly alarmed, because the medicine is inert.; for, when medicine refuses to act, danger must be imminent. He does not remember the adage, equally applicable to his own profession as the legal, *The man who pleads his own cause, has a fool for a client.* If a physician is thus imbecile when at home, he is, in a foreign land, entitled to sincere compassion. Images of death hover round him—no friends to soothe his pains, or smooth his pillow. His little headache is an incipient brain fever; he shudders at the thought of dying in a strange country, away from all his beloved friends. He writes his last letters, makes his will, and—f—iddle-de-dee. I am not sick to-day. The horrible symptoms are all gone; visions of future happiness and joyous union with all that is dear come to occupy their places.

The flower markets are pretty and quite numerous. But a market here must not be thought to resemble the Quincy market in Boston—a large substantial structure of stone; nor one of wood even. No—many of them cannot even boast of such sheds as those of New York. Some indeed are built of stone, but without the smallest pretensions to elegance. Others are merely places, which may or may not have trees around them, and a small fountain in the middle, like the flower market in the *Cité*. Some of the marketmen, especially in the markets, which are held every day, as those for vegetables and others, protect themselves and their merchandise from the weathers' inclemencies by huge umbrellas of canvas, which screen them from sun and rain. The flowers themselves have no other shelter than the puny trees around the square. The air is loaded with odors from these charming productions of nature, offered in great profusion, variety and beauty; at least they are beautiful to me, pent up within gray old walls, encrusted with the smoke of centuries. With the same tact, which the French possess in such an eminent degree, so evident in the merest trifle, these flowers are disposed in captivating arrangements. The pots, which contain them, are unwashed; but a sheet of white paper envelops them and the plants also, except the foliage. The earth is hidden too, and so the bright blows and verdant leaves are strikingly displayed in contrast with the white ground relieving them.

It is astonishing what a quantity of them, such as the pansy, daisy, and little rose-bushes, are sold to the poor grisettes. Their prices, from the knowledge we have of the depth of the purses of these simple girls, must be very small. From her day's wages of twenty cents, she cannot possibly resist the desire to spend two of them for a pot of those sweet violets. She stands on one side looking at it from a distance. Presently she goes nearer; then takes the pot in her hand. Three beautiful violets fully blown; another just begins to show its purple colors; and see, under the green leaf at the side, there is another still. Two sous are not much; their absence will make a scanty dinner still more meagre, it is true, but when the meal is eaten, it is gone; but the delightful flowers will solace many a lonely hour. Such is her mental soliloquy, as her countenance plainly enough betrays: "*Voila jardinier!* here are your sous—and the flowers, yes—they are mine." And they go home with her, pressed to her heart, and tasting her rosy lips. Who would not be a violet? though to mount—mount—five flights of stairs are not enough? No, still a sixth. Ah! the lot of a violet may be pleasant, but that of the poor girl, its mistress, is not so enviable; her path is not always flowery.

I begin to flatter myself on having at last seen Paris. With my numberless visits to most of the principal places, and my views of it from the environs, I had considered, that the city had been pretty thoroughly explored; but it was necessary to make another trial yet. One of the most magnificent edifices had been from day to day postponed, merely because it could be viewed at any time. Now, however, the great *Pantheon* has been seen. In one respect it is much like the State House in Boston, for its beautiful dome is conspicuous from all portions of the city, and serves as a beacon for a wide circumference. The reason that the little dome of freedom's temple in Boston is so prominent to the citizen and sailor, consists in its situation. Placed on the summit of an eminence, and isolated by the smallness of the surrounding buildings, it possesses unusual elements for the fine display, which it really makes. It covers one of the lofty headlands of the bay with its crown, which however would long since have been broken, like that of Jack, (of the firm of Jack and Gill), had it adorned a human brow, instead of that of Beacon Hill.

But the Pantheon owes nothing to its situation. The whole city is built on nearly level ground. Real greatness is the only thing, that can cause one constituent part of it to rise above its neighbors. Two hundred and eighty two feet are the measure of the distance from the pavement to the top of the dome; and to this height an easy access is provided, if the visitor has the strength to ascend it, by four hundred and seventy five steps—a march which will give him a feeble notion of the punishment of the treadmill; on that account I entreat those legislators to try it, who are in favor of that description of exercise. When once this elevation is surmounted, an extensive prospect opens on the eye.— Every other building is below, though, with the cathedrals of St. Sulpice and St. Eustache, many still tower around. From no other place can a better idea be obtained of the actual magnitude of the city. In whatever direction one in the streets may turn, the same mass of hoary walls stops the view, save when here and there it is diversified by some conspicuous structure, for the number of which the city is remarkable; or by the gardens of the Tuilleries, or the Luxembourg. It is from this uniformity of structure and material, that Paris seems so much smaller than it really is. A single color paints it all. In our cities the red brick, white spires, and wooden buildings variously painted, not only render the *coup d'œil* bright and lively, but by their diversity communicate an impression of extent, which does not belong to them. This metropolis, viewed through a foggy atmosphere, might be taken by one not conversant with what he was observing, to be a heap of rocks; for it presents no object to correct the natural illusion; the steeples, chimneys, roofs, being all of stone.

He might indeed be puzzled, by numberless smoke jacks and funnels, two or three of which on an average spring from every chimney in the city, for I question whether one exists that does not smoke.

But to return to the pinnacle of the Pantheon, which we were not wise to leave perhaps after the labor of climbing to it—let us examine the interior; for, strange to say, we have got upon the top without entering the structure. The world looks gloriously from the temple, and the temple looks finely from the world. The approach is from dirty, narrow streets, whence we step into a spacious, well paved square around it. The buildings, that stood there, have been torn away to make it; and those, which are to be erected in their stead, must be formed with hollow fronts, that the square, agreeably to the laws of Irish perspective, may lie in the form of a ring. One only has yet been erected, the *Ecole de Droit.* From this, an excellent view may be had of the principal front. This is a magnificent portico, composed of twenty-two fluted columns, sixty-feet high and six in diameter, supporting a triangular pediment, one hundred and twelve feet broad, and twenty-two feet high, which is embellished with a large composition in relief by David;—France—a figure sixteen feet high—bestowing honors on her distinguished sons. Among them are Fenelon, Mirabeau, Voltaire, Rousseau, Lafayette and David the painter, on one side; on the other are soldiers of the republican and imperial armies, with Napoleon conspicuous at their head. At the feet of France, Liberty and History, seated, are weaving crowns to reward the great, and illustrate their names. In the corners, children are endeavoring to imitate the example, thus set them, and below is the inscription:

AUX GRANDS HOMMES LA PATRIE RECONNAISSANTE.

From the centre of the edifice rises the great dome, springing from a circular gallery, surrounded by thirty-two Corinthian pillars. Above this is a lantern, formerly surmounted by a ball and cross, which are to be replaced by a bronze statue of Immortality seventeen feet in height, a model of which is now in the temple. She stands with one hand open to record, and holding in the other a crown to reward, the deeds of the worthy. The whole elevation to the apex of the monument, will be *more than three hundred and twenty feet*. The dome, pillars and all, are of stone.

On entering the Pantheon we find within but a single room, which is in the form of a Greek cross, two hundred and eighty feet by two hundred and fifty-eight. Its superbly sculptured walls and ceiling, eighty feet in height, are supported by one hundred and thirty pillars with rich pedestals and cornices. All is white and pure within. From the shape of the structure the effect of the dome is greatly diminished. It cannot be seen, til one arrives at the centre, and almost breaks his neck in straining to get a sight of the magnificent painting by Gros, who received for it not only twenty thousand dollars, but the title of Baron from Charles X. It extends over three thousand two hundred and fifty-six square feet.

This edifice, when erected in 1764 by Louis XV, was intended for a church, and has been vacillating a long time between that and a hall of philosophy, till it has finally become a temple devoted to the reliques and glory of the illustrious dead. This picture therefore has a mingled design. The dome represents four groups, rendering homage to St. Genevieve, to whom the temple is dedicated. These groups are encircled by angels, each of whom is a king of France, who by the lustre of his reign, or the influence of his age, has created an epoch in the history of his country. There is a circle, in which are seen Louis XVI, Marie Antoinette, Louis XVII, and Madame Elizabeth, and in the centre the glory of Deity. The *pendentives* are allegorical pictures of France, Justice, Death and Glory embracing Napoleon. The picture in the dome can scarcely be seen distinctly from below, on account of the inconvenient but necessary position of the beholder; but one can mount to it almost, and then he may not only examine the painting well, but from an inner dome look down upon the people, who appear below like pigmies. People, who are seen from above or from beneath, always appear much smaller, than when they are at the same distance on a level, as the moon in the zenith shows scarce half as large, as the same satellite in the horizon, though not for the same reason. To give one an idea of the magnitude of this noble picture, a mosaic circle is placed immediately beneath, and of exactly the same span —thirty-three feet.

Under the temple are the tombs of those, whom France has pronounced worthy of a place of such distinction. The guide proceeds with a lantern through its chilly passages, and, as he comes to each monument, arranges his company, so that they can have an advantageous view, taps it with his cane, and after a suitable preparatory hawking and hemming, commences his history. But his recital is almost as unintelligible, as the reading of a well-fed priest. Voltaire and Rousseau have suffered the penalty of greatness in being torn from a quiet country Abbey, and the beautiful pleasure grounds of the Marquis de Girardin in the isle of Poplars. And now with others, who have the misfortune to be famous, their memories, like wild beasts in a menagerie, are "stirred up" by a chattering guide, and their merits canvassed by the stupid Englishman, who says "well that's did," —and the curious Yankee, who asks "have you ever saw?"— neither of whom have ever read a syllable of their writings, and know them only by the anathemas, which have been showered upon them.

Voltaire is also brought to more vivid recollection by a fine statue of Houdon's, which is placed on a niche near the mausoleum. Lagrange, the distinguished mathematician, reposes here. With all his mathematical powers he could not calculate the absurdities uttered over his tomb, multiplied, as they are, by the echo in a neighboring portion of these vaults. It seems to me that so fine an echo might be better employed, than in repeating the shouts and dialogues of the guides, and the blows inflicted by them with their canes upon a sounding board, which they have placed there for the purpose. The loud responses appeared to my imagination to issue from the bodies of the dead, complaining of the unseemly sacrilege. The ashes of about thirty eminent persons now find a resting place in these caverns, enclosed in marble cenotaphs or urns. The fickleness of the people is exhibited in their treatment of the remains of the illustrious Mirabeau, which in 1797 was buried with much pomp by the National Government, but were afterwards disinterred and banished from the precincts. Marat shared the same fate.

Near this building is a reservoir for water obtained from the Artesian Well almost a mile distant.

From the tone of several recent letters, I am afraid, you will think I am engaged in dead-letter writing. Whatever the fact may be, you may be assured that such is not my intention.

XLIV.

MINT—REPUGNANCE TO THE USE OF STEAM POWER BY GOVERNMENT—GREGORY XVI.—CABINET OF COINS—MEDALS—JEWELERS—ACADEMY OF INDUSTRY.

The *Mint* is a large building of three stories, situated on the bank of the Seine, and from its length makes a striking figure, when viewed from the opposite side of the river. Perhaps the arrangements of this institution are farther behind the age than any other similar one in Europe or America. Those who are acquainted with the workshops of the Mint in Philadelphia, pronounce them infinitely superior. Not only are these dark and dirty, but everything is inconvenient. It is almost impossible to believe, from the appearance of the utensils, that such fine coin, as is current in the kingdom, could be possibly produced; though it must be admitted to be still inferior in beauty to that of England, the United States, and several other countries. All the machines are worked by hand. From the foundery, where the bars are cut, I passed to the room, where they are flattened and punched—all by hand labor. The punching requires a force, which an unaccustomed arm is unable to command. In a succession of apartments the coin is baked, weighed, whitened, and struck. This concluding operation is executed now by means of a steam engine, placed here within six months. The various steps are explained, in a satisfactory manner, by the workmen, who oddly enough complain, without a single exception, *that it is very warm here*—French way of asking money!

This government are extremely slow in introducing steam into their works. They contend, that every steam engine makes paupers of all workmen, whose places it supplies; and, acting on this opinion, their work is consequently inferior to that of other nations. The Pope of Rome (Gregory XVI.) taking a similar view, has recently announced, that no railways shall be constructed in his dominions, as long as he shall live. The whole nation living on the money which drops from the pockets of strangers, his Holiness may be right; since few more perhaps would visit it, if the facilities for traveling were greater, while those who went would obviously spend less. Churchmen in that country, as well as our own, have a kind of *second sight*, where money is concerned. Besides, the Vatican has never been fond of new discoveries at any period, as Galileo found; and it ought not to be wondered at, if the courteous old gentleman of the keys and triple crown is a little nervous about the introduction of the exciting locomotive among his uneasy lieges. He knows it is a Protestant invention, as much as the terrible *Alliance;* and, like another sensible and prudent Laocoon, may exclaim, *Quicquid id est, timeo Danaos et dona ferentes.* And why should not the fiery *horse*, which has burnt the woods and barns along Long Island Sound, also scatter light, and perhaps flame, among the dwellers on the banks of the Tiber?

In another part of the building is the *Cabinet of Coins*—an immense collection. These are arranged in glass cases round the room, with statistics connected with them. The oldest is a French coin of Childebert I., of the date of 511. There are English and Spanish coins in great profusion. In a small case are shown the coins of America; those of the United States are very poor. With these there are a great number of *medals;* one of Charlemagne is a unique specimen of the time. Those of the Louises, Napoleon, and Louis Philippe, are almost innumerable. A case of some of the most common and recent ones is marked with the prices, at which they can be purchased. Many cases contain specimens of the medals and tokens of various societies and commercial companies. In an adjoining gallery are the dies, from which the coins and medals have been struck, since the reign of Charles VIII., and specimens of the various metals, used in coining, in their native states, as well as in their pure and refined form. The whole collection is richly worthy of a visit, and to the antiquarian must be a delightful treat, for it contains many relics, extremely valuable and rare.

Old coins are very easily obtained in France, abounding in the shops of the gatherers of old rubbish. Among them, a few days ago, was found a two sous piece, coined by Napoleon, but never circulated—a few only having been given to the ministers of the cabinet. It consists of a bit of silver, encircled by a ring of copper, raised above the interior, to save it from wearing away. Its price was fixed at five dollars. The admirable collection of *Roman* coins belonging to the government is deposited in the Bibliothèque Royale.

To this edifice, the jewelers, silver and goldsmiths, bring all their manufactures to be stamped. This is not performed, unless they possess a certain fineness; the gold must be of eighteen carets; ten per cent. is charged on the value of the gold. This proceeding insures the purchaser against deception in the quality of the wares. Having very little money in my pocket, I gazed upon these rich and glittering commodities with the same pleasurable emotions, as one may be supposed to feel on looking into the kitchen of the Astor House just before the dinner hour.

I will conclude this letter by telling you an anecdote of the great composer, Rossini, and the great cook, Careme. On second thought, I will omit this for the present, which, like Careme's own preserves, will not spoil by age, and give you a hasty sketch of an exhibition of works and industry made by the *Academy of Industry* of Paris, in the Orangerie of the Tuilleries. It was on a somewhat similar plan to those often seen in America, in Boston especially. The commodities however were entirely French in their character and uses. Our shows consist of instruments and works of utility with very often little pretension to beauty; such as labor-saving machines and substantial fabrics, designed for the use and consumption of working men. These, on the contrary, were all articles of luxury, fitted to the wants of the rich and voluptuous, and to a highly artificial condition of refinement. The cabinet work was of the most beautiful description; but such as would very far transcend the means of any person less than a peer at the least. Beside each different variety of wares sat a young girl, who displayed their uses, beauties and advantages; distributed cards to every one, who passed, of the makers' city address; and prospectuses of every novelty. I remarked to one who had the oversight of one of these pieces of furniture—a table of ebony, with a rich blue velvet top, inlaid with other woods,—"Ah!" said I, "that is for no one less than a little king." "*Au contraire*," was the answer, which, reinforced with a sweet smile, and bewitching words melted together—*tout à fait Française*—left one in doubt, whether to believe or not. "On the contrary," said she, "it is for any one that will buy it. It is a mere *cadeau*, only eight hundred francs." I could scarce refrain from telling her, that my *thrice great* grandfather made his own table of pine boards with hemlock legs, and on that he ate his frugal meal one hundred and fifty years ago in the wilderness of unexplored America, with a keener relish, than I fear the buyer of this gew-gaw will know. Passing by *suspender makers to the king*, my eye was caught by a *new method of roasting coffee*, which has such an operation upon the grain, as to preserve all its aroma, good taste and fine qualities without producing the least effect upon the nerves;" and the civil attendant took a quantity, and applied it to the noses of all that passed, giving each a card, and hoping he would come and try it. There was a musical instrument, called *Concertina Nouvel*, which I had never seen before; it was claimed by the seller as a new invention. But it is on the principle of the accordeon, in one respect at least, for like that it must swell and contract in order to be played. The tones are also not very unlike. This instrument is, however, much more extensive in its compass, comprehending five octaves. From a very hasty inspection I think it cannot be very different; the extraordinary compass it possesses may be attained by the method of playing it, which is on both ends. Its form is octagonal; but the keys are not arranged precisely in the same manner, and this serves to lend it an air of novelty. The price is from a hundred and fifty to a hundred and ninety francs, according to the case. It is capable of application to piano fortes and organs.

Near this was a vender of *hollow, flexible tubes.* These were of any length ; their use was to call to one in another room. For example, in the night a sick person has this cord passed round the baluster to an apartment below, and placed near the bed of the attendant there. If any thing is wanted, the sick man fixes a small whistle to his end of the cord, the blowing of which arouses the watcher. This friend, or servant being thus awakened, one has only to substitute the mouth instead of the whistle, and his wishes are at once communicated to him, who has his ear at the other end of the tube. The price is sixty cents a metre, or a little more than a yard.

Then we came to a little shaver, who showed off the beauties of a *traveling trunk*, which he had, with a volubility more amazing than his merchandize, which, my friend observed, must infallibly make his fortune. The glib-tongued youngster did not understand our language, but concluding with national politeness, that it was something fine, laughed heartily. The trunk was not an ill invention. It was provided with small slides, making the interior of any form desired ; allowing one to carry a bonnet, hat, or other dainty thing, without injury. Next was one, who had a *box of paste*, which, put upon a pair of white kid gloves, would instantaneously remove every particle of dirt without the least rubbing. Perhaps it might take gloves and all. *Bonbons* and *chocolate* of all varieties were there ; *meats* of every sort preserved for a voyage ; *turkeys* and *chickens*, that will retain all their original flavor after a lapse of twenty years.

The *lockmakers* to the king—there was a time, when a French king made his own locks—have, among other things a new invention, which has some utility. It is a small lock, which is put upon the outside, after the door of a room or house is locked, and completely closes the key hole, so that no one can enter by picking. There were *lamps* worse than ours at home, but highly praised ; *umbrellas* in canes, &c. in great numbers. *Sick chairs* of new invention are singular things to be shown by the prettiest girl in the room, who freely commented on all their advantages. *Painted fans*, of the most beautiful description, superior even to Dorr's, were exhibited ; and diamonds manufactured to order of such brilliancy, as to easily deceive, when not compared with the genuine monarch of the mine. This species of the gem is so much worn in France, even in a common company, that almost every body is connoisseur enough quickly to detect a counterfeit. Whoever wishes to cut a figure among Parisians with false stones will find it decidedly safest to do it with *small* ones; as in their estimation, when an ornament is not real, the less there is of it the better; a base coin of a low denomination only having any chance for currency. Some *cameos*, that I saw cut there, will not drop out of my memory for many a day.

But what seemed most extraordinary was the specimens of *hair work*. One piece comprised a *representation of 'Père la Chaise*, wonderfully true to nature, containing every monument, and all within a moderate compass. These were all standing independently of each other, without any mutual support. The willow trees, the common grass, the clover and the bouquets placed there by affection, were entirely of hair, and all perfect. I could read the names of the deceased upon the monuments, which a single hair appeared to write. Behind, moved by machinery, advanced the funeral of a soldier, who was carried on the shoulders of his compatriots. The whole was charming. And these clever people work on chains and bracelets equally well. Shall I not do my friends a favor by directing them to the great establishment Rue de la Coq, where all is done cheerfully and in a superior manner? I think so. If they can make even a cemetery attractive, what must be the consequence, when they exert the full power of their exquisite art upon the already beautiful sex? It is the plainest problem in the Rule of Three.

XLV.

CHAUMIERE—MONS. COSTE—FOURIERITES—LA DEMOCRATIE PACIFIQUE—
MONS. BUREAU AND FAMILY—FREDERIKA BREMER—PROF. LONGFELLOW—OBSERVATORY—MONS. ARAGO.

I HAVE just sent you letters by Dr. G. B. S., of Philadelphia. How I longed to be *en route* with them for New-York! As I returned, it began to blow; and in half a minute the rain descended in torrents, accompanied with thunder and lightning. I stopped under a *grande porte cochère*, to wait for the tempest to be over, and saw *au fond du cours*, a sign, on which was written *Bains*. I had no need of a bath, for the streets were immediately flooded, and neither pavement nor *trottoir* was to be seen. As, under existing circumstances, I did not wish to swim, there was absolutely no choice, but to remain where I was, and act upon the *statu quo*, until the deluge should subside, and the street be fordable. In the evening, feeling intolerably *ennuyeux*, I set off for the Chaumière, a ball-room, celebrated for its beauty and pleasures. Notwithstanding the glowing panegyrics I had heard on this popular resort, my raised anticipations were far surpassed. The place seemed, to my imagination, the fabled gardens of the genii. Nature and art conspired to captivate the senses. The air was redolent with sweet odors, stolen from lilacs, laburnums, acacias, and innumerable flowers; music intoxicated; lamps, brilliant with gas, reproduced, through elegantly cut shades, a softened day, and beauty, seen through the green leaves gracefully turning in fairy waltzes, colored the whole scene with the rose hues of sentiment and feeling. Even Juno, Venus, and other shining divinities, left their celestial abodes on this occasion, and from the numerous winding alleys, and buildings around, appeared to enjoy their evening's visit very much, if I could judge correctly by their radiant smiling faces. The dancers are grisettes and their cavaliers; the spectators are delegations from every class of people in Paris; and the English tongue is almost as common as the French.

I was surprised to see at these balls the great men of the city, the most distinguished in the fields of letters and science. I have already mentioned, as you may remember, that I attended the celebrated lectures of Mons. Coste, Professor at the College of France, on Embryology. He is soon to publish a work, which will be the completest on the subject, to the aid of which the Government has advanced twenty thousand francs. I was walking leisurely about, absorbing as much as possible of the joyousness, that was overflowing and running to waste everywhere, when accidentally I met him. He inquired, "if I intended to dance." My answer was, "I did; for a physician is not permitted to enjoy a rational pleasure in America; and I must seize the few dancing moments that are left me." "Come," said he, "I am looking for the extravagances;" and we found them easily, you may be sure. In one place a mulatto girl was floating in the waltz and polka with her Caucasian lover; and many a fair spectator would have assumed her yellow skin, could she have taken with it her fine silk dress and jaunty hat. An ample heel proved not the least impediment to superior waltzing. A young girl, in another quarter, herself without attractions, contrived to draw a crowd around the set where she was pirouetting, by the peculiar way she had of showing a fat, and not particularly taper——hose distender, for it just occurs to me, that American women have no *legs*. "Ah," says M. Coste, "the human specimen, in a state of perfect development, is a strange animal." For a moment, I fancied myself listening to his lecture at the college; but glancing at the speaker, and then at the surrounding audience, I was quickly reassured; the great lecturer and the learned *sage femmes* vanished; M. Coste and the beautiful grisettes happily reappeared, and the scene became brighter than ever for the shadow, that had passed. A little farther on, we found a throng applauding a young fellow, who, in the midst of the dance, was turning somersets, rolling wheels, and performing similar absurdities, without losing a note of the music. In another portion of these elegant gardens were the *Montagnes de Russe*. This is an inclined plane, elevated to the height of an ordinary three-story house, on which several railways were sunk. Ascending to the summit by winding-stairs, for five sous one may enter and go down the railway in a little chariot. From the steepness of the descent at the commencement, the velocity is very considerable. The wheels of the vehicle are checked at the end of the course by running into loose sand, and thus it is stopped. No danger can arise in enjoying this miniature avalanche, for a leather band confines the rider to the coach, and the sides, raised some eight inches, are nearly on a level with the small wheels; nevertheless, there is plenty of screaming among the fair adventurers.

The organ of the Fourierites in France is the newspaper, *La Democratie Pacifique*. In the saloon attached to the editor's department, there were assembled the other evening several of the most musical of the Phalansterians to hear some music composed by Mons. Prudent, one of the first Parisian piano players. He had sent his grand piano before, following it himself, as fast as a game-leg would allow; and gave us a delicious treat. Mons. Bureau, the musical editor, apprized me of the entertainment, as he had of similar ones before. Another part of the evening's amusement was a recitation of his works by a poor poet. In his rough grey coat he contrasted strongly with the smooth, sleek, well-dressed gentlemen in white kid gloves around him. Being a fine reader, he succeeded, by the aid of a sonorous voice, in passing off some rather indifferent rhymes, as their nice dresses did his genteel critics, for all that they were worth, and a little more perhaps. This man gets his living by vending the works of the Fourierites, and procuring subscribers for this newspaper, selling occasionally a copy of his poetry, which is all clear gain. He is called the apostle of the Phalansterians, and his face gives indication of considerable talent.

Having mentioned the name of Mons. Bureau, I must not omit to remark, how much he and his wife sympathized with Horace Greeley, of New York, on the burning of his office. His interesting family reminds me more of the United States than anything I have seen in France. Their history would adorn a tale, and is not entirely destitute of romance; but my account shall be concise. He was a captain of artillery; she a poor tailor's daughter. He was not handsome; she quite pretty and graceful. He not rich; she without a sou. If any one in the army marries, he is obliged to take a wife, who has a *dot* (dowry) equal to his rank, varying of course with his position. The private courts by sous; the officer by francs; there is a fixed price. Poor Mons. Bureau wished to marry the indigent working-girl. In doing this he forfeited his rank, espoused poverty, and now lives in more contentment, than any Frenchman I have ever seen. He does not pass, like them, all his days within a café; his home is too enticing. There he is surrounded with a charming educated wife, and three smiling boys and girls, precisely at the age when they are most pleasing. Madame occupied herself in putting them to bed one night, soon after my arrival, and the whole operation was so vividly home-like, that it went directly to my heart, and the memory of it warms it still.

I frequently spend a portion of an evening there, and read to her from Thiers' French Revolution, while she corrects my pronunciation. Once she consumed some time in trying to teach me the euphony of the word *usurpateur;* after all, it was left as an exercise for the next visit. When the throat gets husky, I give her, in return, a lesson in the polka, which she is anxious to acquire; and I have actually received compliments at a small party for the proficiency of my graceful pupil. She is naturally so *gentille*, and the *messieurs* so accustomed to applaud her waltzing, that they do it more, perhaps, from habit. Never mind. Mr. B. comes home in time to play for us. Then Mons. S. and his silent wife are frequent visitors. She is from the nobility, and gave her hand and purse to obtain the fine countenance and superior talents of her husband.

Just hear him talk of the *garde nationale*—the militia of the kingdom. He was formerly an officer of the army under Napoleon; but now a militia private; and his commanding officer is a butcher. Every inhabitant, who has any property to protect, is included in this corps, whose duties are no amusement. Clerks and all subordinates are excluded. It numbers in the city of Paris 55,000 men, splendidly equipped, and by frequent drills exceedingly effective. They are bound to fight, not for their "sacred honor," but solely for their "lives and fortunes." Every member, if not sick, at certain intervals, once in two months, perhaps, must don his uniform, shoulder his musket, and give the day to the service of his king and country. The man of ease or science—the poet, too, if one can be found, who possesses any property rights to secure, but those of *copy*—is forced to spend twelve hours of the day, warm or cold, wet or dry, marching and countermarching; eyes, now right, now left. Should business render it desirable, instead of these, his all-powerful commander may assign him, as a matter of favor, the agreeable duties of mounting guard and making the night patrols. There is no excuse whatever; he must go; the only privilege ever granted is an absence of three or four hours, on application to——the butcher! I have often, when attending the lectures of Ricord, Dubois, and Sechel, seen them in their uniforms, presenting a ridiculous contrast to their usual dress and duties. But, as you can't hear Monsieur's laughable exposition of the benefits of the *garde nationale*, listen to the beautiful song which Mons. Bureau is performing, and you will hear his words vocalized. It is called *Le Roitelet;* and the singer is giving you his own music. (This song will soon be published by Atwill, 201 Broadway, with English and French words, in his "Beauties of the Opera.") Mons. B. has composed and published many very sweet songs and waltzes. They are superior in my estimation to the generality of French romances, which seem to depend for their interest entirely upon the words, as the music is quite common-place.

Much of my happiness here springs from these charming people, whose kindness has greatly endeared them to me. I cannot give them fame, I know; but it is a pleasure to express my gratitude in these letters, some of which Madame B. has read, and say that the memory of the family, in whose bosom

I am welcomed, is a pressed flower, destined to be one of the sweetest *souvenirs* of my European visit.

The myriads of strangers, attracted to this city, are really marvelous. Not many evenings since, I chanced to have a seat at the Opera Comique by the side of a Swede of considerable intelligence, who spoke English with much fluency and ease. One cannot long converse with a countryman of Frederika Bremer, without mentioning a name, which, as a sort of middle term, makes mutual acquaintance of all her readers in the most distant lands. Such is the power of intellect and goodness in union with truth and nature, to draw unknown individuals, and even nations, towards each other. "Your translations," he asked; "from what language are they made? from the original?" I replied, "that I believed, they were almost wholly from the German; for I had a doubt, if there were a dozen persons in the Union, competent to translate a Swedish work at the period of the first publication of her interesting tales." "Ah," he answered, "I think they are not so rare, for I myself knew one of your countrymen at Stockholm, who was a very talented man, and so beautifully translated the exquisite *Children of the Lord's Supper* by Bishop Tegner. I have seldom seen better versions than those executed by Professor Longfellow. Ah, if he would translate the writings of Frederika, she would then obtain that credit in America, to which her works entitle her; at least it may not be too much to hope, that he might superintend one." "I should regret extremely," I rejoined, "that he should devote his time to the labor of translation, for we are in the constant hope of another work from him, sparkling with fresh gems of beauty, such as those so lavishly strewn in his exquisite Hyperion, which has a charm, like that of the Opera we are now witnessing, *La Syrène*, one of Auber's best."

At the extreme end of the garden of the Luxembourg, crossing the space, where the brave, though unfortunate Marshal Ney was shot in 1815, one comes to the Observatory, erected in 1672, in most respects after the designs of the celebrated astronomer, John Dominic de Cassini, who was summoned from Bologna for the purpose. The edifice is entirely of stone, neither wood nor iron entering at all into its construction. During later years, this building proving inconvenient, the astronomical observations have been made in one near it of smaller dimensions. In this is the meridian line, by which all French calculations are made. On the first floor of the main structure is a telescope twenty-two feet in length and twenty-two inches in diameter, which is however not now used. In this building are many other instruments of ancient and modern manufacture. Here is a *Bureau des Longitudes*, consisting of two geometricians, four astronomers, two navigators, and one geographer, with numerous assistants, who hold weekly meetings, and present an annual report to the king, which is published.

This edifice contains one of the most beautiful amphitheatres in the city, which is used for a lecture room by the renowned Arago, one of whose elementary works has recently been edited by Dr. Lardner, and published in New York. Eight hundred persons can be accommodated in this hall; and so eager is the desire to hear him, that it is filled with beautiful ladies and wise men long before the hour of commencing. The room is embellished with fine statues in marble of Newton and Herschel; busts of La Place and others; a painting of an appropriate allegory adorns the ceiling. The entrance of the philosopher was greeted with demonstrations of pleasure and honor, which are indeed the usual compliment to the popular lecturers in the various academies and schools. He is of large stature, and five feet ten or eleven inches in height. His head is bald upon the top, and elsewhere covered with long gray hair; and his capacious face betrays the vestiges of some sixty-five winters. All his features are large and coarse, and his black and sparkling eyes, which constitute the best feature he possesses, are overshadowed, and nearly buried, beneath shaggy brows covered with hair, once black, but now thick-sprinkled with autumnal frosts. His mouth would be remarkable, were it only for its uncommon size; but it absolutely engrosses the attention, as soon as it is observed how wonderfully it varies, and adapts its shape to every word that is uttered, displaying teeth yellow and *mummified* by years. No hair is suffered to remain upon his cheeks. In point of dress one might be tempted to call it *slouchy*, could such an epithet be thought of in connection with so distinguished a personage. His clothes are black, but have not any of the spruce, attractive look, that sometimes divests a widow's weeds of all their woe, and almost all their sadness. Those, on the contrary, of the great astronomer have an air of sincere sorrow; and, as there was no especial reason for it, probably it was for being no better than they were. This uncourtly toilet is rendered more conspicuous by his white cravat.

As a lecturer, M. Arago is plain and distinct in his articulation and explanations, so that even while calculating the distances of the moon and sun from the earth, he was so perspicuous, that a child could follow him with ease. In the first portion of his lecture, which was concerning winds and storms, his frequent citations of experiments made in the United States brought to my mind Professor Espy again lecturing at Harvard College; where the numerous collegians, who attended his course, complimented him by coming to a man, with open umbrellas over their heads. M. Arago, in common with the French generally, employs much gesticulation; and his performance, interspersed with frequent amusing allusions, elicited often repeated applause during its continuance of two hours.

The weather in Paris has been extremely unpleasant, generally cold with constantly recurring showers. Occasionally a day quite warm, by inducing a removal of some portion of one's clothing, exposes him to take cold from the chill, which is certain to succeed. The French assert, they never knew such unpleasant weather at this season; but the American residents affirm, that last year was just the same. The probability is, that very few of either have known what kind of weather it was any day they ever lived, and if they did, forgot it in a week.

XLVI.

HOPITAL DE BICETRE, AND ITS OCCUPANTS—THE MORGUE.

HALF a league from the barrier *D'Italie* is the *Hôpital de Bicêtre*, one of the most interesting of all the charities, with which Paris is adorned. The first building on this spot was the chateau, erected by John, bishop of Wincester, in 1204, and thence called after him Wincestre, which, twice altered in the lapse of ages to Bichestre, and Bicester, at length assumed the name of Bicêtre, by which it is now known. In 1632, Louis XIII. bought it, and and established there a military hospital for invalids. Louis XIV. annexed it to the *Hôpital de la Salpêtrière;* and it is now in all respects a similar establishment, except that it is entirely devoted to males, as the other is to females. It is an immense range bearing the scars of antiquity, though well preserved. In an architectural view, it is not so striking as the Salpêtrière, for it wants its grand church dome rising majestically from the centre of masses, which appear to be one entire structure.

This building is divided into five departments. First, the *reposans*, who are the servants of the various hospitals of the city. At a certain age they withdraw to this retirement, where a comfortable home is afforded them during the residue of their lives. Then come the infirm, who are at least eighty years of age—the oldest in the house having reached ninety-seven years. Persons, who have turned their three score years and ten, compose the third department. The fourth consists of the infirm poor, and those of all ages, who are infected with an incurable disease. A melancholy miscellany of insane, idiots, cretins and epileptics, constitutes the fifth and last department. The first four departments number four thousand persons; the fifth alone nearly nine hundred. The air of comfort, which surrounds these aged men, is grateful to a lover of humanity. There they are, with their locks of silver, seated around the courts and gardens, contented and happy, chatting together; or, if still pretty strong, pursuing the avocations of former days, and selling to visitors the products of the industry which amuses them; such as carved work, cocoa rings for napkins, pin-cases, little boxes, and other things. I noticed the table of one division set for dinner; and the pewter service, brilliant as silver, proved the care and neatness that pervaded their domestic economy. Four hundred persons sat at this board. The individual daily allowance is a portion of soup; one and a quarter pounds of bread, white and good, four ounces of meat for dinner, accompanied with some vegetable, a dessert of cheese, and a quarter of a pint of wine. To those over seventy years of age the quantity of *wine* is doubled; while they who have been thirty years in the house, receive a double allowance of *everything*. The cost of each is about eighteen cents a day, and the whole annual expense, one hundred and eighty thousand dollars. There are no private dormitories, but from twenty to a hundred sleep in a single room. When sick, they are transferred to the hospital, and receive every requisite attention.

It is the fifth division, however, that demands our deepest sympathies. Poor creatures! sunk below the level of humanity, wanting the faculty of reason, yet without possessing instinct, its substitute in brutes, they form the saddest spectacle, that can be presented to human eyes. Tenderly should they be cherished by human hearts. And well has that obligation been here redeemed. How soothing it is, even to the ordinary feelings of our nature, to behold the humane attention which is paid to them, though subject, as many are, to the most filthy and disgusting habits! Their dormitory is perfectly pure, and free from the least odor; the waxed floor reflects the face of the visitor; and the beds are scrupulously clean and neat. This ward is a model for all similar ones, that I have ever seen. The most faithful and unremitting labor alone could have accomplished this herculean task. The buildings appropriated to the lunatics are long and low, rising to a single story only. The most strenuous exertions are used to sustain them in complete order. The oaken floors of palaces cannot surpass the brilliancy of the daily waxed floors of these cells. Their food is little better than that of the other tenants of the hospital. I thought it strange that wine, which has more or less effect on the head even of a sane man, should be served to them at the rate of half a bottle a day—sufficient surely to plant

"A dagger in the heat-oppressed brain."

The patients are distributed into three divisions, each under the charge of a separate physician, who has nothing to say in regard to the treatment of the others. This distribution has no reference to distinction in the maladies of the patients. Each of these primary divisions is subdivided into three others with respect to their degree of tranquillity. Among the notabilities is an Albino, said to be eighty years of age. He is exceedingly active, and a living proof that this peculiar people are not necessarily short-lived.

The curative efforts vary from those in all other lunatic establishments in the city. Every motive is used to induce the patient to employ himself on something of his own free will. Many are consequently engaged in regular labor; some making hats of straw, others fancy baskets, and the like. In connection with the institution is a farm, where numbers are employed with distinguished advantage to the crops and their own health. There is an establishment upon it for the raising and fattening of swine, where every operation is performed by these invalids, in preparing them for the market, down to the moment of their quitting the yard, dressed and quartered. But this particular department I did not see. Some of the patients, whose health or tastes give them a preference for other employments, are provided with such as suit them.

Among the various means adopted for their improvement is the establishment of schools. The patients generally belong to the lower orders, which in France and through Europe indeed, are lamentably ignorant. Few know even how to read and write, which of course become the principal branches of instruction.

There have been some, though none are here at present, who have prosecuted more advanced studies. The walls of the school room are embellished with pictures drawn with a pen, like those which decorate the writing academies, so numerous in every city in America, to which oil paintings and other ornaments are added. This treatment, I am told, succeeds beyond expectation; but I do not know what was expected.

One ward is appropriated to those, whose minds habitually brood over plans of murder and arson; some were pointed out, who had killed a mother and a sister, and one who had murdered two men in a diligence. The friend who accompanied me began to ogle the door. The guardian, however, re-assured him by stating, that no attempt ever was made on the safety of visitors, nor even of the medical attendant, in his diurnal round, for they regarded them as beings endued with superior power, whom it would be idle to attack. It was the guardian himself, who was the object of all their persecution and vengeance. But on glancing at his muscular frame, I felt quite at ease on the score of his security. Yet notwithstanding his commanding presence, he frequently receives blows from their fists and wooden shoes. You must not suppose, however, that his strength is used in contending with his patients; it is, on the contrary, merely employed for their necessary restraint. In no lunatic asylum is a patient permitted to be struck.

There are not many objects of general interest connected with this establishment. A well of prodigious dimensions may, however be considered as one; said to be five hundred feet in depth, and fifteen feet in diameter. This statement seems extravagant; yet it is certainly immense; for the sound of water thrown into the awful abyss, requires a great length of time for its passage to the surface. It is worked by machinery, propelled by twenty-four insane men, and is but little used, as an aqueduct from the river now supplies the hospital with water.

Near the Pont St. Michel is situated a structure, which attracts the notice of every stranger visiting the city, in consequence of the publications of travelers; and yet it is a building possessing no interest in itself. Composed of stone, without pretension;

plain, and even insignificant; without a sign or flag, or anything else to distinguish it, every body would be in danger of overlooking one of the most extraordinary places in Paris, were it not for the number of people seen constantly entering, and soon returning from the enclosure. Following the multitude to-day, I entered a small room, divided into two parts by a glass partition, to which the company is prevented from making too near an approach by an iron railing. The crowd of dirty blouses, charcoal-men, washer-women, and hucksters of all sorts, is so great, that we are kept for some time at a little distance. A quantity of clothes is hanging on nails around the apartment; such as are near are of poor quality, an old cap, and the well worn garments of a man, having the appearance of being rough-dried, wrinkled, and much soiled. Beyond these, in the middle, hangs the apparel of a woman;—a pretty, open worked straw bonnet with a neat riband, a crape shawl, a dress of white cambric and body linen of fine texture; from all which the water is dripping. Still farther on, are male garments of costly materials, dabbled with blood.

The enormous straw hat, which has obstructed our view for a long time, is now attempting to retire, and we can begin to see through the glass—"Oh, horrors!" said my fair companion, "what an awful sight is this! 'Tis the Morgue!—the dreadful spot which I have shuddered to think of, and never wished to see.—Oh, let us go." I had seen enough myself, though a contemplation of so many hospitals, museums of anatomy and *abattoirs* had given me nerve, and I was not so easily disturbed, as my pale-faced friend; so we went out. Iron frames supporting inclined boards to the number of eight or ten were arranged round the room, into which we had looked. On these, directly underneath the collections of clothes, were outstretched the bodies of their wearers, stripped naked, with the exception of a slight covering of small size about the loins. Of these unfortunates, after inquiry, I obtained the following account.

The character of the first might be read without much difficulty in his red and bloated face, bearing indelible traces of the ravages of strong drink. He had been drawn from the Seine, into which he had thrown himself, or unintentionally fallen. The body had evidently remained some days in the river, and becoming thus putrescent, a constant shower of water was projected upon it from a cock, which was fixed above, as well as all the other inclined frames. The owner of the feminine apparel was a girl of twenty-two years, and more than commonly handsome. Her delicate features were as white as marble, contrasting strongly with her hair of jetty black, which fell in deranged, but luxuriant masses upon her beautiful shoulders and naked breasts. She had just been taken from the water, and there she lay in such sweet repose, that, but for the associations of the place, one might have imagined her a Nereid in placid slumber. The morning papers gave her name and history. She was not a goddess, but only a poor grisette, who earned a meagre subsistence by daily labor. She was employed in a shop to sell goods, and had lived in pleasant harmony with a young clerk in the same establishment many years. But latterly, it seems, he felt her charms to be less attractive, and, growing tired of her society, he had fomented a dispute on purpose to effect a separation; and so he left her to seek another companion. The poor girl, however, being not gifted with the same selfish facility, or heartless infidelity, found herself unable to support the estrangement, and sought a reconciliation. But in vain. Her false lover had accomplished his object, and, thus abandoned, she felt that the only way

"To bring repentance to her lover,
And wring his heart-strings, was to die."

A leap from the *Pont Neuf*, where the swift Seine runs most rapidly, and all was over.

The other body was a Spaniard from the West Indies. A long purse in Paris very shortly exhibits to view the terrible epitaph:

"Mene, Tekel, Upharsin."

but when the gambler puts his fingers into it, the catastrophe is too sudden to admit any premonition. Constant losses had nearly exhausted the ample funds of this unhappy youth, when one day, in the private apartment of a café, the report of a pistol was heard, and he was instantly found entirely dead, having his head shockingly mangled by this awful act of self-destruction.

To this building are conveyed the bodies of unknown persons, who meet with accidental or violent deaths. If not claimed by any friend, they remain three days, and then are interred at the public expense. The number thus annually brought is about three hundred, of which one-sixth only are females.

XLVII.

ROYAL LUNATIC HOSPITAL—DR. FOVILLE—PRICE OF BOARD—TREATMENT—CURIOUS PRACTICE IN A PART OF FRANCE—PYRAMIDAL HEADS—FLAT HEADS—BLOCKHEADS—ILL TREATMENT OF INFANTS—NEW JERSEY HOSPITAL FOR THE INSANE—DEPARTURE FROM PARIS.

YESTERDAY morning I heard a lecture on Insanity at *La Salpêtrière*, and this morning I went to the great Royal Lunatic Hospital at Charenton, about seven miles from Paris. By means of the omnibuses and early rising, I got there at nine A. M., and attended the visit of the physician, the celebrated Dr. Foville. This institution was founded in 1644 by the minister Sebastian Leblanc; subsequently converted to a boarding house by the Brothers of Charity, for the care of lunacy, and in 1797 changed again to a government establishment. It is most beautifully situated on the summit of an eminence, which commands an excellent prospect of the city, the Seine and the country around, now in the pride of its glory. The bank of the river, and a small island, which is a dependence of the hospital, are covered with trees of various descriptions, of which poplar, maple, and horse chestnut are the most common and conspicuous. The poplar is not here the same miserable ragged runt as in the United States. In its native soil, uninjured by the mild winters, it towers aloft a very handsome ornament to the landscape. It is said, with how much truth I cannot vouch, that those in America are all of the same sex, and reproduced by offsets mostly; and that, even when springing from the seed, like the races of mankind, they have deteriorated from want of "crossing," so essential among animals to the raising of a vigorous and healthy offspring.

The edifice itself, though but partially built, is a pattern of the kind. Some years ago a bill passed the Chamber of Deputies appropriating one million of dollars to its construction. More than one half has been finished at a cost of six hundred thousand dollars, which completes the accommodations for males; the females are still in the old building, soon destined to give place to one in correspondence with the male department. Dr. Foville, the physician, resides in the city, and makes four visits to the patients every week. There are a resident physician and apothecary beside, who have the charge in the meantime. Few men are better qualified than Dr. F., for the care of such an institution. An uncommon union of suitable qualities renders his superiority evident. In person he is of good size, and endowed with strong athletic powers. His countenance has a peculiar expression of gentleness, decision and reflection. Were we to notice his voice alone, so particularly sweet, soft and winning, we should be disposed to characterize him as a good-natured man, but deficient in firmness; but when one remarks his treatment of the patients, and his general conduct, it is easy to recognize his possession of that resolute determination, so indispensable to his office. In no situation perhaps are the scrapes and *congés* of a Frenchman so productive of real good, as in the management of the insane; the angry passions of the furious are calmed and softened by the deference which such manners habitually display. In going his rounds the doctor had some ten or twelve hundred bows to execute in the space of three hours. Thus polite to the patients, he certainly was not less so to myself and friend—Dr. Selden, of Norfolk, Virginia;—and from this visit we bore away with us not only a knowledge of the construction of the building—erected after the plan of the distinguished Esquirol—the method of classification and treatment of the patients; but many hints and ideas of value, which he communicated. As the feelings of patients might be sometimes injured by hearing observations made respecting them, he chiefly spoke in English, which he had at perfect command.

The patients are of three classes, who pay respectively thirteen hundred, nine hundred and seventy-five, and six hundred and fifty francs a year, including washing. Fuel, private servants, and incidentals swell that amount of course. The rooms, which those of the highest class occupy, are really very fine. They have a charming aspect, commanding the delightful view before alluded to, and are handsomely supplied with mirrors, clocks and other furniture. During the periods of exacerbation, no distinction is maintained in the classes; they are removed at once from their rooms to another department, where their noise would be heard only by those as furious as themselves. In the treatment of the patients, very little, if any, medicine is given; opiates and sedatives with extreme rarity. The cold douche is not an uncommon means of soothing the excited state into which they frequently relapse. The doctor in speaking of it expressed his opinion, that it was a remedy of great power, but—should be used with extraordinary care, and by no means so indiscriminately, as it is frequently done. Cold baths, and sponging the body with cold water, are often employed. As a means of confinement, the strait jacket is the principal. A treatment of kindness is now generally adopted throughout the world; rarely indeed do we hear at this day of murders or other outrages perpetrated by the insane. Take a sane person, plunge him in a dungeon, enveloped in filth and exposed to the inclemencies of the weather, load him with irons, throw him his victuals, as you would toss bones to a dog, and it would not be very marvelous if he should revenge his wrongs sometimes by deeds of violence as startling as any that have ever been committed by the crazy man. An instance of the powerful operation of kindness, on a disordered intellect is furnished in a young girl, not wanting grace or beauty, who in another institution killed two of her fellow-patients. She is calm and rational here, and needs only kind words and gentle management to render her, what she has become, an agreeable tenant of an apartment adorned in a style of costly luxury.

In this institution there is less apparent confinement, than in any similar one, that I have ever seen. The windows have none of those horrid looking iron bars, which characterise a prison. A grating of wire, nearly the size of a pipe stem, seemed designed more for the protection of the glass, than the security of a captive prisoner. The doors were open with few exceptions, and their clothes were in their rooms, so that they could take them, when they wished to promenade in the court below. Though one hundred and eighty persons were attached to the establishment having the care of the patients solely, without including the private servants, there was no symptom of surveillance. As a peculiarity in the practice of Dr. F., I noticed that he made no concealment of their malady, but conversed with them on the subject, as he would have done of any bodily disease. This I think much better, than the subterfuge and evasion so commonly resorted to for the concealment of the patient's complaint, which is sure, sooner or later to be discovered by him; and information, thus obtained, is likely to be productive of much detriment to the patient.

As we went round the long galleries, Dr. Foville pointed out to us several persons, whose heads were of a very peculiar form, more or less perfectly approaching the pyramidal; the face might represent the base, and the occiput the apex. Their foreheads were particularly flat and narrow. In reference to them he remarked, that this species of head was peculiar to a particular department of France, in the same manner as the flat-heads of the Indians are peculiar to one tribe. In this district more children die at an early age than in any other; the diseases being principally convulsions and other maladies, which depend on the health of the brain. More insane come from this, than from any other quarter of the kingdom, in proportion to the population; and finally, more cases of idiocy, epilepsy, and the like, than elsewhere What is the cause? Evidently the peculiar shape of the head, which pervades the people of that whole region, who all participate in this deformity, in a greater or less degree, without a single exception. So universal is it indeed, that some painters and sculptors, regarding it as the natural head of man, have drawn from this source their beau-ideal of beauty; and fixed upon the sloping shoulders of their Venuses and Apollos, heads gracefully rising in tapering pyramids.

An investigation of this extraordinary phenomenon has been made, and the cause discovered. The Flat-Head Indians are known to alter the form of their infants' heads by pressure on the skull, when its bones are in a more or less cartilaginous state, and not yet firmly united. From this fact it was suspected, that some such prank was practised on these children of France; and, sure enough, it has been found, that mothers and nurses have been employed for centuries in the wholesale business of driving mad, maiming, and murdering the children of a particular district. This enormity has been committed by putting a peculiar cap upon the heads of their tender offspring, and fastening it tightly there by means of a strong band; and this simple cord has killed its hundreds, and diseased an entire region!" With the Flat-Head Indians the pressure is in another direction, and may affect the intellect, while the nutritive organs are unimpaired. Dr. Foville mentions an autopsis made on one of these countrywomen, who had the venous circulation so impeded, that a large plexus was formed, for the accommodation of which a deep cavity was sunk in one of the lobes of the brain. So that from the silly ambition of improving the beautiful proportions of nature, men have succeeded in producing the valuable varieties of *pyramidal-heads, flat-heads*, and *block-heads*. In the meantime, the other sex have not been idle; but their abilities, it is well known, have been principally displayed, at least of late, at the other end of the human specimen.

And now what is the use of such a narration, which is not to be read by medical men? It appears to me, I confess, though probably in pure simplicity, to enclose the kernel of something capable of a fruitful application. In Yankee land the head is not thus hooped; the fact is granted; but—the body—is the body free to grow, as God designed it? The swath bound tightly round the body of the infant—does that do nothing? Are the internal organs left to their perfect development? Is the pressure on the liver nothing? How often do the helpless creatures vomit the healthy nourishment they swallowed just before! May not that be caused by pressure on the stomach? I have seen the liver of a woman marked with a deep furrow, plowed by the screw of the corset; cannot a similar mark be seen in the liver of a young child? Should any one deem these interrogatories foolish, pray do not impute the folly to Dr. Foville; he is entirely innocent, for they are none of his. One thing is certain—no injury can be done by guarding against tight bandages on the flexible, half-ossified body of the young child.

The patients are resolved into three classes; the most turbulent, the comparatively quiet, and the convalescent. There are also rooms, where some in intermediate stages are temporarily placed on trial. One young man from the West India Islands, entirely nude, was bouncing about a room, whose floor was covered with straw. He was a recent inmate. In another was a man, who came from the country to bring a neighbor just attacked. He was returning homeward with his companion in a state of excessive excitability; but before he reached his house was seized himself in a similar way, and the same manacles, which he had put upon his friend, were fastened on himself.

Notwithstanding the excellent accommodations, which are here afforded; the healthy situation of the hospital; its real beauty, with the high reputation of its physician, I was informed, that few of the nobility or rich bourgeois were sent hither, but that private establishments were preferred, where high charges were thought to guaranty superior care and attention. For myself I must acknowledge, that I never saw in any similar institution so many advantages combined. Of the beauty of the situation I cannot say too much, though at the hazard of frequent repetition; it is indeed unrivalled, and with the sanguine aspirations of a life just commencing, I can say from my heart, that here I should be extremely happy to spend my days.

The accommodations are now sufficient for five hundred and fifty patients; the future buildings will in some degree enlarge them; beside, one wing, having been recently finished, is not yet occupied. I observe by your Daily Advertiser, that New Jersey intends shortly to build an Insane Hospital within her borders. Let not, I pray, the Hospital at Charenton, constructed from the plan of the greatest man, who has ever been engaged in the treatment of these unfortunates, be overlooked or disregarded. At any rate whatever else is neglected, it is to be hoped, that the *form* of this edifice will be adopted—a building of a single story. This will necessarily occupy a greater extent of ground; but it will create numerous courts between its walls, allowing free exercise to the patients in apparent liberty under the trees, which should be planted there. To crown the enterprise with success, may the State be so fortunate as to secure for a superintendent a learned and gentlemanly—in short another Dr. Foville! Without a competent physician, the State will, after all, have only turned some thousands of dollars into stone and mortar.

This is my last letter from Paris, which I leave with emotions of sadness, in two hours for London, through Holland and Belgium, by Switzerland and the Rhine. A month or more probably will be consumed upon the way, of which I will attempt some hurried sketches taken on the wing.

And now I must take a reluctant leave of thee, *ma belle France*. I did not think, when I came among thy people eight short months ago, alone and friendless, that it would ever give me such a pang to part. But they have twisted themselves around and within my heart, and I have begun, I feel, to shoot out radicles of affection, which are fast rooting me to thy beautiful country. Farewell to the land of the apple, the grape, and the olive. For these, and thy mild skies, thou hast a name, and others may admire thee. But I love thee for thy great and famous men, thy refined and lovely women, and the many dear friends; that I have no sooner found, than I must lose forever. Alas, that is a melancholy word to say, and wraps up a serious and momentous thought. Yes—we shall never meet again. The scenes in which we have mingled with such delight the past few bright months, will be repeated here another year; but we shall no more see them together. In two hours I depart in the diligence for Geneva, and shall travel several days and nights, without intermission but for the usual meals. Adieu, then! my heart beats tumultuously for all, who have been so kind to me, and I try to articulate—Farewell!

> "But wherefore could not I pronounce Farewell?
> I had most cause to bless them, and yet Farewell
> Stuck in my throat."

Paris exists to me now only in the memory. That city of the world, and all that it contains to captivate the antiquarian, or philanthropist, the man of letters or of taste, has vanished, for aught I know, into some such stuff as dreams, or the bodiless spirits of the air, are made of. But the acquisitions I have made, and the pleasures I have enjoyed, I cannot be deprived of—they are yet mine. How great these are, it does not become me to assert; but it will not be deemed assuming to observe, that few days passed away, when nothing new or curious was seen. No grand celebrity scarcely has been omitted, of which I am aware, except the catacombs, and the tomb of Napoleon, now in the process of erection. The reasons assigned for refusing the admission of the public to the former, are various; the principal of which are, that their lives would be at hazard from a possible downfall of the roof; and also, that gunpowder might be introduced underneath the city, and jeopard its safety, if not existence. Yet, though the pen may describe these wonders with more or less of vividness, it is a personal inspection only, which can set the living attributes of reality before you. Our country is so wanting in those things, of which Paris is so abundantly productive, that a narrator is seriously embarrassed to find objects of comparison.

Paris is left behind, and the friends I made there can never more be seen by me; but while l live, their sensitive hearts, their sweet and fascinating manners, and their tears so freely shed at parting, will be nursed like tropic flowers in my warm memory, flinging their bright colors and perfume over many a wintry day, that will doubtless overtake me. In a world of perpetual change, absence, like death, will embalm these summer friendships, and preserve them forevermore the same. My worthy hostess, good soul, with a kindly disposition, but wayward as the wind, was at the starting place to see me off. She brought with her a bouquet, composed of a rose bud surrounded by forget-me-nots—her own gift; and another from her neighbor, which was a bunch of *pensez-a-moi* with a simple rose bud in the centre, enveloped in green leaves. I had also in my pocket a pretty purse, the handiwork of a dear friend given me just before I left my lodgings, as a *gage d'amitié* with a note accompanying it. Should modesty prevent my showing it to you, as a characteristic specimen of the taste these graceful creatures throw around every act of life? I think not. And so, premising the very flattering fact, that the less the truth, the greater the compliment, here it follows verbatim:—

"Souvenir de l'intérêt, que Mons. A. K. G. a su inspirer en France aux personnes, qui ont eu le plaisir de le connaitre.   Anais D——."
le 17 Juin, 45.

We kissed one another *a la Française*—on both cheeks, and between—in the court yard; and a tall, robust cavalry officer from Sardinia went through a similar evolution with a grenadier of Paris. The clock struck twelve—the *conducteur* gave breath to his horn—the postilion cracked his whip—the horses bounded forward—the *Barrière de la Gare* was passed, and——we were *hors de Paris*.

BOOKS

PUBLISHED BY

C. S. FRANCIS & CO, 252 BROADWAY, NEW YORK,

AND JOSEPH H. FRANCIS, BOSTON.

In one volume, handsomely printed, put up in paper, same style as the Waverley Novels. Price 25 cents.

THE EPICUREAN,
A TALE,
BY THOMAS MOORE, ESQ.,
AUTHOR OF LALLA ROOKH, ETC., ETC.

A new Edition, revised and corrected by the Author, with Notes.

In one volume octavo, handsomely printed, in cloth gilt.

WRITINGS
OF
CHARLES SPRAGUE.
NOW FIRST COLLECTED.

Consisting of his Poems and Orations.

"Mr. Sprague's poetry is of the highest order, and every piece has been stamped with the admiration of the best critics."

In two vols. 12mo, cloth.

JULIAN;
OR,
SCENES IN JUDEA.
BY THE AUTHOR OF ZENOBIA, OR LETTERS FROM PALMYRA, AND PROBUS, OR LETTERS FROM ROME.

These works, ZENOBIA, PROBUS, and JULIAN, for beauty of style, classical taste, and interest of narrative, may challenge comparison with any works in the English language.

In one vol. 12mo.—For Students.

A NEW LITERAL TRANSLATION OF

LONGINUS ON THE SUBLIME.
BY A GRADUATE OF TRINITY COLLEGE, DUBLIN.

PUBLISHED BY C. S. FRANCIS AND CO., NEW-YORK.

THE THOUSAND AND ONE NIGHTS; OR, THE ARABIAN NIGHTS' ENTERTAINMENTS. Translated by Rev. EDWARD FORSTER. With an Explanatory and Historical Introduction, by G. M. BUSSEY. Carefully revised and corrected, with some additions, amendments, and illustrative notes, from the work of E. W. LANE. Illustrated with Twenty large Engravings from designs by DE MORAINE, and numerous smaller Wood Cuts. In three volumes.

Contents.

VOL. I.

INTRODUCTION.
THE SULTAN OF THE INDIES, THE SULTANESS SHEHRAZADE AND HER SISTER DINARZADE.
THE OX, THE ASS, AND THE LABORER.
THE MERCHANT AND THE GENIE.
THE FIRST OLD MAN AND THE GAZELLE.
THE SECOND OLD MAN AND THE TWO BLACK DOGS.
THE THIRD OLD MAN AND THE MULE.
THE FISHERMAN AND THE GENIE.
THE GREEK KING AND DOUBAN THE PHYSICIAN.
THE HUSBAND AND THE PARROT.
THE VIZIER WHO WAS PUNISHED.
THE YOUNG KING OF THE BLACK ISLES.
GANEM, THE SLAVE OF LOVE.
THE ENCHANTED HORSE.
THE PORTER, AND THE THREE LADIES OF BAGDAD.
THE FIRST ROYAL CALENDER.
THE SECOND ROYAL CALENDER.
THE ENVIOUS MAN AND THE ENVIED.
THE THIRD ROYAL CALENDER.
STORY OF ZOBEIDE.
STORY OF AMINA.
NOUREDDIN AND ENIS ELJELIS, THE BEAUTIFUL PERSIAN.
THE THREE APPLES.
THE LADY WHO WAS MURDERED.
NOUREDDIN AND HIS SON, AND SHEMSEDDIN AND HIS DAUGHTER; BEDREDDIN HASSAN AND THE QUEEN OF BEAUTY.

VOL. II.

THE LITTLE HUMPBACK.
THE CHRISTIAN MERCHANT'S STORY.
STORY OF THE SULTAN'S PURVEYOR.
STORY OF THE JEWISH PHYSICIAN.
STORY TOLD BY THE TAILOR.
STORY OF THE BARBER.
THE BARBER'S FIRST BROTHER.
THE BARBER'S SECOND BROTHER.
THE BARBER'S THIRD BROTHER.
THE BARBER'S FOURTH BROTHER.
THE BARBER'S FIFTH BROTHER.
THE BARBER'S SIXTH BROTHER.
CAMARALZAMAN AND BADOURA.
PRINCE AMGIAD AND PRINCE ASSAD.
THE SEVEN VOYAGES OF SINDBAD THE SAILOR.
PRINCE AHMED AND THE FAIRY PARIBANOU.
ABOU HASSAN, THE WAG.
ALI COGIA, THE MERCHANT OF BAGDAD.

VOL. III.

ALI EBN BECAR AND SHEMSELNIHAR.
ALADDIN, OR THE WONDERFUL LAMP.
ADVENTURES OF HAROUN ALRASHID.
BABA ABDALLAH.
SIDI NOUMAN.
COGIA HASSAN ALHABBAL.
PRINCESS GULNARE OF THE SEA.
KING BEDER BASIM AND THE PRINCESS GIOHARA.
ALI BABA AND THE FORTY ROBBERS.
PRINCE ERYN ALASNAM AND THE KING OF THE GENII.
PRINCE CODADAD AND HIS BROTHERS.
THE PRINCESS OF DERYABAR.
THE THREE SISTERS.
PRINCESS PERIZADE AND HER BROTHERS.
CONCLUSION.

" A beautiful American reprint of a book which furnishes, perhaps, as much of the 'stuff that dreams are made of,' as any other that we could mention. This has long been needed and wished for, and the book produced is just what was wanted. Paper and print unexceptionable; illustrations graceful and suggestive, and price extremely moderate; nothing mars the pleasure of possessing a work without which not only no library, but no youthful imagination, can be considered thoroughly furnished."—*Union Mag.*

" The republication of these fascinating stories, in so good and cheap a form, will be very acceptable to the community. No good American edition, to our knowledge, has as yet been published, and it has been difficult to find it, except in the very expensive illustrated French or English editions."—*Boston Daily Adv.*

PUBLISHED BY C. S. FRANCIS AND CO., NEW-YORK.

THE BOOK OF ENTERTAINMENT,—OF CURIOSITIES AND WONDERS IN NATURE, ART AND MIND;
Drawn from the most authentic sources, and carefully revised.

Forming a thick volume of nearly one thousand pages. Illustrated by more than one hundred Engravings.

A PORTION OF THE CONTENTS.

Part I.—Thebes, its origin and rise, extent and internal arrangement, hundred gates; its splendor, decline and ruin, &c. Manners and Customs of the Irish peasantry. Abstinence. Affection. Agricultural operations. Useful Arts described. History of the Battle of Cressy; of China and its customs; of the Falls of Niagara; French Gypsies; Hindoo Pilgrims; Leaning Tower of Saragossa; Lion of Africa; Beaver Hat manufacture; Usefulness of Birds; Causes of the Earth's fertility; Crops, their preservation, &c. Experimental Science; Feats of strength, Fortitude of Women; City of Mexico, its great temple, idolatry of the people, magnificence of the King, besieged by the Spaniards, mode of writing, &c. Voyage on the Mississippi. New-Castle Coal Trade, &c., &c.

Part II.—An account of the City of Venice, giving a history of its origin, rise, greatness, and decline, with a description of the interior of the city, and the most remarkable public and private buildings. Excursion in Arabia. Cathedrals of Auxere and of Kirkwall. Cordova, in Spain. Elephants, and the manner of catching them. Blackbirds. Errors and superstitions. Coroboree Dance. Gizzard in birds. History and description of Kirkwall. Man overboard. Mines of Great Britain. Mermaid. Voice in man and animal. Passenger Pigeon of America. Account of oysters, muscles, and cockles. Greek islands. Useful arts—the ox and cow; milk and butter; making cheese. Account of the sheep, goat, and hog. Wanderings in the American forests, &c., &c.

Part III.—Account of Madrid; its capture by Napoleon, situation, and form. Palaces and Churches. Prado, and streets, &c. The Main-Truck, or leap for life. Lady Harriet Ackland, and her sufferings. Animals used as food. Eugene Aram. Aromatic Vinegar. Savings Banks. History of Bees. Chinese duck-boats. Method of preparing Coffee, Chocolate, &c. City of Cologne. Different Dispositions. Remarks on Cooking. Egyptian mode of hatching eggs. Female Excellence: a tale of real life. Moscow, and its Churches. Mode of preserving Insects. Account of the Coast of Ireland. Ratisbon. St. Robert's Chapel and Cave. Cathedral of Winchester; of Durham; Colchester, &c. &c.

AMONG THE ENGRAVINGS ARE THE FOLLOWING:

City of Muscat.
Western Steamer.
Breaking Stone on a Man's Chest.
African Lion.
Manufacture of a Hat.
Eltham Palace.
Norris Castle.
Agricultural Instruments.
Rocking Stone.
Mississippi Overflowing.
Gypsies.
Mexican Paintings.
Russian Travelling.
Hieroglyphics.
Windmill.
Plains of Cressy.
Ruins of Karnac.
Bridge of Sighs.

Roman Coins.
Shells.
Launceston Castle.
Mowing.
Reaping.
Inclined Plane.
Mushrooms.
Churns.
Cheese-Press.
Sir Francis Bacon.
Stones of Stenis.
Stornaway.
Stromness.
Catching Elephants.
The Ceylon Elephant.
Views of New South Wales.
Mermaids.
Women of Scio.

Wild Pigeons.
Snowdon.
Fairhead.
Ducal Palace, Venice.
Colonnade, Venice.
Palace of the Escurial.
Coffee Tree.
Dropping Well.
Water Clocks.
Snake Charmers.
James Crichton.
Pearl Fishery.
Palace at Madrid.
Church of St. Basil, Moscow.
Natives of New South Wales.
Rocks of Ragherry.
&c., &c., &c.

"Made up from all sources, describing whatever is most wonderful and worthy of admiration in the world, it cannot fail to prove highly attractive, especially to the young, for whom, of course, it was mainly intended, though all persons will find in it much matter of decided interest."—*Journal.*

PUBLISHED BY C. S. FRANCIS AND CO., NEW-YORK.

THE BOOK OF ENTERTAINMENT,—OF CURIOSITIES AND WONDERS IN NATURE, ART AND MIND.
Drawn from the most authentic sources, and carefully revised.

Second Series.

Another volume, of nearly a thousand pages, illustrated by more than one hundred engravings.

A PORTION OF THE CONTENTS.

Part I.—Natural and Civil History of Ceylon; the Natives; Boodhism; Trial by Jury, &c. Sugar maple. Coverings of Animals. History of the Arch. Arabia and Mocha. Attar of Roses. Fall of Babylon. Instinct of Birds. The Hermit of Switzerland. Cathedrals of Caen and Saragossa. Colombo in Ceylon. Debt and Misery. Division of Labor. Convent at Saragossa. Female Fortitude. Festival of the Bairam. Mode of measuring heights. Manufacture of Pottery. Manners and Customs of the Turks. Mexico, account of the modern city, its streets, churches, police, population, &c. Hotbeds, Hothouses, Conservatories, &c. Woman, the solace of man. Robert Raikes. Poisonous Plants, &c.

Part II.—Cemeteries and Burial in Turkey. Information concerning Barley, Bread, Vermicelli, Brewing, Charcoal Coal and Coal Mines. Anger and Madness. Account of Benares, Basle, Highlands and Islands of Scotland, Owhyhee, and its Volcano, Liege, Londonderry and its famous Siege, Luxor and its Ruins, Malvern Hills, Thebes and its Ruins, Karnak and its Temples, Society Islands, &c. Anecdotes and Tales of Bonaparte, Addison; Burke, Bishop Hall, Jenner, Irving, Johnson, Lavater, Locke, Mungo Park, Wilberforce, &c. Old Castles, viz: Dunvegan, Ennandowan, Shirbourn, &c. Dialogue between a Clergyman and Deist. Druidical Remains. Old Cathedrals, Ely, St. David's, &c. Clock at Rouen. Druidical Cromlechs. Wild Beasts, Rhinoceros, Elephant, Lemming, &c. Gypsies. History of Writing. Natives of Swan River. Skating Soldiers of Norway. &c. &c.

Part III.—Account of the City of Brussels, its history, situation, and climate, streets, squares, parks, palaces, public buildings, manufactures, &c., with a description of the Battle of Waterloo. Agriculture and Gardening in Japan. Allahabad in India. Description of Domesticated Birds; the common fowl; the Turkey and Guinea Hen; the Goose and Duck; the Pigeon. Early Rising. Deaths of eminent persons. Forest Trees. Greek Islands, Chios, or Scio. Harvest in Nassau. Hog Hunting in the East Indies. Culture and Manufacture of Indigo. Instances of insect sagacity. Experiments concerning Jugglers. Study of Material Nature. Self-taught Mathematician. Great Square in the City of Munich. &c. &c. &c.

AMONG THE ENGRAVINGS ARE THE FOLLOWING:

Church of N. S. de Guadalupe, Mexico.
View of Mocha.
Natives of Ceylon.
View of Colombo, Ceylon.
Measuring Heights and Distances.
Different Cider Mills.
Potters at Work.
Festival of the Bairam.
Street in Rouen.
Harbor of Havre.
Turkish Funeral.
Etruscan Vases.
Charcoal Burning.
Skating Soldiers of Norway.
Ruins of the Memnonium.
The Lemming.
Colossal Statues at Thebes.

The Druid Stone.
Dunvegan Castle.
Orders of Architecture.
Bridge of Saragossa.
City of Mexico.
Cathedral in Mexico.
Mexican Water Carrier.
Pulque Plant.
Coining Press.
Shawl Goat.
Indian Corn.
Fort at Allahabad, E. I.
Hop Picking.
Nimbus, from Teniers.
Abbey of St. Stephen.
Volcanoes in Owhyhee.
Shirbourn Castle.
Ruins at St. David's.
Ennandowan Castle.
Ruins at Medeenet-Habou.

Colonnade at Luxor.
Rhinoceros and Elephants.
Egyptian Vases.
Domestic Fowls.
Hog Hunting.
Place-Royale, Brussels.
Botanic Garden, Brussels.
Indigo Works in S. Amer.
Diamond Cut and Polish.
Carlisle Castle.
Town Hall at Bologne.
Barnacles.
Crystals of Snow.
The Sumach.
Crossbows and Arrows.
Night Scene in N. S. W.
Dunluce Castle.
Throwing the Lasso.
Modifications of Clouds.
&c. &c. &c.

"The contents of this very thick volume, which contains a great amount of reading, are both instructive and entertaining. It is admirably adapted to improve the mind, and to give the readers, especially the young, a taste for useful information, and an inducement to the further pursuit of practical knowledge."

THOUGHTS ON THE POETS:

By HENRY T. TUCKERMAN, Author of "Artist Life," etc.

Being Essays on the Lives, Characters, and Writings of the following

Poets:

PETRARCH,	GOLDSMITH,	GRAY,
COLLINS,	POPE,	COOPER,
THOMSON	YOUNG,	ALFIERI,
CRABBE,	SHELLY	HUNT,
BYRON,	MOORE,	ROGERS,
BURNS,	CAMPBELL,	WORDSWORTH,
COLERIDGE	KEATS,	BARRY CORNWALL,
HEMANS,	TENNYSON,	BARRETT,
DRAKE,	BRYANT,	

This volume does credit to the critical taste and imaginative faculties of the author, who passes in review the works of between twenty and thirty of our more modern poets, quotes them, points out their beauties, and estimates their qualities in an enthusiastic spirit, congenial to his subjects, and yet not so unchecked as to lead him into indiscriminating admiration. He displays taste and judgment, in fact, as well as fancy and feeling; and though verging toward praise, is not blind to the claims of criticism; and is it not better, as well as more just, to be somewhat gentle in your visitings, and rather lavish than otherwise of encomium and encouragement, than to suppose that the critic's true office consists in detecting microscopic blemishes, magnifying them, and parading your superior talent in ill-natured carping and dogmatic abuse? Be assured that censure is not only the easiest, but the worst species of inquisition: any fool can find faults, but it requires a competent person to point out merits, and institute faithful comparisons. In performing his pleasing task, Mr. Tuckerman has shown that he possessed this power; and he has made a volume of a very agreeable nature, studded with poetical quotations, in support of his opinions.—*London Literary Gazette.*

Almost any man's true, unaffected, living thoughts on the poets, whose verse makes part of our mental substance, could hardly fail to be acceptable. We all love to talk about our friends, and to hear others talk about them, in the right spirit. But Mr. Tuckerman's talk is as if we heard from a fine genial soul, who had seen our friend since we had seen him; and knew him and loved him quite as well as ourselves; minute and discriminating accounts of his excellence—made extra-piquant by personal anecdotes, and reminiscences of amusing and pathetic passages in his history.—*Mirror.*

Mr. Tuckerman is one of our especial favorites. There is a grace, delicacy, and earnestness about his writings, which we admire and love; while his candor, his warm appreciation of the merits of others, and his critical nicety of discrimination in literary matters, constitute him, in our opinion, one of the best guides to those who, not being able to give much time to study, are yet desirous of cultivating a taste for elegant letters.—*New York Gazette.*

This volume does great credit to Mr. Tuckerman as a writer and critic. No work has appeared from an American source, within our memory, so thoroughly imbued with the belles-lettres spirit, as this. It is the result of much patient thinking on the most attractive of all subjects, and is admirably calculated as a guide to a large class of the reading public, who have the means and the time to gratify literary tastes, but are ignorant of the relative rank and importance of the different English poets, and of the best method of reading them to advantage. This volume is well calculated to convey knowledge as well as opinions. We cordially recommend it to the lovers of poetry.—*Boston Courier.*

PUBLISHED BY C. S. FRANCIS & CO., NEW-YORK.

Writings of Orville Dewey.

DISCOURSES ON HUMAN NATURE,

Human Life, and the Nature of Religion. By ORVILLE DEWEY, D.D., Pastor of the Church of the Messiah, in New-York.

As the former volume is chiefly controversial, and is an admirable exposition of the religious opinions of Unitarians, and of the general principles and modes of reasoning by which they are sustained, so this is almost exclusively practical, and affords an exhibition of the spiritual results of those views, of the modes in which the religious life and character are conceived of, presented and urged by Unitarian preachers.—While both volumes, therefore, are excellent books to put into the hands of those who would learn something of what Unitarianism is, and what are its practical tendencies and results, they are yet more valuable to instruct and establish the minds of those of our own body who would have "a reason" for the faith that is in them, the faith in which they have been educated, and to quicken and direct their efforts to attain the Christian character, the true spiritual life. In rich, deep, noble thought, in apt and forcible illustration, in impressive appeals, in an earnest, manly eloquence, in a living spirit and power,—power to convince the reason, to sway the affections, to move the conscience, guiding while it quickens its action, to wake up all the slumbering energies of the soul, make it feel its responsibleness, make it feel that religion is a reality, the great, solemn, and blessed reality of its being,—in all these respects we are willing to compare the twenty-four sermons of this volume with any similar volume given to the world from any other denomination of Christians.—*Christian Examiner.*

These Discourses abound in the purest and most exalted precepts, beautifully adapted to almost every condition of life, and replete with instruction, such as becomes the minister who himself feels that the religion he preaches is divine. We may venture to say that no reader, whatever may be the form of his creed, can rise from a serious perusal of this work without feeling his faith strengthened, his charity enlarged, and his reverence for the Christian religion, and for all holy things, increased by the exalted and ennobling views in which they are here set forth.—*National Intelligencer.*

Dr. Dewey has been characterized as a preacher for clergymen; and we would that numbers of them could sit as learners at his feet. We earnestly hope that multitudes who have never enjoyed the advantage of hearing his expositions of the Christian life from his own lips, will embrace the opportunity afforded by this new edition of his works, to ascertain for themselves "what manner of man he is," in this his great office.—*Christ. Inq.*

CONTENTS.

On Human Nature.—I., II. On Human Nature. III. On the Wrong which Sin does to Human Nature. IV. On the Adaptation which Religion, to be true and useful, should have to Human Nature. V. The Appeal of Religion to Human Nature. VI. The Call of Humanity and the Answer to it. VII. Human Nature considered as a ground for Thanksgiving.

On Human Life.—VIII. The Moral Significance of Life. IX. That Everything in Life is Moral. X. Life Considered as an argument for Faith and Virtue. XI. Life is what we make it. XII. Inequality in the Lot of Life. XIII. The Miseries of Life. XIV. The School of Life. XV. The Value of Life. XVI. Life's Consolation in View of Death. XVII. The Problem of Life, Resolved in the Life of Christ. XVIII. Religion the Great Sentiment of Life. XIX. The Religion of Life. XX. The Voices of the Dead.

On the Nature of Religion.—XXI., XXII., XXIII. The Identity of Religion with Goodness, and with a Good Life. XXIV. Spiritual Interests, Real and Supreme

PUBLISHED BY C. S. FRANCIS AND CO., NEW-YORK.

Writings of Orville Dewey.

DISCOURSES AND REVIEWS.

Upon Questions in Controversial Theology and Practical Religion. By ORVILLE DEWEY, D.D., Pastor of the Church of the Messiah, in New-York.

CONTENTS:

THE UNITARIAN BELIEF:—
On the Nature of Religious Belief; with Inferences concerning Doubt, Decision, Confidence, and the Trial of Faith.

CURSORY OBSERVATIONS ON THE QUESTIONS AT ISSUE BETWEEN ORTHODOX AND LIBERAL CHRISTIANS.

I. On the Trinity. II. On the Atonement. III. On the Five Points of Calvinism. IV. On Future Punishment. V. Conclusion; the modes of attack upon Liberal Christianity, the same that were used against the Doctrine of the Apostles and Reformers.

THE ANALOGY OF RELIGION WITH OTHER SUBJECTS CONSIDERED.

DISCOURSES AND REVIEWS:—

I. The Analogy of Religion. II. On Conversion. III. On the method of obtaining and exhibiting Religious and Virtuous affections. IV. Causes of indifference and aversion to Religion.

On the original use of the Epistles of the New Testament, compared with their use and application at the present day.

On Miracles.

The Scriptures considered as the Record of a Revelation.

On the Nature and Extent of Inspiration.

On Faith, and Justification by Faith.

That Errors in Theology have sprung from false principles of Reasoning.

On the Calvinistic Views of Moral Philosophy.

It is the highest pleasure to meet with a volume so replete with earnest thought, tempered with the kindest charity. Besides the intellectual pleasure of studying the works of an essayist so accomplished and eloquent as Dr. Dewey, the reader enjoys the greater satisfaction of considering the highest religious principles and problems with a writer who looks at them with the simplicity and dignity of study which they deserve.—*Boston Daily Advertiser.*

The profound learning, cultivated taste, and eminent ability of Dr. Dewey give an interest to this work that will secure a large class of readers without the circle of his own religious denomination.—*Journal of Commerce.*

There is no living writer to whom we feel ourselves under greater obligations than to Dr. Dewey. We have been touched and moved by him as by no other preacher now living to whom it has been our privilege to listen. We need not commend this volume; and yet, as we have been reading it, we could not help wishing, that its spirit, at least, of reverence and charity, might find a place in every heart; that those, who are not convinced by its reasoning, might yet be profited by its teachings, and go from its pages better, and, therefore, wiser men.—*Christian Register.*

We rejoice whenever a competent writer feels moved again and again to discuss subjects involving the best interests of humanity. Such we conceive to be the topics in the present volume, and which Dr Dewey has invested with fresh beauty and interest —*Christian World.*

PUBLISHED BY C. S. FRANCIS & CO., NEW-YORK.

Writings of Orville Dewey.

DISCOURSES

On the Nature of Religion; and on Commerce and Business; with some Occasional Discourses. By ORVILLE DEWEY, D.D., Pastor of the Church of the Messiah in New-York.

We know not where to point to a series of moral and religious writings superior in compass and power to those contained in these three volumes of Dr. Dewey's works. A happy unity connects all the constituent parts. The principles, so clearly stated in one volume, are carried out to their practical results in the discourses and orations that fill the other two. If we were to state the peculiar charm of Dr. Dewey's style, we should say that it lies in the remarkable combination of colloquial ease with depth of thought, and frequent pathos and solemnity.

This volume presents specimens of three departments of composition,—sermons upon personal religion, discourses upon business morality, and addresses on various literary and ethical topics. No respectable American library can be without Dr. Dewey's volumes. Wherever his views are peculiarly his own, they are stated with a force and candour that must win the respect alike of theologian and reformer.—*Christian Exam.*

This volume contains a selection of the ablest discourses of this eloquent preacher, on his views of the nature of religion, and relating to the common events and duties of civil and political life. They strike the reader as remarkably sensible, clear, unpretending, and often thrillingly eloquent ... The earnest truths which he utters in behalf of honesty, justice, mercy and humanity, we could wish to be read by every one, and by none more thoughtfully than by orthodox Christians.—*N. Y. Evangelist.*

Dr. Dewey is one of the most eminent divines, of the Unitarian faith, in this country; while, as an eloquent and forcible writer, he has few superiors in the whole range of the clerical profession.—*Tribune.*

We have never before been so deliberate in reading a book of sermons, as this one. It is well printed, and well bound, and has altogether a very taking appearance. The most substantial reason, however, for our interest in the work, is its general intrinsic excellence. There are, to be sure, opinions and views, expressed and insisted upon, which are at variance with our own; but which we can more than tolerate because they seem to be part and parcel of the moral and intellectual stamina of the writer; and which, therefore, we believe him to be perfectly conscientious in supporting.—*Christian World.*

CONTENTS.

On the Nature of Religion.—I. Spiritual Interests, Real and Supreme. II., III. On Religious Sensibility. IV., V. The Law of Retribution. VI. Compassion for the Sinful. VII. God's Love; the chief Restraint from Sin, and Resource in Sorrow. VIII. The Difference between Sentiments and Principles. IX. The Crown of Virtue.

On Commerce and Business.—X. The Moral Law of Contracts. XI. The Moral End of Business. XII. The Uses of Labour, and the Passion for a Fortune. XIII. The Moral Limits of Accumulation.

Miscellaneous and Occasional.—XIV. Oration before the Society of Phi Beta Kappa, at Cambridge. XV. The Arts of Industry, with their Moral and Intellectual Influence upon Society.—An Address before the American Institute. XVI. The Identity of all Art.—A Lecture before the Apollo Association of New-York. XVII. The Moral Character of Government. XVIII. The Slavery Question. XIX. Public Calamities.

PUBLISHED BY C. S. FRANCIS AND CO., NEW-YORK.

Cabinet Library of Choice Prose and Poetry.

X.
THE EPICUREAN: A Tale. By THOMAS MOORE.

"A romance of antiquity, and one of the most exquisite of its class. A choice volume, that may be read with relish in our most languid moods and moments."—*S. Patriot.*

XI. XII.
ZENOBIA; OR THE FALL OF PALMYRA. A Historical Romance. By WILLIAM WARE. 2 vols.

"An ancient classic, from the pen of a modern writer. A fine specimen of that form of moral romance, of which the samples are few."—*S. Patriot.*

"One of the most brilliant additions to American literature."—
N. A. Review.

XIII.
MEMOIRS OF MADAME DE STAEL AND OF MADAME ROLAND. By L. MARIA CHILD. A new edition, revised and enlarged.

"In a gallery of celebrated women, the first place unquestionably belongs to Anne Maria Louise Germaine Necker, Baroness de Stael Holstein."

XIV.
WRITINGS OF CHARLES SPRAGUE. Consisting of his Poems and Orations.

"Mr. Sprague's poetry is of the highest order, and every piece has been stamped with the admiration of the best critics."

Works of Orville Dewey, D. D.

A new edition, carefully revised by the Author; containing most of the Sermons and Essays that have before been published; together with some not before printed; also, Reviews and Occasional Discourses. 3 vols. $1 each.

I.—DISCOURSES ON HUMAN NATURE,—HUMAN LIFE, AND THE NATURE OF RELIGION.

II.—DISCOURSES, REVIEWS, AND MISCELLANIES.

III.—DISCOURSES AND REVIEWS UPON QUESTIONS IN CONTROVERSIAL THEOLOGY AND PRACTICAL RELIGION.

PUBLISHED BY C. S. FRANCIS AND CO., NEW-YORK.

Cabinet Library of Choice Prose and Poetry.

I. II.
HISTORY OF THE CONDITION OF WOMEN,
IN VARIOUS AGES AND NATIONS. By L. MARIA CHILD.

"A most attractive subject, treated by a very delightful writer; so treated that the reader is instructed as well as pleased."—*Commercial Advertiser.*

"A work that should find a place in every family library."—*Mer. Mag.*

III.
THE DREAM, AND OTHER POEMS. By Hon. Mrs. NORTON.

"This Lady is the Byron of our modern Poetesses. * * * The Dream is a very beautiful Poem"—*Quarterly Review.*

IV.
THE CHILD OF THE ISLANDS. By the same.

"This is poetry, true poetry—the genuine product of a cultivated mind, a rich fancy, and a warm, well-regulated heart."—*Edinburg Review.*

V.
MEMOIRS OF FELICIA HEMANS. By HER SISTER. With an Essay on her Genius: by Mrs. SIGOURNEY

"These Memoirs, from a sister's hand, with their authenticity, combine all those attractive graces of style and language peculiar to the tracings of a female pen."—*Albany Journal.*

"Prefaced by a beautiful Essay on the Genius of Mrs. Hemans, from the pen of Mrs. Sigourney."—*Com. Advertiser.*

VI.
TRAGEDIES, SONNETS AND VERSES. By T. NOON TALFOURD.

The only complete American edition of Talfourd's poetry.

"A most acceptable addition to the truly choice reading of the day."—*Knickerbocker.*

VII.
LALLA ROOKH. By THOMAS MOORE.

A new edition, thoroughly revised by the author, and enriched by additional notes, and a preface giving its literary history.

VIII.
BIOGRAPHIES OF GOOD WIVES. By L. MARIA CHILD.

"This book is worth a quarter at a boarding school to any young lady."—*Tribune.*

"All that are, and all that hope—expect—to be on the list of married ladies, would do well to read this work."—*Com. Adv.*

IX.
THOUGHTS ON THE POETS. By H. T. TUCKERMAN.

"No work has appeared from an American source, within our memory, so thoroughly imbued with a belles lettres spirit as this."—*Boston Courier*

"No book more worthy of a permanent place in the standard literature of the country has yet been produced by an American."—*N. Y. Gazette*

PUBLISHED BY C. S. FRANCIS AND CO. NEW YORK.

Mrs. Norton's Poems.

THE DREAM AND OTHER POEMS:
BY THE HON. MRS. NORTON.

"This lady is the Byron of our modern poetesses. She has very much of that intense personal passion by which Byron's poetry is distinguished from the large, grasp and deeper communion of Wordsworth. She has also Byron's beautiful intervals of tenderness, his strong practical thought, and his forcible expression. It is not an artificial imitation, but a natural parallel; and we may add, that it is this, her latest production, which especially induces, and seems to us to justify, our criticism.

"The Dream is a very beautiful poem, the frame-work of which is simply a lovely mother watching over a lovely daughter asleep; which daughter dreams, and when awaked tells her dream; which dream depicts the bliss of a first love and an early union, and is followed by the mother's admonitory comment, importing the many accidents to which wedded happiness is liable, and exhorting to moderation of hope, and preparation for severe duties. It is in this latter portion of the poem that the passion and the interest assume a personal hue; and passages occur which sound like javelins hurled by an Amazon."—*Quarterly Review.*

"We find it difficult to overstate the deep interest we have taken in this volume, or the mingled sentiments of admiration, sympathy, and respect with which we offer to the writer our very sincere, though very imperfect praise."—*Examiner.*

THE CHILD OF THE ISLANDS: A POEM.

"There can be no question that the performance bears throughout the stamp of extraordinary ability—the sense of easy power very rarely deserts us. But we pause on the bursts of genius; and they are many . . . . . . The exquisite beauty of the verses is worthy of the noble womanly feelings expressed in them. . . . . . . We wish we had room for a score more of these masterly sketches—but we hope we have given enough, not to excite attention, for that such gifts employed with such energy must at once command, even were the name on the title-page a new one—but enough to show that we have not observed with indifference this manifestation of developed skill—this fairest wreath as yet won in the service of the graver Muses for the name of SHERIDAN."—*Quarterly Review.*

"This is poetry, true poetry, and of the sort we unfeignedly approve—the genuine product of a cultivated mind, a rich fancy, and a warm, well regulated heart. The aim is noble, the tone elevated, the train of thought refined and chastened, though singularly fearless, the choice of images and illustrations, judicious, and the language often beautiful, and always clear.

"We find in almost every page of this elegant volume, some bold burst, graceful allusion, or delicate touch;—some trait of external nature, or glimpse into the recesses of the heart—that irresistibly indicates the creating or transfiguring power of genius."—*Edinburgh Review.*

"Under cover of addressing the young Prince of Wales, Mrs. Norton has written a very beautiful poem upon the great domestic question of the day—the condition of the people. . . . . . The poem is divided into four parts—Spring, Summer, Autumn, and Winter. No connected story binds them together, but a succession of remarkably pleasing pictures from nature are presented to the mind."—*Times.*

In preparation, and will be shortly issued,
BY THE SAME AUTHOR:
SORROWS OF ROSALIE, and other Poems.
THE UNDYING ONE, and other Poems.

PUBLISHED BY C. S. FRANCIS AND CO., NEW-YORK.

MENTAL AND MORAL CULTURE,

AND POPULAR EDUCATION. By S. S. RANDALL, Gen. Dep. Superintendent of Common Schools in the State of New-York. To which is appended a SPECIAL REPORT on COMMON SCHOOL LIBRARIES; prepared in pursuance of the instructions of the Superintendent of Common Schools; by HENRY S. RANDALL, Superintendent of Cortlandt County.

CONTENTS.—Chap. I. The Philosophy of Education.—Chap. II. Physical, Intellectual, and Moral Culture.—Chap. III. The Nature and Mission of Genius.—Chap. IV. Mental Philosophy.—Chap. V. Formation and Development of Character.—Chap. VI. Moral Responsibility.—Chap. VII. Public Instruction.—Chap. VIII. Colleges, Academies, and Common Schools.—Chap. IX. Report on Common School Libraries.

"The object which the author of this work has proposed to himself has been to direct the attention of the reader to considerations intimately connected with physical, moral, and intellectual education, and the formation of the character, and to point out the facilities, as well as obstacles, to mental culture, which are presented by the varying circumstances of life, by the institutions of society, and by public sentiment."

Encyclopedia of Cooking.
THE COOK'S OWN BOOK

AND HOUSEKEEPER'S REGISTER; being Receipts for Cooking of every kind of Meat, Fish, and Fowl; and making every sort of Soup, Gravy, Pastry, Preserves, and Essences; with a complete system of Confectionery; Tables for Marketing; a Book of Carving; and Miss Leslie's Seventy-five Receipts for Pastry, Cakes, and Sweetmeats. By a Boston Housekeeper.

Containing *several thousand* receipts, arranged in alphabetical order, preceded by general observations on the Management of Families, Cooking Utensils, Diet, Boiling, Baking, Roasting, Frying, Broiling, Broths and Soups, and various articles used in cooking.

This book is a complete Culinary Encyclopedia, there being few words or phrases or receipts that cannot be found in it; and it embraces all the improvements of modern times. It is made very convenient for reference, by being arranged in the form of a dictionary.

Extracts from the Preface.—"The Cook exercises a greater power over the public health and welfare than the physician, and if he should be a charlatan in his art, alas! for his employers."

"After insanity, the most grievous affliction of Providence, or of improvidence and bad diet, is Dyspepsy. This malady is beyond the science of the physician, but within the art of the Cook."

"More than health depends upon the proper preparation of food: our very virtues are the creatures of circumstances, and many a man has hardened his heart, or given up a good resolution, under the operation of indigestion."

"The study of the author has been to make every recipe plain, and the proportions certain; little is left to discretion that could be reduced to measure. The system of confectionery is perfect; and if strictly followed, every cook may become a first rate confectioner. Labour, care and expense have been bestowed upon the work, and the publishers feel secure of its merit."

"It will not be beneath the solicitude of a good wife diligently to study this book, by the help of which a neat and well-dressed repast can constantly be provided."

BOOK OF CARVING.

THE HAND-BOOK OF CARVING; with Hints on the Etiquette of the Dinner Table.

Containing directions for Carving all kinds of Meat, Poultry, Game, Fish, &c., with illustrative engravings.

PUBLISHED BY C. S. FRANCIS & CO., NEW-YORK.

Writings of L. Maria Child.

LETTERS FROM NEW-YORK
First and Second Series.

"Mrs. Child is a wonderful woman. It is not likely that all her thoughts will find currency in the world, at this day, and be received as the common-place of the mind but those, who will regard her as visionary and enthusiastic, will yet admire her originality; and those who think the visionary to be weak in mind, will be startled by such boldness of thought, as none but the strong can conceive; yet visionary and enthusiastic as some may pronounce her, and bold to think what the present thinks itself unprepared for, there is nothing of harsh statement to be found in her expressions. So far from it, that her mind rather resembles the vine which hangs in graceful festoons upon the oak; and its visions remind one not of the splendours of a thunder-storm with gleams of lightning at night, but of the soft light of the morning, or the clouds which crowd around the west to see the sun go down. A gentler, purer, happier spirit, it has not been our fortune to meet with in print."—*Best. Cour*

HISTORY OF WOMEN.

The History of the Condition of Women, in various Ages and Nations, from the earliest to the present times. 2 vols. A new edition.

Vol. I. Women of Asia and Africa.—Jewish, Babylonian, Assyrian, Lycian, Carian, Trojan, Syrian, Arabian, Affghanistan, Circassian, Georgian, Armenian, Turkish, Persian, Hindoo, Thibetan, Burmese, Siamese, Malay, Chinese, Corean, Tartar, Amazons, Siberian, Javanese, Sumatran, Japanese; Women of Borneo, Celebes, Bali, Timor, New Holland, Van Dieman's Land, Loo Choo, and other Islands.—Egyptian, Carthagenian, Moorish, African, Hottentot, &c.

Vol. 2. Women of Europe and America.—Grecian, Roman, Scandinavian, Danish, and other Northern Nations. Women during the Middle Ages, and the Centuries succeeding. English, Irish, Scotch, French, Spanish, Portuguese, Italian, Polish, German Austrian, Tyrolese, Dutch, Swiss, Russian, Swedish, Icelandish; Modern Greeks; Peasantry; Modern Amusements, Marriages, Laws, and Customs; Women in slave-holding Countries. American Indians, Arctic Regions, South American. Of the United States. Of the South Sea Islands, &c.

THE MOTHER'S BOOK.
New Edition—Revised and Amended.

The value and usefulness of this little book is well known,—it having passed through eight editions in this country and twelve in England.

Contents of the Chapters.—I. On the means of developing the bodily senses in earliest infancy.—II. Early development of the affections.—III. Early cultivation of intellect.—IV. Management in childhood.—V. Amusements and employments.—VI. Sunday. Religion. Views of Death. Supernatural appearances.—VII. Advice concerning books. List of good books for various ages.—VIII. Politeness.—IX. Beauty. Dress. Gentility.—X. Management during the teens.—XI. Views of Matrimony.—Concluding observations.

FLOWERS FOR CHILDREN.
A Series of volumes in Prose and Verse, for Children of various ages.

"These are flowers which have budded and blossomed for others beside children; and as none may now look upon the lilies of the field, bowing their heads in pure effulgence, or in gorgeous luxuriance of show, without remembering a lesson impressed upon every petal, by that mild look of the Saviour's, which he gave them while observing that human hearts might be instructed by them, so these little flowers, gathered in the fields of Christian wisdom, in the company of the spirit of the Saviour, suggest lessons to instruct the minds of the wisest, and open the springs of pure emotion in the hearts of the best."—*Boston Courier.*

"Verily, we are delighted ourselves, and congratulate our readers who are blessed with the heritage of children, upon this accession to our juvenile libraries, and hope that Mrs. Child will not be chary of her volumes. These "Flowers" are so sweet and unfading that we would make our youngsters' libraries redolent of their perfume and beauty."—*Commercial Advertiser.*

In cloth, plain. Also, in ornamental binding, for Presents.

THE POPULAR POEMS OF SIR WALTER SCOTT.
NEW EDITIONS.
With the Author's latest Corrections, Introductions, and Notes;
EACH IN A SINGLE VOLUME, WITH BEAUTIFUL STEEL ENGRAVINGS.

THE LAY OF THE LAST MINSTREL.
BALLADS AND SONGS.

"For vivid richness of coloring, and truth of costume, many of the descriptive passages of this poem stand almost unrivalled. It carries us back in imagination to the time of action; and we wander with the poet along Tweedside, or among the wild glades of Ettrick Forest."

MARMION.
A Tale of Flodden Field.

"This poem is superior to all that Scott has hitherto produced, and with a few faults of diction, equal to any thing that has *ever* been written."—JEFFREY, *Edinburgh Review.*

THE LADY OF THE LAKE;
In Six Cantos.
THE VISION OF DON RODERICK.

"There is a richness and spirit in this poem, a profusion of incident, and a shifting brilliancy of coloring, that remind us of the witchery of Ariosto."—JEFFREY.

ROKEBY.
THE BRIDAL OF TRIERMAIN.

"The interest inspired by the fable, the masterly delineations of the characters by whose agency the plot is unravelled, and the spirited, nervous conciseness of the narrative, we think will satisfy the expectations which the author's reputation has excited."—*Edinburgh Review.*

THE LORD OF THE ISLES.
THE FIELD OF WATERLOO, AND OTHER POEMS.

"Another genuine lay from the harp of that indefatigable minstrel. The same glow of coloring, the same energy of narration, the same amplitude of description, are conspicuous here, which distinguish all his other productions."—*Edinburgh Review.*

PUBLISHED BY C. S. FRANCIS AND CO., NEW-YORK.

TRAGEDIES, SONNETS, AND VERSES:

BY T. NOON TALFOURD.

Price 50 cents.

"This is the first complete American edition of Talfourd's Plays and Poems. It will meet with a hearty welcome from his admirers, and their name is 'Legion.'" — *Com. Adv.*

"Talfourd is a thoughtful and purely classic writer, and this new volume is indeed an addition to the select library." — *Boston Transcript.*

"Talfourd's poems are too well known to require praise. A chaste, elevated, and even style—a perfect model of grace and melody; and withal pervaded by a generous and humane philosophy." — *New Haven Herald.*

"A most acceptable addition to the *truly* choice reading of the day. If the volume contained only 'Ion' alone, it would be worth twice the price at which it is sold, to any reader of pure and classic taste." — *Knickerbocker.*

"This remarkable poem (Ion) has justly called to itself more attention than any other work of the times. It has given more pleasure to the reader, and more fame to the writer, than all the red-hot productions of the intense school put together." — *N. Amer. Review.*

"Ion is an eminently chaste and poetical creation, graceful and polished in its style, pure and elevated in its sentiments, full of thoughts, which, without being forced, appear original, and adorned with images of great beauty." — *Edin. Review.*

MEMOIR OF FELICIA HEMANS:

BY HER SISTER.

With an Essay on her Genius; by Mrs. Sigourney.

Price 37½ cents.

"Who that has read, and re-read with fresh delight, the works of a gifted mind, does not long to become familiar with the private life of the writer? Who, of all the poetesses now living, could pen so truthful an essay on the genius of Mrs. Hemans, as Mrs. Sigourney?" — *Albany Spectator.*

"These memoirs, from a sister's hand, with their authenticity, combine all those attractive graces of style and language peculiar to the tracings of a female pen." — *Eve. Journal.*

"A well-written biography, prefaced by a beautiful Essay on the genius of Mrs. Hemans, from the pen of Mrs. Sigourney." — *Com. Adv.*

LALLA ROOKH:

AN ORIENTAL ROMANCE. By THOMAS MOORE.

A beautiful Edition, on fine paper and large type. Price 37½ cents.

This exquisite poem is so well known, and its reputation so fully established, that notices of it would be superfluous. It is sufficient to say, in the words of Professor Wilson, that, "This poem, from the hand of beyond all comparison, the most ingenious, brilliant, and fanciful poet of the present age, is the most beautiful and characteristic of his compositions."

PUBLISHED BY C. S. FRANCIS AND CO., NEW-YORK.

Interesting Games.

THE PICKWICK CARDS,
Invented by SAMUEL WELLER, for the Entertainment of his Friends, Old and Young.

Twenty-five cards, enclosed in a neat case; each card having on it a scene or character from the writings of Dickens; with directions for playing three different games, for the amusement of evening parties. Price 50 cents.

SHAKSPERE IN A NEW DRESS.
Thirty cards, containing fifty-two choice quotations from Shakspere, with a list of questions, to be answered from the cards. So arranged as to form an interesting round game, with forfeits. Price 50 cents.

NEW FORTUNE-TELLER.
THE ORACLE OF FORTUNE, and Guide to Wealth and Success.

"These interesting cards combine all the information necessary to secure Wealth, and Success in matters of Love or Money; they are constructed on the principles which the late Baron Rothschild found so eminently successful, and combine the requisite mixture of shrewd suggestions, wise calculations, and cautious admonitions, to direct any one in the way to good luck." Price 50 cents.

THE BOY'S OWN BOOK.
A Complete Encyclopædia of all the Diversions, Athletic, Scientific, and Recreative, of Boyhood and Youth.

Including Games with Marbles, Tops, Balls, Sports of Agility and Speed, Toys, Archery, Cricket, Gymnastics, Swimming; Arithmetical, Optical and Chemical Amusements; Checkers, Cards, Legerdemain, Puzzles, Riddles, Angling, Fencing, &c. &c. &c., with very numerous engravings.

THE AMERICAN GIRL'S BOOK;
Or, OCCUPATION FOR PLAY HOURS. By Miss Leslie.

Including all the Sports and Pastimes suited to Girls; Plays with Toys, Games with Cards, Riddles, Amusing and Fancy Needle-Work, Card-Work, &c. &c.

PARLOUR MAGIC
Or, BOYS' BOOK OF AMUSING EXPERIMENTS.

Containing Transmutations; Experiments in Sight and Sound; on Light and Heat; on Gas and Steam; on Fire, Water, and Air; Sleights and Subtleties; Miscellaneous Experiments.

GYMNASTIC EXERCISES.
Paul Preston's Book of Gymnastics; or Sports for Youth to promote Health and Long Life.

Containing directions for Exercises on the Parallel Bars, Horizontal Pole, Horse Exercise, Running, Leaping, Throwing the Spear, Climbing, &c. &c. &c., with illustrative diagrams.

www.ingramcontent.com/pod-product-compliance
Lightning Source LLC
Chambersburg PA
CBHW050738170426
43202CB00013B/2289